IN A VALLEY SURROUNDED BY HILLS

STORIES OF GROWING UP IN A PENNSYLVANIA TOWN

by
DON SKINNER

FRANKLIN STREET BOOKS

Love,
Adam &
Josh

To Patricia:
life companion
who came to Meadville a stranger
was embraced by its people
made it her home
and doing so helped to make it more fully mine.

And
To Ruth Ann, Clifford and Frank:
who never got to decide
whether they cared to be players
in a book written by their little brother.

Table of Contents

Acknowledgements

Let's confess, in all candor, that the acknowledgements printed in books like this one constitute a waste of paper, because so few people read them. This is unfortunate, because no one completes a book like this without a lot of help. Every author is indebted to someone for something.

In my case, this is especially important—which is why you should keep on reading. The people I name here made tangible contributions that I cannot possibly repay, and deserve every bit of the credit I mean to bestow on them. They are four.

Virginia Linnman, director of writer's services at First Books, displayed monumental patience and panache in guiding me through the essential steps to publication. In the aggregate, my dumb questions and her patient answers constitute a body of correspondence at least as weighty as this book. I seriously doubt that she is paid a fraction of what she is worth.

Tim Woodworth, the genius behind HighTech Computing, Inc. of Meadville, took time off from a demanding schedule, on no notice whatever, to reduce my pen-and-ink drawings to an electronic format that would satisfy the requirements of First Book's design staff.

Rebekah Woodworth—who, as her name suggests, is related to Tim by marriage (I did the wedding)—drove me nuts as my copyeditor. I mean, the woman was merciless, pointing out errors, suggesting word substitutions that should have occurred to me three drafts earlier, and fearlessly scribbling helpful comments like "awkward" and "inconsistent" all over my manuscript. If Rebekah wasn't so creative as a wife, mother, musician, and HighTech Computing staffer, she could earn a living as a fine-toothed comb.

I can think of no greater blessing than "May you have friends as thoughtful as Tim and Rebekah."

Finally, I plan to nominate Patricia Skinner for sainthood. It's not just that she suggested the topic for the book; or that she read through innumerable story drafts, offering helpful criticisms; or that she kept me focused on the original concept when I started to wander off in unhelpful directions. It's that she puts up with me—and that alone ought at least to merit beatification.

In a Valley
Surrounded by Hills

PART I

Getting Under Way

CHAPTER 1

A Simpler Time

L et's be clear about three things.

First, anyone leafing through this book searching for a central, driving plot will certainly be disappointed. Our personal histories do not follow plots. They unfold in seminal moments of growing awareness. In most of our minds—certainly in mine—those moments do not even organize themselves chronologically. They impose their own standard of what matters.

Second, this book is not a history of my hometown. There will be no dwelling on the vital statistics of the place, its industrial output, mercantile opportunities, municipal organizations or political history. Nor will I chart the "big changes" that have overtaken my corner of Pennsylvania, or not, during my lifetime. I touch on these things only as they help me to sketch a series of personal vignettes set in the Meadville of my childhood, not its modern incarnation. Current residents who pick up this book looking for the Meadville they call home will find many things out of place. On the other hand, I hope that those who grew up there in the 1930s and '40s will recognize the place!

Third, it isn't even a history of the Skinners, as my siblings will be quick to assure you. Were any of them moved to write this book, they would not tell the same stories; and if they did their interpretations would differ from mine. In some cases, when I spoke with them to confirm my memory, we found that we shared common ground, but in others their reminiscences are not mine at all. And even where we recall the same events, we sometimes interpret them differently. If I had not fully realized it before, writing this book helped me to recognize the extent to which all memory is necessarily subjective. Nor is there anything wrong with that. Indeed it cannot be otherwise: objective childhood recollection is an oxymoron.

These are stories of feeling—somewhat disjointed, often emotional, always sensate, and necessarily subjective: the recollections of one child who grew up in a small and hilly Pennsylvania town that was as much forest as village, as much family as community. As a town it was a work in progress. The settled and manicured landscape of established neighborhoods flowed seamlessly into open acres of meadow and scrub, where surrounding farms pressed against the city line to remind us where our daily sustenance came from.

Half a century later I still feel the place shaping my life through the mediums of memory and story. If we are what we eat, as the biology of nutrition asserts, it is equally true that, spiritually and psychically, we become our stories. There is a fundamental truth in the words of the corrupt priest in the movie *Robin Hood, Prince of Thieves* who, meeting Robin after years of separation, observes, "I see the boy I knew in the man before me." Even those who are pleased beyond words to have moved away from their hometowns remain the psychic children of the roots they strive to escape.

Psychiatrists tell me that my personality, attitudes, and view of how the world ought to treat me were largely formed within the first three or four years of life. Thereafter, as they say, it was all downhill. Once established, personality changes only under extraordinary pressure from powerful influences; and simply moving to a new town is not one of them. Wherever I go, whoever I meet, whatever I do, I carry my story with me; and my story was imbedded in my soul a lifetime ago in my old hometown.

———

Not to ride a dead horse, but let me note that it really was a simpler time. By way of setting the clock: the world into which I was born got along pretty well without the help of a monstrous list of things that we (and especially young people) now take for granted: computers, e-mail, cell phones and PalmPilots; television of any size or definition; microwave ovens; antibiotics, MRI's and organ transplants; nuclear energy for any definable purpose; Omnimax theaters and stereophonic sound; jet aircraft and lunar landers; pre-nuptial agreements, quantum physics and digital anything; interstate highways and automobiles equipped with the whole long list now considered standard. The cars of my youth had four wheels and an internal combustion engine, and not much else.

Some technologies, like rotary-dial telephones, $33^{1/}_3$ and 45-rpm records and wire recorders were invented, marketed and became obsolete in less than half my lifetime. Most painfully, the current explosion of DVD burners threatens to consign my videotape collection, which I didn't even begin to gather until 1988, to the status of the dodo and the passenger pigeon.

"So what's left?" my grandchildren ask in consternation. More than you can possibly imagine, I respond. What's "left" is what these stories are about.

————•——

The place is Meadville, and while it is not now my home, it remains in many ways my hometown. To locate it for you: Meadville lies in northwestern Pennsylvania ninety miles north of Pittsburgh, forty south of Erie and twenty east of the Ohio border. Interstate 79 brushes its western flank and intersects with three of the old federal roads that merge getting through town: U.S. 6, 19 and 322. In spite of the temptation to think parochially, the joke about a man seeking directions from a Maine native only to be told "yew can't git theah from heah," doesn't apply to Meadville. It really is possible to get from there to any place you want to go and back again. I know because I've done it. And let that be sufficient on the topic.

————•——

As a citizen of Meadville, I may be unique in one peculiar regard: I have moved there four times thus far (I feel safer being dogmatic about the past than about the future!). I take no credit for my first arrival, it was my parents' doing: my mother was five month's pregnant with me when they arrived. On three later occasions, however, I left only to come full circle and land back where I started. This fragmented history has given me a different view of the place than that possessed by those who never left, or left and never returned.

It seems to me, on later reflection, that I may have had the best of both worlds. Thirty-four years of living there, at several stages of life, provided me with progressive memories of the place. The intervening years during which I lived a number of elsewheres gave me the perspective of distance, and acquaintance with other towns against which to compare my own.

It would be presumptuous to assume that, having come to the end of this book, a reader will feel intimately connected to my small Pennsylvania town—although, should that occur, I will accept their adoption as a compliment. But I do hope that the book provides useful clues for those reflecting on what it was like to have grown up in other places, the more fully to discern the gifts they received from their own hometowns.

Forest Grove, Oregon
December 2001

CHAPTER 2

Westbound

I t was Sunday, June 6, 1993, a day so totally northwest-Pennsylvania! Sunlight fell less as light than glare, laced with so much heat that the land, still in thrall to winter's last deep frost, could not absorb it. Humidity hung about thick enough to stir, resisting evaporation. By mid-morning, clothing we had climbed into fresh from morning showers had grown mottled with sweat and clung to our skin like it had grown there.

Sixty years of my life had been spent east of the Mississippi River, thirty-four of them in Meadville, just not all at one swat. When a change of jobs brought us from Minnesota to Pennsylvania in 1978, only a year after Patricia and I married, I made her a promise: when I retired, we'd take her home to her beloved Oregon. Almost before we could have imagined it, the time to fulfill that promise had arrived, and we stood on the curb exchanging hard farewells with people dear to us. My final task as chaplain of Allegheny College was completed that morning, and a happenstantial mix of family and friends gathered for lunch at a local restaurant—except it felt more like the Last Supper. And then we were in the parking lot, the siren song of the westering road a discordant counterpoint to the blubbering of loved ones about to part with no certainty when they might see each other again. When the road finally won out, we climbed into our packed car and, exchanging waves in the rear view mirrors, started west for six days of hard driving.

Perhaps it was inevitable that our leaving would prompt us to recollections of our coming; and we reflected, as we crossed into Ohio, on how interesting life had been during the days of 1978 that brought us to Pennsylvania as a couple.

That return to Meadville (my fourth, actually) was less a matter of choice than serendipity. Or perhaps it was grace. I will not second-guess all the forces that were at work that consummately difficult year. Nine years into a deanship at Hamline University in St. Paul, Minnesota, I experienced for myself the pregnant portent of Exodus 1.8: "Now a new king arose over Egypt, who did not know Joseph." Private college administrators serve at the pleasure of presidents. Presidents are known to change with some frequency. And new presidents have a habit of issuing terminal contracts to those they want to replace with members of their own team. Enjoying our life in St. Paul, we really didn't want to leave. But as sometimes happens, the sadness veiled a blessing: in one of the supreme ironies of our married life, we discovered that the chaplaincy of Lewis and Clark College, a stone's throw across the Willamette River from Pat's home town of Milwaukie, Oregon, and the dean of students position at Allegheny College, in mine, were both vacant. But Lewis and Clark called someone else, and Allegheny called me, launching us into the most rewarding period in my professional career.

"Meadville," Mrs. Dunham intoned, "is in a valley surrounded by hills." Elizabeth Dunham taught geography at Meadville's First District School in an era when it was still thought important that children know where things were in the world—things like continents and countries and the peoples who inhabit them. My siblings, who labored in turn under Mrs. Dunham's tutelage, apprised me of what to expect. And part of what I learned to expect, though not yet acquainted with the pedagogical vocabulary, was that Mrs. Dunham taught by rote memorization. When she said something was so, it was our cue to commit it to memory, verbatim. The durability of the product showed thirty-four years later, on another hot and sultry summer day, when Patricia and I came cruising up I-79 and topped the curve where signs of Meadville's presence first become visible on the wooded slopes ahead. Opening mindlessly, my mouth chanted the sacred mantra: "Meadville is in a valley surrounded by hills."

"What?" Patricia inquired with an inflection that really asked, "What *are* you talking about?" Then and there, as we rolled up exit ramp 36-A and onto Smock Highway, Patricia learned more about Mrs. Dunham than she probably cared to know, along with a gaggle of eighth-grade geography to mold her first impressions of my hometown.

Whatever else one might say about Meadville, it changes slowly. As we drove through town and I regaled Pat with a running commentary on just about everything we were seeing—buildings, families, history—she silently absorbed it all, sponge that she is, before commenting matter-of-factly, "It sounds like nothing much has changed since you were a child." That simple assessment so struck me that it cut off my verbose rambling like she had turned off a faucet. Meadville's newest resident (at least we knew of no one competing with her for the title right then) recognized in three minutes what my small brain had not absorbed in half a lifetime: the rapid growth, the razing and rebuilding of whole blocks of cityscape, the breathless transformation that our largely urban population finds exciting—or tolerable—doesn't happen in Meadville. There is a stubbornness there that makes it possible to discern, behind its present face, a pentimento of the town it was a century ago.

Some will find that boring at best, intolerable at worst. Change is an urban American preoccupation; the vestigial remnant of a frontier mentality that sees everything now existing as a resource to be exploited for economic gain or self aggrandizement or personal comfort. Paradoxically, it is Meadville's failure in this regard that makes it so appealing to those who value the tenacity of small-town America. A man can go away for ten or thirty or sixty years, only to discover on his return that he still recognizes most of what he sees. Not every detail, to be sure; Meadville is conservative, not stagnant. Half the buildings that lined the business streets when I was born no longer stand; and among those that do, few house what they did during my childhood. And other buildings now standing, already showing early signs of aging, didn't yet exist. A few streets I traveled as a child are gone, and a couple new ones got laid down in my absence. But in the main, the town's character persists and its neighborhoods abide.

Most important, the people endure: dependable and neighborly, interested in one another, engaged in the political and economic management of their community. That they are largely a new generation goes without saying. But familiar family names are still in evidence; and far more of their children, proportionally, grew up there and by choice remain there than is typical of our peripatetic urban society.

The truth of that assessment was brought home to Pat when, half a dozen times during our first weeks in Meadville, someone approached to ask, "Are you related to ol' 'Doc' Skinner?"

"He was my father," I'd respond.

"Well, he put me to sleep when I had my appendix out."

Then they'd laugh when I said, "My father put half of Crawford County to sleep at one time or another."

What struck us about those encounters was less that people remembered ol' "Doc" Skinner than that he had been dead for forty years. The continuity that retards physical change in the town enhances its sense of neighbor relations—of who people are and how our families are connected, and how our identities help us to define our place in the scheme of things even through generational changes-of-the-guard. If there is parochialism in this, there is also deep security. I have traveled widely across this land. I enjoy every patch of it. We Americans are vastly more friendly and caring than the daily fare of shock media insists, or even than we are wont to credit ourselves with being. But when I am on the road I am the visitor, the customer, the guest. When I arrive in Meadville I am home. I know in a palpable way who I am, because I know my family's place in the exquisitely interwoven relationships of families whose collective histories define the town.

———·—·———

Such were the reflections that first accompanied us as we rolled southwest through Ohio's waning afternoon that June Sunday. Once opened, however, the windows of reminiscence are not easily shut, and memories of my earlier Meadville lives tumbled out one after another. I felt like the proverbial drowning man whose whole life passes before his eyes in a split second. Those memories are foundational; they shape my sense of who I am and where I come from. They, and how I interpret them, constitute the substance of this book, starting with a few that are not even my own. They came as gifts, in stories my mother told me— like the one about the haste of my arrival.

CHAPTER 3

Old Mat

My birth at 5:10 a.m. was noteworthy not because of the hour, but because Mother didn't go into labor until after 4:00. Ruth McCafferty Skinner's ability to birth a child was legendary. She credited this to a "toughening" she underwent when a siege of ungulate fever (a malady acquired from un-pasteurized milk) took her out of high school for most of a year. I suspect that genetics had more to do with it. Whichever it was, if she does not hold the Crawford County record for alacrity in childbirth—maybe even the record for the whole state— she must surely be in the running.

I imagine it was one of the few times when sleeping with a physician was an advantage. How many times Dad was called out in the middle of the night on medical emergencies was never recorded; but each time it happened, it must have disrupted her sleep as often as his. On this occasion, she not only turned the tables on him, she had a knowledgeable consultant right there at her side. Not that she needed one. It was, after all, her fourth run at it. But they were a bit unnerved by the speed with which things appeared to be moving. In a matter of minutes the frequency of her contractions were such that she and Dad quickly concurred on the need to get moving, lest my first view of the world be not through one of the maternity building's soaring Victorian windows, but the windshield of the family car. With little wasted motion, they disrupted a neighbor's sleep to come stay with my soon-to-be sister and brothers, hastened into their clothes and climbed into the car. The drive down North Main Street hill and one block left on Prospect Street, even in the snowy pre-dawn of mid-December, consumed only minutes. It was, after all, a whole mile from our house to the hospital. But it was all the time they had: I was born ten minutes after Mom was admitted, with Dad the attending physician.

Mother once commented that it was probably a good thing that I was her last. I can think of several reasons why that might be true. She herself once observed dryly that I had been the sweetest infant she ever knew, and she never could understand what happened to me when I became a teenager. What she had in mind in counting her pregnancies, though, was more pragmatic: she figured that if she'd had a fifth, she might never have made it out the door.

She also made sure I never forgot how much it cost them. At the birth of each of her children, Mother bought a baby book in which she posted all our vital—and some not-so-very-vital—statistics. Glued to the first page of mine is the hospital's bill for my birth:

<u>To The Meadville City Hospital</u>

12/17/32 to 12/24/32 Days 7 @ $5.00	$35.00
10% Discount	- 3.50
Sub-total	<u>$31.50</u>
Delivery and Dressings	10.00
Laboratory	<u>1.50</u>
Total	$43.00

I presume that the 10% discount was a benefit of Dad's standing as a physician. God only knows how much I would have cost had Dad charged for obstetrical services.

———·+·———

Shortly after we moved to Meadville in 1978, Pat was hired as secretary/receptionist for a department of City Hospital housed in an old brick building that sat in the hospital's parking lot like the outrigger of a canoe. Her duties included delivering documents to the office of Jim Werle, the hospital administrator, where she experienced for herself the "Doc" Skinner connection. During an early visit, Jim—knowing of my appointment at Allegheny—stepped out of his office and introduced himself. Having confirmed Pat's relationship to me, he wondered out loud what she might have learned about my father, and shared several stories about him.

During the conversation, Pat mentioned that I had described to her a photographic portrait of Dad that, for some years after his death, hung in the physician's lounge of the hospital. Jim's brow knit as he told her that the lounge had disappeared several years earlier during a construction project to modernize the hospital's lobby. A bit apologetically, he confessed that he remembered the portrait, but did not know what had become of it.

One day that spring, Jim's well-over-six-foot frame filled Pat's office door, bearing the lost portrait. Face wrinkled by an irrepressible grin, like a kid touting an unexpected achievement to his parents, he described how he had scoured through several storage areas in the basement of the hospital, finally turning up the picture among some historical items. Would she, he inquired, be kind enough to return it to me?

By the time Mother came for a visit the following winter, the portrait was hanging in our front hall, and Pat recounted the story of its recovery. When she described the specifics of where she worked, however, Mother abruptly redirected the conversation. "Oh," she exclaimed brightly, looking at me, "that's where you were born." It was news to me. I always assumed that I and my whole generation of friends had been born in the hospital. Not exactly. At the hospital, yes; in the hospital, no.

Around the turn of the twentieth century, Meadville's birth rate outpaced the capacity of City Hospital's maternity ward. With gifts from two prominent Meadville women as a foundation, the Ladies' Advisory Committee raised funds to erect a separate maternity building that came, in time, to be called "Old Mat."

The Old Mat
1910

"I'd like to see that again," Mother said pointedly. "Why not?" we replied, and off we went. It being a weekend, the office was closed and the building empty. Mother paused only briefly in the parking lot, her eyes scanning the building for the first time in a generation. Notably unadorned for a late Victorian structure, its simplicity was a concession to economy. But it had an evident functionality, as if to say that it knew what it had been built for and did the job well, thank you very much.

Pat's key opened the front door, and we stepped into the cavernous hall that ran the length of the building. Once in, we stood aside, watching Mother's face for clues that memories were flooding back. They were. Eyes narrowed and lips pursed, she considered the large room to the left of the entry, then brightened as she told us that it was the fathers' lounge. Looking at its gaping emptiness, my imagination peopled it with young men who paced nervously or perched on chair edges, waiting for tidings of larger responsibility. Across the hall a side room, then as now, housed a receptionist, while several smaller rooms adjacent provided office space for staff.

Right there public access had halted: enormous swinging doors, their curtained, wired-glass windows as opaque as their solid frames, barred the way. Swinging open momentarily and closing again at the passage of a physician or nurse, they offered no more than a glimpse into the largely woman's world beyond, the only clues to its purpose revealed in the periodic wail of an infant, or the encouraging prattle of a nurse attending a young woman straining in the thrall of labor.

The doors stood agape now, and the darkly silent rooms seemed to stare back at us.

By the 1950s Old Mat, too, became obsolete. The maternity program was moved back into the newly enlarged and modernized main hospital building, after which Old Mat served a variety of purposes. For a time it was a dormitory housing unmarried and student nurses. Indeed, as a student at Allegheny College a few blocks uphill to the north, and clueless to how close I was to my point of embarkation, I dated one such, and spent a number of evenings on the stolid front stoop engaged in activities the nature of which are not included in the scope of this essay. Later, after City Hospital abandoned its student nursing program, the building was used mainly for storage, and continued in part to do so even after the advent of the program for which Pat was employed.

Thus it was, on the day Mother visited, that we wandered through the building and back in time. Getting her bearings, Mother started off briskly through the huge doors and down the hall, passing the ornate and dysfunctional elevator without so much as a sidelong glance. (Pat said it resembled a bank vault more than a people lift anyway. Large enough to accommodate a bed, it had become just another storage space, crammed with surplus hospital paraphernalia.)

Slowly, guided by Mother's barrage of chatter, my imagination eliminated the reigning confusion and imagined the building as it was that snowy December morning that she and Dad raced the clock to the moment of my birth. One by one, the pale yellow and green lying-in rooms came to life, as if our passage furnished each one anew with a metal bed and matching chair lacquered sterile white, an adjustable bedside stand with ornate cast iron post and base, and a plain dresser with a large swivel mirror. Only the sheer curtains, as long as the too-tall-for-their-width Victorian windows they graced, softened the spare simplicity. The fantasy of transformation was even easier once we passed beyond the storage area, where the empty hall and naked, high-ceilinged rooms echoed every word and footstep.

Climbing the broad and shallow-pitched stairs, Mother turned into the second floor hallway with the unfaltering instinct of a migratory bird in flight, never hesitating until she came to the last room on the right. "This is it," she announced, turning in and standing in the middle of it, her reedy alto voice, undiminished by her seventy-nine years, careening around the bare walls.

"This is where we stayed when you were born. The bed was over there in that corner. And," (she glanced out the door) "Susan Hawkey's mother was in the room across the hall." Susan, a childhood schoolmate and middle daughter of another Meadville physician, was born that same week. "We had the nurses move our dressers so we could see each other in the mirrors, and talked to each other across the hall." In a day when women routinely remained "confined" for a week following childbirth, they had plenty of time to talk.

We had brought the camera, and Pat took a picture of us in the corner of the hollow cavern of a room where the bed had stood. Looking at the frozen image now, the tiny woman beside me barely reaching my shoulder, my 200-pound bulk easily twice hers, I am mindful that I was her fourth and, save for my sister Ruth Ann, am her shortest child. And I muse on the mystery of childbirth and inheritance, and hear God's primordial proclamation to Jeremiah: "Before I formed you in the womb I knew you, and before you were born I consecrated you."

PART II

Seen Around Home

CHAPTER 4

Voice of the Door Monster

T he wind was hard out of the northwest, browsing along the front of the house and probing for any chink that might offer entry. Happily tangling with Mother's pots and pans on the kitchen floor, I hardly noticed. Though it made walking through the kitchen an adventure, Mother tolerated my rummaging through her kitchen cabinets, dragging everything out onto the floor. She said she'd rather I was under foot than her having to chase through the house looking for me.

One instant I was banging away; the next, the racket stopped mid-clatter as fear crowded my ribs and such hair as I had on the back of my toddler neck stood on end. A mournful moan from somewhere in the front of the house traveled the hall and filled the kitchen. It began softly, in a low register; but the pitch ascended in proportion to its volume. Or perhaps it was the other way around. At two years of age, I wasn't concerned about the dynamics of frequency modulation. Something out there was alive, and I was not happy about it. Pots and pans flying in all directions, I scrambled to my feet and ran to Mother, wrapping myself around a leg and pleading with her to make it stop.

As always, Mother's reassurance was mildly dismissive. "Oh, that's only the door monster," she said offhandedly, "and it only sounds mean; it intends us no harm, really, and is quite friendly as monsters go." Gently prying me loose, she returned to her work. I stood in the middle of the kitchen, ignoring the clutter of utensils as if the tears wetting my face had dissolved my interest.

This would take some thought. Door monster, Mother said. That told me where the dreadful noise was coming from, but it did little to ease my fear—not as long as the monster's mournful squall continued to fill the house. I stepped gingerly into the breakfast nook, just off the kitchen and within easy reach of Mother's comforting leg should courage fail me. Without going further, I could look down the length of hall at the front door, watching intently as each revival of the wind raised another yowl. But the Dutch-hung door was unmoving, as oak-solid as ever. The wrought iron thumb-press latch still held, as did the crescent clasp that coupled the upper and lower halves of the door, and the twin

slide-bolts that locked both haves of the door to the jam. If the monster was there, it sure knew how to keep out of sight, even as it continued to complain.

I glanced back into the kitchen to be sure Mother was still there. She was, eyeing me sidelong every few moments, a smile seeming somehow to play inside, but not outside, her lips. Summoning my nerve, I stepped into the hall and moved—ever so cautiously—toward the door. If familiarity doesn't always breed contempt, it at least engenders confidence: no matter how often the door howled, it was still just the front door. As each gust of wind moved the door monster to howl, I ratcheted up my courage another notch and took another step, until finally I was close enough to feel my skin tremble in unison with the door as it fought the press of the wind. That came near to being too much. Fighting the urge to bolt, I thought again of Mother's words: "It's quite friendly as monsters go." Standing my ground and quivering with audacity run amok, I took a deep breath and reached out, putting my hand against the door just as a moan started, ascended, peaked for a terrifying second, and faded to stillness. Exploding with exhilaration (not to mention relief), I tore down the hall, cornered through the breakfast nook so hard that I almost overshot the kitchen door, and trumpeted, "I petted the door monster, and it didn't bite me!"

Soon I was running to pat the door at the first hint of moan, intoning sympathetically, "Good monster. Don't cry. It's okay." So passed my first crisis with the unknown.

It would be several years before I understood how the brute acquired its vocal dexterity. While an architect prepared the blueprints, the design of our home—an imposing colonial reconstruction built the year I was born (allowing me to presume that it was my first birthday present)—was Dad's. Building houses was not new to him. Some long-ago mutation embedded the craft in the genetic map of Skinner males. Dad and his brother Edgar had built several houses, including their mother's boxy-simple but sturdy New York State home. Dad meant our house to be his crown jewel, and it must be prefect in every detail. Doors, inside and out, were equipped with hand-hammered black iron strap hinges and latches, none more elaborate than those gracing the home of the door monster. Too, being parsimonious about re-sources decades before "energy-consciousness" entered the na-tional lexicon, Dad ordered brass-shim weather stripping installed on the exterior doors. And therein resided the voice of the door monster: every stiff breeze crept around the door's edges and set the brass shims vibrating. So dolefully did they moan that a Hollywood sound man would be hard put to create that melan-choly a lament.

There is a lesson here, and a paradox: though among my earliest memories, the door monster ranks among my most vivid. What if it was only imaginary? To my young mind it was real enough, and certainly as real as ever I cared to have any monster become. Mother's willingness to accept my anxiety at face value, neither dismissing it as infantile silliness nor patronizing it as the harbinger of some developmental crisis, allowed me to ex-plore the fear and overcome it. Is this not often the case with our fears? Faced by something strange to us, yet not as alarming as we are prepared to imagine, we fabricate dread out of ignorance. By naming the monster and reassuring me about its character, Mother gave me a gentle tug into a rational world without trying to persuade me to abandon the imagination that my infant mind thrived on. It was the same kind of having-our-cake-and-eating-it-too thinking that allowed us, as children, to admit that Santa Claus was a fable, but still to go to our beds Christmas Eve hoping that, if we could just stay awake long enough, we'd hear reindeer hooves on the roof.

At the time, I experienced it simply as growing self-confidence. Life would be filled with weird things that would frighten me if I let them. The lesson I learned was that I needn't let them, because many would turn out to be nothing more than the wind. The validity of that lesson stayed fresh over a lot of years, and helped me to be of some use to my children and grandchildren when they struggled with their own fears. And whenever they did, I'd pause once in a while when no one was looking, and glance over my shoulder to smile and wink at my old friend, the Door Monster.

———•———

My encounter with the door monster was nothing compared to Frank's discovery, about the same time, of a serious flaw in the design of our new home, and that only a few feet away. Our wailing front door opened into a central foyer—a small but complex space that hinted right off at the character of the house. A hammered copper chandelier suspended from the brocaded plaster ceiling looked down on wide, varnished floorboards doweled to the sub floor. The whole formed an open stairwell, up the right hand wall of which ran an open staircase, beckoning to the second floor.

Regrettably, the maple banister that climbed the stairs atop a run of plain square balusters did not, at the bottom, rest on a newel post. It was set into the side of a slender pillar that went floor to ceiling. Children inattentive to this detail discovered, on their very first slide down the banister, how abruptly and painfully that pillar ended the trip. Still, no first-and-final ride down it ever ended half as painfully as Frank's unintended descent of the stairwell without the aid of steps. The miracle is not that he lived to tell his grandchildren, but that he lived at all.

It began innocently enough. Confined to the house one afternoon, we were busy making the best of our three-dimensional playground—yelling at one another in the open stairwell, clattering up and down the bare wood treads, and racing along the open balcony that wrapped around three sides of the second floor, off which doors opened to the family's bedrooms and the children's bathroom. If Mother thought we were intent on making as much noise as possible with our running game of push and shove, she was probably right. It was during such a frenetic moment that Frank exposed the critical design flaw by suddenly vanishing. While Dad's architect had a fine taste for aesthetics, he either wasn't thinking about children when he determined the spacing of the balusters, or wasn't thinking at all. They were a full ten inches apart, more than wide enough for a small child to step between them or, playing among them, to lose his balance and fall through—which is precisely what Frank did.

Let it be stated right here, however, that Frank is not one to do anything halfway. My next oldest brother is nothing if not thorough. He didn't fall through the railing along the side somewhere, or near the top of the stairs where he'd just tumble a few feet onto one of the upper steps. He fell through at the far end of the balcony, opposite the top of the stairs, where there was no stopping short of the bottom step. Which is just where he landed—on his head.

The expression on Mother's face as she came flying out of the kitchen can only be described as a cross between "What now?!" and "God help us!" Little wonder: by her account, Frank's landing shook the whole house. She had no idea what to expect, and what she found was not reassuring. Her third child lay prone on the hall floorboards, an awesome hematoma swelling from his forehead like a volcano about to erupt. He probably had a fractured skull. We'll never know. Whether it was a symptom of the time or the fact that our parents enjoyed an intimate acquaintance with the practice of medicine, we visited the doctor only if unconscious or bleeding profusely. Frank wasn't bleeding—not on the outside, anway. And he assuredly wasn't unconscious: he was wailing up a storm. And since he made it through the rest of the day without wandering around like a duck that had been hit on the head, colliding with small obstacles like door jambs and refrigerators, Dad and Mother concluded that he'd survive, and that time would remove the goose egg on his head. It didn't, at least not entirely. To this day, Frank carries a striking lump where the weight of his three-year-old frame was concentrated when his forehead met the step.

Skinners, we were told as children, have strong bones, a quality presumably inherited from our progenitors. Not everyone has chosen to express it that way. More than one observer has suggested that "hard-headed" would be a more apt adjective than "hard-boned." Still others—clearly not intent on flattery—prefer "thick" to "hard," but I favor the latter as suggesting inherited strength as opposed to willful stupidity. If that be so, it must in candor be said that Frank was blessed that day with an extraordinary measure of inherited strength.

For reasons requiring no elaboration, Dad quickly corrected the architect's oversight, securing panels to the balusters that even a tiny child couldn't get past. While not pretty, they served to prevent several generations of children from a reprise of Frank's inaugural, and sensational, solo flight. I hardly found them necessary. One look at the goose egg on Frank's forehead—and it was around to look at for a long time— eradicated any thought I had about trying to fly in the stairwell.

I was less immune to the seductive lure of the telephone. A few paces from the home of the door monster, on the wall opposite the bottom step that reverberated so lustily when Frank's head assaulted it, a narrow niche was cut into the floral-papered wall. Equipped with a single wooden shelf of the same honey-toned maple that was used to finish the entry hall, it housed the family telephone. I specify family, because there was a second phone in the house: it sat on a bedside table in the master bedroom where Dad could easily answer it in the event of a late-night medical call. But it was off-limits, like everything else in that room. From my point of view, it wouldn't have mattered if it wasn't there at all.

But the family phone sat right out in open sight, all tantalizing and easily within reach of even a toddler. That I found it so tempting was Mother's fault. The phone, she instructed, is not a toy. In our household, that was code for "this is off-limits;" a declaration that mainly served to transform some item I might otherwise have ignored into forbidden fruit pleading to be plucked. Passing the niche one day, my thoughts somewhere else, I looked up and found myself eyeball to eyeball with that phone. Had it been a huge snake, swaying rhythmically in a hypnotic dance intended to eliminate my resistance to becoming lunch, it could not have been more seductive.

Like all phones of the day it was black from its round base to the mouth horn that swiveled atop its ten-inch post. Even the wire cord that attached the earpiece was black. In time it would become so frayed and twisted that it began to resemble an oriole's nest. But on the day of my temptation, it was still new. And even though it made not a sound, I could hear it purring: "Come play with me. Pick me up. Talk to me." More than once, on days when I was more ready than on others to be tempted, my hand had reached out almost involuntarily, hanging me on the edge of a first-rate scolding. Each time, however, I was saved by the admonition Mother recited every time we entered one of the stores down on Chestnut Street: "Keep your hands in your pockets." Cramming my hands halfway to my ankles, I rushed past and avoided censure.

But this time was different. I was almost three, and fresh out of resistance. I looked up and down the hall furtively, even though I knew that Mother was upstairs. It would not have been the first time that I began to do something, sure that I was secure, only to hear Mother speak my name in a tone that made the question that followed redundant: "What are you doing?" Satisfied that my indiscretion would remain hidden, I cautiously lifted the receiver off its hook and held it up to my ear. For an instant, nothing happened. I was about to pick up the phone to say "hello" into the mouthpiece, as if speaking would bring some answer, when a woman's voice came from the receiver: "Number, please?" For a split second, it seemed that someone had crept up beside me and spoken right into my ear, startling me enough that I almost dropped the receiver. To my untutored ear, it also seemed loud enough that I was sure Mother must have heard it, no matter where she was. Jamming the receiver back onto its hook, I jumped back in the same way that I did on a dry winter day when, scuffing through the house absent-mindedly, I reached for a light switch. It didn't matter how many times I did it; there was no holding still when the tiny spark jumped from the light switch to my fingertip.

I hadn't fully realized the thing was wired to another human being. But it made sense of the conversations I had heard whenever Mother picked up the phone before it ever rang. Next time she went to the phone, I squirmed in beside her, watching

in fascination as she lifted the receiver off its bracket, opening
the circuit to the central exchange. Soon the same woman's voice,
nasal and pinched as though traveling a length of ventilator duct,
twanged out of the receiver:

"Number, please?"

"Two-four-five, please, " Mother responded.

"Thank yew," said the ventilator voice. A brief pause and a
few clicks later, the burr of a phone ringing in someone else's
hallway or kitchen announced that the connection was made.
That settled it. I knew that if I tried to make a call I'd have to talk
to that woman, and she'd call Mother back and ask her if she
wanted me using the phone, and I already knew the answer to
that. Besides, I had no idea what my friends' numbers were, or
even whether they had any. Sneaking calls would just have to
wait until I was older.

CHAPTER 5

Living Room

I never think of our living room without remembering the fireplace; or the fireplace without reflecting on the origin of my middle name.

The north and east walls of the room were clad in honey-colored maple paneling, in fine contrast to the plaster on the south and west walls and a brocaded plaster ceiling supported by hand-hewn oak beams spanning the width of the room. The space above the narrow fireplace mantle was framed to form an arched triptych, its center panel occupied by an old linen sampler in a plain wood frame. It was typical of its genre, by which generations of girls mastered an essential homemaking skill. Two complete alphabets, one of upper and one of lower case letters, were lined between double ranks of numerals, the whole bordered by an intricate acorn motif and garnished with species of birds, trees and flowers that reside only in whimsy. Across the center appeared a complex if syntactically dubious proverb:

"A deſire to excel others in Virtue is very Com-
mendable and a delight in obtaining Praise
deſerves Encouragement becauſe it Discovers an
Excellent mind."

But its attraction for me was anything but abstract: paneled
across its bottom center was the ascription: "Elizabeth Covill •
Aged 9 years • 1810."

I was twenty-seven before I learned just where Elizabeth
perched on our family tree. After my maternal Grandmother
McCafferty died in 1959, Mother handed me a small, hinged metal
case clad in maroon leather and secured by minute, twin metal
hooks-and-eyes. I had never seen it before. Opening the velvet-
lined cover, I found myself looking into the frank eyes of an old
woman, perhaps eighty, who gazed impassively out through an
arched mat of gold, her visage frozen in time. Remarkably, the
image was in color, adding to the uncanny sensation that we were
being introduced. Her hands, enlarged and hardened by labor, are
folded on her lap, palms together, a hint of book visible between
them, and a wide gold band glistens on the fourth finger of her
right hand. A black-and-white plaid stole, pulled taut about the
shoulders of her black satin blouse, is pinned at the breast. Her
face is cuddled in an ornately-frilled white dust bonnet through
which a wide satin ribbon is threaded, black like her blouse, emerging at the bottom and tied in a large bow under her chin.

Let it be admitted that Elizabeth Covill was not a comely
woman. Dark brows, masculine in weight and arch, shelter asymmetrical eyes, one higher than the other on her long and narrow
face. An extraordinary nose, flanked by prominent cheek bones,
looms above a mouth aligned as true as a ruler's edge, beneath
which her chin juts as if to put the world on notice that it would be

unwise to take this woman lightly. Yet there is a twinkle to her eyes and a play of smile about her lips, as if she really wants to break out into a grin but must not, in deference to the deliberate pace at which silver nitrate responds to the impulse of light. If I had to guess, I'd suppose her to be a kind person, but businesslike.

A small piece of yellowed paper fell from the case as I opened it. Stooping to pick it up, I recognized Grandmother's meticulous handwriting: "Elizabeth Covill—my great great grandmother." That made Elizabeth my great great great great grandmother—a scope of heritage hard to comprehend. Born and raised in England, Elizabeth immigrated to America as a young woman, married, and raised a family.

But long before I knew any of that, I stood in front of our living room fireplace, musing on how I came to share my middle name with this little girl, and gained my first imprecise sense of ancestry and blood kinship.

Our living room played the role of a nineteenth century front parlor: we seldom used it. It was reserved for company, with

seasonal exceptions. Our Christmas tree always stood at the east end, in front of the door to the dining room. If I hadn't known better, I'd swear it was the same tree every year. Mother insisted on a balsam fir, six feet tall and symmetrical. She preferred balsams, a taut, short-leaf variety, because she was convinced they held their needles longest—not that it made any difference in the end. After six weeks of dry heat, there was no way to crawl under the branches to pour water into the reservoir at the base of the tree stand without getting terminal prickles. Every scrap of life that might have clung to the poor things had long since been wrung out of them. Dragging the tree outside on New Year's Day never failed to lay a highway of needles from the back of the living room to the front door. And every April, at spring cleaning time, we were still scooping up the last of them.

I never knew for sure, but I think our Christmas tree lights were manufactured a few weeks after Thomas Edison successfully fabricated his first light bulb. Their twin wires were sheathed in fabric, and the narrow fluted bulbs, in six colors, had been smacked around so much that their painted surfaces were scored to the glass, creating a random sparkle of white light among the branches. But they were durable beyond belief. I doubt that more than a dozen of them burned out during my entire childhood, and those were easily replaced at Murphy's 5¢ & 10¢ Store down on Chestnut Street.

On blustery winter Sundays, when the door monster howled and snow churned past the windows, afternoon was family time in the living room, and Dad built a fire in the best fireplace I ever knew. It was on a side wall, offset toward the back of the room where it served as the focal point for most of the comfortable furniture, and Dad designed it himself. Taller than it was wide and barely deep enough to fit two logs side-by-side on the andirons, it was far too shallow by the measure of boxy modern fireplaces, and demonstrably superior. The thing heated up a storm. Flame licking up the back wall fired the bricks to an iridescent red, and we sat on the couch against the opposite wall, fifteen feet away, and baked our knees. Or, gathered about a board game on the rug a few feet from the hearth, we children could rotisserie ourselves to a turn. On such days, I was sure that we lived in the coziest house in town

It was about the same time, in the same room, that I began to absorb Mother and Dad's notion that reading is not only pleasurable, but important. Over the years, several family friends told me of observing Dad sitting in a room filled with talking people, absorbed in a complex medical text as completely as if he had been alone. Likewise, Mother was never without a book nearby. Late in life, when she lived alone, she kept a reading stand on her dining room table so that a book or magazine could serve as a side dish to dinner.

The back wall of the room, evenly flanking a door to the dining room, featured matching maple built-ins with bookshelf tops and cabinet bases. I paid little attention to what lived on the shelves to the left of the door, which was reserved for grown-ups' books; but the ones on the right were devoted to us children— Junior Literary Guild books like *The Wizard of Oz, Robinson Crusoe* and *Robin Hood,* and magazines like our *National Geographic* collection that grew larger with each passing year. One exception to Mother's general "stay out of the living room children" rule was blanket permission to pick out a book or magazine and settle down on the couch to read.

I wonder what it is in us as children that we so quickly lose when we become adults. As kids, we devour books or magazines like a starving man handed a ham sandwich, reading them time after time. Then we grow up and become so entangled in the busyness of the adult world that we can't seem to find time to sit down even with books we claim we want badly to read. Still, I suspect that I learned vastly more of the mechanics of reading, and of its infinite pleasure, in one afternoon on that living room couch than I did in ten years of public school. I mean, how can "See Spot. See Spot run. Run, Spot, run" compete with the likes of my favorite issue of *National Geographic* that featured the whales of the world in living color? I pored over that magazine until the pages fell out, and I could identify it on the bookshelf by its frayed spine long after the table of contents had faded to illegibility. And while I can't recall a single story I read in grade school, I consumed books like *Bambi's Children* and *Green Grass of Wyoming* so many times that I lost count.

—————

In reality, our living room was two rooms. The offsetting of the fireplace and its accompanying furniture toward the back of the room left the front end open to serve as a music studio. Having been born the year our home was built, I accepted the layout as natural. It would be a while before I appreciated how unusual the front end of our living room really was; and even longer before I realized how basic music was to the courtship and bonding of our parents.

So different were their backgrounds that it seems a wonder, on the face of it, that Clifford Skinner and Ruth McCafferty got together at all. Dad grew up in the southwestern New York village of Ashville, population at his birth in 1892 maybe 200, but I wouldn't bank on it. Dad's father, Aaron Skinner, was a country doctor who carried a black leather satchel that served as peripatetic office, ER and pharmacy. When his patients couldn't get to him, he hitched horse to buggy and went to them, at whatever hour the call for help came and in weather that would tie modern urban commuters in knots. He was obstetrician attending a birthing mother, pediatrician treating a child with whooping cough, orthopedic specialist repairing a limb crushed by a wagon. Aaron was such a mush-heart that his family lived on the short end of economic necessity; the man couldn't bring himself to lean on his mostly poor patients to pay their bills, especially when treating a child, so his own family made do with what was left over.

Making it happen was the job of the woman whom Aaron "took to wife," according to the idiom of the age, in 1877. Emma Weld was the daughter of another modestly situated family, most of whom settled across the border in northern Pennsylvania. She was a study in placidity, a veteran of the hard life with a genius for transforming "make do" into "sufficient." Without bitterness or complaint, and against serious odds, she struggled to sustain her husband and raise her children. She bore seven. The eldest, a girl they named Rachael, died at birth. Their second child Frank, after whom my brother is named, succumbed to scarlet fever in his ninth year. Three girls and two boys survived to adulthood, carrying typically nineteenth century names: Gertrude, Maude, Edgar, Mabelle and Clifford.

In such a setting, religion was earthy and unsophisticated. Clifford was raised in a matrix of Methodist piety, high moral standards, hard work, personal modesty and social generosity.

And love. Whatever other impressions crowd my mind when my thoughts turn to those dear people, I feel still the enveloping tenderness of a love as consummate as any I can even imagine. They did not always approve of my childish behavior and even less would they—had they known—approve of my youthful experimentation in the ways of the world. But that I was loved was never in doubt.

After graduating from high school and business college, Clifford taught school for several years while contemplating entering the ministry, and married a girl from the neighboring village of Panama. She died carrying their first child. A widower at 24, Clifford pulled himself together, enrolled in Allegheny College and changed his vocational goal to medicine. Older than any in his class, friends soon nicknamed him "Doc," a sobriquet he carried for the rest of his life. On campus, it was reinforced by an old doctor's grip in which he carried his books and (his 1921 classmates averred in the college yearbook) all the "A" grades available in any class he ever took, leaving none for them. Nor did it hurt that he was named laboratory instructor in biology while still an undergraduate. After he was inducted into Phi Beta Kappa in his junior year, it was no surprise to anyone that he was named valedictorian and elected president of his graduating class. He was admitted to medical school in Cleveland, but had to withdraw his application because of a lack of funds. Always adept at transforming a setback into an asset, he quickly accepted Allegheny's offer to stay on as biology instructor while earning a master of science degree.

This was a good thing, because Clifford's interests at Allegheny had by then broadened considerably: his teaching duties put him in more than casual contact with Emma Ruth McCafferty, a petite and vivacious Pittsburgh socialite. Emma so detested her first name that she refused to own it, choosing to go by her middle name. Indeed, she was sufficiently determined in this that even her family got confused, on several documents recording her name as Ruth Emma. The transformation was completed when she and Clifford married and she became Ruth M. Skinner, excising

"Emma" from the family history. Ruth was known to chastise her children for stubbornness. We know where we got it.

Ruth was fond of recalling that she "grew up on the lap" of Pittsburgh food magnate Henry J. Heinz, to whom her father was personal secretary and legal advisor. Taken early into the inner circle of Heinz's friends, the McCaffertys were invited to reside next door to H. J. in Heinz Circle, a cluster of fine homes in Sharpsburg, a suburb of Pittsburgh. A doting grandfatherly type eager to spoil, H. J. was smitten with Ruth and her older brother Tom. The grandly mustachioed and sideburned man of business and the little girl would sit and swing on the veranda of his palatial home, chatting like family. In spite of what seemed an idyllic life, Ruth bridled under her parents' firm hand. They were loving, often generous. Nothing that was needful (a valuation the McCaffertys never confused with "desired") was lacking from her life. But they were firm to the point of being domineering. Ruth yearned for the chance to take charge of her own affairs.

For a time, it seemed the opportunity might be indefinitely delayed by that siege of ungulate fever that took her out of school for most of a year. Whether her opinion that the experience toughened her is medically supportable or not (she was hardly sick another day in her life), she recovered in overdrive and determined to catch up. Completing her work at Pittsburgh's Peabody High School in record time, she enrolled in Allegheny mid-year and hit campus with a trunk brimming with flapper gowns and a determination to graduate with her class. She did.

It is not clear whether Ruth's decision to major in biology grew more out of a love of science or her attraction to the darkly handsome lab instructor—nine years her senior, a widower of modest means from a tiny agricultural village in southwestern New York. Following her graduation in 1923, newly engaged, she took a job as teacher in a one-room school in Erie County, PA, an experiment that soured during her second year when a belligerent teenager threw a book at her. (Those who believe that aggressive behavior in American schools is a recent development may want to take notice.) Her way out was clear, however: in 1924, Clifford enrolled in Northwestern Medical College, later to graduate from Rush Medical College at the University of Chicago. One book-throwing incident being one too many, Ruth happily left teaching; and when, in 1925, Clifford started west to the Big Windy for his second year of medical school, she accompanied him as his wife.

In Chicago, Ruth was introduced to what Clifford had been intimately acquainted with his whole life: how to skirt the edge of poverty without slipping over. She would later relate how they hawked the Chicago dump, scavenging for discarded furniture to equip their small apartment. They managed in part by engaging in several years of itinerancy. By an arrangement that now seems preposterous, Clifford commuted between Chicago and Richmond, spending part of each year at the medical college of the University of Virginia, where he progressed from associate in anatomy through associate professor to assistant dean. By such peripatetic choreography, my sister Ruth Ann, their eldest child, and Frank, their third, were born in Richmond; but Clifford Jr., their second, was born in Chicago. I alone was born in Meadville—which undoubtedly qualifies me to be the one writing this book!

———————

Ruth and Clifford's match might have seemed less likely had Ruth's wealth been more than one generation deep. It wasn't. I need only travel to her parents' Ohio birthplace to discover how similar the soils were in which she and Clifford were rooted. Ruth's parents grew up in the village of Harrison, west of Cincinnati astraddle the Indiana border. Although Harrison was more prosperous than Ashville, because Ohio's alluvial plains are naturally more fertile than New York's foothill valleys, the two towns yet harbored the same Midwestern values. After attending Michigan's Adrian College, where he excelled academically (and suffered written reprimand, with threatened dismissal, if he did not desist immediately from playing ball on the college's front lawn), Ernest Dair McCafferty worked his way through law school at the University of Michigan.

Along the way he courted and won demurely shy Florence Emma Bowles. His employment by H. J. Heinz promising economic stability, they married in 1897 and left for Pittsburgh. There Florence bore a son and daughter, and Ernest began the career with H. J. Heinz that brought wealth and social status to his family and created, on the surface, what some might consider an unbridgeable gap between them and a New York country doctor's family.

But in fact, Ruth and Clifford shared in common several things that strengthened the bond between them and influenced their children's development. And at the heart of it was a mutual love of music. Ruth was an accomplished pianist and organist, able to sit down and play a strange piece of music as if she'd known it her whole life. She was sought out as an accompanist by instrumentalists and vocalists who valued her ability to adapt to their idiosyncrasies—and thereby to make them look good! Clifford, though not trained to read keyboard music, possessed a wicked ear. He could attend a concert, listen to a number he had never heard before, then sit down at the piano and play an impressive facsimile of its main themes.

So it was natural that there would be a piano in our home. But I soon discovered how unusual it was for there to be two of them. They filled most of the front wall of the living room, leaving only the broad front window, overlooking North Main Street, uncovered.

Add the antique pump organ that sat against the south wall, by the door to the screened porch, and there wasn't space for much of anything in the front of the room *but* music. More music was made in that living room during the sixteen years we lived there than most houses experience in their lifetimes, and not much of it was of the halting, pick-and-poke method of children struggling to master keyboard basics or trying to decipher an instrumental score. There was much of that, to be sure: piano lessons were as mandatory for Skinner children as hot cereal breakfasts in February. And if the sound was as bruising to parental ears as it was to our egos, they had no one to blame but themselves. It was Mother and her friends and associates, who came often to rehearse in preparation for one performance or another, who flooded the room with music, all of it competent, much of it downright professional. If it wasn't a string trio it was duo-piano; or if not an instrumentalist seeking Mother's skilled accompaniment, a vocal soloist. Or it was one of the young musicians that Mother seemed to attract like a July herb garden draws bees. Many went on to make music an avocational joy, and not a few to become professional musicians and teachers.

It was hard to grow up in that house and *not* develop a love of classical music. Whatever other appetites we might gather up along the way—pop, jazz, folk—classical music ("good music," in Mother's lexicon) was always, and remained, the foundation.

But it was the old pump organ that captivated the youngest Skinner. For sure, the Estey Company in Brattleboro, Vermont, which built it, didn't spare the rococo. Every aspect of it seemed to mimic a Gothic cathedral, further evidence if any were needed of how indelibly twelfth-century European architecture continued, eight hundred years after the fact, to define "church." The old girl was a casualty of time, however: only one of the two pump pedals worked, the canvas strap connecting the other to the bellows having long since frayed and separated. But a one-legged organ was good enough for a no-count musician. I didn't even care that every song I poked out seemed to have passed through a tremolo box stuck in slow motion, the volume enlarging and fading in direct proportion to the speed with which my small leg was able to work the single pedal: "o GOd ouR HELp in AGes PAst..."

The instrument had come into Dad's family years before, by way of his mother, and everyone claimed ignorance about how to fix it—an odd confession in a family that could repair just about anything. It would finally pass on to our cousin Harold, only child of Dad's brother Edgar and himself a professional musician. Harold had the thing repaired and up to speed in short order. But for the time being it was ours to abuse, and I sat pumping with one-legged ferocity, alternately pulling out the piston stops singly or in combination to see how much of what kind of noise I could generate, whether flute, trumpet, diapason, or full orchestra, thrilling at the reverberations that careened around the room. When I could manage it, I used one knee to work the pistol-handled lever under the keyboard that controlled the swell box, enlarging or suppressing the volume.

To my untutored musical taste, long on enthusiasm but short on finesse, it was almost as good as church! For such a small instrument, it made a lot of noise when driven at ramming speed and everything playing in concert. That may explain why Mother passed it on to Harold as soon as the opportunity presented itself. It's just possible that she'd had about all the one-legged organ music she could tolerate.

CHAPTER 6

A Shot in the Arm

It's hard to say how often Dad's home office was actually used for medical purposes. By the time I was old enough to take notice, he was gone. But only one memory is necessary to convince me that it served its intended purpose: the vivid imprint on my tender brain of a teenaged boy sitting atop the examining table with blood oozing from his mouth and soaking his shirt front. Head wounds bleed worse than just about anything, and busted tongues are the bloodiest of all. The boy looked like he might keel over dead any instant; but his case was probably less serious than just terribly inconvenient. He and his friends were playing baseball on a farm a few miles north of town when he caught a smartly batted line drive, not in his mitt but squarely in the mouth. That several teeth were knocked out was probably the enduring consequence. But for the moment, his pain was complicated by the fact that his tongue had been between his teeth when he got hit, and it was largely from the resultant gash that blood was soaking his front. Throwing him into a car, several friends raced him into town to get medical help and, knowing that "Doc" Skinner lived right there at the city line, roared into our driveway and frantically pounded the front door knocker.

For just a moment, while everything was still in uproar and no one had yet regained their composure—save Dad, who seemed never to become discombobulated by this sort of thing—the doors to his office stood open. From the front hall, bug-eyed astonishment playing all over my four-year-old face, I gawked at the boy. Perched there on the end of Dad's examining table in obvious and intense discomfort, he must have been dreading what was coming even as he realized that, whatever it was, it couldn't be a lot worse than what already had. Me, I couldn't imagine how it *could* be any worse. Then Mother intervened, the door was calmly but decisively closed, and we were instructed, just as decisively, to go outside and play. I didn't even want to imagine what the boy endured as Dad cleaned him up and sutured his gashes. But when he came out the door, Dad patting his shoulder reassuringly, he looked like his face had become the baseball—round and hard with the skin cross-stitched at the seams. Whether he ever played ball again is anyone's guess.

My personal anxiety about what went on in Dad's office predated by some months the young man's mistaken attempt to chew on a line-drive. Somewhere around my third year, Dad decided that all of us, including Mother and him, should receive some kind of inoculation. I don't recall what it was supposed to prevent, but it hardly mattered. I didn't yet know measles from Monday. All I knew was that Dad was going to give me a shot in the arm and the prospect didn't please me one bit. To sweeten the deal, Dad made a promise that I would later recognize was nothing but a come-on for the credulous: if we didn't cry when he gave us our shots, we could watch him give the shot to himself.

Properly primed, I obediently—and gullibly—lined up with my siblings at his office door to get my shot. For reasons no longer remembered, we went inversely by age, which put me first in line. Maybe Mother and Dad thought that if I got it behind me quickly, not having to wait for the other three children to get their shots, I'd have less time to get anxious. If so, they were mistaken. To make short of it, I bawled and my siblings didn't. But my complaint at being stuck with the needle was nothing compared to the noise I made when, true to his word, the door closed behind the others, and Dad punched the needle into his own arm while I stood in the front hall with Mother and loudly belabored the injustice of it all.

Some lessons are learned so subconsciously that their origins are discovered only after reflection that is years in coming. Among the things Dad taught me was the value of reliability. I could depend on him to do precisely what he said he would do, because he consistently proved it on occasions like this. Thirty-five years later, having been appointed (some would say condemned) to the post of dean on a college campus, I instinctively applied that lesson without at first recognizing where it came from. Students, I sensed, must be able to trust me absolutely, and nowhere more so than in campus discipline, never making a threat that I was not prepared to carry out. If I couldn't be trusted by students in trouble, why should anyone trust me at all?

———

As a child, it never occurred to me how much our life was influenced by the fact that Dad practiced medicine at a time when physicians still treated patients at home—not just house calls to the home of a patient, but in the physician's own home, as with the young ball player. Doing so required a space that had both the

requisite privacy and the medical equipment to treat patients who
appeared at the door. That need was clearly on Dad's mind when
he designed our house. Dad's office occupied the northwest corner of the main floor between—and a few steps inside—both
the front and side doors of the house, allowing patients to enter
or leave his office by way of either door without passing through
any other part of the house or disrupting family routine.

Although it was his medical office whenever the need arose,
it was a lovely room all of the time. A low doorway, identical to
one serving the living room across the way, opened off the front
hall. Each appeared to be a simple, paneled passage, but the side
panels were actually narrow, recessed doors, fitted with brass ring-
pulls, that swung out to meet in the center, insuring privacy. Walls
clad in wide-board paneling again contrasted with a brocaded plaster ceiling supported by more hand-hewn oak beams. Like the
other formal rooms on the main floor, the walls were studded
with copper sconce light fixtures. A large square-bay window, looking out toward North Main Street to the west, surmounted a sill
both high enough to accommodate a couch beneath and wide
enough to hold magazines and house plants, and mementos like
the ornately carved Philippine mahogany strong box H. J. Heinz
brought home from one of his world tours as a gift for the
McCaffertys.

Opposite the bay, against the back wall, stood Dad's maple
veneer secretary. Its writing desk closed to cover an upper compartment fitted with small drawers and cubbyholes that disguised
two "secret compartments." Carved in the form of miniature
amphorae perched atop simple pillars, they slid out in the manner of a book being taken from a shelf. Their hollow interiors
could hold only a few small articles, but were a perfect lodgment
for the family's safe deposit box key and savings account books

embossed with gold letters: "First National Bank of Meadville" or "Crawford County Trust Company." The piece lacked the traditional bookcase on top; but three shelves affixed to the paneled wall above the desk served the same purpose.

To the right of the desk, bunched into the corner of the room at a 45-degree angle, stood a Dutch fireplace, its semicircular hearth of dark red brick elevated two feet off a floor of the same doweled, random-width boards as the entry hall. Except for the exposed hulk of the hearth, the masonry of the fireplace was wrapped in paneling like that in the living room, leaving only the lip of the firebox brick exposed. A slender, built-in cabinet with paneled doors was sandwiched between the fireplace and the front hall passageway, pierced by a small opening about waist high. It was another demonstration of Dad's ingenuity. A small door hidden in its left wall allowed Dad to draw the telephone in from the niche in the front hall whenever need demanded that the talk be confidential.

In the corner opposite the fireplace, also angled forty-five degrees to the room, stood Dad's examining table—the one occupied by the bloodied ball player—its white enameled frame and legs a sharp contrast to a fine-grained black leather top. The positioning of the table let Dad approach a patient from either side with equal convenience. To the right of the table, a small glass-fronted cabinet stood against the north wall beneath the room's second window, its shelves stocked with medical instruments, bottles of antiseptics and salves, and carefully aligned boxes of gauze and adhesive tape. Those, and the obligatory college and medical school diplomas hung on the wall, were the only evidence that the place was a medical office—except maybe for the real human skull standing on one of the shelves above the desk; or the mortar and pestle on the fireplace hearth that one of our physician grandparents had carried into the fields in search of medicinal herbs to be crushed and dried and added to his supply of palliatives; or the exquisite balance-beam apothecary's scale standing atop the secretary, its small drawer holding brass weights tiny enough to measure the breath of a bird. But those were there mostly by way of decoration, curios from the past in the midst of "modern" medicine.

———·—·———

After Dad died, his office underwent the most material change of all the rooms in the house. The examining table and medicine cabinet were passed on to some other Meadville physician, and the diplomas, taken down and replaced by pictures, were laid away, eventually to pass to my eldest brother, Cliff Jr., when he earned his own M.D. degree. Mother took over Dad's secretary and, together with several of his personal effects that had made the desk his, like his matching scissor and letter-opener set, used it for the rest of her life. (Because her legs were too short comfortably to reach the floor, she rested her tiny feet on the front strut of the ladder-backed chair on which she sat when using the desk, eventually stripping it of varnish.) But for the duration of our time in Meadville, it served as the family desk, repository of essentials like paper and pencils, erasers and paste, paper clips and rubber bands. I don't even care to calculate how many arithmetic and algebra problems I failed to solve while sitting at that desk, staring up at the philodendron plant that had replaced the skull on the shelf above and wishing with all my might that I could be somewhere else.

After Mother died, and the secretary passed to us, Patricia set about to restore the finish on the exterior of the hinged writing desk, which was marred by handling and age. In working her way down through sixty years of wax, each with its filmy burden of grime, while trying to preserve as much of the original finish as possible, she was surprised by the gradual emergence of a name scratched into the face of it. In awkwardly formed letters, as if carved with a sharp metal point (perhaps Dad's letter opener?) was the name "Clifford." Thinking it not only odd but unlikely that Dad would scratch his name into the front of his own desk, she asked Cliff Jr. about it next time she had opportunity to talk to him.

"Oh, I remember it very well," he confessed. "I also recall that Dad allowed me to select the switch with which he would whip me for doing it!"

Some of life's mysteries are more easily solved than others. I concluded that though I had cause to regret many losses incurred by the untimely death of our father, the switch ritual was not among them.

CHAPTER 7

Aesculapius

I t is probably safe to venture that few Americans, indeed
hardly anyone at all except classics scholars and residents of
Greece, ever heard of Aesculapius (say Es-kuh-láy-pee-us).

This is hardly surprising. Every physician in the country takes
the Hippocratic Oath, the essential covenant to which all who
enter the practice of medicine are expected to adhere. On the
other hand, and while you'd think it would be advantageous for
them to know what it says, few of their patients ever read it, or
are aware of its arcane reference to Aesculapius, whose name it
invokes. In Greek legend, which held that he was the son of the
god Apollo and the nymph Coronis, Aesculapius was the god of
medicine. His skill in curing disease and restoring the dead to
life roused the ire of Zeus, who became fearful that Aesculapius
might make all humans immortal, which could really make a mess
of things. So Zeus slew him with a lightning bolt.

Leave it to Dad to name our first dog after him.

It is a truism that among canines, some possess natural beauty and grace, some are not bad looking, and a few are as homely as a wart hog. Aesculapius (how can I say this kindly?) took no ribbons for beauty. We never called him by his full name, actually. It was simpler to say "Eskie." Come to think of it, if we called him Aesculapius he probably wouldn't come anyway; and it was difficult enough to get his attention without confusing him into putting on airs. But whether called by his Greek patron or his easier-to-say nickname, he was a mongrel, and there's no use being subtle about it: he was short-legged and scruffy-faced with a coat of enough colors to make Joseph blanch with envy. To deduce that dog's genealogy would tax the aptitude of Sherlock Holmes. He may well have been the very dog about whom the joke was coined that his breed was "Heinz," as in fifty-seven varieties. Certainly we had the family connections to make the claim.

He was also a creature of habit. Once he adopted a pattern—and it generally seemed to require two or fewer repetitions to establish one—it was a waste of time trying to get him to change. Had his customs been divinely ordained, and I certainly do not suggest that they were, he could not have been more resistant to amending them.

Two cases in point:

Dogs, like people, trusted Dad, whether they knew him or not. Eskie and Dad hit it off the first time they met: after the manner of puppies, Eskie demonstrated his delight by piddling on Dad's shoe. It didn't appear to be intentional and certainly wasn't full-bore, if you take my meaning. He just got so excited he sprang a leak. There's nothing particularly remarkable about it. Many puppies do it. Except that Eskie did it every time Dad came home for the rest of his life. No one else was so honored—or minded being excluded. Nor did Dad get upset about it. But then, as a matter of routine, doctors deal with a lot of things the rest of us don't much care to be associated with.

As a result, Eskie was readily, and daily, forgiven for his selective breach of etiquette—but at no other time. Much as she loved animals, Mother's conditions for allowing pets into her home were firm and nonnegotiable. That dog was housebroken in a matter of days, and was smart enough never thereafter to challenge Mother's rank as the alpha female who got to set the ground rules for every critter, two-legged or four, living under her roof. So every time Dad came through the door the dog ran to him looking ecstatic and guilty at the same time, circled Dad's legs while pressing against his pants like a cat, and wet on his shoe. The rest of the time he was the soul of self-control.

Another of Eskie's scheduled customs was harassing the mailman. Not the milkman or the parcel postman, none of the meter readers or the paper boy or guests just dropping by. He didn't even get upset by the man who backed his loud and dirty truck into the driveway, laid a chute through the foundation window into the dark chamber that served as our hopper, and sent coal scuttling noisily into the basement (until natural gas came to our neighborhood and Dad, to Mother's everlasting gratitude, had a gas burner installed in the furnace firebox). Part of the time, Eskie didn't even rise to the occasion; he just snoozed on like nothing was happening. The rest of the time, allowed outside, he sniffed around the truck and stuck his head so far into the basement opening that the passing coal threatened to entrain him and deposit him onto the coal pile below.

No, the mailman alone was privileged to arouse Eskie's wrath, which was too bad, because he really was a nice man. Eskie never actually attacked him. There just seemed to be something about his daily passage that drove that dog over the edge.

Mother thought it was his uniform, but Eskie seldom actually saw the man. Hearing his footsteps padding mutely up the flagstone walk as only a dog can hear such things from clear at the other end of the house, the animal was up and running. As the mailman rounded the corner, Eskie was flailing through the kitchen, his toenails clawing frantically at the dark red linoleum in a vain effort to get a grip. And as the mailmen reached out to clack open the lid of the wooden mailbox on the side porch, Eskie was already in the back hall sounding like he meant to take the varnish off the door. Then the effect reversed itself: by the time the mailman had cut across the side yard and disappeared up Hamilton Avenue, the dog was like as not asleep again. It was a totally bizarre performance that made no sense whatever. So Eskie repeated it every day but Sunday.

It worked to the mailman's advantage, actually: Mother was so embarrassed by the dog's behavior that she gave him a generous gift every Christmas.

———————

Eskie's most recalcitrant trait was his dim-witted penchant for chasing cars. Once allowed to the curb on North Main Street, that animal would take off after any moving object that had four or more tires. He didn't chase bicycles (he was on tail-wagging face-licking terms with every kid in the neighborhood). Nor did it appear that his need to chomp rubber was based on a hatred of automobiles. He certainly vaulted into one fast enough when invited to go for a ride. He simply enjoyed the thrill of the chase. Mouth agape, tongue hanging out, ears at full forward alert, he waited, his center of gravity thrust so far out over the gutter that his front paws threatened to slip off the curb, tumbling him into the street. And he'd wait for ten minutes if he had to, however long it took for some unsuspecting Studebaker coupe or Dodge sedan to chance down the street, minding its own business, wheels a-ripple on the paving bricks.

Vibrating in anticipation, every muscle taut, Eskie waited until the front of the car was abreast of him before rocketing off

the curb as if he was chasing salvation. He seemed not to care about the back end of a car—maybe it struck him as lacking bravado; he must have the front tire, and he must taste it. Emitting a throaty stream of barks so rapid that they merged into one— something like ohwohwohwohwohw—he chomped ferociously at the rolling front corner of a tire until it outraced him. Then, head high and exuding triumph with every paw-prance, he trotted back to the curb to catch his breath and get ready for the next ambush.

It was an exercise in futility. He never even managed to puncture a tire, much less capture a car. But he never gave up, either. No matter how many times his neck was jerked by catching a tooth on a knob of rubber; no matter how many creative ways we devised to break him of the habit (all of them failed), he was *Don Quixote* at the windmill for his whole life.

In the end, perhaps inevitably, it was his undoing, not on North Main Street but on some nameless country lane. Among the earliest of Mother's passions to revive in the year following Dad's death was her lifelong love affair with Chautauqua Institution in southwestern New York State. In spite of economic realities, or the constraints imposed by wartime gasoline rationing when it came to that, she was determined to take her family there, that year and every year, and not just for the eight-week season but for as many days before and after it as her budget and Meadville's public school schedule would afford.

For the first couple of years Eskie was boarded at a kennel; but it was expensive at a time when money was in short supply, and three months in a cage was an unhappy experience for so free-roaming a spirit. So it was, in the summer of 1943, that Eskie went off to spend the summer at the farm of Mr. Baldwin, a small man whose grizzled face was forever wrinkled by a crooked grin that revealed a huge heart. Mother routinely stopped at Baldwin's Market House butcher shop, preferring, for all the reasons known to friendship and trust, to buy much of our meat from him. But even when she wasn't sure she needed anything, her children pushed her in that direction: "Puh-leeze, Mom, *can't* we go to Mr. Baldwin's?" It's not just that we adored the man, or that he returned our affection in full measure. It was how he expressed it: by reaching into his refrigerator case and handing each of us a frankfurter on which to chomp while Mother made her decisions. So when, one May Saturday, Mother broached the subject of Eskie spending the summer on his farm, he didn't even hesitate. The deal was struck.

It was a wonderful summer for the dog: dozens of strange new animals to become acquainted with and a thousand new scents to absorb, catalogue, and memorize in ways that only a dog's brain understands. He had a splendid time, and we never saw him again. His old addiction caught up with him one misty August morning and he sneaked out to the road in front of the farmhouse for a fix. Mr. Baldwin found him lying by the side of the road.

He was crushed. Not Eskie, Mr. Baldwin. (I suppose Eskie could have been too, but Mother preferred not to inquire too closely into the details.) To think that he had let down Ruth Skinner distressed Mr. Baldwin deeply, and how could he explain to her children? He needn't have worried. Mother had a pragmatic attitude about animals. They were to be cared for dependably, trained properly, and treated with unfailing kindness. But beyond shedding a few tears to wash away the loss, she never grieved unduly when they died. Besides, she had known for years that Eskie had a rendezvous with Goodyear. She admonished Mr. Baldwin not to trouble himself any more about it; and if any explaining to her children was required, she'd handle it herself.

Too, there may have been something in her reaction, and ours, having to do with Eskie's devotion to Dad. Whatever the reason, Eskie never really recovered after Dad's death. He seemed always to be going about the house, worrying its corners and sniffing out his questions about where his beloved master was, and why he never came home. Looking now at pictures of him, I wonder whether there might have been some German shepherd folded into that little body, together with the single-minded, single-person devotion that characterizes the breed. One can, I think, find solace in the idea that all the creatures in the history of the world, whatever traits might appear to distinguish us as discrete species, are united in our common bondage to time. Physical immortality is illusion. There truly is, for each of us, a time to be born and a time to die. This is not some sort of cosmic cruelty, but an act of mercy by which one's death makes way for someone else to experience the privilege of being, their moment under the sun to strive and grieve and rejoice before making way for yet another. In the final analysis, it is not individual survival, but the thriving of our kind, which satisfies the creative intent of God.

Eskie had a good life; and if it was not as long as it might have been, he determined his own end time. Think of it: he died doing the dog-thing from which he derived the greatest thrill in life. And if I wouldn't choose it for myself (*that* goes without saying), I can think of worse ways to go.

CHAPTER 8

Lionel Blue

W hen Henry Ford's manufacturing plant began production of the Model T, America's first mass-pro-
duced motor car, Ford reportedly quipped that
Americans could have any color car they wanted as long as it was
black. Our grandparents McCafferty understood that kind of language. They made it clear that Mother and Dad could spend Christmas anywhere they wanted as long as it was at the McCafferty
home in Allison Park, north of Pittsburgh. We sometimes visited
Dad's Ashville family around the holiday season, but Christmas
itself was not up for discussion.

As a small child, I wasn't aware how intensely Mother wanted
to celebrate Christmas at home. I was a teenager before she mentioned it; but when she did, I could remember only once that we
had. Nor did I mind. From the first, Christmas in Allison Park—
attending the richly musical, candle-lit and poinsettia-brilliant
Christmas Eve service at the Presbyterian Church in nearby
Glenshaw; Christmas day dinner with Mother's brother Tom and

his family in their handsome, colonial-style home a hundred feet down the bluff rise from our grandparents' home—embodied the image of Christmas for me. I never wanted to be anywhere else.

Ruth Ann also preferred it, but she had another reason: being both the eldest and the only girl, she got to stay with Tom's daughter, Betty Jane, who was Ruth Ann's age and our only McCafferty cousin. The two of them were inseparable; a non-stop pajama party went on from the moment we arrived until we left. We rarely saw them. We boys, in contrast, stayed with Mother in her parents' home, where we had to contend with a few uncertainties, like where to sleep. There were only two bedrooms, so someone had to accept temporary quarters. I use "temporary" advisedly: sleeping on the folding, wood-and-canvas army cot was only marginally preferable to being consigned to the brown mohair living room couch. It wasn't pretty, that couch; but in coal-driven Pittsburgh it was demonstrably practical, as were the dark rugs and the sheer, washable curtains. (Grandma never even removed the cellophane wrapping in which her lamp shades arrived from the store; it kept the shades clean.)

On either cot or couch, a sheet was folded in half and covered with a wool blanket, and we crawled in between the folded halves of the sheet as if into a sleeping bag, but with no way to button it up. Inevitably, by 2:30 a.m., I had squirmed around enough to work my way out of the sheet, and spent the rest of the night rubbing wool on top and either canvas or mohair on the bottom, and I didn't care for any of them. Too, both cot and couch were in the living room, the fireplace mantle of which was home to a wind-up clock with Westminster chimes. Its incessant tick-tock was loud enough to waken even children known to sleep through thunderstorms. But the chimes, shattering the pure stillness of the wee hours, could waken a mud turtle from hibernation.

On the other hand, breakfast with Grandma and Thelma Fuge, the family's long-time and incomparably loyal housekeeper and companion, and more family than either, was a highlight of each day. Lined up on one side of the McCafferty's diner-booth breakfast nook, we chattered like squirrels as Grandma and Thelma asked us about home and school and friends. More, the breakfast nook was the site of modernity run amok: an electric receptacle under the window allowed Grandma's Westinghouse pop-up toaster to live right there on the table. This was a wonder. Our toaster lived in the kitchen; and no matter how fast I worked, by the time I got my toast buttered and onto our breakfast nook table, it was cool on the way to soggy.

And that didn't end the contrast. Operating our toaster was an adventure. Powered by a cord so twisted it looked like a black-snake with severe arthritis, it had no switch and a single operating temperature: plug it in, it was on; pull the plug, it was off. Each of its sloping sides was a door hinged at the bottom that, when closed, held the bread against the heating coils. When one side was toasted, the doors had to be opened and the bread turned over. Inattention led to disaster; an eruption of pungent smoke put us on notice that "bread" was already beyond "toast" and was approaching "ash."

Grandma's toaster, by contrast, was right there on the table, a gleaming stainless steel case with a temperature control knob on one end. A spring-loaded handle lowered bread into twin slots in the top and popped it back up when it was toasted to the desired color. Automated amazement! Hot toast with the butter still melting beneath a dollop of apple butter and laid right there beside my steaming bowl of oatmeal fresh from Thelma's kitchen... well, it just doesn't get any better than that.

Like everything else in their lives, in which quality was the driving motive and doing without was preferable to purchasing cheap, Christmas presents from Grandma and Granddaddy were substantial. Not that there wasn't some good old seasonal junk stuffed into our stockings along with the healthy and useful items—an orange or apple and a pair of socks or mittens or pocket comb. Filling those stockings was a pretty good piece of work, actually, since we were theoretically asleep right there in front of the fireplace. It required some fancy footwork on Moth... uh, Santa's part. Any lingering doubts in my growing agnosticism about Santa Claus died my fourth Christmas Eve. Lying there with mohair chafing my flesh on one side and wool on the other, deprived of sleep by the mantle clock, I watched through barely slit eyes as Mother stuffed our stockings. It didn't matter. I had just as much fun dumping the stuff out and pawing through it come morning.

The serious exchange of presents, however, had to wait until after Christmas dinner, when we gathered in Uncle Tom and Aunt Helen's brightly decorated living room while Granddaddy and Grandma distributed the sort of presents we otherwise would never have received. Their choices were not entirely wise, because the six-year age range among us children did not mesh with our grandparents' desire to treat us alike. There was, for example, the year each of us received a fine Bulova wrist watch. Everyone was thrilled, and four of the watches presumably served their owners faithfully for many years. Still too young fully to appreciate either its value or its mechanical limitations, and wanting to keep it clean and bright, I took mine into the bathroom soon after we returned home and scrubbed it thoroughly in the bathtub. I didn't own another watch for years, and when I did, Timex was the brand of choice.

With customary generosity, and in a manner that was very McCafferty, we each received a U.S. Savings Bond each Christmas, graduated according to age. Emphasis was definitely on "saving." Within hours of our return to Meadville, my bonds disappeared into our family safe deposit box at First National Bank and didn't see the light of day again until I was engaged to be married, by which time most already had matured to their face value, rolled over, and done it again. Thanks to McCafferty generosity, I finished seminary and set up housekeeping with resources to spare. Whatever else I might think of Mother's parents, they taught us not just to dream a future, but to prepare for it.

In light of such well-rehearsed tradition, 1935 can only be considered unique: it was the Christmas of Lionel Blue. I don't know what got into Granddaddy that year, but he didn't even wait until after dinner to give us a present that would be shared among us for years. In fact, he barely got past breakfast. Maybe he didn't care to haul its hefty bulk down the hill to Uncle Tom and Aunt Helen's. Then again, maybe he was too excited himself to wait. Whatever his reason, once the temporary bedding had been folded into the front hall closet and the breakfast table was wiped, we were summoned to the living room where a large box had appeared, a patch of color against the prevailing coal-resistant brown motif. It was an impressive box, almost as tall as I was and certainly heavier. By adult consensus, Dad was delegated to open it, which should have told us something. But not until he lifted the first item out of the box and peeled off the packing paper did we realize how much magic it held: it was the locomotive for an O-gauge Lionel model train. Cries of delight followed in succession as Dad unveiled each piece—a coal tender followed by a mail car, passenger car, and club car complete with minute wrap-around railing on its rear platform and red taillights at its roof corners. Then out came the track, enough of Lionel's signature three-rail design for a large oval, with half a dozen switches for crossovers and sidings, and the hefty transformer needed to power it all. That was all it took. Next thing we knew, Dad was on his knees assembling enough track for an inaugural run.

I thought it the most beautiful thing I had ever seen: it was royal blue, with silver fittings and black trim—as sharp an assembly as ever rolled off an industrial line. And when the wheels were aligned and the transformer powered up, igniting the passenger car windows and sending the locomotive surging forward, its headlight agleam, Dad pressed a button atop the transformer and the room filled with the sound of a whistle so persuasive that I could close my eyes and imagine I was in my bed at home, summoned from sleep by the beckoning whoop of a train smoking down-valley on the Erie main line.

Oh, it was a splendid gift, like none ever received before or likely to be repeated.

And no one's face shown with greater pleasure than Granddaddy's. He fairly glowed with satisfaction, self and otherwise, as pieces of train came one by one from the carton to be assembled on the silver track gleaming against his dull brown rug. And when the train came to life, its whistle warning everything out of its path, he burst out in a grin the likes of which I don't ever recall seeing, before or after. I rather think it was one of those things he would have loved to own, but could never grant himself permission to be that frivolous—except to treat his grandchildren.

My own excitement was tempered. I ached to play with it, but was denied the chance. Standing next to the track as the sublime assembly rolled smoothly past my toes, my three-year-old feelings smarted under the clearly articulated judgment that I might damage it, and I wondered what good it was to have a train I couldn't play with. Time would prove their anxiety unfounded— though not because they underestimated my capabilities. Lionel got the credit. That train was so tough it could have survived war and come churning home without showing a scratch. But it was Christmas morning, and the train was brand new, and no one was taking any chances until we got it home and set up in a secure place.

The secure place was Dad's rock-solid workbench in the basement furnace room. His demanding schedule didn't leave him much time to use it for anything else, and we boys wouldn't begin to do so for several more years. The bench so perfectly accommodated the track that the two might have been designed for each other: a completed oval of track covered the length of the bench with about four inches to spare. Each 180-degree end-curve fit precisely between the basement wall and the front edge of the bench, making it critical that the train not be sent careening around an outside curve at too great a rate of speed. If it jumped the track, it wouldn't stop short of the concrete floor. And I doubt that even Lionel designed its locomotives with that in mind.

Dad wasn't content for very long merely to run a passenger train service, however, and next Christmas provided sufficient excuse to purchase a box car, hopper car, tank car, flat car, and— bringing up the rear—a suitably scarlet caboose. Now the blue locomotive and tender had two trains to pull, and a siding was laid down for whichever set of cars was out of service while the other roamed the countryside of Dad's workbench.

To say that Dad delighted in the thing would be understatement. It's not clear whether Granddaddy intended to give a model train set to his son-in-law as opposed to his grandchildren, but he might as well have. In theory, the train belonged to all of us; but like Aesculapius, there was no doubt as to whom it truly belonged. Whenever Dad was home with a minute to spare, he was in the basement watching the blue locomotive churn its way around its oval world, chrome pistons and drive wheels flashing and whistle broadcasting its warnings; and if we knew about it, we were down there with him. I couldn't see much the first year or two, actually; my eyeballs weren't yet up to track level. In my earliest memories, the train is visible only along the front edge of the workbench, the engine hoving into view at one end and the club car or caboose chasing it out of sight at the other.

That Dad was like a kid with a long-coveted toy was most clear to Mother. It wasn't just the moments he spent down there with one or more of us when he arrived home in the afternoon, or following dinner when he lingered a few minutes before going out for an evening appointment. It was the times he was down there alone in the middle of the night. Mother would already have climbed into bed, lying there half awake waiting for him to come home (even in later years, when we were grown up and just visiting, Mother never really slept when one of her family was not yet home.) Suddenly, the hesitancy of her sleep would be penetrated by the faint, almost-like-real song of a train whistle, and she felt the indiscernible vibration of a model train rolling along its track on the basement workbench. Then she'd know that Dad had driven into the garage and come in through the basement, but was loathe to come upstairs until he had stopped in the furnace room. He didn't even turn on the light, preferring to stand there in the dark while the lights of the train, especially the gleaming locomotive headlight, worked their model magic. For a brief moment, the boards of his workbench and the white-washed stone walls were transformed into the rolling night hills of open country, where a passing train momentarily illumines the face of things before vanishing around a bend or receding into the mist. Then Mother would roll over and smile and fall asleep, knowing that for a minute or two, her grown man had recaptured the joy of his never-to-be-regained boyhood by the grace of Lionel Blue.

———

We were never quite sure what to do with the train after Dad died. It had been a source of family joy, and joy was in short supply around our house after he left us. For a time, it was boxed up and stacked among the other accumulations in the old coal bin turned store room. Later, we occasionally got it out and set it up, usually at Christmas time. Some Decembers, it ran around the base of the tree. A few times Mother even encouraged us to make a holiday spread that covered most of the dining room rug. Given constraints on the family budget, we couldn't afford the kind of model buildings and electrified gadgets that turn a model train set into a "layout." But we made do with what could be had around the house, assembling a crazy-quilt spread in which no two articles were of the same scale or sophistication, and none remotely close to the O-gauge scale of the train. Under Mother's encouragement, however, we discovered that tuna fish cans, washed out (thoroughly!), coated with aluminum paint, and turned upside down with petroleum company logos from *Life* and *Saturday Evening Post* magazine ads pasted to their sides, made a convincing oil refinery.

It was in the dining room that we learned just how tough old Lionel Blue really was. Bored with simply watching it run in endless ovals, we turned to sabotage. As Cliff recollects it, this demonic shift came in the wake of Dad's death, hinting at the possibility that the train became the whipping boy for the loss of our father. Maybe somewhere, down deeper than thought forms words, we assumed that beating up on the train Dad had loved would dispel the anger and hurt we didn't otherwise know how to vent, as if the train had borne him away from us.

Whatever our motive, the train took a terrible beating. The gist of the activity was to calculate what aggregation of stuff, laid on the track in what configuration, would most dramatically catapult the train into the air—the more violently the better. We experimented with dozens of combinations, sending the train to its doom at ramming speed. I have no idea just how many times we did it, but it was a lot, and surely far more than Lionel's builders ever anticipated. It was a tribute to the company that a model train could be reassembled and wrecked like that, time after time, apparently no worse for the wear. When, years later, the locomotive did stop working, it wasn't as a result of our abusiveness. The rollers mounted under the locomotive's belly—the ones that made contact with the middle rail, completing the electrical circuit to the motor— became so scored by electrical jolts that their wires melted away. That was one tough train.

Only once did it return to Dad's workbench. As years passed and we boys grew older, the workbench was more often used for its intended purpose—to repair bicycles or re-wire lamps or glue chair legs—whatever Mother wanted done. Having finally accepted that her sons had inherited their father's fix-it gene and really could do that sort of thing, she increasingly took advantage of it. Thereafter, when one of us was home from school on vacation, or later when we returned to visit with our wives and children, we were greeted first with a hug, then with a list of things around the house in need of repair.

Once, however, during our last year in the house when Mother and I were the only ones of our family still at home, I set the train up on the workbench again, intent on going the whole nine yards. I messed up half the basement making plaster of Paris to splatter over fly screen shaped and nailed to the workbench to create mountains and tunnels; gathered weeds and twigs from the yard for trees and shrubs; carved up empty cartons to create buildings; and finished off several derelict cans of oil paint trying to make it all look natural. It was wasted effort. There's just so much you can do to mimic reality when limited to chocolate brown, forest green and black. Besides, it was hard work. I have no idea how many years those cans had stood undisturbed in the paint cupboard; but by the time I pried off each rusted lid with a screwdriver, the surface of each had dried to a skin the consistency of boiler plate, and I had to pound a hole through it to reach what was left of the paint—if it could still be called that.

Yet even as I labored, time was running out. It was 1947. Ruth Ann had been away at Allegheny College, and Cliff at Mercersburg Academy, for two years. With Frank's departure that September, I had only one more school year at home. In the spring, when Mother issued the order, I set to work to undo it all, discovering in the process that I would have been better advised to use papier maché than plaster of Paris. Talk about building for eternity. If I hadn't beaten those mountains apart with a hammer, they might have outlasted the house. And even when I finished, and the workbench was again stripped to its boards, the footprint of the train layout was clearly visible where I had slopped green and brown and black paint beyond the edges of whatever I was painting, or where it had sunk into holes and score marks in the battered wood. For all I know, it's there still.

———

A footnote: Mother never could bring herself to dispose of the old train. Packed into a carton, it went into temporary storage the year she left Meadville, then was moved to Chautauqua, where she had been named registrar of the Institution's summer school program. And there it sat, seemingly consigned to oblivion in the back of a dark attic. Reprieve came a few years later when Mother learned that Cliff's youngest son Roger was a serious train freak. She sent the engine away to Lionel to be repaired; and next opportunity she had she lugged the carton out to the trunk of her car and headed west, where she added the train to Roger's growing collection. There's something fitting, to my mind, about having it end up in California. The very image of an American train, after all, is of a steam-belching behemoth powering across the Great Plains, through the Rockies and over the Sierra Nevada to the Pacific Ocean. And I truly believe that, if it was possible to collect enough Lionel track to stretch from coast to coast, and to start Lionel Blue rolling across the nation's midsection, that old train was tough enough to make it all the way to California on its own.

CHAPTER 9

Breakfast Nook

T here are rooms that cannot be entered without unleashing a torrent of feeling; not just discrete emotions associated with particular moments in time—although such inevitably ride in on the flood—but some cumulative sense of everything experienced there. Our breakfast nook was for me such a room. I know, because I have visited twice in the decades since Mother sold the property and it ceased to be home; and every time I step into that room, more than in any other in the house, the torrent floods my senses all over again. If it could be said that our family lived in any single room, the breakfast nook was it. Whether we spent so much time there because we loved it, or loved it because so much that made us a family happened there, is hard to say. That it is at the center of our family memory is evident.

And the heart of that memory—indeed, the heart of the room—was the table. Of trestle design, its top was more than half as wide as it was long and made from three pine boards, each more than a foot across and joined to its neighbor by a pair of hardwood butterfly joints. The soft pine didn't hold varnish well, so Mother periodically buffed it with steel wool and brushed coats of shellac on it until stroking it was like caressing satin. Over time, its surface acquired a patina of scuffs, scratches and gouges so complicated that it seemed a hieroglyph with no Rosetta Stone, a history that only family could interpret.

On rare occasions, a simple piece of furniture takes on an independent life. That table was such a one. In 1977, when Pat and I were newly married, we had occasion to travel from Minnesota to Washington, D.C. on business. It was the first time she had been further east than Wisconsin, so we took the opportunity to visit places in the Northeast where I had lived and gone to school—"a tour of Don's roots," we called it. Our route took us through Pennsylvania to Meadville, where we paused at the corner of North Main and Hamilton Streets, looking at the house where I grew up. Seeing us pointing and gesturing from the curb, surveying her home, Sue Henry came grinning out the door and called brightly, "You must be Skinners. C'mon in!" Sue's father purchased the property from Mother in 1949 as a wedding present for Sue and her husband Bill. They were only the second couple to live and raise a family there.

When we stepped into the breakfast nook, it was, in the words of the eloquent Yogi Berra, *déjà vu* all over again. There stood the table, exuding memory as palpably as a wood stove radiates warmth. Indeed more so, because the memory of places that nurtured us, in contrast to the heat of an iron stove, does not fade when we walk away, but warms us against the cold of time. Sue explained: when Mother sold the house, she couldn't bring herself to remove the table; it was too perfect for the room. Like a cat, the table was understood to belong to the house, not to its temporary occupants.

More radio programs were listened to, games played and stories read while sitting around that table than any of us can count—and none more engrossing than the stories Mother told. Wanting her children to become as avid readers as she, and knowing that a love of reading is born of a love of story, she often read to us—not three-minute bedtime fables but whole chapters of books. Finishing dinner on an evening when nothing pressed for her attention, she'd ask if we'd like to hear a story. She never had to ask twice. In less time than it might take us on some other evening to argue about who should clear the table, put away the food, and clean up the kitchen, we had it done and were back at the table, waiting with less patience than we would accord a theater delayed in starting a movie.

Taking her place at the end of the table closest to the kitchen (the chair at the far end had been Dad's, and largely remained empty after he died, no one presuming to occupy it), she began to read. Immediately, the room filled with word-borne visions of far-away places, curious events, and interesting people, and we absently played with the napkin rings or laid our heads on our arms to stare vacantly at her, or at nothing at all, because what our eyes saw was at that moment unrelated to what our minds envisioned. On and on she read, sometimes for more than half an hour; and the room remained still but for the unwavering pulse of her voice as it tracked the lines, lifted them from the page, and transported them to our waiting ears. Her reading was measured, steady, never freighted with intensity or emotion. Knowing that our imaginations could pick a story line out of thin air, she left it to us to set the scene, provide the props, dress the actors; and while no two of our minds conjured the same images, all were held equally in thrall.

I can't speak for my sister and brothers, who had their own favorite stories, stimulated in part by the Junior Literary Guild subscription that Grandma McCafferty gave us each year for Christmas. But my favorites so captured my affection that I still own the books—a series by naturalist Sam Campbell. Sam spent his summers in Chequamegon-Nicolet National Forest in northeastern Wisconsin's lake country managing a wilderness retreat he called the Sanctuary of Wegimind. And when the gales of winter drove him from his lakefront cabin, he took to the lecture circuit, weaving tales of nature and showing movies that he filmed himself. Sam came to Meadville several times, each time bringing copies of his latest book. Observing my fascination with nature and wildlife, Mother took me to hear Sam's lectures, where I had the opportunity to meet him. Drawn to his warm and congenial manner, I later wrote him a letter, hardly expecting a response. But he did respond, and we exchanged letters for several years. A thoughtful man, he readily offered encouragement to a young teenager who looked on him as a hero.

As an author, Sam was nothing if not prolific. Between 1943 and 1957, he wrote eleven books with never-to-be-forgotten names like *How's Inky?, Eeny, Meeny, Miney, Mo—and Still-Mo, The Seven Secrets of Somewhere Lake, Fiddlesticks and Freckles*, and *Loony Coon*, each as fresh and transporting as the one before it, and as funny as they were informative. So well did Sam understand his animal friends that he could step out of the way and let them tell their own often whimsical, sometimes hilarious stories. Sitting around the breakfast nook table, laughing until the tears rolled down our cheeks and even Mother's measured elocution threatened to break up, became the stuff of cherished memories.

If it wasn't a story that drew us around the table, it was a game of a nature and difficulty that advanced as we matured: Uncle Wiggly, Old Maid, Chinese Checkers, Pick-up Sticks, Parcheesi, Monopoly, Hearts. Those were the good times, because it seemed to matter so little who was there to play on a given day, and even less who won or lost. Maybe I am guilty of Pollyanna memory, but though I recall periodic outbreaks of conflict around home ranging from petty friction to full-bore yelling, my memory of games around the breakfast nook table comes wrapped in an aura of good-natured competition and teamwork and the unbreakable rule of fairness. Mother would not tolerate cheating, but she plain detested squabbling. Apparently the lesson was learned early and well; recollections of good times that filled a rainy spring Saturday or winter Sunday afternoon come tumbling out of my brain in such bounty that I can't even begin to sort them one from another.

And if not a story or game, it was a radio program. The family radio—the only one we owned until Mother, in an uncustomary burst of self-indulgence, bought a small one for her bedside stand—stood on a small table behind Dad's chair. A bulky, walnut veneer box with a Gothic arch top and a single dial in its face, it resembled our grandparents' noisy mantle clock more than an electronic device. Much of what we learned about the world beyond Meadville—the economy's improvement (or lack of it), the progress of our arms during World War II, or the worlds of music and entertainment—entered our home and lives through that radio's single, tinny speaker which, depending on the weather, might carry more static than program.

While we were free to read all we wanted, listening to the radio entailed some parental accommodation. Mother disliked noise, and considered much of what came out of a radio as nothing but. Some of it also sounded more violent than she thought appropriate for children (although by today's standards... well, never mind). In any event, if it wasn't classical music, Mother didn't want to hear it and that's all there was to it. Ruth Ann, being a child of her time and the time being World War II and the era of swing, defected to the musical enemy. She fell head over heels for trumpeter Harry James and crooner Frank Sinatra and other noise-makers who—given my age and her budding notions about romance—made me want to throw up. Or so I pretended. It didn't really bother me, but it sure got her goat; and that, as we all knew, was one of the main reasons God created little brothers.

Even at that, Ruth Ann sometimes joined us boys for our preferred menu of adventure programs featuring stories of improbable heroes doing less probable things. With the sheriff passing-out drunk or off in Abilene, and the townspeople peeping helplessly out between dotted Swiss curtains or cowering in abject terror behind the cracker barrel in the general store, there was no one—no, not one—to stand up to the diabolical Dastardly Gang. So it fell to the Lone Ranger, riding in from twenty miles away at the last possible moment, with naught but his faithful Indian companion Tonto at his side, to head them off at Vulture

Pass and save the day for virtue and womanhood. Never mind that there were six of them and every one armed to the teeth with rifles and pistols and sixteen-inch knives; our hero needed only his trusty brace of six-guns to disarm them all, shooting their weapons out of their hands while riding past at a full gallop on his magnificent stallion Silver. Thus we absorbed the absurd fiction of radical individualism and drove Mother out of the breakfast nook.

And if it wasn't time for the Lone Ranger, others waited just beyond the lighted dial to step forward and entertain us. The adventurous Jack Armstrong the All-American Boy engaged in heroics that we could almost imagine doing ourselves, while the Green Lantern or the Shadow ("What evil lurks in the hearts of men?") reassured us that good would triumph over crime and malevolence; and the Inner Sanctum—its door hinges so creaking rusty that the table vibrated—alarmed us with the thought that it might not.

But more than anything, especially during the wearying war years, we yearned for a chance to laugh; and nothing conjured the explosive guffaws and long-running belly laughs like the infectious stuff that came daily from the radio: Amos and Andy's entirely preventable predicaments; Fibber McGee and Molly's innocent marital bantering and overstocked, avalanche-prone closet; the hysterical caricatures living along Fred Allen's famous Alley; and "Jello again, this is Jack Benny," noteworthy because his was the only program that Mother consented to listen to with us. These were servants of the public well-being, reminding us that there was still innocence and humor in a world gone stark raving mad. I wonder, had they not been there to remind us, whether we might have forgotten.

It was probably not until the advent of television that I began fully to understand how privileged we were to be raised with

books and radio. To be appreciated—indeed, simply to work—
each depended on responsive minds and imaginations willing to
take wing. Neither the stories Mother read to us, nor the oral
tales flowing from the family radio, demanded that we accept a
stage setting devised by some writer or producer.

They provided the central, the indispensable, thread, but
we were unconstrained in how we used it to weave a whole gar-
ment of story. Our minds knew no limit but the range of our
imaginations, and we learned the secret magic of Rumpelstiltskin's
spinning wheel, spinning straw into gold.

I will never accede to the illiterate proposition that I was
underprivileged because I grew up with "only" books and radio.
To the contrary, I grieve for those among today's children who,
sadly, have "only" television.

———·•·———

A friend once observed that a truly appealing room requires
no furniture; it is charming standing stock empty. Our breakfast
nook was like that. Even on a cloudy day it was a sunny room.
Its east-facing back wall was a hanging bay fitted with metal casement windows with diamond-shaped panes, through which the
morning sun burst to ricochet off unpainted walls of bone-white
straw plaster, an effect enhanced by checkered orange, yellow
and green café curtains that Mother had hung at the windows.
That plaster was Mother's favorite feature in the whole house,
and the bane of her existence. For small children, a wall permeated with chips of dry-gold cut straw was irresistible: it insisted
on being picked at. And every piece of straw extracted by tiny
fingernails left a telltale groove in the wall. By the time the youngest of us had been broken of the habit, there were as many
grooves as straw chips in the bottom three feet of wall. So exas-
perated did Mother become that straw-picking was right up there

with lying and stealing as conduct guaranteed to earn parental retribution.

The floor was equally striking, clad with hand-made Mexican tiles, a mix of square and rectangular pieces a few inches long and wide laid to resemble a woven basket of yellow and orange and garnished with earth green. Crossing it as morning flooded through the windows, snatching up shards of yellow-orange and spraying them against the lower walls, was like splashing through sunlight. But practical it was not. All those little tiles were embedded in lines of grout, creating ten thousand cracks to trap spilled food and tracked-in dirt; and anyone who thinks it possible to raise four children without spilled food and dirt-encrusted feet has never raised four children. Wherein lay a serious work assignment.

About the time each of us children reached our third birthday we joined a well-trained child labor force, and not just for minor chores (bring in the milk, set the table, do the dishes, clean your room, change your bed). Such lightweight tasks were augmented by weightier jobs, indoors and out: sweep the basement, dust and dry-mop the halls and stairs, mow the lawn, shovel the driveway, rake the leaves. The list was endless, not only because Mother knew that idle children were a danger to both themselves and the neighborhood, but because she never thought her house was finally cleaned, only in process of being.

Among the recurring and weightiest of assignments was the breakfast nook floor. Now there was a job to lay waste to a boy's Saturday plans. Down on wet knees, soapy bucket at my side and scrub brush in hand, I worked that floor end to end and corner to corner more times than I care to remember. A second transit followed, with a bucket of rinse water and a rag. And after the floor was thoroughly dry, and Mother had granted it her Good

Housekeeping Seal of Approval (never a sure thing), it was down for a third time, with a rag, to rub Johnson's paste wax onto the tiles—and into every crack and cranny between.

That waxing rag was an institution living in a can. It resided there, as far as I know, my entire life. Now that I think of it, at the rate we went through paste wax, it probably resided in more cans than most people occupy homes in a lifetime. I don't think anyone remembered its original size. It was folded and refolded to fit neatly into a child's palm; and by the time I was old enough to handle the breakfast nook job, it was so permeated with wax that the fabric had melded into a blob. Any attempt to unfold it would have been like trying to unwind a lump of well-kneaded bread dough. It wouldn't surprise me to learn that the thing had obtained eternal life and is still out there somewhere, defying decay.

Finally, after yet another wait for the wax to dry, Mother let me move on to the only part of the job that was both fun and mechanical: polishing the floor with the electric buffer. That's not as impressive as it sounds; the buffer was a small device that Mother picked up as a premium somewhere. The buffing drum measured about eight inches in both width and diameter and was studded with stubby, densely-packed bristles. Still, when the small electric motor mounted on the end of its four-foot handle kicked in, it polished up a storm. Well, at least an eight-inch wide breeze. It took a lot of passes up and down the room to polish all those tiles, with time out to move the table and chairs back and forth as the polishing progressed. Nor was the buffer always cooperative: it had remarkable torque for so small a motor. Every transit of an uneven joint or canted tile catapulted it into the air, threatening to pull my arm out of its socket. There was also the danger, if it broke my grip, that it would run amok around the room or, if properly aligned, would fly right out into the kitchen.

But when the job was done, that floor shown so bright it hurt to look at it. Little wonder Mother took such pride in it.

Until about two months later, by which time enough food would have been spilled and dirt tracked in to dim the burnish of even Johnson's paste wax, and to start Mother thinking that it would soon be time again to hand one of us the scrub-and-wax assignment.

My most difficult memory of the breakfast nook occurred the evening I learned the pain of empathy—not through any earth-shaking event, but a haunting one. The temper of it became hard-wired into my psyche, one of those seminal lessons of infancy that endures to the end of life. I must have been about four, because Dad was at his place at the radio end of the table, but I was still too small to possess the perspective by which to make sense of what happened.

The issue was parental authority, and the victim was Cliff.

It was a winter evening, clammy cold and close enough to the solstice that the world had gone dark a full hour before suppertime. A distorted specter of snow, illuminated by the starburst glare of street lamps and porch lights, was visible through the humid-wet coating on the diamond-shaped window panes. As we took our places at the table, Cliff's chair was empty. I looked up from the essential business of assessing the plate in front of me (thank God, no mashed turnips) to see Mother and Dad exchange a glance. After a brief prayer, Dad muttered, "Excuse me, please," and left the table. He moved through the house, even down the basement stairs, and we heard the click of each door bolt ramming home. We sat and waited, observing a cardinal social grace of our table: no one's food was touched until everyone else, especially she who prepared it, was seated.

The instructions had been clear: if we were out playing with friends, we were—without hesitation—to come home when called, to wash up and be ready to sit down when Mother put dinner on the table. Cliff hesitated. When the deadline came and went without him, the doors were locked and he would be privileged to remain outside until the meal was over. Then perhaps he would be allowed in to eat his own supper, but don't bet on it. Being sent to bed without supper was never out of the question around there. Indeed, Mother thought it so severe a form of punishment that she never could quite see it through. Feeding her children, amply and dependably, was as essential to her parental self-image as breathing was to her life. Not to feed a hungry child when it was within her power to do so tore her insides up. For her, it really *was* a case of "this is going to hurt me more than you, dear." On the few occasions that my behavior was so egregious that I was packed off to bed on an empty stomach, feeling dreadfully sorry for myself even as I knew I had it coming, she crept into my room late in the evening, gently woke me, and asked softly if I wanted something to eat. Oddly, once having fallen asleep, I never did. But I cherished her tenderness more than any banquet she could have prepared for me. By morning, the lesson was learned and never had to be repeated.

Nor would Cliff ever be late for supper again! But I still cringe when I think of that meal, because memory and emotion are one; time has proven the event and the response it invoked in my psyche to be inseparable.

Trying the doors in turn, Cliff found them bolted. By the time he got around to the basement door he realized that he really was locked out. The light cascading out the breakfast nook windows told him that we were gathered around the table eating dinner, and he had to be hungry. Cliff was *always* hungry. And as it dawned on him that his exclusion was deliberate, he dissolved in tears, knocking on the door with the persistent drumbeat of the damned and pleading to be let in. It was cold out there—not cold enough to endanger him, but who has not felt cold intensify when it comes edged with the fear of not knowing how, or whether, one can escape it?

Sitting at the table, my heart broke with his, and I started to cry. My brother was hurt and it seemed to me that, somehow, I ought to help him. I looked at Dad, wanting to say something on Cliff's behalf, something to make it all right, to be the reconciler whose words would heal the divide—and was struck dumb by the grin that creased his face as he happily wolfed the dinner Mother had prepared for us. I can't recall another occasion on which I became so angry with my father, or one that hurt so much. The incomprehensible sense of having to challenge my father in order to help my brother was too distressing to unravel.

Psychiatrist Alfred Adler observed that children are excellent observers but lousy interpreters. That was me. I saw and heard it all, every shred; and my anguish was every bit as substantial as the detail I observed. But I neither understood the triviality of what was happening to Cliff, nor appreciated the benefit of the lesson he was learning. Even less did I grasp the fact that four children, not one, were learning it. The momentary embarrassment was Cliff's to endure, but all of us were chastened.

All that aside, the message I absorbed that evening went way beyond simply knowing enough to come home when called. I felt for the first time the imperative of justice. The compassion that propels me in any encounter with suffering may be the product of my whole nurturing; but I don't know how to make sense of something that large. I need something tangible, a specific

moment, to focus upon. The totality of my childhood is too complex to grasp, but the discrete sensation of feeling my brother's
hurt is branded in my gut. To this day, it is my point of reference
on the world's pain. And that's an awesome lesson to have
learned—especially since I wasn't even the one locked out.

CHAPTER 10

Yesterday's Produce of the Cow

I n general, Mother's alarm clock was the sole wake-up authority in our household. We might get up earlier as long as we kept quiet for the benefit of those who didn't need to. But we depended on her clock if we needed to rise early, or if we had stayed up too late the night before—an uncommon occurrence in our early-to-bed household. Most of the time, we didn't require prodding to get out of bed. Some evidence of a waking neighborhood usually roused us from sleep—a loud-beaked robin warbling the sun awake, dogs out for morning constitutionals announcing their inane discoveries to the world, or simply the increase in traffic on North Main Street.

My favorite was the clank of the Hilgendorf dairyman's glass bottles. Pulling up to the end of our driveway in his snub-nosed white truck, its sliding door closed only in sub-zero weather— and not always then—he was out and running almost before the vehicle rolled to a full stop. His crunching trot up the gravel drive-way was the first clue to his arrival, followed quickly by the clack of the wooden milk box lid striking the lattice wall of the side porch. And if I somehow managed to sleep through all that, there was no escaping the brittle clank of glass against glass and glass against metal as he dropped the empty bottles into his wire car-rier and left the standing order of two quarts of milk and one pint of cream, or more or less as a note from Mother, rolled up and stuffed into the mouth of one of the empty bottles the night before, might instruct. The ritual music of his passing found its way up to the open window, invaded our room, and stirred my brain to the arrival of a new day—and of a new batch of miracu-lous milk.

But unless I had wakened early for some reason, I never saw him. In this regard, our milk man was akin to Santa Claus: he could arrive, complete his errand and be gone before a child had opportunity to leap out of bed and catch a glimpse of him.

The first chore to be performed by the first child downstairs each morning was to bring in the milk and put it in the icebox.

(Odd, how words cling to habit: we owned an electric refrigerator for years before we stopped calling it "the icebox," because that's what our parents grew up with; and for years after vocabulary finally overtook technology, we called every refrigerator "the Frigidair," because that was the first brand of refrigerator we owned.)

One would not expect so mundane a chore to be the occasion for temptation, but for the attentive child the opportunity for misbehavior was ever at hand. Along with microwaves, Pop-Tarts and Hamburger Helper, the process of homogenization had not, in my childhood, been invented. It was still a vision in the mind of some agricultural chemist who, in my humble opinion, ought to have focused on something more important, like a cure for the corn borer or bole weevil, and left milk alone. In those pre-homogenous days, milk still behaved as God intended, and each quart bottle bearing the scarlet logo of the Hilgendorf Dairy was a cream separator in microcosm. Left alone for a time, the cream rose slowly to the top, and the longer it stood undisturbed, the thicker the cream got. By the time the Hilgendorf dairyman passed our porch, every bottle displayed a clean line a third of the way down from the top, demarking the line between cream and milk.

Which meant that—standing orders from Mother to the contrary notwithstanding—the first child able to get hold of a new bottle of milk, and to open it without shaking it, got to pour out a glass that was demonstrably more cream than milk. The ruse seldom worked. Circumstance and group appetite militated against it. Hogging all the cream meant that the other children around the table got something akin to chalk water. There was no way, under such a circumstance, that three aggrieved victims would fail to raise a hue and cry: "MUH-THURR, FRANK TOOK

ALL THE CREAM OFF THE TOP!" Nor was there need for a jury trial. The incriminating evidence was right there in front of the accused, or painted in a creamy-wet streak across his upper lip. Guilty as charged.

There was a more secure variation on this theme that I early learned to take advantage of. The milk box on the side porch was just that: a simple box with a hinged lid that Dad banged together from scrap lumber and painted white with a robin's egg blue lid, matching the clapboarding and window trim of the house. I was never exactly sure why the box was there. Most Meadville families just stood their empty bottles on the porch, to be replaced with full ones as Meadville's dairymen worked their rounds. A few privileged homes even had metal-lined passageways, perhaps fifteen inches square, built into the outside wall of their kitchen or back entry, with doors both inside and out: the milkman opened the outside door to remove empty bottles and replace them with full ones, and the family took their milk in through the inside door and put their empties out. That was some modern convenience. But it deprived the children of those houses of one incomparable privilege that we enjoyed every winter: our milk froze. It seldom got hard enough to shatter a bottle, though that did happen on a few occasions when the mercury plummeted to fifteen or twenty degrees below zero. The result was a slurry of half-frozen milk and shattered glass in the bottom of the milk box. Take my word for it, cleaning it up was no one's favorite assignment.

In general, however, the time lapse between the milkman's visit and my arrival at the side door was just sufficient to allow the bottles to start to freeze. As they did so, the contents expanding in proportion to their drop in temperature, freezing cream lifted the paper cap and followed it right out the neck of the bottle.

Under just the right conditions, the frozen column rose four or five inches, a pillar of crystalline succulence and an opportunity to die for! If I was the lucky child (and, being the earliest riser, I most often was), I'd carry the bottle gingerly into the kitchen, slice the crystal column off into a glass, replace the cap, and stuff it into the refrigerator. Kept chilled, the liquid would remain frozen for several hours, its enlarged substance creating the illusion that the bottle was full; so, set into the refrigerator, it would not thaw and shrink, leaving a tell-tale gap, until after I left for school. And if I was really lucky, Mother either didn't notice, or had forgotten, by the time I returned home for lunch.

On the 4th of July, or any other summer day on which we could convince Mother to bring home some strawberries, we engineered an excuse to whip some cream. It never took much begging, actually; Mother loved strawberries, in all their known varieties and uses, about as much as anything I can think of—except whipped cream, which she loved more. Permission granted, we poured the cream into a bowl (never a drop less than what was permissible) and set to work with a will, small hands powering the egg beater as if the effort would fail unless we gained three feet in altitude. On we strained, until arm muscles burned from the effort. Sometimes, when the cream was reluctant, we traded off, passing the beater hand to hand with such practiced technique that it barely stopped spinning in the transfer. And always, Mother cautioned us not to go too far and turn it into butter. Slowly, the cream began to thicken and the beater's tracks to remain in the stiffening stuff, like footprints in wet snow. Then of a sudden it heaped up into a mound of sweet indulgence, and we grinned, wide-eyed and panting, at the reward of our labor. "Quick,

Mother, where are the biscuits and berries?" There cannot be, I thought, any flavor in the entire world equal to that of crushing a ripe, whipped-cream-coated strawberry between tongue and palate, sending the sun-sweetened juice of a dozen rain showers cascading across my tongue and down my throat. Is there a better definition of ecstasy? And if I knew of one, would it be moral to put it into print?!

Well, maybe one, at the other end of Pennsylvania's growing season. To this child, Thanksgiving without pumpkin pie was not simply unimaginable; it was sacrilege, a betrayal of religious tradition inaugurated at Plimouth Plantation and handed down through generations of Americans until it got to *me*. If I learned anything at all in early primary school history, I learned about the Pilgrims. I even knew about their wardrobe, because I dressed just like them for school pageants: saggy knee-length white socks imperfectly tucked into corduroy knickerbockers; a heavy belt cinched about my waist outside my jacket (I never did understand how that was supposed to hold my pants up—nor did it); shoe buckles cut from cardboard wrapped in tin foil and fastened to my loafers with rubber bands; and a flat-brimmed hat with a conical crown, made of poster board and colored with tempera paint that left a black ring around my head when I took it off (though somehow I didn't think the Pilgrims had to put up with that).

But whatever else I knew about the Pilgrims, I knew what they had for Thanksgiving dinner: oven-roasted turkey with cranberry sauce; mashed potatoes with giblet gravy; garden peas and sweet potato casserole with marshmallows baked on top; grated carrots imprisoned in molded lemon Jello; and of course olives and pickles and hot cloverleaf rolls dripping with butter. But all that was prelude. The highlight of the meal, the dish that surpassed everything before it, was desert; and on Thanksgiving Day, only one desert truly reflected the genius of the Pilgrims: pumpkin pie with whipped cream gobbed on top.

It was a lucky thing for me that strawberry shortcake with whipped cream, and pumpkin pie with whipped cream, came at opposite ends of summer; having to choose between them would have constituted one of life's few, genuinely insoluble dilemmas.

———·——

Would it be an error to assert that the vast majority of children today do not even *realize* that, left undisturbed, cream rises to the top of whole milk? The disengagement is not, after all, a simple datum about the dairy. It is a wonder of nature, a mystic event that liberates cream from the role of a flavor additive that lends richness to milk and exposes its true identity as ambrosia, the food of the gods.

While this predilection of cream and milk to part company had been recognized and taken advantage of for centuries before my birth, the mechanics of the process were little understood, and had been improved upon even less. Generations of human beings simply waited for the commingled fluids to reorganize themselves, a process that occurred only as rapidly as its natural composition allowed. Then, in the late nineteenth century, technology came to our rescue: the waiting abruptly ended with the invention of the dairy "separator," a device that employed specific gravity to force the issue. Fluid fresh from the cow, poured into the top of the machine, emerged seconds later from twin spigots—thinner milk from one, fatter cream from the other, and far more of the former than the latter.

The gadget could be adjusted to control the degree of separation desired. Leaving more cream in the mix made milk "creamier." Conversely, more milk in the cream made it "lighter," while less made it "heavier." My preference was uniformly to maximize the process until the milk flowed thin as whey-water and the cream was so thick that it no longer flowed at all, but piled up in the collection bowl like cookie batter. Sadly, my preferences never influenced the Hilgendorf Dairy folks. The only time I was actually able to affect the outcome was when we visited Dad's brother in the tiny crossroads village of Blockville, New York, a few miles out of Ashville. Edgar Skinner was a teacher who, for thirty-five years, taught all the math and science in a centralized high school. Through those years, however, he also maintained a farm and kept a small herd of Guernsey cows that required twice-daily milking seven days a week. After setting aside milk and cream for the Ashville family, he sold the rest to a local dairy.

Thus it came to pass that I actually got my hands on a separator. Not that it did much good. About five at the time, I learned first-hand that a separator took a strong arm, which Uncle Edgar had and I didn't. But he was always willing to let us try our hands at things around his farm, like steering his red Farmall tractor, which was easy, or milking a cow, which wasn't. So he stood patiently aside with a bucket of fresh milk, gentle amusement playing about his wide wise mouth, while I tried in vain to get the beast up to speed. I heaved on that sixteen-inch crank until I almost imploded with the effort, and managed to work it up to about one-eighth of the required revolutions-per-minute. Frank and Cliff had a try at it next, and while they managed to triple my contribution, we'd still be standing there creamless had not Uncle Edgar, a full-fledged grin now creasing his weathered face, taken the crank and set the machine humming with about two turns. It was a lovely illustration of how great strength creates the illusion of effortlessness.

Uncle Edgar appreciated what we were after, too, which is to say that he attended to our begging by setting the dial to squeeze the maximum amount of milk out of the cream—or the maximum amount of cream out of the milk. Whichever. We were far less interested in the particulars of the operation than we were to sit next morning at Aunt Mabelle's breakfast table, drooling like rabid dogs over a pitcher of cream the consistency of soft butter. And when the permissive nod was given, and we walloped a dollop of the exquisite stuff onto a bowl of corn flakes and brown sugar, I thought I'd died and gone to heaven. Indeed, could I have known with certitude that heaven was half that alluring, I might have volunteered to get up a group and start the trip right then and there.

It should be evident by now that milk was more than simply the beverage of my childhood. It was that, to be sure; water never held a candle to a big glass of ice cold milk for soothing a throat seared by hard work or vigorous exercise on a hot summer day. But it was more: an erstwhile form of entertainment; an essential weapon in the practice of sibling rivalry; a beginning physics lesson—and a set of olfactory clues by which events are translated into memory.

When the private automobile rules, super markets dominate the shopper's landscape, and most food is so thoroughly processed as to achieve featureless uniformity, it is easy to forget that dairymen once delivered freshly bottled milk and cream to people's doorsteps. And therein is a difference worth noting. Whatever benefits derive from central processing, flavor is not among them; nor is uniqueness preserved by collecting all the milk in half a state, combining it in one enormous slurry, and redistributing it in plastic gallon jugs to every store within two days' journey by truck. It matters little which brand you buy: they all taste the same anyway, which is to say hardly at all.

The villain in this piece is homogenization, as demonic a procedure as ever was forced upon an innocent and unsuspecting populace. It accomplishes two things, both bad: it prevents whole milk from separating into its natural constituents, and it renders all milk tasteless.

Homogenization does not allow for the kind of breakfast-table worshipfulness that Uncle Edgar made possible for us. Indeed, its very purpose is to prevent it. But that's not its only consequence: it also interferes with a fundamental law of nature. Call that, rather, a fundamental law of flavor. The marvel of bovine chemistry is its ability to transform cellulose, in the form of grass, into protein. No other creature does it so well. Cows do it without thinking about it—or about anything else for that matter, including what else beside grass they are tearing up out of a meadow and ingesting. And that "what else" gets processed right along with grass to flavor the next milking. This leads to some swell surprises. We knew when the ascending sun of spring had driven the last vestige of frost from riparian pasturage and wild onions had emerged from the soft stream banks, not because anyone told us, but because their pungent aroma informed our nostrils the minute we pulled the paper cap off the milk bottle the following day. Who needs a calendar to explain what month it is as long as wild onions spike the pasture? Other fragrances betrayed other seasons and events, the appearance of mint and wild thyme or the release of the herd to browse among fallen apples or corn stubble. To the olfactorily gifted, each herd's milk was a diary of what was happening around the dairy.

And that was one of the sublime benefits of independent dairies: the unique signature of each herd was marketed intact. Even now, turning back my sensory clock, I revel in the liquid substantiality that parents and school health classes and *Saturday Evening Post* ads early taught me was *the* essential food for growing children. Peeling the cap off a bottle brimming with yesterday's produce of the cow, I nosed the sweet bouquet of milk churning into my glass and savored the robust flavor as it tumbled into my throat and etched a trail of coolness all the way to my belly. When, I ask you, was the last time you could *smell* the sweetness of milk?

Don't look for it to happen with the generic stuff in your glass-fronted supermarket cooler, with its ranked shelves of plastic gallon jugs and paperboard containers on which the butterfat content is labeled in fractious percentage points. I'm talking milk that is unique to each herd if not each cow. When sampled farm by farm, even a blindfolded novice could quickly learn to differentiate the produce of a Guernsey from a Holstein from a Jersey. Those signatures registered with us. Part of the fun of being invited to a friend's house for lunch was to taste the difference between milk produced by the dairy that supplied his family and what we were accustomed to. Each trip to Pittsburgh to visit Mother's family, or to New York State to visit Dad's, received a gustatory boost from the uniqueness of their dairies, making each outing more pleasant to anticipate, more palpable in memory.

Can homogenized milk do that? Not by any stretch of the imagination.

CHAPTER 11

A Clear Case of Harassment

A s noted earlier, it is a sacred obligation among little brothers to harass their big sisters. Being the eldest, Ruth Ann enjoyed the benefits and endured the liabilities of her station—and counted three younger brothers as being in the latter category. I'm not sure that I even remember all the things that Cliff, Frank and I did to make Ruth Ann's life miserable. I suspect that if the four of us were polled, each of us (particularly Ruth Ann) could name more than a few incidents the other three have long since forgotten. But then, such a list is superfluous anyway: our mere existence caused her as much grief as joy, and more than any young girl would consider tolerable. To her demure female mind, we were a nuisance, all the time making crude boy noises or rolling around on the floor wrestling.

Still, in my memory, Ruth Ann endured me with more than a measure of grace and good humor. Bright and cheerful of disposition, she giggled at the slightest provocation, especially with her large group of girlfriends. If I pestered her it was not to bother or harass, but because I enjoyed being with her, and longed for the affection she bestowed in greater measure than Mother who, while she clearly loved us, was still a McCafferty. And among McCaffertys, affection was nothing if not reserved.

It should also be stated that we boys did not spend a lot of time plotting and scheming about ways to get on Ruth Ann's nerves. For one thing, Mother would not have tolerated it, and what Mother did not tolerate did not long survive in that house. So we just went along, stumbling into whatever opportunities naturally presented themselves, and Ruth Ann was stuck with it. And among the opportunities that presented themselves was one incident that lives as fresh in my mind as the day we perpetrated it. It cannot be considered anything but premeditated and willful, a clear case of harassment. It was a midwinter Saturday afternoon, and Ruth Ann was getting ready for a date with her midteen friends later that evening.

Why we boys felt driven, that particular day, to commit a known misdemeanor I no longer recall. I suppose it could have been boredom, though not likely. Boredom, too, was banned from our house; we were not permitted to indulge it. We were thoroughly indoctrinated in the core imperative of the Protestant middle class: don't waste time! Any activity was superior to none. Further, there was a hierarchical ranking among the options. Reading a book was, except in rare cases, superior to listening to the radio; raking the lawn better than a game of cards; playing with friends preferable to wandering about the house getting underfoot; and all of them superior to going to a movie. Not that any of these was bad in itself. We were spared the injunctions against dancing and playing cards still observed by Dad's Methodist kin up in Ashville. No, the intolerable evil was jaded idleness, moments when—in the trenchant prose of Luke the Evangelist—

Satan might demand to sift all of us like wheat. Whining to Mother that I had nothing to do was always a mistake: she could find something for me to do faster than I could retract the confession, and generally something I'd rather not have to do. But once I'd put the agenda in her hand, backing out was no longer an option.

I suspect the events of that afternoon unfolded because we were not bored enough, a case of rowdiness run wild among three brothers straddling the cusp of puberty, with too much energy and looking for an outlet. Watching our bathrobed and barefooted sister padding off to the shower, we woke as one to the opportunity presented us by the conjunction of her absence and a fresh supply of crisp, dry snow coating the yard.

It took less time to contrive the deed than to execute it. With consummate stealth—necessary to preclude Mother's hindering intervention—we sneaked out the door, scooped up fistfuls of snow, and crept back upstairs to Ruth Ann's bedroom. This in itself was a flagrant act of trespass. Being the only girl, Ruth Ann enjoyed a dual privilege: not only did she have a bedroom to herself while we three boys were required to share one; she was able to make it her sanctuary. Her door was more often closed than open, and her favorite winter pastime was to curl up atop her small hope chest to read, luxuriating in the warmth-oozing grate of the radiator set in the wall beneath her back window.

Male Skinner children were firmly instructed that the room beyond that door was off-limits, no ifs, ands or buts. Even a door left ajar, but showing more door than ajar, read "Keep Out!" as clearly as if the words had been carved into the lintel. That afternoon, for unwitting reasons, Ruth Ann committed a tactical blunder: she left her door standing wide open. To three adolescent males on the prowl, and receptive to any plausible excuse to ignore sibling privacy rights, that was enough.

Had I dared so provocative an act on my own, I probably would not have lived to see Sunday morning. Fortunately for me, I had observed the doctrine of safety in numbers. While Ruth Ann was turning off the shower, we were ascending the stairs. While she was drying herself, we were in her room spreading fresh snow on the rug. As she emerged from the bathroom and started down the hall, I jumped behind her door, Frank slipped into her closet, and Cliff slid under her bed. There, in consummate conspiratorial silence, we waited until she entered the room.

I confess, in all modesty, that our timing was flawless. My leap from behind the door, "Boo"-ing on the fly, occurred at the

precise instant that one bare foot touched down squarely on a glob of snow. I had never seen my sister screech in mid-air like that—or jump so high while doing it. It was impressive. But before she could turn her startled fury on me, Frank leaped from her closet—and to my rescue—yelling "Boo!" as her foot touched down on another patch of snow. Again she squealed, although by now the ballerina leap had faded into a rapid two-step as she bounced from place to place, searching frantically for a bit of dry rug. We hadn't left her much. And before she could regain even a semblance of composure, Cliff was out from under her bed with a final startling Boo-bellow.

By that time, Ruth Ann was utterly discombobulated. But where your average teenaged girl might be expected to start sobbing, denouncing our low-life nastiness, Ruth Ann reacted in trademark fashion: she broke down in a hopeless giggle-fit. If she tried between twitters to lash out at us, it was a futile effort. She had been had and she knew it, and the four of us stood there, laughing raucously at our impeccable teamwork.

Though I never heard, I'd be surprised if the episode did not figure prominently in that evening's conversation among her friends. But I don't recall Ruth Ann going off to the shower leaving her door standing open again; and ever after, when she returned, her entry was a bit more cautious. Oh, yeah—and she probably remembered to wear her slippers.

———◆———

A footnote on hidden treasure: the hope chest on which Ruth Ann loved to curl up and read was in reality a wooden shipping crate, a foot and a half wide and deep and three long, that traveled back and forth between Chicago and Richmond carrying Mother and Dad's sparse, medical school era belongings; but they never mentioned it, and their children remained ignorant of its history for the next sixty years. In 1931, after completing his medical residency, Dad was called back to Allegheny to become the school's first college physician and to teach biology. Arriving in Meadville, the old crate underwent a sow's-ear-to-silk-purse transformation. The inside was painted with the cream enamel we would later recognize as Mother's favorite hue, and cotton batting was tacked to the outside, upholstered with yellow fabric in a floral pattern—an instant hope chest for a young girl. After Ruth Ann married and left home, Mother kept the crate, eventually consigning it to her Chautauqua basement as a storage box. When Mother died, Pat and I hauled it back to Meadville and removed the frazzled fabric and mildewy batting, thinking it just a sturdy old box for which we could surely find some use, and were startled to discover a family travelogue.

Stenciled on the front in the oval shape typical of late Victorian business logos were the words, "From Arthur Thomas Co., Philadelphia, Pa." Glued to one end, and surviving the years remarkably well in spite of its newsprint-like quality, was a diamond-shaped label: "CAUTION: Hydrochloric Acid. In case of leaking package, wash acid off with water." Apparently Dad had acquired it from Allegheny College's chemistry department. A closer examination, however, revealed how well-traveled the crate really was.

Across the top, in rough swatches as by a brush stiffened by dried paint, appeared the address: "Clifford Skinner, Chicago, Ill" and scrawled across the front in blue-green crayon: "To E.D. McCafferty, Allison Park, Pa." Further, fastened to the top and one end with carpet tacks were two orange shipping tags, printed: "From C. W. Skinner, Allison Park, Pa. To Jacob Umlaut, 2510 West Main St., Richmond, Virginia." Oddly, the "from" address was in Mother's hand, the "to" address in Dad's. We can only guess how many trips that box made from Pennsylvania to Illinois to Virginia and back.

The final bit of whimsy turned up when we removed the orange tags in hopes of cleaning the wood while preserving the history. Absent-mindedly turning one over, I found more printing—this done on a commercial press—revealing that they, too, had an earlier incarnation: "For the Moore Milk Company, Cincinnati, Ohio. From Thomas Bowles, Harrison, Ohio." Thomas was Mother's maternal grandfather who abandoned farming in midlife to attend medical school and become a physician, eventually to attend to her paternal grandfather as he lay dying. All those winter afternoons, Ruth Ann curled up atop a travel odyssey of thousands of cumulative miles, touched by four generations of genealogy, without knowing it. Little wonder the old box was able to be a flying carpet for her imagination.

PART III

One Death
Changes Everything

CHAPTER 12

A Very Low
Regard for Death

Mother and Dad had a very low regard for death. They understood it to be life's concluding event, nothing more. They much preferred that everyone have a fair shot at living. But they knew that life isn't fair; some souls get only a momentary glance and are, of us all, the only true innocents. For those who are granted an extended run, the object is to live in such a way that, at the final curtain, the actor can leave the stage content with a job well done, and honest critics will report that the play was worth attending.

None of these variations makes it easier on those left behind. When Dad died in 1940 at the age of forty-seven, leaving Mother with four young children and negligible means of support, grief and apprehension dropped more weight on her than she had ever borne or ever would again.

Dad and Mabelle, his next oldest sister, never knew their oldest brother Frank. He lost a bout with scarlet fever before they were born. When they were old enough to grasp the meaning of mortality, and to understand that they'd had an older brother whom they would know only in story and picture, Grandmother and Grandfather Skinner took them to the attic and opened a trunk in which Frank's clothing and toys had been laid away when he died. A few days later Mabelle and Clifford came down with scarlet fever. The family believed that the spores of the disease had survived those years in the trunk. A physician to whom I once related this story scoffed at that idea, branding it an impossibility. I have no expertise to challenge his judgment, but you would never have convinced Dad's family circa 1897. The loss of one child to scarlet fever was one too many; the trunk and its contents were hauled down to the back yard and burned.

It was precaution too late. Mabelle recovered, apparently no worse for the wear—never a sure outcome in those days before the discovery of penicillin—and died a month before her eighty-fifth birthday. Dad wasn't so lucky. His illness progressed into rheumatic fever and a compromised heart, leaving him with nothing to do for it but to get on with life; and get on he did, pressed to pack everything he could into a span that he knew would be short, and unalterably so. He meant, in the words of Henry David Thoreau's trenchant Walden Pond reflection, to "not, when I came to die, discover that I had not lived."

In that he could not have found a more congenial companion than Mother who, all her life, thrived on activity and social interaction every bit as much as he. Both had long since come to terms with life's finitude. Dad made no secret of his damaged heart or his lousy survival odds. Taking his brother's vital signs one day after graduating from medical school, Dad commented, "I'd give anything to have a heart like yours." Indeed. Edgar survived to age ninety-six, twice as old as his little brother, before his good heart gave out. So Dad and Mother talked frankly about his condition while courting, understood the outcome, and knew that it was a matter of when, not if. But if death meant to catch them it would have to do it on the run; they felt under no compulsion to cooperate.

Dad's Allegheny colleagues clearly saw this. Three of them, charged by the faculty to prepare a memorial statement at the time of his death, wrote, "In fraternal and civic organizations, in church and in professional groups, he was always a leader; few men in Meadville have ever had a larger circle of friends from more walks of life than he. He was friendly, sincere, helpful; he lived a sacrificial life. When he knew that activity would lessen his life span, he was active; he willed to live his life for others."

———·———

It was predictable, then, that Dad would be stricken in some such manner as he was, attending a concert of the Meadville Orchestral Society. He, Mother and Ruth Ann (old enough by then both to appreciate the music and to sit still) were seated in the balcony of Meadville High School's cavernous auditorium when Dad collapsed with a cerebral embolism. A blood clot escaping from his damaged heart had lodged in his brain. For several weeks he lay in Meadville City Hospital, unable to speak, half his body paralyzed, while fellow physicians and the nursing staff struggled to mitigate the damage and the *Tribune-Republican* printed daily notices reporting on his presumed progress. A turning point seemed to have come when, early one morning, a nurse asked him if he would like more orange juice, and he answered "yes."

In utter disregard of hospital protocol, which mandated the maintenance of serene calm both in the building and on the streets outside, she ran down the hall screaming, "Dr. Skinner talked! Dr. Skinner talked!"

It was false advertising. Dad was moved home several days later, where a hospital bed was set up for him in the dining room. The mongrel Aesculapius promptly lay down beside it and steadfastly refused to move. A week later Dad suffered a second and fatal embolism and the dog stopped eating for two weeks.

———·•·———

To us children, Dad's loss was devastating in ways we still may not fully comprehend. As shadows of physical wounds remain for years in our flesh, reminding us of the journey we have been on, so scars left by parental loss mark a young child's psyche for life. Each of Dad's children, in our own time and way, would recover, if that is the legitimate word. We would sort through our feelings, own our grief, and store away our individual fragments of memory. But we would do so differently because we understood differently. In my case, the confusion of losing Dad was

compounded by the low estimation of my elders of how much a seven-year-old comprehends. They thought I was too young to understand, and therefore too young to grieve. So I was never given the opportunity.

The last time Frank and I saw Dad was from the passageway between the front hall and the living room. He lay under a blanket on the couch opposite the fireplace, a tongue depressor wrapped in adhesive tape jammed between his teeth to prevent him from chewing his tongue while a nurse leaned over him in compassionate futility.

Cliff remembers seeing him from there, too, but not being allowed in. Mother, distracted beyond reason, told him to go to his room. Climbing the stairs, confused and frightened, he began to cry. It was Aunt Mabelle, he recalls—she who survived the same siege of scarlet fever that would now, finally, take her brother's life—who heard and followed him up the stairs to offer tenderness and comfort.

Frank and I were treated even more curtly. Not to put too unfeeling a tone on it, we were banished to the homes of boyhood friends, Frank several blocks away to the home on Woodland Place of classmate Charlie Ufford whose family, in a touch of irony, lived in the house our family occupied in 1931 while waiting for our North Main Street home to be built; and me across town to the home of playmate Clark Davis, the son of City Hospital's chief of medical staff. I never saw Dad again. When I arrived home the following day, most of our extended family had gathered. Eyes red and swollen, they bustled about helping Mother, or sat around the breakfast nook table, drinking coffee and talking quietly. I moved from caress to embrace, but it was comfort to small purpose. No one spoke of the finality of the event that had summoned them there. Ruth Ann, Cliff and Frank were in the living room, making the pretense of looking at magazines. Eyes brimming with tears, they could not possibly have seen anything on the pages they turned, slowly and mechanically.

"Where's Daddy?" I asked, glancing around the edge of the door at the empty bed in the dining room. No answer.

"Is he upstairs?" I pressed. "No," one of them (odd that I don't recall who) said dully.

"Is he in the hospital?" I pressed harder. Again a monotonic, "No."

"Then where is he?" I insisted, growing increasingly frustrated.

"He's dead!" Ruth Ann erupted through her tears.

That was it. No explanations. No reaching out one to another. The reserve and self-control that the Skinners and McCaffertys jointly valued was more evident that day than it ever would be again. And that day, for one of the very few times in my life, it caused my family to fail me. On more than one occasion, that toughness carried both families through harsh events and tragic times when giving way would only have compounded the loss. On that day, it left their children with no place to turn. And with preparations for the funeral moving rapidly forward, Frank and I were exiled again.

If news accounts and mementos are to be believed, it was a remarkable occasion, expressive of the quality of neighbor relations that typified life in my Pennsylvania town, and of the esteem in which Dad was held within the professional and social groups that comprised it. At that age, I could not possibly have appreciated the depth of feeling that the event registered, any more than I am able to recognize all of the 340 guests who must have stood in line a very long time to sign the book of remembrance that we found among Mother's effects after her own death. I still have difficulty envisioning how the front of the Presbyterian Church ever accommodated 115 floral arrangements, but the donors' names are also inscribed in the memorial book in Mother's determined hand. The entire faculty of Allegheny College, dozens representing Meadville's medical profession, the Masonic Lodge and Kiwanis Club, and more from congregation and community, crammed into the church and overflowed onto its sidewalks. And as if any greater gesture of esteem was needed, the mourners included a gentle and appreciative coterie of ten Roman Catholic nuns from Spencer Hospital who, under the prevailing religious custom of the time, ought not even to have been there.

But I have neither knowledge nor memory of it. By the time I was brought home from Clark's house the funeral was over. Our relatives, whose bustling about even in grief spoke reassuringly of the durability of family, were gone. An uncomfortable quiet had descended over my home—not the soft calm of serenity, but one as cold as the angel of death whose unwelcome entry brought it. Ruth Ann, mature enough to grasp what was happening, and to be more fully included in the ceremony of Dad's passing, remembers seeing Mother sitting alone on the living room couch where her husband had died, staring blankly into space, her face a consuming countenance of despair. She seemed, Ruth Ann recalls, to be utterly lost. Yet even then, somewhere deep in that tiny frame, the brave determination that was a hallmark of her whole life was stirring, picking itself up and brushing itself off. Life would return to normal, whatever that might mean. She had understood from the outset the temporary nature of the terms life offered her in the love of the man now lost to her, and had embraced them willingly. She would not now, after the fact, whine that they had been unfair. She would reassemble the fragments and move on.

On this point my siblings and I agree: after his burial Mother never spoke to any of us about Dad's death again. Even when I asked her, years later, it was evident that it was not something she would willingly discuss. It was as if the passion I know that she and Dad shared had been buried with him, and it would be too painful and unseemly to resurrect it to memory.

———·—·———

Dad never wanted to be buried. He considered cemeteries a waste of good farmland, and thought cremation the logical alternative. I never really understood why he *was* buried; it was clearly one of those things Mother didn't care to revisit. Perhaps she just couldn't bear the thought of having him cremated, though she was pretty hard-headed about such things herself. It may be that social or familial pressures were too great. Few Christians chose cremation in those days; it flew in the face of the common wisdom about resurrection. The idea seems to have gotten abroad that reducing someone's body to a handful of scraps and scattering them all over the landscape precluded reassembly on the Great Gettin' up Mornin'. It seems to me a notion of profound unfaith. If God, as we profess, can call a universe into being by uttering a word, then compiling the ingredients needed for resurrection surely presents no problem. Besides, if the Apostle Paul was right in asserting that flesh and blood can't inherit the Kingdom of God, because something perishable cannot possibly inherit what is by definition imperishable, then the issue is moot. But then, we Christians are not always long on the logic of these things.

So Dad's physical body (nothing more than that, Mother *was* willing to assert) lies in Greendale Cemetery, atop a broad hill on the eastern edge of town at the top of Randolph Street. If one's body must wait through time for whatever it is that yet lies in store for Earth, then Greendale is as nice a place to wait as any. It is by any definition a surpassingly lovely place. Narrow cobbled lanes curve among weathered and lichen-clad gravestones, some almost as old as Mead's Settlement, surrounded by rhododendron, arborvitae and forsythia, and dappled by whatever sunlight works its way through the dense overstory of centenarian maple, oak, and beech trees. Through a few breaks in the landscaping, it is possible to glimpse the Presbyterian Church steeple and the Courthouse dome, three-quarters of a mile west and three hundred feet below—a congenial reminder that, at least in small towns, church and state really can abide in convivial relationship.

Greendale is a history of Meadville engraved in granite. I have reflected, when walking the grounds with Pat during June's rhododendron explosion, or when the hilltop is aflame with October leaves, that as many members of Meadville's historic families probably lie there as live along the tree-lined streets below. But while we still strive with issues of wealth and social standing and who gets to decide what, they share the ultimate egalitarian peace that is death.

———•———

A postscript: Ruth died in the fall of 1991, half a century after Clifford. She had remarried after twenty-seven years of widowhood; and when her second husband died peacefully in their living room at ninety-eight, she saw him buried with full military honors at Arlington National Cemetery in Washington. At the time of her own death, she was still living in her Chautauqua home, preparing her own meals and driving her own car. And while the inevitable penalties of age were evident, she remained mentally and spiritually vibrant.

At her memorial service, a woman approached me to relate that, five days before Mother died, there was a parish dinner. Mother had called the church that morning and asked the woman, who was in charge of arrangements, whether anyone had come to help her.

"No," she replied, "I'm here alone so far."

"I'll be right up," Mother said. And she was, pressing her ninety-year-old frame to the task of arranging tables and chairs and setting places. That evening, she sat by the door, the pastor's baby son perched on her lap, making change as people paid to attend the dinner.

I could not escape the delicious irony of the scene. When she moved to Chautauqua, Ruth settled into Clifford's native

southwestern New York and joined the only church in town—a United Methodist congregation. So doing, she ended her life in communion with the denomination that her husband had abandoned fifty-five years earlier to join her Presbyterians, in the congregation that his sister Mabelle served as organist for half a century.

Maybe things really do balance out in the end.

In May of that year Ruth Ann, Cliff, Frank and I and our spouses, sixteen of Ruth's grandchildren and thirteen of their spouses, and the eleven great-grandchildren that had thus far

joined the family, gathered in from nine states to celebrate
Mother's ninetieth birthday. And on a chill and gusty-bright afternoon that November, those able to make the trip a second time
gathered in Meadville's Greendale Cemetery, joined by a clutch
of Allegheny student friends who, simply by coming, earned my
enduring gratitude. Being the family's minister-in-residence, I
officiated at grave side, while her eldest sons and two of their
sons lowered her gently, by hand, into the ground near Clifford.
I had come full circle: the child never given a chance to weep at
the end of our Dad's life was privileged to speak on the family's
behalf in celebration of our Mother's. Good thing, too. I would
not gracefully have been denied a second time.

CHAPTER 13

The Shadow on the Ceiling

For the most part, how substantial our memories of Dad are is proportional to how much time transpired in their formation. But not always. Ruth Ann and Cliff, who knew Dad the longest, recall the most details, Frank and I the fewest. Yet curiously, my most enduring memory, the one that comes first to mind when someone asks me about my father, is the shadow on the ceiling.

Early on, we three boys shared the second floor bedroom at the northwest corner of the house, over Dad's office. I will not pretend that we were cramped. Even three-to-a-room was hardly close quarters in bedrooms the size of those in our Main Street home. With Cliff's bed against the north wall and Frank's the east, there was ample room for my crib against the south wall, behind the hall door. Even adding two dressers and a couple of chairs to the room failed to crowd the floor. Any insufficiency of space we thought we suffered was psychological and self-imposed.

No three boys in the whole history of the world, required to grow up sharing a room, ever did so without tangling once in a while.

To remember bedtime—hanging my clothes in the smaller of two closets, smaller because of a steeply sloped ceiling imparted by its location under the attic stairs—is to recall a rush of air pouring in the twin double windows. One pair opened west toward Main Street, the other north toward Hamilton. Together, they gave our room a light and airy aspect. More importantly, they satisfied Mother and Dad's requirement that every room must have cross-ventilation. Summer or winter, we never settled down to sleep without the windows being thrown open to "air out the room." Each night she was home, Mother tucked us into our beds, reminded us to say our prayers, and kissed us goodnight. Once in a while, but rarely, Dad was with her. He seldom made it home early enough to find us still awake. Even on evenings when he arrived home in time for supper, he often left afterward. My overriding sense is of his absence. If not at the hospital, he was speaking before some group in town or attending a church meeting or Masonic Lodge event or other point of community engagement. There seemed always to have been something, almost never to have been nothing.

But when he got home, even if we had long been in bed, he tiptoed into our rooms and kissed each of us goodnight. I was usually asleep by then, or should have been. It was a rare evening when he returned home early enough that he and Mother would think it appropriate for any of us to be awake, certainly not the baby of the family. Still, there is that thing in children that senses when something important is *going* to happen, especially if it is a matter of cherished routine: they take almost as much satisfaction from the expectation as the actuality, even though unconscious of what time it actually occurs. Though Dad's kisses were most often planted on my insensate face, just knowing that he would come in, and that I would not go long into the night without my father pressing his lips into my cheek, was all it took to reassure me that God was in heaven and all was right with the world—at least with my world. Maybe it was the imprint left in my impressionable skin by his whisker-grizzled lips that convinced me, when I stirred during the night, that I had indeed been kissed.

But then there is that shadow indelibly imprinted in my brain. For whatever reason, I was not deeply asleep one evening when I heard his footsteps climb the stairs and come down the hall. Oddly, the sound roused some anxiety. It was the two-year-old thing: too old to enjoy an infant's bliss of ignorance, not yet old enough to distinguish between real and imagined wrongs. Regarding my father with blended awe and adoration, I turned a late-evening ritual of affection into a problem: if he found me awake when I was supposed to be asleep, mightn't he be angry with me?

No fear. Can a shadow convey a smile? Can assurance float like a corona about the edges of a silhouette? As he opened the door I recognized him, and could have told at a glance if it was not him, by the shadow on the ceiling; and I knew, though I am unable to say how—perhaps by some aura—that he was smiling. Oddly, the memory ends right there, as if the light went out and took his shadow with it and left me alone again in the dark.

In the intervening years, my mind has learned to read that brief, luminous moment and the shuttering darkness that followed as the defining metaphor of my experience of my father. It remains as vivid in my mind as on the night when it happened. He was there in our lives, not fully understood because we were still too young to look with discernment, and then he was gone. And even as I have succeeded by hard, almost wearying reflection to recapture other fragments of my experience of him, they always come filtered through the smiling shadow on the ceiling, and evoke the confused blend of love and dread that I never was given the opportunity to outgrow.

———•+•———

Mother's ninety years took her way beyond the final chapter of this book and into a whole new life—indeed, several of them. Her influence on her children was inestimable. As Polaris, hanging high in the northern night, orients us to our position on Earth, so Mother was the point of light from which everything we did took direction, almost entirely so after Dad's death. Of necessity, she is the constant star in these stories.

In contrast, Dad's passage was like the evanescent flash of a meteor. His death at forty-seven took him early from our lives, our home, our town and my story. And while his influence on us was considerable, our memories of him are disconcertingly fragmentary. Conversations among my siblings and me, occasioned by my launching into the writing of this book, make clear that while we possess mainly yarns and anecdotes based on third person accounts from friends, we possess few narratives based on personal experience. In the elegant phrase of *Star Trek's* Commander Spock, our sharing has consisted largely of "long dormant memory remnants" reactivated by our very effort to relocate something of him. It is as if, running about in our yard, we had looked in and seen him momentarily through one window or another, and were left with nothing more than snatches of him gathered on the fly.

For all these reasons, I was surprised and delighted, years later, by the observation of an old family friend. Among the Allegheny freshmen given a physical exam by Dad in 1933 was a young man named D. Armour Hillstrom. Armour developed a deep admiration for Dad. They remained friends until Dad's death, and the relationship continued with Mother until hers. By the time I returned to Allegheny as dean in 1978, Armour was a trustee of the college; and when I became the college's chaplain in 1985, he sometimes attended chapel services at which I presided. After one of them, he remarked to Pat, "Don reminds me so much of his father when he speaks. He even has his father's stance."

Never let it be said that we do not incarnate our parents. I never saw or heard my father speak in public. I have no memory whatever of how he carried or expressed himself, how he advocated his ideas, or how he employed the sense of humor that his contemporaries described as spontaneous and infectious. Such models of public address as I studied, and those I mimicked because they somehow impressed me, came years after his death. Yet here was a man who knew my father half a century earlier, before I reached my first birthday, exclaiming on how closely I resembled my father in stance, expression and humor.

The observation affected me deeply. It was as if Armour had rekindled the light that threw Dad's shadow on the ceiling of our bedroom, igniting an insight that I should have acquired on my own years earlier, and which ought not to have caught me so by surprise when it came: if I want to see Dad, I need only look at his other three children or—equally important—look in the mirror. We are of his flesh and blood. It wasn't that I had never reflected on such things during my own study of humanity and its vexing and wonderful complexities. I simply had never made the connection to me: that to the degree to which posture and gait, aptitudes and interests, and manners of speech are genetically wired into us by our inheritance (and I believe they are to a much larger extent than most of us recognize or admit), then we are our parents—not just the mother we knew into her ninetieth year, but the father we did not, and thought we never could. We are, at least by half, him; and he was, at least by half, us.

It turned out that the shadow on the ceiling was a great deal more substantial than I had any reason to imagine.

CHAPTER 14

Dining Room

Two giant corner cupboards dominated our dining room, wood-paneled doors on their lower halves and arched ones with multi-paned windows on top. Standing with my nose to the glass was like looking into a china shop that bore witness to the divergence between Mother's and Dad's origins. Mother's bone china, embossed with a delicate green and brown border pattern, covered one set of shelves. Behind it, a dozen ironstone plates from Dad's family stood upright against the back of the cabinet, plain white fading to age-induced gray. Most decrepit among them was Grandma Skinner's "oven plate," the one reserved for keeping things warm in the oven of her kerosene-fired stove. It had made enough trips into the heat and back out to bake it brown and crackle its glazing so finely that I couldn't fathom why it had not long since disintegrated into a pile of shards.

Which is as Mother would have it. Much as she enjoyed the glitter and formality of well-to-do society, she was not herself a formal person, and loved knickknacks. Small pieces of pottery, brass, wood, or glass, from anywhere in the world and bordering on kitsch, were gathered in such abundance that half an hour was required to dust a bookcase from which two or three artifacts had first to be set aside in order to remove a single book. How she ever managed to mix it all together so successfully is a bit of a mystery. But she had a knack for making it all charming without becoming cluttered, creating the kind of informal and lively place in which guests felt immediately at home and where, as a result, they loved to gather and talk away the evening hours.

Long before I started school, I was intimately acquainted with every decorative piece in that dining room—the Mexican clay water jar shaped like a pear, the hand-painted wooden relish tray from Czechoslovakia, the olive-wood candle sticks from the Middle East, and the three Chinese bells suspended on a single cord from a wall bracket, one above another and made not of metal but of lacquered wood as thin as paper and as brittle as ice.

But the lights were my favorite. Whenever Mother wasn't there to tell me not to (even more than the living room, the dining room was off-limits to sticky-fingered little kids), I'd sneak in and flip the light switch that controlled six faux-candle sconces hung around the walls. The illumination from their round, creamy-orange bulbs was not entirely effective to begin with, and was made less so after bouncing off glistening, hand-hammered copper reflectors that scattered it all over the room. They were puzzling, those reflectors: five-pointed, they looked less like stars than deep-dish gelatin molds. As lights, they were suitable for occasions on which adults gathered to dine under "atmospheric" conditions, but they weren't very useful for actually seeing anything. Dad fixed that: he installed reflector lamps out of sight in the two-foot gap between the tops of the corner cupboards and the ceiling, and fitted them with bulbs that, to my young eye, compared favorably with basketballs. Between them, they bounced so much light off the ceiling that Mother could use her 16-mm wind-up movie camera to full color effect without supplementary light. We've got the movies to prove it.

Then there was the chandelier, though it was largely aesthetic—more so than originally was intended. A genuine eight-arm candelabrum crafted of wood, it was Mother's favorite thing in the room. But she only used it once. The first time it illuminated a table set for a gathering of dinner guests, the eight candles coated half as many square feet of ceiling with waxy soot that defied scrubbing and resisted a new coat of paint. Sam Rayburn is reported to have observed that there's no education in the second kick of a mule. Mother, as already noted, was a quick learner. She had no desire ever to clean that ceiling a second time. The candles were never lit again. But they were never replaced, either. She enjoyed them too much, half-burned and coated with graceful if lumpy wax melt; they remained there until she sold the house, a charming but pointed reminder of one of her and Dad's few bad ideas.

Our dining room was the Dr. Jekyll and Mr. Hyde of the house. It wasn't planned that way. Time and events just brought it to that. When it was new and Mother had the opportunity to use it as she had dreamed, it was a formal room, but warm and inviting. Bone-white upper walls, contrasting with wainscoting and woodwork of Williamsburg blue, provided the setting for a dark veneer table and matching chairs. Two doors served the room. A narrow one in the northwest corner led to the kitchen by way of the breakfast nook, which doubled as a butler's pantry during formal dinners, while a broad passage centered in the west wall opened into the living room, where guests gathered while waiting for the meal to be served, usually around platters of hors d'oeuvres. These were never elaborate; Mother's taste in entertainment fare was both uncomplicated and abstemious, running to the likes of crackers and cheese, carrot sticks, and stuffed celery, accompanied by small glasses of tomato juice.

Reportedly, there were some lovely parties in that dining room. Invited to the table, guests filled their plates at the free-standing buffet under the east window—a triple affair set high enough into the wall to accommodate the buffet beneath, and bordered by in-set curtains of soft, almost transparent gold. When they took their places around the table to break bread together, they filled the room with laughter and conversation. But I never witnessed it. If the gatherings weren't mid-day luncheons or afternoon teas that ended before we children got home from school—or from the homes of friends willing to take us out from underfoot so that Mother could focus on her guests—they began after we were in bed. Mother and Dad held firmly to the conviction that young children should be in bed by 7:30 p.m. (though they never revealed whether this was supposed to benefit our health or theirs). Since the house was exceptionally solid and we were sound sleepers, we couldn't have told you whether our parents were in their own room preparing for bed, downstairs quietly reading in the living room, or yakking it up around the dining room table with a clutch of their boisterous friends.

While Dad's work schedule confined his social activities to lunchtime or evening affairs, Mother was under no such constraint. During an era when few married women of her social station worked outside the home, she was free to socialize as occasion allowed. And socialize she did. Allegheny's Faculty Wives and the Meadville Women's Club, the Philo-Mathesian Club (founded for "social enjoyment and intellectual improvement"), student leaders of Allegheny's Kappa Kappa Gamma sorority that Mother served as alumnae advisor, and the officers of the Civic Music Association all enjoyed her home. Mother loved to entertain, and her dining room, with its proximity to the living room, was the perfect place to do it.

———•+•———

All of which makes me think that the enjoyment Mother derived from her dining room died with her husband.

She was an inveterate compiler of scrapbooks, not just for herself but for her children. There is a price to be paid for delving into them, to be sure: a tour of her mementos, especially the earliest ones, necessarily exposes the delver to an awesome array of allergens that have accumulated in them through a lot of years. More than one case of a stuffed-up nose and tingling fingers has been contracted in the writing of this book—distracting if not terminal. But the scrapbooks provide an entrancing look into the past, a window into a time when an evening's entertainment focused on other human beings, not electronic desperation. Cumulatively, those pages reveal a couple enjoying a life vibrant with diversity and untiring in the nurturing of neighbor relations. It is startling, then, to arrive at 1940 and find... nothing. Not a single item was saved for most of a year, a twelve-month void imposed by grief.

That Dad lay on the edge of death in their dining room, the table and chairs shoved back to make room for the hospital bed in which it was hoped that he might recover, cannot have helped. After he died, the bed was dismantled and carted back to City Hospital and the furnishings were returned to their customary places. But the doors were closed and forbidding, the room cold and silent. The star-shaped reflectors lost the pale, orange shimmer of new copper, darkening with age and neglect until they were almost black. Mother seemed to find motivation neither to polish them nor to assign the task to one of us children during a family workday. The room was opened now and then for a reception or social event, but then was closed up tight again. Such events as did occur seemed somehow half-hearted, and as often as not were hosted not by Mother, but by one of us children—a birthday party or a function of one of Ruth Ann's high school sororities.

With social formality gone, the room was open to activities that were unheard of before Dad's death, including that peculiar period when the floor was covered by Lionel Blue. Maybe Mother had grown weary of solo entertaining, or was simply looking for an excuse to remain silent during those awkward pauses in group planning meetings when everyone waited to see who would volunteer to host the next gathering. In any event, once the large oval of O-gauge train track was laid down, there wasn't room for much of anything else.

That too would not last. Mother was too proud of her home to devote any part of its main floor to playroom status for long. It must be restored to its formal appearance, even if closed behind those forbidding doors. Nor was she one to allow her enjoyment of friends, or of the places she loved, to be diminished by life's harsher realities. Once she'd had opportunity to compass the dimensions of her grief, she again took pleasure in the rest of her home, but not the dining room. It appeared to have been touched by a deathly finality, as if it held a burden of grief such as defies balm or healing, and never again could be her room. It would, in time, ring again with the exuberance of family and friends gathered to dine and celebrate, but not until the house had passed to new owners.

And while Mother mused in later years that if houses, like furniture and clothing, could be packed up and moved, she would have taken ours with her when she left Meadville, I can't help but wonder whether that included the dining room.

CHAPTER 15

Say 'Mote-sart', not 'Moze-art'

T he chattering gaggles of ladies standing around the room, or twisting about in their chairs the better to see their sister conversants, grew hushed when the chairwoman tapped on the lectern and called them to order. Standees quietly tiptoed about as if someone was napping, looking for seats.

"Welcome to the October meeting of the Meadville Garden Club," intoned Madam Chairwoman, or words to that affect. Any of a dozen other beneficent societies would illustrate the case as well; in my mental file labeled "Memories / Age Eight," they all blur into a homogenous mass. And as British comedian Anna Russell was wont to emphasize, "Perhaps you think I meant homogeneous; but I mean homogenous, as in milk!" (But I already exhausted that topic.)

"And thank you for coming," she continued. "Out of deference for our guests, we're going to postpone today's business meeting until after the program. Now it is with special pleasure that I introduce the Skinner Ensemble."

That was my cue. The Skinner Ensemble consisted of Mother, piano; Ruth Ann, violin; Clifford, flute; Frank, cello; and Don, mouth. This generous arrangement, conceived by Mother, allowed me a share in the family's musical accomplishments when I did not yet (nor ever would) play an instrument well enough to participate musically. So I got to be the Deems Taylor of the Meadville chamber music circuit, announcing the program. Stepping confidently to the center of the room, I informed the ladies in a ringing voice that "The Skinner Ensemble will now play a classical medley...," and reeled off a list of works by Schubert, Mendelssohn, Beethoven, Chopin and Mozart.

There was nothing spontaneous about my speech, you understand. Mother's musical training had long since taught her that only amateurs are dumb enough to try to be innovative during a performance. Spontaneity on the part of one performer simply confuses everyone else and sacrifices the whole effort to the demons of chaos. Or, to quote Allegheny choral director Dr. Ward M. Jamison (who was among those blubbering on the curb of the restaurant that humid Sunday when Pat and I started for Oregon), "There will be no surprises during the concert; we're going to perform it like we rehearsed it!" Mother was in complete agreement: hard practice and "performing it like you rehearsed it" are the twin pillars of professionalism. And that applied even to the Skinner Ensemble's mouthpiece. Mother had me practice that menu until I could rattle it off backward without thinking. I have no idea how many repetitions that entailed. My single discrete memory is of my first attempt: the final number was composed by Wolfgang Amadeus What's-his-face and I pronounced his last name "*Moze*-art." Any eight-year-old American child, seeing "Mozart" for the first time, is going to say "Moze-art" until taught otherwise. We don't speak of "Botes-mun, Montana," and slothful children are not called "lait-sy." So why isn't it "Moze-art?" Mother was right there: "Say '*Mote*-sart,' she instructed gently, 'not '*Moze*-art'." And *Mote*-sart it was, then and forever.

Truth be told, I disliked the assignment. It wasn't just that I had to take a bath and put on my church clothes and stand in front of an audience for forty-five seconds correctly pronouncing Mozart's name. Nor was it sitting off to the side ("...and sit still, for heaven's sake!") listening to that same program until I detested it as much as I did summer squash and it made me gag. It was that sitting aside after my brief public appearances, while the rest of my family performed with a precision that even professionals applauded, was a constant reminder of failure.

Mother and Dad made music a part of our lives from the get-go. Singing in the car or around the piano at holidays was a family pastime. In constancy, music was exceeded only by food and work assignments. We were taught the basics almost as early as we learned to talk and joined choirs earlier than we can remember. Knowing that study of the keyboard is an excellent foundation for any musical endeavor, and especially for playing another instrument, all four of us were started early on piano lessons, at which three of us did well. Each in turn moved on to take up an instrument, from which an early pattern developed: Ruth Ann's choice of the violin put her among the stringed instruments; when Cliff followed on the flute, we were represented among the woodwinds (an odd label, I thought, for a metal tube with a bunch of holes in it); and Frank tilted the balance string-ward again by choosing the cello. All did exceptionally well, and the foundation for the Skinner Ensemble was laid.

Unfortunately, our collective achievement stalled right there. Had I chosen a second wind instrument right off, the balance might have been maintained. But I broke the pattern, asking to take up the French horn, a member of the brass family. It is also among the most difficult of instruments to master, and discipline was not my long suit. My grade school music coach suggested the E-flat Alto—a small, tuba-like horn that requires mastery of the same techniques but is easier to play. So I tried it, but it was like wanting to ride a horse—the hairy prancing four-legged kind with steaming breath and tornadic spirit—and being told that for now I'd better hone my scooter skills. My heart wasn't in it, and it didn't take the coach long to see it. So he suggested the bass drum, which had the virtue of simplicity. You know, boom boom boom is a lot easier to master than the fingering required to drive an instrument up and down the scale in just about any key you might care to pick. At least I could count and had a sense of rhythm; but going boom boom got boring real quick, and opportunity for promotion was lacking. If I could have shifted to the timpani, I might have become a half-serious percussionist. But funds for a set of those big kettles were not in the grade school budget, nor would be anytime soon, and they were hopelessly beyond Mother's resources. And in any event, no drum in the world would secure me a chair in the family chamber group.

Finally, as much out of desperation as real interest, I returned to the woodwinds and chose the clarinet. I also received an impressive gift from an unlikely source. The source was Rudy Bosch, and he had fled his native Austria to escape the devastation then engulfing Europe. Immigrating to America, he became a piano tuner for the Steinway Company in New York. But Rudy wasn't a run-of-the-mill tuner; he was blessed with perfect pitch, and could dismantle, repair and reassemble a piano blindfolded. Steinway soon had him traveling to Chautauqua each summer, not simply to care for the Institution's numerous practice pianos, but to maintain the majestic concert grand pianos played by visiting artists appearing with the Chautauqua Symphony.

So it was that he came to the door of our cottage one day in response to a call from Mother, a young widow with three and a half musical children and an out-of-tune piano. Yes, even the Chautauqua cottage Mother managed somehow to purchase as World War II ended must have a piano; and the beating it took over the winter, when the cottage was unheated, would tax the skills of the best tuner in the business. And Rudy was the best. But it went beyond that. He took an interest in us, and we in him. He came often then, not to tune the piano but to be among friends. He even took Frank under his wing, touring Chautauqua's performance studios and practice shacks and teaching him the fundamentals of piano tuning.

A few months into these visits, Rudy happened to see my metal clarinet, on loan from First District School, lying on the piano bench. "Oh, my," he said, "we can do better than that!" And when he next visited, a black case the size of a standard dictionary was tucked under his arm. Watching me out the corner of one eye, he opened the case. Nested into its five velvet-lined compartments were the segments of a dark wood clarinet, an Austrian-made instrument of exceptional quality and timbre that he had brought to America with him. We were stunned, me not least, when he announced with obvious pleasure that it was not a loan; it was a gift. Neglected when he acquired it, and hard-traveled since, it was not in the best of shape. Several key pads were missing, making it unplayable; and the register key (which allowed the instrument to shift octaves from a "lower register" to the "upper" and back), was broken in half. Exercising his knack for teaching by doing, Rudy soon had me removing the worn pads, cleaning the key cups and gluing new pads into place. A local metal smith, once the delicate nature of the job was explained to him, so expertly brazed the register key back together that when I reinserted the tiny screws on which it pivoted, it fit perfectly.

And when, finally, I attached a reed to the mouthpiece and blew into it the first time—oh, what a sound! "Heavenly" may have been too grand a word for it, but "mellow" was surely too meager. Even as the family's musical dumbbell, I appreciated both the exquisite tone and the value of that instrument, so much so that I actually learned to play it. Not exceptionally well to be sure, but well enough at last to hold my own among my school peers. But all of this came much too late for me to carry my weight in the Skinner Ensemble, by then disbanded because several members had moved on. Which is why, in the ensemble's heyday, I was stuck in the role of announcer and unwilling member of the audience.

Had I been older or more perceptive, or had Mother been more forthcoming about what was at stake, I would have participated more eagerly, even as the announcer. The inspiration to form an ensemble was clearly musical. Mother never missed an opportunity to expose us to good music, and constantly encouraged us to perform it. But during those lean years following Dad's death, musical imagination was driven as much by economic necessity as artistic temperament. The Ensemble, we would later understand, was one of several survival schemes Mother hatched to get us through hard times. Each performance added some small largesse to the limited funds that her ingenious money managing skill would make do.

—————•—————

Supplemental income wasn't the only benefit derived from the Ensemble's activity, however; it also opened the door to one of Meadville's historic homes. Halfway up Chestnut Street, a few blocks above the business district and Diamond Park—Meadville's community "living room"—stood some of the town's most substantial homes. Among them was a boxy but well-appointed Victorian brick house called Hill Home by three generations of its owners. By the time the Skinner Ensemble was occupied entertaining half of Meadville's civic groups with its immutable medley of chamber music, Hill Home was occupied by a lone widow and a couple of servants. Elizabeth Heidekoper Kidder was the widow of Henry Purkett Kidder of Boston. More to the point, she was the granddaughter of Harm Jan Heidekoper, an immigrant Hollander and agent for the Holland Land Company, broker for thousands of square miles of northwestern Pennsylvania and southwestern New York.

Arriving in Meadville in 1802 at age 26, Heidekoper became one of the state's largest landowners and leading citizens. A sometimes controversial figure—largely because of his habit of evicting settlers from land claimed by the company—he was yet capable of great generosity, and sought to repay his good fortune in his adopted land by civic service. It is reported that he instructed

so many pensioners and petitioners to buy a plow or garden seed
and "charge it to Heidekoper" that the words became a catch
phrase recognized throughout northwestern Pennsylvania; and
he was co-founder of the Meadville Society for the Encouragement of Manufactures and Arts, effectively one of the first cham-
bers of commerce in the nation.

Born a decade before the Civil War and a widow at 35 (which
may have contributed to her empathy for Mother), Elizabeth was
childless and wealthy. Along with some of his money, Elizabeth
inherited her grandfather's belief about the social obligation of
wealth, and continued his custom of generosity. I would not learn
until doing research for this book that she and her Aunt Elizabeth Heidekoper were the two prominent Meadville women
whose gifts provided the initial funding for construction of Old
Mat, where I was born.

It was to Hill House, on a warm Spring Sunday in 1942, that
the doctor's widow and her children were invited to dine with
the elderly and frail heiress.

We climbed the broad brick steps and crossed the iron-railed
porch about which floral-cushioned wicker furniture stood in
groupings that made it seem larger than our living room. I instinctively moved closer to Mother's side as we paused at the
double-hung walnut door and rang the bell. The etched glass windows permitted no unseemly spying into the vestibule, so we
stood, our anxiety rising in proportion to the length of our wait.
It seemed minutes, though probably was 20 seconds, before the
large brass knob, ornate in spite of its patina of tarnish, turned
slowly and the door swung inward. It took a second for our eyes
to adjust from bright daylight to dim interior, during which fraction of time I wasn't sure anyone was there, as if the door had
opened itself. Then as my eyes adjusted to the dimness of the

entryway, he came into view: formally dressed and radiating unbelievable dignity, a real-life honest-to-God butler like I'd never seen except in a Cary Grant movie. This was really something!

"Good afternoon, Mrs. Skinner," he said graciously, seeming to find it unnecessary to confirm that she was Mrs. Skinner. But then, I suppose young middle-aged women with four children in tow did not come to Mrs. Kidder's door with any frequency, and certainly not uninvited.

"Please come in. Mrs. Kidder is waiting for you in the parlor." Given her upbringing, Mother was accustomed to this sort of thing. But her children's eyes bulged like golf balls as we were ushered through the foyer, gawking at the fringed glass-and-satin lamp suspended above the ornate walnut table that stood precisely at its center. Actually, I think we walked on tiptoe, so overwhelming was the sense of being in some sort of library, or even a church.

Mrs. Kidder sat opposite the parlor door as we entered, her fragile frame slumped into a plush upholstered chair surrounded by mementoes a lifetime in the acquiring. Her dress, high-necked and lace-yoked, would have been fashionable half a century earlier, yet epitomized the way that finely made clothes, even when hopelessly outdated, radiate quality. Her hair, long since devoid of color, haloed a face of a thousand wrinkles. It was deceptive camouflage: her eyes, contradicting her outward frailty, shown with the intellect of a facile mind. And it seems to me, looking back six decades, that I witnessed that day something that must be called (for lack of a better word) breeding. Hunched down in her old chair, the woman's ancient frame still managed to bear itself erect, as if it were possible by sheer dignity to annul the unyielding weight of ninety years.

Breaking into a smile like sunrise, she reached forward to touch and greet us, gazing intently into each face as she repeated our names with an inflection that made each sound like a salute. Immediately the questions began to pour out of her, as if she meant to know everything she could possibly learn about us and had such a short time to find it all out. The conversation hardly faltered when the butler came in to announce that dinner was served. Rising slowly, the cumulative stiffness of a lifetime hobbling every effort, Mrs. Kidder leaned heavily on her cane and made her way across the hall into the darkly paneled dining room, its table laid with the elaborate detail of Victorian linen and china and silver. And formal. Oh my, formal. How would we possibly know which spoon or fork to choose for the soup or salad, entrée or dessert? Though a social gaff might have embarrassed Mother (she had, in fact, tutored us to start from the outside and work our way in and, when in doubt, to watch Mrs. Kidder), I don't think our hostess cared a whit. She lived this way not because she needed somehow to be fabulous, but because it was her custom. And it seemed not to concern her at all that it wasn't ours. She would not let social convention stand in the way of her enjoyment of her young guests; she must have answers to her questions, and the recess in the conversation necessitated by her halting trip from parlor chair to dining room table ended before the soup tureen made it out of the butler's pantry.

I no longer recall all that was discussed. Okay, I confess: I recall none of it. But I remember that old woman, her hand-painted china hearing-trumpet crammed into her ear, engaged in the hard work of listening, and meaning to miss nothing. And I grinned as she listened, because she violated a sacred rule pounded into us since infancy: she propped an elbow squarely on the table, because it was otherwise too taxing to hold the trumpet to her ear.

And at each new turn in the conversation, her fork stopped in midair, suspended halfway between plate and palate, her eyes intent upon whichever of us was speaking, because it was more important to learn about new friends than to eat.

Maybe, in her ninety-plus years, she really had gotten it right, and understood what truly mattered. And maybe, if we were attentive and took our cue from her, just as Mother recommended, we'd get it right too—not just pronouncing Mozart correctly, but the equally important business of living with class.

CHAPTER 16

Making Ends Meet

D ad's professional career wasn't long enough to yield a nest-egg from which his young family could draw support after he died. Mother was left to create her own, and it was no small job. She must have sensed how instantly thin our financial thread would be stretched by Dad's death. And if that seems an odd conjecture, as if I don't know even now how close we were to losing everything, I don't. Nor do my sister and brothers.

It was a different time. Americans were not yet stricken by the virus that ravages the privacy gland, disabling reticence and concocting the belief that guarding privacy is some form of social retardation. High on any list of things that were no one else's business was a family's financial affairs. While we might surmise from their behavior whether our neighbors were well-off or struggling, of the details of their family fortunes we were privileged to know nothing, and that's the way every one wanted it. Almost as common was the assumption that children need not to be aware, indeed ought not to know, about family finances. Mother's fierce guarding of her privacy, even from her children, prevented us from knowing how close to the edge we really were. It also spared us the anxiety that would come with knowing: unaware of how ignorant we were, we realized neither the extent, nor the tenuousness, of our bliss.

Fortunately for Mother—and more fortunately for us than we were told, then or ever—she was never truly alone. Quietly, always remaining in the background, her father came to her rescue. Cliff once observed, to rueful smiles from Frank and me, that Ernest McCafferty's motto was "All work and no play makes Jack." There was much truth in the remark. Granddaddy's job at H. J. Heinz consumed by far the largest part of his life, and even when not working he exhibited little by way of either humor or playfulness. We used to joke that his idea of a perfect vacation was to sit in a rocker on the veranda of the Riverside Inn in Cambridge Springs, a spa fifteen miles north of Meadville, and read the *Wall Street Journal.*

But those, like most caricatures, were demonstrably incomplete, and not simply due to the omission of the phrase about Jack being a dull boy. In spite of what other traits we observed in him, Granddaddy was not about to stand by while tragedy threatened his family's welfare. For more than a decade, he provided Mother with a monthly allowance. It was only enough for a barebones budget, to be sure, with little wiggle room and nothing for luxuries. Nonetheless, it freed Mother from worry about how she would buy food and pay the utility bills; and that was enough, because it gave her peace of mind. And when Cliff asked to enroll in Mercersburg Academy, because he hoped to follow Dad into medicine and wanted the strongest preparation he could secure, it was Granddaddy who picked up the bill. He did it again for

Frank, and then for me. It was an unmistakable indicator that Ernest McCafferty, who appreciated investment more than just about anything, thought no investment equal to education of children for value, or likely to earn so generous a return.

———·———

With those exceptions, life consisted largely of making ends meet, and Mother's ingenuity was more than adequate to the need. Her first and continuing avenue was, of course, music, the pace never slackening as long as she remained in Meadville. Soon after Dad died, she accepted the position of organist at Grace Methodist Church. And with that simple decision, our family church life abruptly changed. We went every Sunday as always, but not to the same place. For the rest of our school years, Sunday morning meant parting company: we children were dropped off at the Presbyterian Church, or walked there if Mother had an early service; and she went on to Grace Methodist.

Still, for a performing musician to make anything close to a living in a community the size of ours wasn't possible. Something steady was needed, like a salary; and for the first and only time in her life, Mother took the kind of job for which she had prepared in college. The saint in the wings this time was Chester Darling, long-standing chairman of Allegheny's biology department and Mother's mentor when she was a student. Chester was hard hit by Dad's death. It was Chester who secured Dad's appointment as laboratory instructor when funds for medical school were lacking. It was Chester who advised Dad through his master of science program. And they had been faculty colleagues for the last decade of Dad's life, sharing departmental and teaching duties. Chester was more than anxious to help. And, by coincidence, he was looking to hire an assistant for the department.

On the other hand, convincing the college authorities to budget the funds was hardly a cakewalk. The nation was embroiled in World War II, and the college was under severe budgetary constraints. I have always been suspicious that Chester, who was no one's fool when it came to the internal operations of the school (he even acted as president for a year when Allegheny was without one), turned the screws on his colleagues. I can hear his raspy voice now, appealing to the memory of Clifford Skinner, emoting on how the most severe test of collegial loyalty comes when a colleague's family is in need—and insinuating the while his own need for extra help in the department!

My suspicion notwithstanding, Mother went to work as Chester's assistant, staffing his office, supervising student departmental assistants, and preparing materials for the weekly laboratory sessions required of all students studying biology. In an extraordinary negotiation of needs, Chester adapted the operation of his office to accommodate Ruth Skinner's family obligations, and she adapted her family schedule to satisfy the needs of the department; between them, they worked out an arrangement that remained agreeable until Chester retired and Mother left Meadville.

I won't even describe some of the hand-me-down outfits that this youngest brother wore to school, except to observe that, by the time they got to me, they had already hung on Cliff's and Frank's frames for a collective three or four years. And if kid's clothing of that era could be said to have "fashion" (a proposition I am not prepared to defend), whatever fashion my school clothing might originally have possessed had faded to passé by the time it got to me.

But nothing was required of us here that Mother did not impose on herself. Years later, when she sent me to get something out of her closet and I really studied her wardrobe for the first time, it dawned on me that she probably didn't buy herself a new dress from Dad's death until my high school graduation. What "new" clothes she had came from her Singer sewing machine, which was as old as Ruth Ann, from fabric store patterns reused until her ancient straight pins reduced them to confetti.

Nothing, however, changed our life so much as did the progression of our house from home to dormitory to apartment building.

The transition began before Dad died, actually, when Allegheny found itself with too many women and too few dormitory beds. It wasn't the first time the college faced the problem. When Allegheny first opened its doors in 1815, it owned no facilities at all, and certainly no residence halls. Consequently, the all-male student population (women were first admitted in 1870) were housed with Meadville families. It was not until 1865 that Culver Hall, Allegheny's first dormitory, was erected on the east side of the dirt trail that eventually matured into North Main Street. Culver was a wooden structure, heated by wood-burning fireplaces—not a promising arrangement in light of the structural characteristics of the time. In December of 1882, when the building was a modest seventeen years old, a fire ignited in a third floor student room ran rampant until nothing remained but brick footings standing among smoldering ashes. The only good thing that can be said about the Culver Hall fire is that there was no loss of life.

When the first women students arrived, it was their turn to rent rooms about town. But the college's leaders failed to anticipate just how many women would rush to take advantage of their new opportunity for higher learning, and before long the number of women exceeded the capacity of the townspeople to accommodate them. Besides, the notion was prevalent at the time that a woman's delicate constitution necessitated greater care and supervision than that required for a man. The college's response came in the form of Hulings Hall, its first women's residence, which opened in 1879 and temporarily restored the balance between the college's housing needs and its female student population. It was into Hulings that the young Pittsburgh socialite moved when she arrived on campus in 1920, began the study of biology, and met the widower from New York State who would become her husband.

By the 1930s, with the nation struggling to escape the Great Depression, Allegheny was badly situated to raise funds to expand housing for women, whose numbers were outstripping Hulings' capacity, and the college again turned to the town. Among those who responded was the family of the college physician. Well, "family" is actually a bit hyperbolic in this case: we children had nothing to say about it. Before we knew it, we boys were moved to the attic, half of which was finished off to form two rooms. I use "finished off" reservedly; the walls and ceilings were clad in fiberboard sheeting half an inch thick with thin battens nailed over the joints. And while this provided a semblance of insulation, the rooms were unheated. Warmth reached us only when the door at the bottom of the stairs was left ajar, allowing warm air to flow up from the second floor hall. It seemed to me to do so reluctantly, and benefited Cliff more than Frank or me, because the stairs came up into Cliff's room. Residual warmth, such as it was, reached our room only by making a sharp right turn and passing through a doorway. I don't recall that much ever made it. Habituated as we were to sleeping with the window open, getting dressed on winter mornings became a really bracing experience.

Our move to the attic made way for three young women to settle into our second floor bedroom. They were thoughtful guests, causing minimal disruption beyond the inevitable bathroom crush, and so nice to us children that we might as well have acquired three older sisters. The smoothness of their adoption was aided by Allegheny's requirement that the women take their meals in the college dining hall. Add the hours they spent in class and in the library, and we seldom saw them—except for the time that none of us can forget, or is likely to. That would be the time that one of them, working in the kitchen, got her fingers caught in Mother's Mixmaster.

It was a rock-solid machine, powerful enough to make concrete, though the task of the moment was cake. The batter never made it to the oven. It got spoiled by blood. Even if it hadn't, by the time it should have finished baking, no one had much appetite. Halfway through mixing the ingredients, the girl somehow got several fingers into the turning beaters, and before the motor stalled they had been dragged past her second knuckle into the steel hoops. That had to have been bad enough, but her predicament was compounded by the fact that there was no way to turn the assembly backward to get her fingers out again, and if there were, she probably would have passed out from the pain. I don't understand why she didn't anyway. My stomach churning even more than it had when the farm boy sat bleeding on Dad's examining table, I watched as Dad bent over her, working carefully but urgently to disassemble the beaters without dismembering her already crushed hand. It was a task on which he employed more tools from his furnace room shop than medical implements from the small cabinet by the examining table.

Throughout the process, which took almost an hour, the girl never made a sound, just sat there as if she was getting a manicure, trusting the college doctor to save her hand. Only her complexion, pale as death, betrayed her agony, and Dad kept glancing up at her as he worked, watching for telltale signs that she might be going into shock. I can't even imagine how one would go about measuring that kind of pain tolerance. Oddly, as often happens between people bonded by trauma, the moment cemented the relationship of the girls to our parents. Mother received Christmas cards from them for years, and exchanged correspondence with one for the rest of her life.

————·————

As it turned out, the three women were only the first in a series of tenants. After Dad's death, Mother remembered that financial help could be had by renting rooms, which brought Phil Benjamin into our home and our lives. It was the last time that Mother would be fully in charge of her own home.

Phil was the librarian of Allegheny's Reis Library, and a bachelor. Mother was acquainted with him through Meadville's Civic Music Association, in which both were active, and they struck a deal that would secure desirable new quarters for him and added income for her. The master bedroom and guest room of our home, each with its own door to the second floor hall and joined by a common bathroom, really constituted separate quarters. During the summer of 1941, Phil moved into that "apartment" and his Packard coupe moved into the basement garage, where each continued to live until Mother sold the house in 1949.

The whole family was soon on casual terms with Phil. The bedroom doors to his apartment had privacy locks, but no other security. Phil never asked to have them changed. His quarters

stood open the entire time he lived with us, and he made it clear
that we were welcome to come in, when he was not there, to
play his spinet piano—as if, with two pianos in our living room,
we needed a third—or to read his magazines. I especially appreciated his subscription to *New Yorker* magazine, though I never
read the articles (or would understand them if I had). I was in
his living room soon after each issue arrived to pore over the
cartoons.

It was the kind of trust that children receive with gratitude
and return in kind. We were careful neither to violate it nor to
abuse the privilege—except in one peculiar case when Phil demonstrated his inexperience with children.

Because he enjoyed the four-block walk from our home to
the college library and back, Phil seldom drove to work. And since
our basement garage was designed to house two cars end-to-end
rather than side-by-side, he and Mother agreed that his car would
live in front, with its nose to the back wall. Since it sat there most
of the time, Phil let me play in it; and since it was World War II,
his Packard became my war plane. The garage wasn't well-lit anyway, and its whitewashed walls proved the perfect screen for my
projected imagination. Perched on the edge of the seat, I roared
into the skies over Europe in my P-51 Mustang in search of
Messerschmitt 109Es, or swung my P-40 Flying Tiger into action
against Japanese Zeros. It was all exquisite imagination—until
the day I discovered that Phil had neglected to remove his keys
from the ignition.

As always, I was prepared to take advantage of any error in
judgment that came my way. I was, after all, an eleven-year-old
American male already impatient for my sixteenth birthday when
I would qualify for my learner's permit. I was also securely anonymous in the basement of my own home, in a Packard coupe with

the key in the ignition. For a long time, I fingered the key uncertainly, all thought of enemy planes abandoned. I knew what to do, up to a point; I had seen Mother do it dozens of times. But I was unsure that I had the courage to do it, knew perfectly well that I should not, and heard the command of my internalized parent: "Don Skinner, don't you dare! You get out of that car this instant!" The spirit knew the rule, but the flesh had the key. Succumbing to the seduction of power, I pulled out the choke knob on the dash, turned the ignition key, punched the clutch pedal to the floor with my left foot, and pressed the starter pedal with my right. Phil sure maintained that car well. At the merest kick of the starter motor, the engine roared to life, startling me with how much noise it made enclosed in the garage like that.

My composure took flight faster than any P-51 ever cleared the runway. Instantly aware that Mother would hear it and frantic to get out of the car before she came storming down the basement stairs, I reached to turn off the ignition key and jerked my foot off the clutch pedal. That's all it took. The car leaped forward like it was coming off a catapult and slammed into the pipe that fed the water softener, sheering it off as cleanly as if I'd used an ax. Before I got a grip on the door handle, Phil's Packard was taking a shower. So, coincidentally, were the ceiling and walls of the garage. Racing through the downpour, I reflected incongruously on how much water comes out of a sheered-off three-quarter-inch water pipe pressurized to 80 or 90 pounds per square inch. The only thing that prevented the water from flowing under the doors and into the basement hall was a pair of drains in the garage floor.

I was not even tempted to run upstairs to Mother shouting, "You'll never guess what I discovered in the garage!" It was not a case in which prevarication would be successful, much less helpful. So I just blurted it out: "I got in Phil's car and started the engine and the car jumped forward and hit the water softener and broke the pipe and there's water going all over the garage and..."

"You *WHAT?*"

Her response told me that I'd said all that I needed to, and it was time to shut up, or at most to confine myself to a reiteration of the facts. What the house needed at that instant was a plumber, not a discussion of my stupidity. For once Mother concurred. She was on the phone in an instant, calling a plumber and growling at me to get back downstairs and control the water as much as possible. The plumber, being a prescient man, recognized the urgency of the situation and came immediately. I'm not quite sure, but I think I observed him chuckling and shaking his head a lot while repairing the pipe. Mother, on the other hand, glared at me in disbelief, that day and for the rest of the week. But she knew that nothing she said would be anywhere near as instructive as that ruptured pipe.

Nor did Phil say much when he learned of it. The bumper of his car had absorbed the impact well and appeared no worse for the wear. This was fortunate for me, else my allowance might have been confiscated for the rest of my life to cover the cost of repair. On the other hand, Phil locked his car after that. Not that it mattered; I never would have had the nerve to climb into it again. My flying days were over.

Over the long haul, Phil was one of several people in my life who believed in me long before I believed in myself, and thereby helped to form in me a self-image that was worth living up to. More clearly than at any other time, this was evident at the end of my senior year at Allegheny. I had withdrawn from the college in the middle of my junior year, failing in just about everything, and returned two years later as a veteran. In my remaining three semesters, I amazed even myself by making up the deficit I had spent five terms accumulating. In consequence I was actually going to graduate. But then what? I had hoped to attend theological seminary, but felt like Groucho Marx who, invited to join a club, responded that he would not care to be part of any organization that would have him as a member. I was doubtful that any seminary I might want to attend would have me as a student, and skeptical about enrolling in one that would. Nonetheless, I selected two that I respected and submitted my applications. Next time I ran into Phil on campus, I asked him to write letters of recommendation for me. Few people, certainly, knew me better! Where, he asked, had I applied? I told him. His response stunned me.

"Why not Yale?"

"Oh, Phil," I answered, "what possible chance would I have?"

"Let Yale decide that," he countered.

So I did. To my delight (not to mention dismay), I was accepted. Phil claimed it was because of my improved record. So why am I so suspicious that his letter of recommendation carried even more weight? And I'll bet it never even mentioned his Packard or our water softener.

———————

Like other American colleges in the wake of World War II, Allegheny was inundated by a flood of veterans anxious to resume their lives and educations. Many of them were men who had been drafted out of college, while others had never thought about college until their war experience changed their outlook. Now they all wanted in at the same time. Their sheer numbers taxed the college's facilities to the breaking point. In the case of housing, they exceeded it. Again the college turned to the town, and again Mother, as anxious for the income as she was to help, gave up another piece of her home.

It was 1946, a turning point for our family life for other reasons. Ruth Ann had enrolled in Allegheny. She could have lived at home, but Mother believed that living in the dormitory was an important part of going to college, and didn't want Ruth Ann to miss it (nor did Ruth Ann). That same fall, Cliff left home to attend Mercersburg Academy. Neither would return to live in our Main Street home again. The vacuum created by their departure allowed another shift, this one as dramatic as the last: Mother moved to the attic in Cliff's place, making room on the second floor for four veterans.

In one of those developments that demonstrate how life sometimes circles back on itself, one of the veterans living with us that year was Al Kern. By the time I enrolled in Allegheny, Al had completed graduate school and returned as an English instructor, in which capacity he tried valiantly to teach me grammar and writing. Later, when I returned as dean, we became colleagues. Sitting in the campus Grille one day, recollecting the postwar year that he lived with us, he surveyed me with the mildly cynical look of a man who had been reared among New York City's cold-water walk-ups, survived the war, and taught college for thirty years. His ever-present cigarette curled between index and middle finger, lips pursed, he looked at me piercingly and commented editorially, "I always thought your mother did a pretty good job raising you kids." Mother huffed when I told her that, but she couldn't quite hide her satisfaction.

The housing tradeoff had unanticipated consequences. While living on campus, Ruth Ann met another veteran, a man returning from the U.S. Navy, to whom she would be married after graduation. Less life-amending, if a lot funnier, she was assigned to live in Caflisch Hall, a large brick "U" of a building originally equipped to house men but which, over the years, changed roles numerous times to accommodate the college's gender prevalence *du jour*. She found herself living with a hundred freshman women who were equally at a loss figuring out what to do with the tall porcelain devices built into one wall of each bathroom, equipped with chrome handles that, when pressed, sent a rush of water down the concave interior of the things and out the drain at the bottom. They did not appear, at first blush, to be of much practical use to women. One enterprising girl on Ruth Ann's floor suggested that they plant flowers in theirs and, once a week or so, someone happening by could press the handle to water them.

———————

No year in our Meadville home was more challenging and chaotic than the last.

Chester Darling had retired from the biology department the previous spring, and the college, seeking a replacement of equal stature, invited Robert Bugbee to join the faculty and chair the department. Bob was ranked among the top entomologists in the nation, and could easily have commanded a position at a major university. Like us, however, he had family ties to Allegheny (his grandfather was president of the college during the late nineteenth century), and Bob's educational instincts drew him to a private liberal arts college setting.

There was, however, a hitch: the housing shortage that had plagued Meadville since the opening days of World War II was still in full vigor, and would not be resolved for several more years. Bob and Peg, his wife, had three children and no place to live.

Making the case more interesting, Peg was pregnant. After some mental gymnastics figuring out how it could possibly work, Mother agreed to absorb the Bugbee family into our already crazy-quilt household. Though Cliff had graduated from Mercersburg and was returning to Allegheny, he would, like Ruth Ann, live on campus. And Frank would leave for Mercersburg, easing the body crunch by one. Mother concluded that she and I would continue to enjoy our unheated attic, to which we were well-accustomed, leaving the rest of the house, excepting Phil Benjamin's apartment, to subdivide. So the deal was struck: Mother and I would keep Dad's office as our all-purpose living/dining room, both families would have the use of the kitchen and bathrooms, and the Bugbee family would occupy the rest.

The arrangement had advantages, but I will not pretend it was easy; and it had to be an especially trying year for Mother and Peg who, in spite of the unavoidable tensions attendant upon housing and feeding two unrelated families under one roof, managed to remain friends, then and for years after. Harmony was maintained in part by engaging in the fiction that we were related. Within hours—and for the rest of her life—Mother was "Aunt Ruth" to the Bugbee children, Sandra, Angie and Mac. For us youngsters, the adjustment was even easier: we hit it right off (and though I don't recall applying for the job, I was soon assigned the post of built-in baby sitter). The whole household worked at getting along, and being respectful of each other's privacy helped.

That being the case, there didn't seem to be much that we couldn't handle until Peg put the whole arrangement to a severe test, in two installments. In installment #1, she returned from her new Meadville physician to report that she was not carrying a child. She was carrying two of them. That was surprise enough, especially for Peg and Bob. But the prospect of returning home with twins got complicated real fast in installment #2: minutes after Peg went into labor, she stepped out the side door to get into their car for the trip to City Hospital, slipped on the ice, and fell, fracturing her leg. The wonder was that we didn't have twins right there in the driveway. Displaying immense determination, Peg struggled into the car, went to the hospital, birthed the twins, got her leg set, and returned home, all in four days. Then we really were family, as everyone took turns caring for Janet and Jeannette so that Peg wouldn't have to carry the whole burden on a walking cast. I was still thirteen years away from fatherhood, but the practice I got in the ensuing months sure came in handy when my turn arrived. I suppose it's like the old saw about riding a bike: once you learn, you never forget. Too, I was reassured whenever I saw the twins during subsequent years: they showed no evidence of trauma stemming from my teenaged contribution to their postpartum care.

CHAPTER 17

Civic Music Association

M other was never one to neglect an opportunity. Her job as Grace Church organist was only the beginning. She seemed forever to be playing the organ at the wedding of some young couple or other, if not at one church then at another. She may have played for more weddings than the clergy who presided at them.

But that wasn't the fun stuff. Fun was contributing to the musical culture of her town; and even though she usually received some honorarium for an appearance, the money neither equaled in value the pleasure she derived from it nor matched the effort required to prepare for it. Every minute in performance was underwritten by at least five in rehearsal—and there was a lot of rehearsing. If she wasn't playing piano for some vocal or instrumental soloist—as often as not one or more of her own children who surfaced in every combination that can be worked from the number three—she was preparing for a duo-piano recital or as anchor for a string trio. Glued into our scrapbooks is a bewildering spread of newspaper clippings and printed programs from such performances. (All but the late-bloomer here. Beyond reports of my introductions at Ensemble performances, articles naming me are mainly lists of students our piano teacher pressed into appearing "in recital." And—take my word for it—those were published for social, not artistic, reasons.)

Turning the brittle and darkening pages of Mother's scrapbooks, my tingling fingertips a palpable reminder that sixty years have passed since the *Tribune-Republican* paperboy dropped their contents on our porch, I find it hard to fathom how she did it all. In 1946 alone she performed an average of once every two weeks, most frequently with a string trio. Several were organized over the years, none more enduring than the combination of Ardath Chandler, violinist, Gratia Laws, cellist and Ruth Skinner, pianist.

Ardath was music supervisor for Meadville's elementary schools and she, like Mother, often shared the stage with members of her extended family (a brother-in-law played bass violin in the Meadville symphony and a nephew became an accomplished operatic baritone).

Gratia, whose husband was minister of the Unitarian Church, was an earthy, substantial woman who drove a Crosley—America's short-lived experiment with real life Matchbox cars. ("Small" hardly did the things justice: when I was a student at Allegheny, six of us, finding one parked on the street, carried it into a classroom building and left it in the main hall with the trunk open and hood up, as if on display in a salesroom. But that's another story.) Adapting to such a car took ingenuity. A cello does not bend without suffering irreparable damage. There was no possible way both Gratia and her cello were going to fit in the front seat of that rolling cheese box. The entire instrument wouldn't even fit into the back seat. Whenever Mother informed me that the trio was scheduled to rehearse at home, I ran out the side door at the appointed hour, gleefully anticipating Gratia's arrival. Folded so tightly behind the wheel that she could barely steer, she came tooling up North Main Street with her arm jutting out the driver's window and the neck of her cello case protruding out the window of the back seat. I can't even imagine how she worked the pedals. Her delicious belly laugh erupted out the open window as she turned into our driveway and saw my grinning face. She knew how silly she looked and thought it just fine to share the humor with me.

The humor rolled on as the trio of women got settled in the living room, set up their music stands, arranged their music, tuned their instruments, and agreed on an order of rehearsal—all steps that musicians take to prepare for, and to avoid, getting down to work. It burst out again every time an error, or arrival at the end of the score, brought a pause. But when the music was underway, the effort was all serious, and the house filled with the resonant and elegant sound peculiar to solo instruments playing in parallel. The effect is the same as listening to a vocal quartet as distinct from a chorus. Individual voices predominate, but complement and sustain each other. If I wanted to hear one instrument more than the others, I needed only to listen more carefully. Yet their cooperation gave to each a harmonic magic it lacked when played alone.

It was not an easy lesson for me. I was not born predisposed to enjoy chamber music. My preference ran to full-throated orchestral and choral *tutti*, as the notation appears in musical scores. The word means "all," but translates in my mind as "Okay, everyone, let 'er rip!" For the same reason, I suspect, I preferred organ music *sforzando*—every stop open and the swell box yawning until the vibration threatened to shatter the stained glass. To my young mind, it made no sense to have all that power and not use it, the more vigorously the better.

But Mother and her friends would not let my preference for loud-mouthed gusto stand unchallenged. In spite of myself, I came to see the elegance that resides in delicacy. Doing my assigned chores around the house, or playing quietly (whatever it took to ensure that I would not disturb the rehearsal—a sin equivalent to swearing in church), I was bathed in sound both lyrical and liquid, a kind of artistic baptism by immersion. After those years of mandated exposure, I would never again hear chamber music without appreciating it more, or being thrown back to hear, in memory's ear, three women tilting back and forth between making good music and collapsing in raucous laughter. Just as Mother insisted that I try every food whether I liked it or not, stimulating a global appetite, her insistence that I absorb music I was not born to prefer broadened my taste and exposed the world as an artistic feast.

To this day, you understand, I still prefer *tutti* and *sforzando*. It is difficult to amend congenital partiality. But I am able to taste and enjoy other opportunities as well, and am the richer for it.

———————

It is curious that one small community, with no more reason to be artistically curious than a thousand others across the nation, should prove such a supportive audience for musical performances—including those by its own citizens.

If Meadville's interest was exceptional, it may have originated in an accident of commercial geography. Twenty-first-century Americans traveling between urban centers of the Northeast and Midwest have no reason to pass through Meadville. The majority of travelers on I-79 turn off—if at all—only long enough to visit a restaurant or motel. But from the mid-nineteenth through the mid-twentieth centuries, when airlines were either non-existent or in their infancy and "high speed highway" was an oxymoron, steam-powered rail was king and Meadville straddled a main line.

Equally to the point, the New York to Chicago run took two days as measured by iron rail, and Meadville lay smack in the middle of it. For anyone just passing through, this was of no particular significance. But the route carried a lot of talent—thespians, entertainers and musical companies on tour and seeking an audience. And they weren't simply indulging artistic ambition, they were trying to make a living, and sitting in a train wasn't the way to do it. They needed an audience, and the train stopped in Meadville.

Lacking a professional site, early shows occurred in one of several make-shift halls. During warm weather, tents and open-air platforms were often used. So Meadville's status could only have improved with the completion in 1869 of the thousand-seat Opera House, insuring performers an attractive venue. Among them was John Wilkes Booth, who revealed more of his inner rage than anyone at the time was prepared to appreciate. Playing Meadville on August 13, 1864, at the height of the Civil War and less than a year before gaining infamy by assassinating Abraham Lincoln, he used a diamond ring to etch a frightening confession on the window glass of his McHenry House Hotel room: "Abe Lincoln departed this life August 13, 1864, by the effects of Poison." Booth was apparently referring to a co-conspirator who, even then, was trying to poison prescriptions prepared for the Lincoln family at a Washington, D.C. apothecary.

As too often transpired in those days of large wood-frame buildings with untrustworthy heating and lighting systems, the

Opera House burned to the ground in 1884, two years after similar deficiencies brought Allegheny's Culver Hall to a pyric end. Thus was born the Academy of Music, completed the following year—a Chestnut Street theater halfway between the train station and the Diamond where traveling troupes and artists laid over could once again perform for a paying audience.

It's difficult to say whether people were drawn to town by such cultural opportunities, or the opportunities molded Meadville's citizens into a more appreciative audience. Probably it was a little of both. But it would not last. The landscape of social and cultural life was already in transition, even though few Americans would recognize it until there would be, indeed could be, no turning back. Major transportation systems were abandoning America's small towns, leaving them to strangle on their own insularity. Meadville no longer held their interest. Simultaneously, the flickering light of motion pictures began to draw people like moths to flame, feeding the American penchant for the new and novel and eroding the singular supremacy that live performance had enjoyed since the days of Greek theater. When the government, responding to constraints imposed by World War II, restricted non-essential travel and drafted many young artists into the military, the flow of itinerant performers slowed to a trickle. Looking to survive, the Academy of Music yielded to the inevitable, changed its name to the Academy Theater, and bought itself a temporary future as a movie house. It would be most of a century before a live performance of consequence again mounted its stage.

Fortunately for Meadville's cultural future, human beings evolve more slowly than the systems they create, and interest in art endured. By mid-century, when the Skinner family, and particularly Ruth and her friends, were looking for opportunities to

perform, appreciative audiences were ready to receive them. Indeed, support of culture was written into the charters of several
community groups, like the Meadville Women's Club, which was
founded in part to "promote by education and organized effort
an interest in public welfare and an appreciation of literature
and the fine arts." As both outside talent and the means of bringing it to town shriveled, such groups woke to the realization that
there was a lot of talent right there. It was a serendipitous time to
be musical in Meadville.

———•———

    In 1941, in a touch of mortal irony, Mother was invited to
become pianist for the Meadville Orchestral Society, the town's
fifty-one member, home-grown symphony orchestra. I can't say
whether she approached her first rehearsal without being haunted
by the memory of the night, a year past, when her husband collapsed at a concert by the same group in the same auditorium.
Whatever conversation they shared that evening as they waited
for the concert to begin was the last they would enjoy on this
earth. It could not have been an easy memory. But if it troubled
her, she gave no evidence of it. She threw herself without reserve into her new assignment, like she did every other in her
life. But in this case, money wasn't her motive. The orchestra,
which rehearsed every Wednesday night from September through
May, was voluntary. The opportunity to do what she loved best
was her only compensation, and it must have been considerable:
in seven seasons she missed one rehearsal, never a performance.
    What is it about American towns that people give so much
of themselves in support of the things they value? People in a
better position to know than I am have observed that volunteer
labor, the giving of time and skill for no reward beyond the chance

to benefit one's community, is more characteristic of this nation than any other. Some will even argue that the chance to give, not to be paid, is the best compensation there is, and the only one that truly counts. If that be so, one coterie of Meadville's people, joined by half a dozen volunteers from other towns within an hour's drive, gave generously to their community, and received its demonstrable appreciation in exchange.

In a 1947 feature story remarkable for its detail, the *Tribune-Republican* introduced the people of Meadville to the day jobs of their orchestral musicians. The conductor, Maurice M. "Gummy" Lord, was manager of the local Pennsylvania State Liquor Commission Store that natives euphemistically called "the package store," presumably in reference to plain brown wrappers. The concertmaster, Bruce Frye, was assistant cashier at Meadville's First National Bank.

The group did not lack professional musicians. Seven players were former members of other orchestras, including two who had retired from the Pittsburgh Symphony—one to operate a hotel, the other to become a farmer (there's a story in *there* somewhere). Another five were public school music supervisors, including Ardath Chandler.

Still, that was only 14 of 51 members, a quarter of the total. The rest were a kaleidoscope of the town and all "amateurs." Three came from business—two more bankers and a department store employee. Industry contributed the supervisor of a petroleum company and four Talon Corporation employees (the zipper, originally called the hookless fastener, was invented and first commercially produced in Meadville), including an engineer and a production supervisor. Even city government got into the act with Roy Phillips, the city engineer, as timpanist. There was a dentist, an optometrist, a carpenter, a plumbing contractor and four housewives, among them Gratia Laws. Education contributed a primary school principal and one member each of the faculty and staff of Allegheny, the latter being Mother. Rounding out the adult contingent were two clerks from "Gummy" Lord's package store (suggesting that Meadville may have boasted the most musically literate unit in the Pennsylvania State Liquor Commission!).

Most encouraging for a small town orchestra, the remaining fifteen players were students, ten from Allegheny and five from Meadville High School, among whom were two young cellists who earned their chairs at the ripe age of fourteen: Diane Luvaas, daughter of the founder of Allegheny's choral program, and Frank, who played with the orchestra for two years.

Do you suppose it ever occurred to Mozart or Beethoven that the performance of their music might come to depend on the likes of these? It's right up there with "Would you buy a used car from this guy?" Yet it is the beauty of music that it can be played and enjoyed by anyone willing to accept the disciplines of instruction and practice. If true greatness is reserved to those few who, born with "the gift," consume themselves to develop it, it is also the case that average folk can, with diligence and commitment, transform their high school auditorium into a symphonic hall and bring to life the genius of the masters. And Meadville's citizens responded mightily. Hundreds of them poured into the auditorium at the northern edge of the Diamond on concert nights. Who would imagine that a town of 14,000 would so generously support the classical endeavors of friends and neighbors?

Nor was Meadville the lone beneficiary. "Gummy" Lord believed that the orchestra both had an obligation to its wider community and benefited by broader exposure to it. Enough of his players shared the sentiment to make it worthwhile periodically to hit the road to one of the nearby boroughs—villages like Saegertown and Linesville, Cochranton and Cambridge Springs.

These were "read-through" sessions. There was no rehearsal. Indeed, the group might never have seen a musical score before sitting down to play it. That was the fun and the challenge: to get together and just have at it. If things fell into disarray, orchestra and audience had a hearty laugh and the musicians started over again.

The full orchestra seldom went; job or school obligations precluded it. But it didn't much matter, for two reasons. First, no one cared. These were rump sessions and everyone knew it. Second, "Gummy" had Ruth Skinner to fall back on. Mother's agile sight-reading allowed her to sit down with a score she had not seen before and play through it better than many musicians could manage after several rehearsals. Part of her job on these outings, and even during formal concerts, was to fill in for missing instruments. Was the clarinetist absent that day? Never mind: listen for that melodic line coming from the piano.

Let it be said that the folk of those rural Pennsylvania communities were every bit as appreciative as the home audience. Farmers and shopkeepers, housewives and doctors, their children in tow, packed into a school auditorium or gymnasium and listened in rapt attention as "Gummy" spoke about the composers and the music and the orchestra strutted its unrehearsed stuff. And when it was over, the audience applauded and beamed and mingled with the musicians, examining their instruments and asking their advice. It was heady stuff. It was also *Americana* at its earnest best.

——————

Then there was the Civic Music Association, Meadville's affiliate of the Civic Concert Service, an agency that booked professional performers into small towns left behind when railroads and traveling troupes abandoned them for more lucrative urban markets. The agency offered an impressive line-up, mainly soloists and small groups that promised professional quality. Leave it to Mother to be right in the middle of it. At one point she was treasurer and kept the books. Then she kept the membership rolls, or served on the committee that chose the talent for the following year's performance series, or made arrangements to house guest artists when they were in town or hosted receptions for them after performances, or all of the above. I suppose it's what she did in her spare time.

Each year she purchased memberships for whichever of us remained at home. Since I was last out of the nest, I benefited most; and being Mother's son, and her in the thick of it, I got to rub elbows with some prodigious talent. The Civic Concert Service served up a solid menu: while young and promising artists were given a shot at the circuit, the mainstays were musicians of national reputation. I long ago lost track of how many evenings I spent in the High School auditorium. They loom larger in memory than does the aggregate of my two years attending there, because each event was unique. Still, the whole thing fell into a routine after a while: drive with Mother to the Lafayette Hotel, climb into the back, and shut up so the adults in front could converse— even though they seldom talked about anything that seemed all that important to me. But that just shows how little I knew about the mundane nuts and bolts of performing. I was learning a lot more than I realized, riding along staring at the back of some visitor's head and wondering what about them was so special. The men were balding and the women were overweight. They didn't glow in the dark or anything. Set one of them down on Chestnut Street or at the Market House and they'd fade into the crowd without leaving a trace. They were just like the rest of us.

But when I climbed to the balcony and found my favorite seat, and the house lights dimmed, it wasn't the same. The artist

who strode onto the stage, graciously nodding in acknowledg-
ment of the audience's applause, wasn't the same person who'd
stepped out of our car moments before. Something had happened,
and footlights and evening dress weren't enough to explain it. It
dawned on me, as I grew older and more attentive, that what
made these people exceptional was not who they were but what
they did. On stage, their years of training and consecration to
their art, tested before unnumbered audiences and proven in the
heat of critical review, made them larger than life. They commanded admiration because they had earned it, and we were the
beneficiaries. It might only have been little old Meadville, yet
every month or two our very own high school auditorium was
transfigured by the grace of artistic endeavor. We might as well
have been in Carnegie Hall, and none of us was about to gainsay
the gift.

I suppose it comes as no surprise that hormones, not art,
fire my favorite memory of these events. That would be the brittle
winter evening that the Trapp Family Singers came to town.

Following the burst in popularity of the movie version of
"Sound of Music," it is difficult to get past the American perception of the Trapp family as a cutesy song-and-dance team. But
they came to Meadville, and to our home, decades before Julie
Andrews twirled about that mountain meadow singing synthetic
songs about the hills being alive and all that; and both their lives
and their music were far more demanding than Hollywood came
even close to conveying.

They visited in the middle of World War II, when their family, like so many in America, was stung by separation that too
often proved permanent: they had recently been granted political asylum and the oldest sons had enlisted in the American

military. The women and youngest son performed in Meadville's high school auditorium knowing that their brothers were engaged in active combat theaters. The first half of the program, far from bubbling about "doe-a-deer" or "schnitzel with noodles," consisted of demanding classical music, largely sacred in origin, and the second half of folksongs steeped in generations of European tradition. Their conductor was a young Roman Catholic priest who sang while conducting, a surrogate voice for the missing sons. The program was withal as distant from the show tunes of the movie as Vienna is from Hollywood, which is to say half a world apart.

Their visit presented me with an opportunity unequalled in the annals of the Civic Music Association. Sadly, it came a cropper. Having helped Mother clean the house and prepare the refresh-

ments that afternoon, I knew there would be a reception following the concert, and I had mixed feelings. I liked Mother's refreshments, and kept wishing that she'd fix that kind of stuff for supper instead of ham loaf and scalloped potatoes and Brussels sprouts or something. But the conversations at such receptions were usually over my head, and therefore boring. Tonight, I was about to discover, would not be at all the same. Pre-performance indifference turned to bug-eyed enthusiasm thirty seconds after the curtain went up.

Sitting in the balcony trying to attend to the subtleties of their demanding program, I kept being distracted, my thirteen-year-old eyes migrating to the face of one of the younger singers and getting stuck there. She was twelve and, I thought, uncommonly pretty. Meeting an Austrian girl his own age was not an opportunity that came often to a boy growing up in Crawford County—then or now. It seemed an incredible stroke of luck. The final curtain was still swaying, and the auditorium still echoing a final handclap, when I began to badger Mother about getting home.

Never was I more ready for a performance to end, and never so bitterly disappointed by its aftermath. Arriving home, Mother issued a few last minute orders about turning on lights and getting the platter of cold cuts and cheese out of the icebox, and was engaged in one last fuss over the table arrangements and lighting the candles when the first guest banged the iron knocker on the home of the door monster. Appointing myself concierge, I stood vibrating as the guests arrived. But my heart sank when the Trapps filed in: the two youngest girls—to my mind the only justification to allow all these people to be wandering around in our house—were missing.

"Oh," one of the older girls explained, her tone offhanded in spite of her German accent, "they have colds, and Mama sent them back to the hotel to go to bed."

I was crushed. I knew that about the time I went off to school the next morning, the Trapps would be stepping gingerly down Chestnut Street through the ice and snow to board the train to their next engagement, and that I would lose forever the chance to meet their delightful daughter.

I hid my disappointment pretty well, actually, not from any mature recognition that it really wasn't a matter of cosmic consequence, but because the Trapps were exceptionally gracious people. Well, for the most part. I would not want to characterize the baron as ungracious, but he certainly was intimidating. He strode into our living room as if he owned the place, and pulled a chair so close to the fire that I expected his loden jacket to start to smoke. It didn't, but he did, and it was a lesson in cultural conditioning. Like Santa Claus, he spoke not a word but went straight to his work, puffing contentedly if imperiously on an enormous, ornately carved briar; and all the while, the oldest daughters took turns standing by his side, ready without prompting to light a brand from the fire and hold it to the bowl of his pipe whenever it went out.

But Maria and the Trapp daughters were gracious and gregarious. I had little trouble engaging with them in lively conversation, and was delighted to be treated as a peer by people that famous. Nor did they forget their visit, even though—given their tour schedule—they certainly would have been forgiven if they had. After the war, they purchased property in Vermont's Green Mountains—a reminder of their native Austria—and opened a summer music camp. Mother visited them twice in the ensuing years, and was received as a welcome friend. We still have the color slides that she brought home with her from those visits, evidence of how momentary civic music encounters in a small Pennsylvania town might expand into lifelong friendships.

I was away at school during the first of her visits, and preoccupied with a new professional career during the second. So I never did get to meet the young girl who captured my attention that brittle winter evening during World War II. Following Mother's first visit to the Trapp's Vermont home, I asked what the girl looked like, by then a woman in her twenties. Mother was unsympathetic. Late in her life, I'd mention one girl or another whom I had dated, many of whom visited in our home, some more than once; but she mostly denied having any memory of them. This occasion was no different. "I don't know which one you're talking about," she fussed. "Besides, they're all beautiful, so what difference does it make?"

So much for my Austrian connection.

Frank left the orchestra at the end of the 1946-47 season, following Cliff to Mercersburg. Mother played through the next season, her seventh, until it was my turn to go. Then, the last of her brood gone from home, she left Meadville. During intermission at the May 1948 concert, "Gummy" called her to the front of the stage while he delivered a touching tribute, gave her a bouquet of roses in thanks for her loyalty and labor, and announced to the audience that she would be away from Meadville for a year or so and "on leave" from the orchestra. Perhaps it was gentle subterfuge. But it's also possible that no one, including Mother, sensed the finality of that farewell. It was her last appearance with the orchestra. The following year, her mind settled, she sold our North Main Street home, never returning to live in Meadville again.

Maybe the uncertainty was a good thing. It made lighter what would otherwise have been a very heavy moment for her and for her friends in both orchestra and audience. As noted, Mother never did emotion well. Realizing that, her friends would spare her the burden.

The auditorium stands dark and empty now. The school programs it housed have moved to new buildings out North Street, on the eastern edge of town, reducing the old brick fortress on the Diamond to a topic of endless debate about what to do with it.

The symphony is gone too, its voice stilled by time and the same shifts in public taste that earlier brought the curtain down on traveling theater. But if, visiting home again, I walk the north rim of the Diamond at mid-evening and look across at the old building, I can conjure familiar shapes among the shadows cast by the street lamps that border the park. The transparent images call in greeting as they converge on the sidewalks and chat gaily as they move up the broad steps—elegantly gowned women and bow-tied men come to hear Mozart and Beethoven brought to life again by their neighbors and daughters and sons right here in Meadville.

Among them moves the shadow of a boy who squirms at the unaccustomed chafing of jacket and necktie and stiff-as-board shoes. He climbs the stairs to the U-shaped balcony and moves down the narrow left side, from where he can see down across the stage to the piano. He sits there in the dark alone, but tied by shimmering chords of music to his mother at her piano below, and absorbs, adolescent lethargy to the contrary notwithstanding, the magic of very classical music and the miracle that very un-classical folk, by diligence and commitment, can make it live.

PART IV

Not All Spiritual Experience is Created Equal

CHAPTER 18

A Germ of
Religious Sensibility

I t should be evident by now that Granddaddy McCafferty
was determinedly no-nonsense. Reserved and businesslike, his goal in life—or so Mother understood it—was to
make a million dollars in spite of the United States government.
By contemporary standards it seems a modest enough ambition.
But when Ernest McCafferty first went in search of it, milk cost
5¢ a quart delivered to your door, the average worker earned
$300 a year, and the U.S. boasted a grand total of 144 miles of
paved road. In such an economy, one could earn a fine salary for
a lifetime, invest wisely, and die without achieving the rank of
wealth. Well-to-do, we used to say, but not wealthy. Ernest's success was further tempered by generosity. An intensely ethical
man, he took seriously what he understood to be the obligations
of both his Christian faith and his social station. In religious life,
such a man values sound thinking, dignity, a sense of order.

Besides, he was Scots-Irish. It was inevitable that Mother would be raised a Presbyterian.

I never learned how, or whether, my parents pursued their spiritual life during those hectic years of pounding a rut between Chicago and Richmond, with stops at Ashville and Pittsburgh, the while accumulating three new mouths to feed and three more sets of clothes to pack. Once they resettled in Meadville, however, the decision to join the Presbyterian Church was concluded promptly. There is no way to tell, the principals having left the scene, whether theological insight, or a preference for representative church governance rather than rule by bishops, played a part in their decision. I conclude, however, that for them as for many of their peers it was partly an ecclesiastical expression of middle class reserve: those folks just didn't cotton to religious emotionalism. It doesn't matter. Meadville's First Presbyterian Church was, to this child, both fertile ground for spiritual rooting and a launching pad for vocation. It is not a gift horse into the mouth of which I care to look critically.

———·•·———

The church building faced Liberty Street, one block east of the Diamond and directly behind the Crawford County Courthouse. The arrangement was prophetic. The Sunday school wing, which comprised the back of the church building, backed onto a narrow alley directly opposite the county jail. If ever an object lesson on the wages of sin was needed, that juxtaposition provided it. The consequence of failing to heed the moral injunctions in our weekly lessons was right there, staring us in the face. More than once, gawking across the alley at the barred windows, I found myself looking directly into the eyes of a prisoner looking back.

In actuality, the relationship between church and jail was of long standing. As reported in 1938 in the Sesqui-Centennial Edition of the *Tribune-Republican*:

> About the year 1800, church services were held temporarily in various places, the first regular meeting place being in the room on the second floor of a log building... on the west side of Diamond Park, the first floor of which was used as a jail, and the above mentioned room as a courtroom.

The notion that Presbyterians were fixated on good order may have more to it than we imagined!

First called simply the "Meadville Church," the congregation welcomed the support of all Protestants, regardless of denominational background. In 1818, a building was erected on the part of the Liberty Street property later occupied by the Presbyterian Church of my childhood. Ecumenism survived but a quarter century, however, before sectarianism worked its divisive will. By 1825, Meadville had become large enough, and sufficiently diverse, that denominationalism would no longer be denied. Each new separation drew off more of the congregation until, by mutual agreement, title to the building was transferred to the "Presbyterian division," which continued to occupy it for another half century.

In 1875, a red brick building was erected on the site, mock Gothic in style. Its steeply-roofed front, featuring a trinity of arched, stained glass windows and flanked by asymmetrical buttressed steeples, comprised one of Meadville's enduring landmarks.

Along the way, however, mainstream Presbyterianism contracted a case of national disunion, infecting the local congregation with schism fever. Those who remained in the original

building adopted the name "First Presbyterian Church," while
the disaffected withdrew to Center Street and, apparently determined to be Second to no one, organized "Central Presbyterian
Church." It is debatable whether the repair of the division depended more on the intervention of the Great Physician or the
services of Meadville's morticians. In any event, when First
Presbyterian's pulpit went vacant in 1903, most members who
were party to the original split had gone to their rewards. Their
progeny, concluding that the cause of the breach was no longer
compelling—if it ever had been—invited the Central folk to come
on home and bring their minister with them. The invitation was
immediately embraced and the congregation reunited. In a short
time, both the cause and the fact of disunion were forgotten.
Central's edifice was sold to the Christian Church (Disciples of

Christ); and few today
are able to explain why
a denomination with no
"Second" church in
town, nor likely to ac-
quire one, still titles itself "First."

———

It was into that
place, a few months af-
ter my birth, that my
parents carried me to be
baptized, their three
older children tagging

along in their wake. And though I was oblivious to both the event
and its significance, the symbolic drops of water that constituted
that sacramental bath inoculated me with a germ of religious

sensibility that would grow to shape both my understanding of the holy and my vocation.

Too, my spiritual awakening was mediated by influences in every way as sensual as the water of baptism. The very walls of the building dripped incarnation, and taught me how deftly the spiritual is mediated through visceral things. Their residue inhabits an archive in my sensory library labeled "Holy," subtitled "Spirit." In the simple act of writing about them, I play the conjuring game of the medium of Endor, and summon the church of my childhood back from its refuge in time.

As we stepped through the arched portal at the foot of the sky-stabbing steeple, Liberty Street's sunlight was consumed by the deep shadow of the vestibule, a constricted space taller than it was broad, through the ceiling of which hung the well-handled bell rope. The temptation to grab it and give it a pull was nearly irresistible, but that was a privilege reserved for adults. A pity. Setting the weight of the massive bell two long stories above to swinging, I could have ridden that rope halfway to the ceiling. The sexton, whose job it was to ring it, merely stood there and let the rope slide through his hands—a lamentable waste of an opportunity. I longed to reach out and give it a sharp pull, and several times nearly did. But while Jesus had to confront Satan alone, my parents were right there to insure that I did not deliver myself into temptation.

My having survived that brief moment in the wilderness, we passed through the door to the spacious, high-peaked sanctuary where I was dazzled, first and always, by the deeply hued, frozen-liquid splendor of the stained glass windows. The ten of them, five on each side of the room, were a scriptural library in the best tradition of medieval cathedrals: a tutorial written in ruby and cobalt for an illiterate peasantry. On many a Sunday, while the adult stuff of Presbyterian liturgy washed over me only faintly comprehended, I gazed at the windows and was set to roving through the biblical stories that inspired some stained-glass genius to embed them in light.

Down front, spanning most of the room's width, a dark, wood-paneled platform lifted the action high enough for all to observe, dominated at the center by an ornately carved pulpit. The arrangement was not accidental; it was an architectural expression of the belief that preaching the Word to Calvinists is both an elevated calling and the central act of worship. Behind the pulpit, as if to second the motion, stood three imposingly crafted chairs for the clergy, arguably as uncomfortable as any I have ever seen. There seemed to be some unspoken lesson there—perhaps that suffering is a prerequisite to godly pastoral leadership. My suspicion in this regard was confirmed in 1987 when I was invited to preach at a Sunday service and actually sat in one of those chairs for the first time. The experience was every bit as painful as I'd imagined, and added to my admiration of the church's pastors, who had to sit in the things for years. Those people really were saints!

The floorboards complained crankily underfoot as people stepped down the aisles to their favorite pews, their expressions brightening with satisfaction if they found them empty, or darkening if they didn't. I reached out and let my hand bounce from one pew end to the next as we walked. Caressing the scrolled tops, rubbed to a satin patina by the oil of a hundred thousand sanctifying hands, was to touch the history of my church. It was deposited there, after all, by generations of worshipful people: stooped and elderly folk steadying themselves as they turned carefully out of the aisle to ease themselves, time-worn and weary-jointed, into their seats; strong adults who gripped a pew end to reach across in greeting, renewing their connection by eye and hand and voice; children gripping an anchor to check their inertia as they cornered into their seat at high speed—or as high as their elders would tolerate.

I waited eagerly for the choir to enter the loft and break out in the holy noise of practiced people confident in their work. Surely, such delicious sound must echo the music of heaven's host intoning "Christ, we do all adore thee..." Beyond the choir, massive ranks of gold pipes (fake gold on false pipes!) fronted the arched organ chamber. Balanced on pointed bottoms, they reached almost to the ceiling and prompted my earliest editorial comment regarding church: the first time my parents took me into the sanctuary rather than leaving me in the nursery, I surveyed the pipes and announced soberly, "There are lots of pencils up there."

Finally came the moment I longed for. The organist, screened from view at the console sunk into the choir loft floor like the cockpit of an airplane, struck the first chord of the first hymn, vibrating my small frame with sound muscular enough to weigh and harmony so compelling that it lifted that staid congregation right off its collective chief-end-of-man in full-throated songs of praise. Whatever else you might care to say about Meadville's dignified Presbyterians, they could sing!

And I say with certainty that if, half a century later, the Good Witch of the North told me to close my eyes, click my heels together three times and chant, "There's no place like home," I could enter that house of worship, eyes still clenched, and my nose alone would tell me that I had come home. Call it decaying timbers and antique plaster. Or the evanescent residue of frazzled hymn books and thumb-worn Bibles, of ten thousand burnt candles and half a century of Sunday School paper and crayons.

Attribute it to decades of air trapped in unventilated rooms, or the accumulated redolence of the last hundred pot luck suppers attended by women splashed with cologne and men with aftershave. Call it whatever you like. To my child's mind it was church, the aroma of piety. Nasally penetrating piety, to be sure; but the incense of my spiritual home.

It was at First Presbyterian Church that I first learned the joy—and the cost—of stewardship. Thrift was impressed upon us as children, a mix, I suspect, of poverty in Dad's history and Scots-Irish blood in Mother's. Before we were old enough fully to appreciate their significance, we children were given brightly painted steel trays (mine was canary yellow) divided into four compartments, each labeled with a patch of the adhesive tape that was an omnipresent commodity in a physician's household.

Those labels, printed in a parental hand, branded my sense of fiscal responsibility for life with my parents' values: Church & Charity, Gifts, Savings and Self. Weekly allowances were determined by age, in five year allotments: 25¢ until age 5; 50¢ to age 10, and so on. The arrangement was convenient: each amount divided easily by five, with one fifth to be deposited into each of the first three compartments, and two fifths, plus any extra we might earn, into "Self."

"Church & Charity" was a floating fund: money generally came in and went out each week in equal amounts, but we had the satisfaction of knowing that since we owned it, it was our offering to give. "Gifts" supported birthday and Christmas purchases, accumulating for a time before being drawn down sharply, as the calendar dictated. "Savings" was forever, or so my mind conceived it; with periodic regularity the money vanished into the Crawford County Trust Company which, like Meadville's other two banks, demonstrated its soundness by surviving the "bank holidays" and securing the assets of its depositors against the failures of the Great Depression. Though parental discretion was advised, we early were given the right to choose our own purchases from the "Self" compartment. It was in exercising this right that I came to my moment of stewardship awakening.

The year I entered first grade, my Sunday School teacher approached Mother after church one day in a state of fluster, and apprised her that I had put a $5 bill into the offering plate. Might there be some mistake? Even though it had been dedicated to God in prayer (lending an air of hypocrisy to its retrieval and all), would Mother perhaps like it back? The teacher might have saved her breath. By then surprised by very little that her children did, Mother brushed the offer aside.

"No. It's his money and if he chooses to use it this way we won't interfere."

Mother knew perfectly well how long it took me to accumulate five dollars, especially when that four-compartment tray was factored into the calculation. Whatever motive I had for such profligate generosity is locked in unconscious memory, if indeed it did not slip the bolt and scurry right out of town. But I recall two things. First, while Mother informed me about my teacher's state of shock, she never asked me to explain, honoring both the decision and my right to make it. And second, while I may have forgotten why I did it, I have not forgotten—indeed, I still affirm in my soul—the lesson I learned that day: that in the contest between generosity and stinginess, altruism wins every time.

Two experiences, I suspect, prompted that awakening.

First, the people around me embodied it. Thanks to the consistency of the liturgy, the Sundays of my memory meld into

a blur from which details of particular days are absent. Except
Pledge Sunday, when the people of the congregation, having
weighed what portion of their Depression-battered incomes they
would commit to God that year, processed down the aisle (pew
by pew in orderly Presbyterian fashion) to drop their pledge cards
through a slot in the roof of a replica of the church building which,
at three feet, was as tall as I was. It was all very symbolic, right
down to the light shining out the small colored windows. And it
was the light, not the model's size, that excited my wonder. Surely,
it seemed to say, dropping my promise into the light was an extraordinary act, a sacred promise on which I had better make good
lest I be charged with breaking my word to the One who is the
source of *all* Light.

Even more, there was Christina Collins, our director of Christian education. Never married, she was typed in the labeling of
the time as a maiden-lady. A plain-groomed woman, tall and
slightly stooped but extraordinarily sweet of face and disposition, she was molded to the softness of one devoted to quieter
pursuits. She glowed with an iridescent affection for her charges,
the kind of human being who radiates light even when standing
in a dark room. She set the tone and temper of the church school
program, helping teachers to make scripture live in the minds of
small children and affecting the way I was introduced to Bible
stories.

Gathering with my small peers at the start of some early and
forgotten year, eager but uncertain what to expect, I was delighted
to learn that we were not simply to hear stories, we were to *be*
stories. We were the *dramatis personae* of sacred history, the
people of God struggling to discover the eternal lessons of faith
in the momentary events of our days. A hapless traveler, set upon,
stripped and battered on the road, I fell to the floor beneath our

classroom table, fists knotted and teeth clenched in pain. There I moaned in my helplessness, alternately flush with hope and sunk in despair as priest and Levite came near, saw my battered form, uttered a voluble "Ew!" and crossed the road to pass by on the opposite side of the Sunday School room. Then—oh, sweet mercy—chanced along the despised but compassionate Samaritan! Like a sack of potatoes, I was hoisted across the back of the poor groaning donkey-child and hauled, body parts dragging on all quarters, to the teacher's table and the sanctuary of the inn, where yellow construction paper coins were tendered for my care and the promise given that, if they were not sufficient, the Samaritan would pay more on his return trip. Then we rehearsed it all over again, and I was the despised and unfeeling Levite. Very unsatisfactory. But in the end I was given opportunity to redeem myself in my final incarnation as the faithful and uncomplaining beast of burden.

Is it possible ever to forget a story and its import when it is first played out among a circle of children made secure by a larger circle of faithful adults? My gut recoils at the sight of a bloodied victim, but my heart compels me to reach beyond the cringing in acts of mercy. My blood boils against the callous disregard of the passer-by, never more heatedly than when I am he, prodding my sense of justice. And I am certain that I want to live as a Samaritan but not as his ass! Charity, I discerned, is not satisfied by acts of petit altruism. It must be as profound as the pain it means to address, and as extravagant as a widow's copper coins.

———·——

Our minister was Glenn M. Crawford, D.D. His call to occupy Meadville's Presbyterian pulpit was conveyed December 12, 1932, five days before my birth, and he remained there throughout my youth. A slight man, sharp featured, he was a diminutive rendering of a van Gogh saint, too tall for his girth—or was it that he was too slim for his height? His face was so narrow it was hard to imagine it could accommodate a full set of teeth. But this was not a pinched man. His eyes, close-set beneath a slender brow, were transparent blue. They seemed to my young mind to project two things: an inner joy that infected everyone he came close to; and the God-like capacity to see right through me, penetrating to the secrets of my heart. In his presence I knew mingled affection and misgiving.

I suppose he was a strong preacher. About the time I was old enough to judge with any degree of confidence, my family scattered across the Northeast and I never saw him again. But to this child, his sermons were an impressionistic wonder. The opening portion of the service, with its strong musical component, always held my interest. Long before I could read, the words and tunes of several dozen popular hymns had been mimicked into memory, and I was at home in my singing church. Come sermon time, however, young limbs got squirmy and restless hands demanded an outlet. It was for such times that Mother, wise in the ways of fidgety children (especially her youngest, whose energy could pent up faster than any minister could possibly reel off the predictable introduction, three points and poem), equipped her purse with a generous supply of scrap paper and pencils. And while no one kept track, I am confident that the value of the paper I consumed during the Sundays of my childhood contributed measurably to the nation's recovery from the Great Depression. Mother used to observe that no one on either side of our family had a bit of artistic talent, and she was mystified where mine came from. Wherever, its first expressive outlet came not in school—where we were required to color pre-printed subjects, taking care never to stray outside the heavy black lines—but in church. By the second grade, I found canned coloring exercises to be a crushing bore. In church, freed from anyone's cramped conception of art as indoctrination, not expression, my muse cut the traces and sent me flying off across the world. I can't say whether worship or drawing during the sermon proved ultimately to be more liberating; but they came a blended gift, and for that Our Mother of the Well-Stocked Purse gets part of the credit.

However, my artistic endeavors collapsed at the sermon's climax. Meadville's Presbyterians observed a custom, common at the time, of lowering the house lights for the sermon—whether to heighten the drama or to provide some measure of anonymity to those destined to fall asleep was not clear. In later years I became suspicious that, in too many churches, it was a harbinger of the verbal gloom that was about to envelope us. At the time, though, it served mainly to make Glenn Crawford's face the one thing in the room that was clearly visible. He never lost my parents' interest. And while I hadn't the foggiest idea what he was talking about, his sermons followed a pattern so predictable that even I quickly figured it out, and recognized the telltale indications that we were reaching the mountaintop. It was an impressive show. Dr. Crawford's voice grew louder and his naturally ruddy complexion intensified. By the climax of his message, volume one decibel short of congregational tolerance, words tumbling so rapidly one upon the other as to threaten intelligibility, he flushed with the intensity of the airport beacon atop the hill west of town. It was a spectacle that never failed to rouse my wonder. Pencil poised mid-line, I fixated on the transported and spot-lit face that hovered above the reading desk like the brimstone-blown visage of the disembodied Oz ("Pay no attention to that man behind the curtain!"). Some days, so enthralled that I no longer could keep my seat, I stood to peer between the shoulders of those in the pews in front of us, and completely forgot about drawing.

Candor compels me to confess a secondary reason for my late-sermon attentiveness: often as not, the Rev. Dr. Crawford's sermons concluded abruptly soon after their explosive climax— a habit that struck me with the conditioned anticipation of one of Pavlov's dogs, putting me on notice that church was about over and we would soon go home to dinner. My eagerness was based on a combination of my growing child's appetite and dubious scriptural interpretation: when Jesus said, "Man does not live by bread alone," I thought he must be expressing his appreciation of pot roast.

CHAPTER 19

Salvation by Snowsuit

Ignorance, the old adage holds, is bliss, though the proposition is open to debate. Still, our inability to see what is coming may be one of the main reasons we get up some mornings. If we knew what a day held, we might just choose to pass on it. I'm confident that, had I been aware of what was coming that day in 1937, I would have done everything in my power to avoid it. The event resulted from a convergence of uncharacteristically poor judgment on Mother's part, childish ignorance on mine, and a passing automobile; but the tactile conjunction was between me and the car.

While Ruth Ann, Cliff and Frank, along with all of our usual baby sitters, were off to school, Mother was off to a gathering of the Women's Club—leaving guess who as the dangling participle. What to do with Don? Simple enough: Dad had no classes that afternoon, so they agreed that Mother would drop me off at his Allegheny office on her way down North Main Street and pick me up again on her way home.

It was chilly that day, the late fall air a raw pronouncement that winter could be expected to make a preliminary visit any day. Apparently I had nothing of intermediate weight to wear on such an intermediate day, so Mother simply bundled my four year old frame into my snowsuit, a dark-green one-piece heavy wool zippered and hooded hand-me-down that Frank had out-grown, and Cliff too, for all I know. Sturdy enough to shield a child against the worst of January, that snowsuit tried Mother's patience and broke her fingernails through half a dozen Pennsyl-vania winters. She wasn't alone: no young Meadville mother es-caped the hazards of one-piece zippered wool in winter. And while she might have preferred not to have to pack me into mine that too mild day, I will not complain. For therein lies the theological dimension of the incident: before the day was over, that snowsuit would save me from a hazard far greater than cold.

Running late by the time she got me suited up, Mother was further delayed by the need to hoist me into the back seat of the car. I could have made it on my own but for my "new" snowsuit, which lent me a profile more akin to a basketball than a boy. Had I fallen down on the way to the car, I might have lain there like a turtle on its back, arms and legs flailing in an impotent effort to right myself, until she picked me up and put me back on my feet. Plopped into the middle of the back seat, my legs as straight as a teddy bear's, I sat immobilized as Mother set off to collect three women who had accepted her offer of taxi service to the gathering.

Louise Sturdevant was first into the car, so she got the front seat. Louise, whose exquisite Massachusetts-style home stood a block away at the top of Hamilton Avenue, was the female half of a diminutive couple. Her husband Carl was a dentist who acquired so little altitude growing up that he spent most of his career atop a foot stool in order to see into his patients' mouths. Carl had an infectious sense of humor, and the five-foot dentist and my six-foot physician father became best friends. Carl and Louise had no children, and took a lifelong interest in the Skinner offspring. It followed that Louise Sturdevant and Ruth Skinner saw a lot of each other.

Turning south on Jefferson Street and down Byllesby Avenue hill, Mother stopped next at the home of Dorothy Charles, back at the corner of North Main Street a block below our home. Dorothy's husband Harry was among my favorite Meadville citizens, a jeweler whose Chestnut Street shop was a town fixture for half a century. Harry was a gracious and gentle man who, my entire life, never failed to greet me cheerfully when I stopped by his store for nothing at all but to be warmed by his kindness. Dorothy climbed into the back seat on one side of me.

Turning down North Main, Mother paused for the third time at the Norton home. Helen, wife of school superintendent Warren Norton, was the mother of six-foot-plus David, one of Cliff's best friends, and was herself close to six feet tall. It took some effort for her to fold herself into the back seat on the other side of me.

Her entourage assembled, with me verging on heat stroke between the two ladies in the back seat, Mother continued on down North Main Street to the college, where she pulled over to the curb across from Alden Hall.

Alden was a two-story yellow brick building with a wide overhang to its roof, windows large enough to use as doors, and narrow floorboards which, like those of the Presbyterian Church, creaked vociferously. A small cat couldn't walk three steps down the hall without announcing its presence. It's unfortunate that the building was named for Timothy Alden, the college's official founder and first president. On a campus noted for handsome buildings, Alden Hall was not one of them. Nor did the building date from very early in the college's history; its 1910 dedication put it tenth in line, almost a century after the college's founding. To make matters worse, it was gutted by fire when barely a decade old, necessitating its complete rebuilding. I would think that old Timothy deserved better.

Still, the building played a large role in Skinner family history. Housing the biology department, it was the venue of both Dad's and Mother's academic majors, of Dad's subsequent faculty appointment, and of Mother's employment as departmental assistant after Dad's death. In the late 1940s, Cliff would take a number of biology classes requisite to medical school admission. Unfortunately, I myself would take several courses there in the early 1950s, thereby throwing the Skinner family's reputation for scientific prowess forever into question.

Perhaps, in the karma of things, this is what was in the offing that chill fall afternoon when Mother pulled over to the curb opposite the scene of so many family triumphs: I was about to make an advance payment on the penalty imposed on me for blowing three decades of family achievement.

But all that was far in the indiscernible future. On the day in question, we stopped at Alden because Dad's office was there. His appointment being in biology, it seemed convenient to house the college's brand new student health program adjacent to his faculty office. Both were on the second floor, where he waited as Mother pulled over to the curb.

Fortunately, Dorothy Charles had gotten in the right side of the car. It would have been futile to try to climb over poor Helen Norton at that point. I crawled over Dorothy's lap and out onto the sidewalk, with explicit instructions from Mother to stand on the curb in front of the car and wait for her signal to cross the street. As instructions go, hers were clear enough that even my four-year-old brain had no trouble absorbing them. The flaw was not in the plan's design but its execution.

I never understood, nor could Mother explain, why on that particular day she thought it appropriate to put a small child on the curb while she sat in the car and waved her hand for me to stay or go. All our lives, she let us take risks when it seemed important to understand and weigh their cost (even while her heart was usually in her throat as we did), but her action that day was extraordinarily out of character. It has occurred to me that perhaps she was cooperating, if unwittingly, in something larger; that maybe God had been waiting for an appropriate opportunity to send me a message, something like, "Look, I saved your life; now I expect you to make something of it." If that was the case, it was a pretty risky way to deliver it!

Standing on the curb, I tried, with little success, to look over the car's hood and past the glare of the windshield to see Mother's face behind the steering wheel. (This was not easy under the best of circumstances: in half the cars ever manufactured, little more than Mother's eyes and forehead ever made it higher than the steering wheel, even when she sat on a cushion, which she did most of her life.) It was not an auspicious beginning, even though she had ample help: I could see well enough to realize that all four women were craning their necks about, looking up and down the street as if charged to make a committee decision about how long I should stay planted on that curb.

Then, with a single gesture, Mother hung my life in the balance. Taking her to be saying "go" when she meant that I should stay, I launched off the curb like every small child ever coached on how hazardous streets are but just given permission to cross:

I would get to the opposite curb as fast as my legs would take me there. I never even came close. Darting into the street in front of Mother's car, I slammed right into the back corner of a passing Model T Ford. Before I knew what hit me (amend that: what I had hit), my snowsuit got tangled in the rear bumper and I was jerked off my feet and dragged down the street, my body bouncing along the paving bricks like a rag doll.

I never heard the screams of Mother and her friends that, even if not confined to our car, would have done little good. Neither did I hear the screams and shouts of several college students walking up the street who, seeing me hooked to the rear end of a Model T whose driver was still oblivious to my presence, put up a real fuss and ran into the street, arms gesturing wildly to stop him. By the time the driver—another student, as it turned out—got turned into the curb, the car was in front of Ruter Hall, several hundred feet farther down the hill from Alden and on the opposite side of the street. Jumping out, the young man rushed around to the back, where those who had flagged him down were already gathered around the rag doll lying unconscious on the pavement, snowsuit still hooked to his bumper. Then something happened to change their tears and cries of horror to anxiety-releasing laughter: I bellowed—loudly.

It being apparent that I was by no means dead, they unsnarled my snowsuit, gently scooped me up off the pavement and ran up the street with me, intent on getting me to "Doc" Skinner's office as fast as they could. They hadn't a clue who I was, and I can only imagine their surprise when they found out, which they did soon enough. By the time they came dashing up the street, Mother and her friends, faces white as sheets and eyes streaming tears, were running to meet them, and another student had run into Alden to get Dad. My first conscious recollection after launching off the curb was of being transferred to Dad's arms as he emerged from Alden Hall, his lab coat open and his Phi Beta Kappa key swinging from the watch chain that perennially hung across his vest. His tender smile was all the reassurance I needed as he carried me up to his office and gave me a thorough going over.

The day's plan returned to something bordering on normal as Mother and her friends, satisfied by Dad's reassuring pronouncement that I was fine, went on to their meeting—though I can't imagine they got a lot out of it. And while I didn't much care for the way I came to prominence, I certainly was the talk of town and campus that day, as the small clutch of students who rescued me from my near-death experience basked in the admiration of friends while relating how they scooped "Doc" Skinner's youngest up off the pavement and carried him to his father.

At the time, I knew nothing of all this. I was content to curl up quietly on Dad's examining table and let the terror wear off until Mother returned to take me home.

———·———

Of this I am confident: I was saved that day by that other, earlier quirk of circumstance. Had Mother not put me into my snowsuit, my injuries would have been severe, if not fatal. Through the haze that clouds my memory of just what happened that morning (I have myself no recollection of running into the Model T), I yet retain the sensation of bouncing down the cobbled street, terrified not because of pain, of which I recall virtually none, but by the bizarre nature of the trip, and by not knowing when or even if it would end. My anguish was not injury, but an overwhelming sense of helplessness.

There are some who would say, and did, that God personally reached down from heaven to hold me out of harm's way that day. I am persuaded by a more subtle interpretation. In a wonderful little hymn, William Cowper (1731-1800) declared, "God moves in a mysterious way his wonders to perform." Given the context, our tendency is to think mysterious must imply huge when it just as well can mean covert. I came, when I was old enough to reflect on such mysteries, to believe that there is more holiness resident in mundane little episodes of daily life than in all the spectacular miracle claims made in the history of the world.

And that is why I credit wool with shielding me from the brutal hammering of those bricks. It was salvation by snowsuit. I cannot honestly claim ever to have been touched by an angel, but

I can certainly claim to have been the recipient of mercy mediated through the unintending hands of a mother in a hurry.

Once when my own children were very young and I related to Mother how one of them had narrowly escaped serious injury, she assured me matter-of-factly that children grow up by the grace of God, not the ability of parents. She surely knew what she was talking about. What she failed to add was how often, in spite of preoccupation or hurry or lapses of judgment, grace is still mediated to a child by a devoted parental hand.

CHAPTER 20

It Wasn't the
End of the World

I t was late in the winter of 1942, I think. The malignancy of
World War II was spreading across the globe when the *Tribune-Republican* carried the story: some self-anointed
prophet had declared that the world would end a few days hence.
And—just our luck—it would occur on a school day.

I do not recall just what presumed signs led the man to conclude that the Day of Judgment was indeed at hand. For anyone
predisposed to look for biblical portents in the devastation spreading from country to continent like a wind-driven grass fire, de-
vouring all that lay before it, there were plenty to find. Not that
such a true believer requires anything so tangible; the wispiest of
visions seems often to be quite enough. But in this instance the
omen traffic was heavy and credible. Even though we would not
learn for several years how consuming had been the suffering, or
how appalling the abominations, the world was awash in war

and rumors of war, with nation fighting against nation and kingdom against kingdom.

Whatever motivated the sanctimonious seer who offered the
prediction of the moment, he was not doing us any favors. To a
group of naïve children, it was simply more evidence that the
world we only recently had joined was not trustworthy.

Mother, possessed of a larger faith in the constancy of God,
and enough experience to know what a fool's mouth sounds
like, took the whole thing rather casually, I thought. In our
physician's house, you see, a child who was dying might be excused from going to school, but don't bank on it. Dad and Mother
shared the conviction that trying to protect children from childhood plagues in that pre-inoculation age was a waste of effort.
The shortest route to immunity was the disease. Their response
when one of us contracted chicken pox or measles was to put
the rest of us on the sick child's bed to play. With customary
firmness, Mother even packed me off to school when I had
mumps, instructing me to explain, should the teacher inquire,
that I had swollen glands.

Her conclusion about the world coming to an end that day
was on the same level: the topic did not merit the effort required
to discuss it, and no way was anyone staying home from school
because of it. She was not even disposed to reassure us by explaining the minuscule odds that the man's prediction was correct. I suspect she realized that the only way we would learn to
weigh the words of religious zealots was to encounter a few of
them, and learn to judge for ourselves.

But my young mind, still subject like my young body to socially communicated disease, had not yet acquired immunity from
the contagion of ignorance parading as prophecy. Disconsolately,

I left home not entirely sure that I would ever see my family again.

My friends and I didn't talk much, walking down North Main Street hill that morning. An unaccustomed soberness reigned in our customary gabbiness and the obligatory shoving and pushing of each other all over the sidewalk. Indeed, we were downright orderly, as if we suddenly had a need to move closer together. Nor did the hush lift as we merged into the river of small bodies flowing through the school doors at the opening bell. Jostling and threading my way down the narrow tiled hall to my room, I didn't mention my foreboding to anyone, or they to me. Even though each of us knew it was the one thing on all our minds that morning, it seemed less scary to pretend it didn't exist than to talk about it. And perhaps because we never asked, our teachers offered little comfort.

Expecting to die before nightfall, I was reluctant to shed coat and hat, mittens and boots, and get down to business. While there is no way to judge with certainty, I suspect that the other children didn't learn much more than I did. It made for a pretty useless day. Books and papers lay atop my desk unseen and uncomprehended; and though our bodies remained bolted obediently to our rows of desks, mine was not the only anxious face that could be observed stealing sidelong glances out the window, while a steady flow of information appeared on the blackboard and was erased unheeded.

I wasn't even sure what I was looking for, but such fragmentary images as my memory now recalls came from stories I had heard—doubtless influenced by the lurid scenes in comic books I pored over with friends on rainy afternoons. Were the paving bricks on North Main Street starting to melt? Was there evidence of a thin jagged line in the lawn that betrayed the presence of a grand tectonic crack about to reach under the building, yawn to a chasm, and plunge us all into the bowels of Earth?

It was one of the longest days of my life.

———————

I can't ever recall a day in school when I wasn't delighted to hear the dismissal bell, but few afternoons witnessed giddiness to equal that one. We shot out the school door like grains from the Quaker Company's puffed wheat gun. Turning uphill toward home, our gait quickening to a canter, my friends and I chattered with the frenetic abandon of condemned men just informed that their sentences had been vacated, and pushed and shoved each other as though we were behind on our time and had to make up for the morning's missed allotment of aggression. Surely, I thought to myself, we were out of the woods. Surely, if the world were going to end, it would have done so before the end of school. *Surely*, now that I was eager to hear Mother repeat her scornful dismissal of bogus oracles because I was prepared to believe her, God wouldn't wait until I was halfway home to pull my plug!

Still, true to our superstitious adolescent natures, we continued our conspiracy of silence, lest our premature celebration be misconstrued as arrogance and trigger an incident of cosmic irony. And while the damage done to my confidence in the world was not totally restored (the war was, after all, still out there, and people were suffering and dying in numbers that I couldn't begin to comprehend), that uphill hike through the still chill of a late winter afternoon restored some sense of Earth's reliability.

It would be months, perhaps years, before I'd again feel the degree of certainty about life's hold on the planet that I'd known before that day. But I had completed an essential exercise in learning to balance the certitudes of being against its ambiguities, and would ever after greet with skepticism any who claimed that God spoke to me through them. It was an important lesson. Children who reach adulthood without learning it live at the mercy of charlatans.

As I hiked up our hill that afternoon, I carried something more than the usual load of frayed books and flapping papers under my arm, something at once poignant and consoling. Barely cognizant of what I was doing, I began to reaffirm all in life that I depended on. Perhaps it was an epiphany granted those just delivered from the jaws of doom—or who thought they had been. Maybe it *was* all silliness. Maybe the threat that hung over me *was* in all respects apparent and in no way real, if that truly makes any difference. Still, it became more clear to me that day, as the thought first occurred to me at Dad's death, that everything that I knew and loved and took for granted could in an instant be snatched away by powers beyond my control or anyone else's.

Had I been required—and it was a kindness that no one demanded it of me—I could not at the time have couched my thoughts in sensible terms. To have tried would have been more burden than a child's mind should be asked to bear. But acquiring some appreciation of the terms under which we finite creatures inhabit this Earth is an essential task in the work of maturation. Paradoxically, realizing how tenuous our grip on life is at one particular time permits us to see how nurturing Earth is most of the time, and to wonder at how often we are given, in just the right measure, what we need to survive. No, I did not think such thoughts that day. But I have no doubt that their seeds were planted then, because I recognized them when I stumbled across them again in Robert Frost's poem "Our Hold on the Planet," where he observed that nature

> ...must be a little more in favor of man,
> Say a fraction of one per cent at the very least,
> Or our number living wouldn't be steadily more,
> Our hold on the planet wouldn't have so increased.

As darkness convened in the valley and stalked our passage up the hill toward home, it seemed to me that North Main Street's paving bricks lay more solidly on their base, and pressed more tightly against the curbstones, than I had remembered; and that the elm trunks pushed more insistently against sidewalk on one side and curbstone on the other. Their stark-naked branches, monotonic in the winter twilight, brushed the roofs of the close-shouldered houses behind, and shamelessly interlaced their fingertips over the middle of my street. Mid-hill, the Allegheny campus presented a face of objective disinterest at our passing. Its stone and brick facades, more reflective of sound because bereft of their summer adornment of ivy leaves, echoed the talk and laughter of students wending curved walkways from laboratory and library to dining hall and dormitory. Obviously, *they* weren't preoccupied with the world coming to an end.

Above the campus, our school mates who lived in the Odd Fellows Home across the street, orphaned by who knows what causes or events, turned up the semi-circular driveway to the large, multi-winged building that was their collective home. The one I knew best, because we traveled through primary school together, was a little girl named Irene. (She was a shy child, but trusted me enough to invite me as her guest when the Odd Fellows had one of their periodic group parties, where everybody's birthday was noted in one boisterous celebration.) I wondered, as the heavy doors opened and closed that winter afternoon, admitting small knots of children to their institutional sanctuary, who would explain to her the significance of the day's events—or lack of it— and whether she and children like her would find reassurance about a world in which they already had been abandoned by the very people they should have been able to depend on most.

By the time I reached the upper hill, where the brick and clapboard houses shouldered each other further apart as if to declare a larger importance (though the elms had the good sense to hug each other as closely as before), lights were coming on, their glow escaping through not-yet-curtained windows to paint any nearby patch of snow the color of illumination. The same light that brightened the rooms for those indoors blinded them to the world outdoors, and allowed an innocent passerby, only just redeemed from the jaws of Armageddon, to glimpse the gladness of families gathering oh-so-routinely around dinner tables to break bread and dispense the day's ration of small talk.

A sense of urgency, perhaps a need to be folded into the comfort of my own family, overtook me as the last of my friends turned up his street and disappeared around the corner, prompting me to increase the pace. Gripping both my books and my newfound cognizance more tightly, I ran the last half-block, took the stone steps two at a time, cut across the brown-frozen and winter-parched yard, and rounded the end of the house in a panting rush. Stopping on the side porch, I glanced back toward the west, where tree-clad hills, silhouetted against the fading after-glow, were rapidly becoming one with the darkness. Then, silly with delicious excitement, I plunged through the door into the warmth and glow of Mother's kitchen. Home may never have felt good in quite the same way.

Ever after, a day that started out fearfully and ended hopefully would seem to me evidence not of our frailty, but of our security. As I lay in bed that night, tracing the familiar tangle of shadows projected onto my ceiling by the corner street lamp shining through naked tree branches, it was clear to me that it had been just another day after all. I mean, it wasn't the end of the world. And I rolled over and went to sleep.

CHAPTER 21

Jesus Couldn't Possibly Have Done It this Way

S oon after the end of the war, our church hired a youth minister. We kids never knew where he came from. I don't recall that there was any announcement. He just appeared, and we were told that we were his responsibility. That's pretty much how things were done in those days before anyone had heard of participatory democracy (or would know what it meant if they had). The church Session (the self-same on which Dad had served until his death) was charged to govern and would do so; and the last people whose opinion they thought was germane to hiring a youth minister were the youth. So there we were.

We made the best of it, actually, though few of us found him someone we wanted to emulate. He was far too square for that, and we did not yet realize how square we ourselves would eventually become. But it was clear that he took us seriously and would work to earn our trust. In a short time he did and, trust in place, we developed a degree of fondness for him.

He even invited us into his home, which was disconcerting. We'd never heard of a minister, ours or anyone else's, inviting kids into his home. Parents, maybe, but not kids. And once we got there, how should we act? I mean, ministers being perfect and sin-free and all, what could we possibly have to talk about? We sure weren't going to talk about the things we discussed among ourselves! A minister wouldn't know about that kind of stuff anyway. What if we said something that offended him right there in his own home? Still, he kept pressing us to come, and we didn't want to hurt his feelings, so one afternoon, with two of my friends and more than a hint of trepidation, I approached his modest house on West John Street, a narrow, dog-legged lane five blocks from home west of the Allegheny campus.

Smiling broadly, he greeted us at the door and showed us into the living room. We immediately realized that this wasn't going to be easy, for reasons we hadn't anticipated. There was hardly any place to sit. To call the furnishings sparse would be generous: a couch and one straight-backed chair. No curtains at the windows, no rug on the floor, no pictures on the wall. Had it been a monk's cell it could hardly have been sparer. Mother wasn't fooling when she told me how poorly clergy were paid. True, he was young and just out of seminary, but he sure had a long way to go. I couldn't help but admire how much courage it must have taken for him to invite us into his home at all, where we'd see for ourselves how little his family had.

My friends and I jammed together on the couch, struggling not to squirm too much and searching our minds for where to begin. We were not yet comfortable enough with him to indulge in the small talk that friends use to move by stages into real conversation. In a word, we were tongue-tied, and he was too inexperienced to help us. So we sat there, filling every seat in the room and smiling lamely while our minds cramped from the strain of trying to think of something, anything, to say.

His wife saved the day, if not my powers of speech, simply by entering the room. I had not seen her before, and thought her one of the most beautiful women I had ever seen. Our parents having trained us in the elements of common courtesy, including the admonition that gentlemen stand up when a lady enters the room, we all leaped to our feet. Well, okay, we struggled trying to get to our feet. It wasn't a very good couch to begin with, and with three of us posted on it like the see-no-evil monkeys, there was no way we could get up without using each other to push on. And when three boys are simultaneously the pushers and the pushees, no one goes anywhere very fast. Our awkwardness was not lost on her. She burst out in laughter and quickly excused us: "Don't get up, boys. It's so nice to have you here." And that quickly she made us extremely glad that we had come.

What does it take for a young couple to covenant together in marriage and set out to raise a family under professional conditions that promise hard work, lousy compensation, frequent moves and more than a measure of heartache? I was not yet aware that my own future lay in the ministry, and had not a clue how many appealing young women, once I adopted that goal, would express admiration for my intention but decline the opportunity to share it. My admiration for my youth minister's wife grew markedly through those years that lay yet in my future. And meeting her that day, my appreciation of him increased proportionally!

––––·•·––––

Let's face it, though, the man was a bit long on piety, and Easter provided the occasion on which it almost got the best of us all.

Easter came early that year—very early. Had the youth of the church been more attuned, we might have resisted, or suggested alternatives. But we were preoccupied with the trivia of adolescence and followed like mindless sheep.

According to gospel tradition, it wasn't even light when Jesus rose on Easter morning; therefore, our youth minister held, we should follow suit. We would hold our sunrise service at the crack of dawn. What's more, after scouting around, he determined that a low bluff overlooking Conneaut Lake, several miles west of Meadville, would be an ideal location. If he consulted an almanac to determine the precise moment of sunrise, it apparently didn't register. It was pitch black and freezing cold as we gathered at the church and piled into cars driven by parents who must have wondered what they were thinking of when they agreed to do this. Night did not ease its grip as we drove to the lake, the headlights illuminating little more than the swirl of snow blown up by the cars in front of us. When we pulled off at the bluff, we climbed out into a foot and a half of snow, fifteen-degree air and a twenty-knot wind. This was not a good thing. Beneath the shell of coats and mackinaws, most of us, especially the girls, were dressed in fine new spring clothing. Never mind the absurdity. It is well known that Easter revelers dress for the idea, not the weather.

If the sunrise on the water was supposed to move us to awe, we'd have a long wait: the lake was capped with a solid foot of ice, and the sun was so far from rising that it wasn't possible to find the eastern horizon. Heavy wool mittens helped with the frostbite, but made it doubly hard to handle the bulletins on which the service was printed and impossible to turn their pages in the wind. And for every flashlight aimed at the papers in our hands, another was shining in our eyes, immobilizing us like deer in the headlights. Jesus, I thought to myself, couldn't possibly have done it this way, not in the middle of an arctic night. Faced with these conditions, he surely would have postponed the dawning of salvation until some June sunrise. And I, for one, would have supported his decision. It was the most dismal hour I ever experienced in the name of religiosity.

Still, we knew why we had come, and proved it by completing the liturgy. The word "liturgy," as used in Christian worship, comes from a combination of two Greek words: *leos*, or people, and "*ergon*," work—literally "the work of the people," a deriva-

tion that resonated with new meaning that morning! But the urgency of our labor was driven less by the flame of piety than the dread of being found, weeks later, standing bolt upright and frozen in time like Lot's wife. I could just see the *Tribune-Republican's* headline: "Presbyterian Youth Petrified during Sunrise Vigil."

So we stood very close together; and if our songs were more chattered than sung, it was not for lack of will. Mercifully, the service ended a few degrees shy of the clotting temperature of blood, and no teenaged caravan in history ever took less time to get back on the road. It was still pitch black and we were still chilled to the bone when the cars pulled up at the church and we bolted for the door. We were scheduled to serve a pancake breakfast to people arriving for the early service—another way our youth minister thought we could serve the parish. It seemed an odd twist: frigid adolescents serving hot breakfast to adults who had only recently climbed from warm beds and had no inkling of how truly bracing a sunrise service could get.

———·•·———

It was only the first time that our youth minister's piety led me into unexpected paths. The next time was surely more appealing to my instincts: he convinced me to go to church camp.

Martin Luther derided as credulous the expectation that male priests and female housekeepers living under the same roof would remain celibate. It was, he said, like combining fire and straw and commanding them not to burn. I had not heard about Luther the first time Mother dropped me off at Camp Caladon atop the gray-shale bluffs of Lake Erie's south shore a dozen miles west of the city of Erie. But by week's end, had we been introduced, I would have counted myself a convert to his viewpoint. I learned as much about the ways of the flesh during that first year at church camp as I did about my Christian faith, and way more than I had learned up to that point in my life. Luther was right: anyone who thinks it possible to pack large numbers of beginning teenagers into lakeside cabins for a parentless week in June, and stoke their spiritual fires without fanning other flames, is hopelessly naïve.

Part of the fun was that we came not from one church but many, not from one town but from half the communities in northwestern Pennsylvania. Except for a few friends from our home congregations, we were all new to each other. And while we were well-schooled in the decorum proper to Presbyterian youth, and would escape our time together without anyone doing anything really stupid, it was open season on exploring the edges of our sexuality.

Mine, I confess, had up until then been explored largely in fantasy. In moments of reverie, or seeing a pretty girl across the room and feeling a pull so intense that it hurt, but hindered as much by my own awkwardness as the admonitions of my elders, I had only imagined what it might feel like to be in love with a girl and actually to tell her so. At church camp I found out, and learned in the finding that it was both exquisite and achingly ambivalent. I discovered that the sun-baked skin of a girl is redolent in ways far more alluring and vastly more intimate than perfume. And that the first skill I needed to master when kissing a girl was where to put my nose. I also learned that committing myself to someone like that would require me to sacrifice my freedom. It was not a commitment I could even pretend to make at the time, and I knew it almost the same moment that our tentative reaching toward one another connected me with that first girlfriend that first June at camp. My exhilaration at learning to understand my maleness because of the close proximity of her femaleness, and in doing so to appreciate both in ways I had never imagined, began to fade the instant it bloomed.

Even at the time, I appreciated that the notorious fickleness of those temporary relationships was a good thing. We met on Sunday, held hands on Monday, kissed on Tuesday. And by Thursday, I think we both realized that when we said goodbye on Saturday, we were unlikely ever to see each other again, and it would be okay. Indeed, it would be a good thing. Because while we gave each other the inexpressible enchantment of first love, we knew it was not sustainable. Though we seemed to fit together perfectly during that heady week of playing and swimming and, yes, worship, the tight clench of our fingers as we held hands was a confession that it was all very temporary, and was better so.

When a hundred family cars arrived Saturday morning and the Camp Caladon green murmured with the feeling-full farewells of new-found and never-to-be-seen-again friends, we parted quietly. But I would be forever grateful to her for lovely memories—something actual to dream about in moments of reverie, or seeing a pretty girl across the room and feeling a pull so intense that it hurt, but no longer so hindered by my own awkwardness and even less by the admonitions of my elders.

———·•·———

Something else happened to me during that week at Camp Caladon, something more subtle, more disturbing, and surely more enduring. I got called to the ministry.

Calls come in lots of ways. Some people experience a growing conviction that the ministry—or a particular place in ministry—is where they belong. Others experience a kind of "a-HA!" moment that startles them awake to the conviction that they need to change direction. Others claim that God spoke to them directly, like the war poster of Uncle Sam pointing right at you and saying, "I want you," but out loud. I'll confess to some skepticism about that last. I rather think Susan B. Anthony, who was not only a feminist but a devout Quaker, was right when she demurred, "I distrust those people who know so well what God wants them to do, because I notice it always coincides with their own desires."

For me, the voice has always spoken out of the mouth of another person, generally someone I admired, or who exhibited some semblance of wisdom, or had earned my trust by being trustworthy. I was really unprepared for it to happen at camp, though; I was mainly focused on our youth minister's promise about how much fun it would be, so that's what I went looking for. I certainly wasn't looking for anything serious to happen—like growing up or something. Which is probably why it could happen: having erected no defense, I was unprepared for the invasion of my spirit when it came.

Actually, God ganged up on me: there wasn't one voice but two. Both were parish ministers, and each possessed—I don't mean to be maudlin about it—a gift. One was able to preach in a way that generated enough electricity among that teenaged gaggle that if we all had joined hands and the last kid in line grabbed hold of a power line, we could have lit up Cleveland. The other could sit down with a self-conscious adolescent and, in less time than it takes to tell it, start a conversation at once deeper and more rewarding than I, for one, had ever experienced. Coincidentally, they were both male. Not that I wouldn't have listened thoughtfully had both been female; I was, after all, being raised by a woman, and it never occurred to me not to think of her, or of any woman, as a legitimate authority. Indeed, by that time in our house, everyone understood that while we were all created equal, one of us was created more equal than the rest of us, and she both ran the kitchen and controlled the car keys. So the hierarchy issue had long been settled.

But that was just the point. Fatherless at seven and raised in a school system where I would not meet my first male teacher until I entered high school, to be exposed simultaneously to two adult men who fired my admiration was dizzying stuff. Just to be with them was exciting.

The larger influence, because it was personal, belonged to the second man. Each cabin, housing seven or eight kids, was assigned a live-in adult mentor, and he was mine. For a week, my peers and I lived closer with that man, under more intimate conditions, than I had experienced with a grown male in my entire life. Our appreciation of him only grew as the week progressed, and it started early. Without making a lecture of it, he taught us that to know something that no one else knows lends status to those who know it.

Recognizing that teenagers value group identity, the camp director announced at dinner the first evening that each group should choose a name for its cabin and, by extension, the group. As we sat around chewing it over that evening, our mentor suggested the name "Ikhthus." Undismayed by our circle of frowns, he explained that the word is from the Greek for "fish," and was an important symbol in early church history. During the Roman persecutions, when public admission of baptism could be a death sentence, Christians hid their identity from prying eyes but revealed it to fellow believers by means of a simple symbol that resembled the silhouette of a fish. It was a powerful allusion: time and again, fish appear in symbolic ways in New Testament stories and parables, not least in Jesus' invitation to several fishermen on the shores of Galilee to leave boats and nets behind and follow him, and he would teach them to "fish for people." The symbol was also chosen, however, because the five-letter Greek rendering of the word (ΙΚΘΩΣ) forms an acronym for Jesus Christ, Son of God, Savior. The fish was not just a mark of identification but a confession of faith.

So, our mentor suggested, we could call ourselves the "Ikhthus," post the name on a sign over our cabin door, and challenge the other campers to guess its meaning. Coming years before the ubiquity of fish symbols on the rear ends of cars, his suggestion was a stroke of genius. For six days the camp struggled, and failed, to guess our secret. When we explained it on the final evening of camp, it was with a sense of group triumph, and quiet gratitude to our mentor. Not only did he make us look good, he let us take the credit. His modesty is a cogent reminder that the ability to build self-esteem among the laity, while staying personally in the background, is an important gift of professional ministry.

By the middle of the week, had he told me to swim across Lake Erie I would have thought it possible, because I trusted him.

But that trust included the conviction that he would never ask me to attempt anything remotely as foolish, because he respected me too much to play games with my life. He fully understood the difference between being a mentor and a manipulator, and how vital it is for spiritual leaders to be one and not the other—indeed, how manipulative spiritual leadership betrays both the calling and the disciple.

So, late in the week, as we lounged about in the dry and aromatic grass atop the bluff and watched the sun execute its daily illusion of sliding into Lake Erie, I could neither ignore nor disparage his gentle encouragement to think about going into the ministry. His urging was devoid of pretense: no phony piety, no hint of spiritual scalp-hunting calculated to improve his evangelical scorecard, marred his words. He had simply lived with me all week, watched me at play, listened to my spiritual groping, assessed my character (yes, even observed my too-intense relationship with the girl whose first ex-boyfriend I was about to become), and recognized in me the man searching to be born.

Now that I reflect on it, maybe it would have been easier if he *had* told me to swim across the lake! It is not entirely comfortable to be seen into as clearly or as deeply as I think he saw into me. But there was healing there, too, in having been known almost as fully as I one day would come to know myself. Because, had he not drawn attention to that in me which I needed to discern, I might have missed it altogether.

***

The heady experience of summer camp took a real knock on the head later in the year. The youth minister whom we increasingly appreciated (or would have once we got squared away regarding the climate and the hour of Easter sunrise), who had given us a year of unstinting time and labor, who encouraged me to go to camp where I would discover that physical and spiritual love are not inherently contradictory, got fired. His going matched his coming. There was no discussion, no announcement. We were simply told one day that he was gone. We never even had a chance to say goodbye.

I was not happy about it. For the first (but surely not the last) time in my life I was furious with my church's leaders—so angry that I was prepared to go before the Session and make a stink, with my friends if they would, alone if I must. Mother discouraged me with her usual clear thinking. On the one hand, she urged, you may feel hurt by what has happened. But before you unfurl your battle flags, you need to recognize that the people who made the decision are not mean or arbitrary: if he was let go there must be a reason. On the other hand, she made clear to me that if I publicly humiliated her, I would have cause to regret it. Who would not be persuaded by such compelling logic?

So I never did anything about it, and would someday add the experience to an accumulating body of evidence that injustice ignored inevitably becomes justice denied. The lesson would fester for a long time, resurfacing nearly two decades later in a ground rule I adopted and tried faithfully to employ on four college campuses: even though students may not have the authority to make a particular decision, everyone affected by it has a right to be heard before it is made.

PART V

Being Taught more than I Cared to Learn

CHAPTER 22

North Ward

T he same olfactory recall that brings my church back from
the past on some aromatic breath is able, as well, to
resurrect my school. It's curious that smell can summon memory, but memory cannot summon smell. At least for
me it is so. Just try to distill a specific aroma from some reminiscence. I can recall that someone or something possessed a distinctive scent—sweet or pungent or foul or seductive. But that is
recollection, not recovery. I am able by a kind of mental synthesis
to recollect what it *felt* like to smell my Mother's kitchen, or the
pressure building in my nose from an hour in the Presbyterian
Church, or the tang of pumping gasoline at Hart-Eiseman's Cities
Service Gas Station at the corner of North Main and Randolph.
But I cannot retrieve their corporeal cargo. And I could compose
an entire paragraph unsuccessfully trying to communicate one
of them to you.

As with my church, however, if I was blindfolded, time-warped
to Crawford County in 1943 and escorted into First District School,

I could tell you where I was before the door swung shut behind me. It was an awesome conglomeration of odors—of books so frayed they filled every sunbeam with a dancing trail of lint; jet-black school-desk ink and mucilage and bottled paste that some kids insisted on eating; slate blackboards impregnated with chalk soaked in wash water; teachers' scented with perfume and powder and rouge that revealed to the discerning nose whether the stuff had been purchased at Murphy's 5¢ & 10¢ on Chestnut Street or Horne's department store in Pittsburgh; window cleaner and floor wax and the cumulative redolence of small bodies not entirely housebroken; and enough other smells that just to list them would require the rest of this chapter.

In any contest to identify the most penetrating odor of all, the undisputed winner would be the disinfectant routinely added to the janitor's mop water, especially during winter when children were believed to be at greater risk of getting sick. I had no idea what the stuff was, and still don't; but we breathed its odor long before the chemical industry learned to mask polluting compounds with perfume. That may have been a good thing; we never fell victim to the hyperbole of labeling the stench "fresh air." If I happened into the building too soon after the janitor went down the hall, swiping his antique string mop back and forth in a specious ritual of purification, the stuff brought tears to my eyes. Even after the floors dried, the effluvium haunted our lessons for hours, potent enough to burn tender young noses and throats.

I couldn't imagine, even then, any disease virulent enough to cause greater distress than the stuff that was supposed to prevent it. Indeed, catching one of the several colds that circulated among us during any given winter was a relief. The mucous my immune system generated provided a measure of protection from the chemical pain, and the attendant loss of smell was, under the

circumstances, a blessing. Each cold generated a tad of self-righ-
teous indignation, too: if the noxious brew was supposed to protect us from communicable disease, why were we all sick? But
that logic was lost on school authorities. They continued to slosh
the deleterious stuff around with abandon, damaging generations
of mucous membranes and degrading Meadville's aggregate sense
of smell for a hundred years.

By comparison, the floor wax had the virtue of smelling good.
Each September I joined the hordes of children roaming the gleaming tile hallways searching for classrooms the locations of which
we'd forgotten over the summer, feeling as if I'd stumbled into a
house of mirrors. People, doorways, ceiling lights, colorful wall
displays, all acquired inverted twins reflected in the glint of floors
freshly stripped and waxed, except that the likenesses were distorted by rippling imperfections in the floor. The images shattered with each step up or down the hall, only to be reconsti-
tuted with the next. Had I possessed a literate mind, I might have
pondered how entirely appropriate it all was: primary school sur-
vives in my mind as a surreal experience anyway; it was fitting
that each year began like a weird dream.

The janitor's hard-won perfection faded as the weeks passed,
however. Even as additional layers of wax raised the elevation of
the floor, the incessant scuffling of prepubescent feet, like snow
tires chewing grooves in highway pavement, wore ruts into the
accumulated coats.

––––––––

In spite of its official name—First District School—those of
us growing up in Meadville at the time called it simply North
Ward. It so dominated the un-summer seasons of my youth that
it seemed a life sentence without parole. It was nothing of the

kind, of course; rather, it was more in line with the Psalmist's description of life: like yesterday when it is past or a watch in the night. Only six of my eight grade school years were spent there. Meadville's population explosion saw to that.

In the late 1930s, an influx of young families overwhelmed North Ward: too many kids, too few classrooms. No one had yet invented the temporary, free-standing buildings that were an off-shoot of World War II, when the need for instant military facilities transformed the pre-fab business from quaint curiosity to national industry. So when a flood of children washed up on Meadville's north hill late in the Depression, brick and mortar was the only solution anyone was prepared to consider. Since First District School was already as large as its site would accommodate, the logical alternative was to put a new building where the children were, and North End School was born. Several acres two blocks north of our home, the former site of a trolley turn-around, were available, and construction got under way in 1939.

It was a modest affair: a couple of offices and four class-rooms devoted to grades one through four. It accommodated only half the children of those ages who normally would have attended North Ward, but parents loved it because none of the children enrolled there had to walk more than six blocks. The building was completed during the summer of 1940, in time for my third grade year, Frank's fourth. So it reduced my North Ward life sentence to six years without time off for good behavior (of which, if the notations next to "deportment" on my report cards are any indication, there wasn't much).

Still, six of my eight primary school years were spent sitting in one North Ward room or another, so North Ward resides in memory as the prototype of "school." Even now, when I think back, or hear someone talk about the primary school in whatever

city or town they have in mind, the image of Meadville's First
District School rises out of my unconscious memory to shape my
thoughts.

It stood at the bottom of our hill, where North Main Street
flowed out onto the edge of the fertile French Creek Valley flood
plain that drew the first settlers to the site in 1778.

Boxed in on all sides by an older neighborhood of close-packed
homes and mature shade trees, the school filled most of the land
purchased for it. A thirty-foot wide lawn against Main Street, and
another twenty feet at the south end of the building by Randolph
Street, was all the open ground left, and outdoor recess was unheard of. Several homes north of the building were razed about
the time my generation progressed through school, but a separate
vocational school was erected on the site, doing nothing to re-
lieve the cheek-by-jowl feel of school and neighborhood.

It was a typical building as schools of the era go. Stuck in the
American preoccupation with architectural balance, the front door
was dead center, a precise half of the building extending right
and left respectively. Its stolid, two-story red brick construction
and pancake-flat roof were about as unimaginative as bureaucracy
could fashion. Metal-framed windows, which comprised much
of the exterior wall in each classroom, insured that we would
bake in warm weather and take a steam bath in cold. (It would be
years before I learned about saunas, but when I did, they held
little novelty for me. Enough moisture condensed on those frigid
panes on any January day to support a hydroponic garden.)

Corridors ran the length of each floor, the one on the main
floor differing from that on the second only in the short hall that
cut across its axis, connecting the front entry to the principal's
office. Don't ask me to explain why the ceramic tiles that clad the
bottom four feet of the hall walls reminded me of a zoo. I can't.

But I can say without fear of contradiction that no acoustical engineer could improve upon their capacity to channel sound. Anyone bent on disrupting classes at one end of the building needed only to slam a door at the other.

Classrooms flanked the corridors like stalls at a cattle auction, their heavy wooden doors opening, without exception, opposite the teacher's desk. Filling the middle of each room, arrayed in precise ranks and rows, were desks for "pupils"—a label I detested even as a child. It sounded like we were some species of forest-dwelling grub. Each desk was a separate unit: a bent-metal frame supported a swivel seat facing a sloped writing table, its top hinged so that it could be tilted up to access a storage bin beneath. That writing table was every child's friend; the bin it covered was the one place in school we could hide something

from the teacher and know it was secure—or so we fancied; naïveté does create a certain peace of mind.

Inside and out, those desks constituted a pass-me-down history of North Ward graffiti. Some kids never could advance to the next grade without soaking their names into their desks with a hundred coats of ink, or carving it in letters that reached halfway to the furnace room. And the true obsessives among them carved their initials *and* filled the grooves with ink, insuring that their vandalism would survive most of the millennium. Had I known which desks to look at, I could have traced the progress of a few such vandals, room to room, up through the grades and right on into high school. It was indicative of how seldom our desks were refinished that even simple ink graffiti remained vivid a decade later. The manufacturers weren't exaggerating when they labeled that stuff "permanent."

If the patina of history made each desk unique to the children who had occupied it, the rooms as a whole embodied the triumph of uniformity over creativity—an attitude nowhere so heedlessly imposed as in how students were seated. Desks, the prevailing wisdom insisted, must be positioned so that windows were to their left, insuring that small right hands holding pencils would not shade the paper being written on; but small left hands could not help but do so. By means of such rules-by-pejorative were left-handed children conditioned, through twelve years of public education, to believe that something was wrong with them or, at the very least, that they constituted a troublesome minority.

Little about North Ward's classrooms—save the size of the desks and a few pictures or instructional aids hung on the wall because they served a teacher's needs—gave much of a clue as to which age group was assigned to which. Without exception, the front of every room was the same Norman Rockwell scene: a broad oak desk with the obligatory dictionary, Holy Bible (King James Version), grading book, and similar teacher's stuff lined up neatly and held in place by institution-gray metal bookends. Off to one side stood the corner-dwelling U.S. flag, largely unheeded except at the opening of each day when we stood at attention beside our desks, right hands over our hearts, and recited the Pledge of Allegiance. It was a cookie-cutter environment for cookie-cutter education.

In the front of each room, hung above the wall-to-wall sweep of blackboard, were several long pieces of cardstock on which the alphabet was printed. In rooms assigned to the first and second grades, evenly spaced white block letters, both upper and lower case, marched along three parallel white lines against a black background (remarkably like our Lionel train track, I thought). Among each teacher's equipment was a wood-and-wire device about the size of a slice of toast, into which five pieces of chalk were clamped. When drawn across the blackboard, it inscribed the five equidistant and parallel lines of a musical staff. But with the second and fourth pieces of chalk removed, it drew three parallel lines just like those on the lettering charts, allowing both teacher and students, during board exercises, to duplicate the patterns on the chart above. To insure our dependency, we were given sheets of paper lined in the same manner.

By noon of the very first day, I understood that nothing about the form and placement of letters would be left to chance. Only letters inscribed precisely like those above the blackboard (and only after we were given permission to pick up our pencils and begin) would earn the approval of Miss Wasson, our first grade teacher. Indeed, she made the message so clear that even my five-year old brain swiftly absorbed it. (The law allowed a five-year-old to enter school provided the child would turn six by December 30th, and my December 17th birth date put me comfortably within the law—albeit uncomfortably short of my peer group.)

The shock came the day I entered my third grade room for the first time: no block letters. The black strip had given way to white (well, faded ash would be a more accurate depiction), bearing black, cursive letters. It was the opening skirmish in my war with education. I was pretty good at printing; I suppose it was a function of that artistic ability, origin unknown, that mystified Mother. Block lettering, after all, is mostly a matter of juxtaposing straight and curved lines within a defined space—a piece of cake for one with the ability I had mysteriously acquired. Wherever it originated, whether as a recessive gene left lurking in the family blood line by some unidentified progenitor, or as a genetic mutation that, like lightning, struck me but missed my sister and brothers, it was my salvation through first and second grades. Sheet after sheet of paper (the same quality of stuff that comedian Bill Cosby so perfectly described as having wood chips floating in it) were carried home with glittering stars in the corner. My venture into formal learning was off to a good start.

But not for long. At the door to third grade my confidence imploded like a jack-o-lantern left standing on the porch through a hard freeze: printing was no longer acceptable. No one explained why we spent two years conquering the printed alphabet only to be told, on the cusp of third grade, that we would never use it again. From there on, we would rigorously follow the Peterson Handwriting Method. My doom was sealed.

With a notable lack of success, I struggled to discipline my hand to assume positions and make movements as alien as walking on the ceiling. My grade in penmanship, a high B under the gentle hand of Miss Cook in second grade, plummeted to an equally solid D under the stern third grade tutelage of Miss Watters, and didn't improve in the ensuing decades. (In an impotent but personally satisfying gesture of defiance, I resumed printing the minute no one was looking over my shoulder to enforce the cursive rule, and no one ever seemed to care.)

I hasten to add, however, that comparing my second and third grade teachers in that fashion is hardly fair. Christine Cook was demonstrably one of the most beloved teachers in the history of Meadville's public schools, not only because she was a good teacher, but because of her unwavering affection for, and encouragement of, children. When reminded at retirement how many children she had taught during a career spanning four decades, she instantly editorialized, "And they were *all* good." But Ruth Watters, considerably younger so not yet a candidate for the beloved grandmother award, was no less devoted a teacher, or less moved by her desire to have us succeed. It was just that she was required to teach something my genetic fabrication was not designed to accommodate, and neither of us was able to explain why.

At the door to the third grade, without anyone realizing it, I stumbled over a hidden liability that would haunt me for the rest of my life. Indeed, no name for it had yet entered the popular vocabulary. I was dyslexic.

In the late 1930s and early '40s, this insight was a distant irrelevance. Absent a basis for informed judgment, parents and educators take refuge in common wisdom, and the sense of the time was to label it willful behavior—or misbehavior, as it pleased some adults to assume. No one suggested that I might have a learning disability. My jittery behavior and lack of discipline were simply a failure to apply myself, as my report cards charged. Even when such items as "wastes time" and "distracts other students" were checked off, no one thought to assign any cause other than attitude. I would not appreciate what was happening until thirty years too late, when the genetic markers of my disability appeared in my son. By that time, the tools needed to deal with it were more readily available; but in observing his struggle, I relived my own, able for the first time to grasp the reason for it.

This is not to fault either Mother or my teachers. Human beings can work only with the tools they know, and the insights that might have helped them to help me would not be developed for a generation. Was I then disadvantaged? That is a matter of perception. I was certainly at no disadvantage relative to every other child, in my own time or earlier, who shared an undiagnosed disability; nor was I more handicapped than my peers who labored under known disabilities that I did not share. Still, despair grew in step with stature. Some day, I thought, I will catch on; somehow I will become a good student like my sister and brothers, and earn the approval of my teachers and family. I thought of that awakening as something that would happen to me, not in me, but it never happened, and I was powerless to compel it. With every new school year and every skin-of-my-teeth promotion to a new grade, the questions of my elders taunted and burned more painfully. Like the proverbial pebble thrown into the pool, my initial failure sent ripples expanding out over the surface of my entire school experience, disrupting it all. With shrinking confidence, I began to ask the same questions of myself: Why don't I try harder? Why won't I apply myself? And the hardest question of all: What's *wrong* with me? The dumb silence with which I greeted the questions of my elders reflected the deep silence filling my brain: I had no answers for myself; how could I have any for them?

Later, in high school and college, it would dawn on me that my teachers had no help to give. That they continued to urge me to solve the problem myself was increasingly frustrating, often painful, but it was cruelty born of ignorance. Even as my work was judged wanting, it was my conduct, not my soul, that was under censure. Nothing was said or done to cause me to question that I was loved, or that my teachers cared. Their disappointment matched my own, and must have been every bit as frustrating. Had someone handed them the tools needed to help me, they would have seized them in a heartbeat. In all the years of my growing failure, from my introduction to Peterson's personally impossible handwriting method in 1941 to the day in 1953 when I had an epiphany and took command of my own life by dropping out of college, I don't recall a single teacher who quit on me. (Flunked me, yes; quit on me, no.) They were not all equally sensitive or competent, but I will not fault their ceaseless effort in the face of my nearly uniform failure.

If that seems a harsh point on which to end the recollection of my primary education, it is an accurate one. If educational achievement was the goal, I was a failure. I walked away from North Ward with little satisfaction and a palpable sense of relief, and this was only the first of four times that I would leave school feeling that way. Fortunately, there was more to the story.

CHAPTER 23

North Ward Footnote

I t should surprise no one that, to my mind, the best part of the school year was summer vacation, when Mother took us to Chautauqua Institution in southwestern New York State to wallow both in high culture run amok and in Chautauqua Lake. For Mother, it was a lifelong love affair. Her parents took her there as a child and she never wanted to leave. Later, she would realize her dream by moving there and making it home for the rest of her life. But given the economic constraints under which we lived following Dad's death, it took ingenuity and sacrifice to get there at all.

Mother didn't even let World War II gasoline rationing obstruct our going. For weeks beforehand, the family was on notice that the car would leave our basement garage for essential business only. Mother wanted the gas tank full the morning school dismissed for summer vacation.

That final school day was a subterfuge, actually: it opened with the taking of attendance and closed with the handing out of

final report cards, after which we were dismissed to the streets
for three months of delicious freedom. The whole of it barely
managed to consume twenty minutes, but by treating it as if it
really mattered, the school completed the tally of days we were
annually required to be in attendance. (I recently learned that
our grandchildren's schools employ the same artifice, and am
reassured to know that, even in a society addicted to change at
break-neck speed, some traditions endure!).

For Skinner children, however, that final-day routine was
way different than it was for our friends. Mother's intense love
of Chautauqua transformed our leaving into the kind of high-
speed getaway that a veteran bank robber would envy. The evening
before, after last-minute washing and ironing of summer clothes
was completed and overloaded suitcases had been sat upon until
their bulges were compressed to the point that the latches could
be snapped shut, all hands turned out to load the car. Under
Mother's experienced supervision, our effort put a sardine packing factory to shame. Not a cubic centimeter of trunk was left
unfilled; bed pillows and sundries were jammed into the shelf of
the back window or assembled, like a three-dimensional jigsaw
puzzle, on the front seat between driver and passenger. Sheets
and blankets were folded into precise rectangles and piled on the
back seat until the whole thing gained a foot in altitude. Boxes of
canned and dried foods were squeezed onto the back seat floor.

As dawn of The Glorious Day convened over the eastern hills,
we were up and at it, tidying up our rooms to stand vacant for
three months and helping Mother with last-minute chores. Then,
everything in readiness, we walked off to school so excited that
we were in danger of coming unstrung. When the dismissal bell
announced that the interminable twenty minutes had expired,
Mother's car sat at curbside in front of North Ward with its motor

running. I, for one, left the building with sufficient velocity that I almost made it from school door to car door without touching ground. Two minutes and two blocks later, Mother stopped at the high school to gather up whichever of us was by then old enough to be there. Her family thus reassembled, she circled the Diamond like a homing pigeon getting its bearings, turned east on North Street, and steered the straining Chevy up State Road Hill and out Pennsylvania 77 northeast toward the New York line.

I suppose that Ruth Ann's perennial claim to the front seat was another privilege of being both the eldest and the only girl, though she and Mother could hardly see each other over the stack of stuff between them. In the back seat, Cliff, Frank, and I commanded a view of uncustomary loft from our perch atop the aggregate bedding, our heads scraping the ceiling and our feet resting on the food boxes on the floor.

Even during the war years, when the national 35mph speed limit extended the duration of the sixty-five-mile trip to two hours, we still made Chautauqua, and were largely settled into

our summer quarters, by lunchtime. So complete was this annual transition that for three months we not only forgot about
school, we forgot about Meadville. It was as if we were citizens of
two cultures, and arriving in the one caused the other to vanish.

Nonetheless, the day after Labor Day each September, the
movie was run in reverse. As dependably as Canada geese rise
and bank away from northern marshes, forming up in lopsided
V's like south-flying arrows, we rose at 5:30, swallowed breakfast, packed the last items into the car, locked the cottage, and
rolled out the Chautauqua gate—Mother again at the wheel, Ruth
Ann in splendid isolation in front, and our boys' heads creasing
the ceiling. With the precision of a Swiss railroad, Mother completed the run to Meadville, pulled up to the curb in front of our
schools, and discharged us five minutes before the opening bells.
I never did figure out how she managed it, but in all the years she
pulled off that stunt, not once were we late for the first day of
school. Drat.

CHAPTER 24

Not Everything was About Book Learning

H appily for my psychic well-being in primary school, not everything was about book learning; if my struggle with the three R's was an exercise in futility, there were welcome distractions—like fire drill. Sitting in class, our first-grade hands clasped atop our desks as mandated at all times when not working on an assignment, we learned that we were about to have our first. The instructions were brief: when the alarm sounds, take nothing with you; move immediately to the door, line up, and wait; at Miss Wasson's signal, file out the door (keeping in line), and walk (do not run) to the door at the end of the building; once outside, turn up the sidewalk to the corner, stop, and wait for instructions. Now let's get to work on our lessons.

Fortunately for the progress of education, the initial drill each September was the only one announced ahead of time. There-after, they were sprung on us at the discretion of Meadville's fire chief and Miss Corry, our principal. Their secretiveness promoted learning: once subjected to the ear-splitting clangor of that bell, and told that it was going to ring again, no one could possibly learn a thing until it was over. Our fire bell, you see, was powerful enough to resurrect the dinosaurs. To an inexperienced first-grader, to be forewarned was not to be forearmed: the first time it went off it lifted my bottom clear off my seat and my tender five-year-old brain almost went into seizure. I had stood mere yards from passing steam locomotives that made less noise. Nor was I alone. The entire roomful of toddlers rose as one, as if the building was suddenly jolted by a massive earth tremor. So effective was our collective ascension that we had only to straighten our legs to start running; the rest of our anatomy was already air-borne.

The experience made quick learners of us all. Miss Wasson had explained that they wanted us out of the building as rapidly as possible. They needn't have worried. We cleared the building, well short of the fire department's time limit, on our first try. Indeed, through eight years of primary education, I don't recall that we ever required a second drill to meet it, but not for the reason normally assumed. We didn't fear burning to death; we just wanted to escape that racket as rapidly as possible. Without breaking line, of course.

———

Fifth grade brought an awakening of a different kind. I fell in love—not with one of my classmates, but with the teacher. Mary Blanchard was a local girl, the daughter of the Market House manager. (This fact assumed exaggerated importance in the way that details of my hometown always loomed larger than any from the outside world, just like those of your hometown. The Market House was important because we, and half the town, went there routinely; so he who was its manager must be a man of some consequence.) Mary was twenty-two, I suppose. When you are ten, everyone between sixteen and thirty-five appears to be about the same age. Not that it mattered. The situation was hopeless from the first morning, when I was struck senseless by the woman standing in the front of our classroom where I was accustomed to seeing... well, grandmothers. Blond and petite, with blue eyes to die for, I gazed at her and realized for the first time that mature female curves matter—in tangible ways.

By the closing bell, I was lost in a fantasy that would endure for months. I still walked up North Main Street hill with my friends that afternoon, but I hardly occupied the same world. They were walking on the ground, their feet in contact with the old slate slab sidewalks, while I floated several feet above. I never tried to explain. I could not have told them what I was feeling if my life depended upon it—and at the moment it felt as if it very well might. Besides, their laughter would have been audible in Saegertown. Fortunately, my recovery from the initial shock was rapid, else sooner or later I would have walked in front of another car, this time without my snowsuit to protect me, with who knows what result. Instead, I took refuge in an elaborate daydream that let me admit what I was feeling to myself but not to anyone else, thereby avoiding ridicule.

I can report without fear of contradiction that I recall absolutely nothing of what I did or didn't learn that year in school. I suppose I carried some knowledge away with me, else I wouldn't have survived *sixth* grade, but it appears to have been entirely subconscious. In the mental diary of my education, I am able to recall some fragment of a lesson, some specific content, from every other year of primary school; but of fifth grade I remember nothing. The entire year consists of the one consuming thought of Miss Blanchard.

If I doubt that assessment, a puzzling piece of evidence remains in my scrapbook to confirm it. Among the mementos Mother collected and pasted away for us are our report cards from first grade through high school. I can't speak for my sister and brothers, but mine are a comprehensive listing of rare achievements and frequent failures concealed among the musty pages to remind me of the need for humility. Except for fifth grade. A report card is there, but it assesses my performance for the sixth and final grading period of the year. The first five columns are as perfectly blank as my memory. The signature on the card is not that of my adored Mary Blanchard but of one Mildred Abercrombie, of whom I have not the slightest recollection. There is nothing personal in that omission. I have no reason to believe that Miss Abercrombie was not as dedicated a teacher as all the others. She was simply pushed beyond recall by my consuming fantasy.

And my grief. In March, Miss Blanchard announced that she would leave at the end of the fifth grading period to be married, and would not return. I was crushed. In fabricating my elaborate fantasy, I had left no room for anyone else. Suddenly I learned that there *was* someone else, a man who had been there the whole time and had won her affection long before I even knew she existed. I woke from my dream world to the rude realization that I was the one for whom there was no room. The report card pasted into my scrap book with five of its six columns blank is a suitable metaphor, if not an epitaph, for a wasted year. I don't even have Mary Blanchard's signature to remind me of her gentle hand.

I relate it now with tongue in cheek and a humorous backward glance at the small boy who, all unaware, started down a path of dismal discovery: that relationships are not all about ecstasy and consummation; they are freighted with self-delusion and disappointment. Had I known Mary Blanchard when I was more mature, I would not have made such a fool of myself, even if only to myself. But in making a fool of myself at ten, I learned that emotional maturity is grounded in the courage to live in the real world, not simply in fantasies of our own creating.

Then there was the School Boy Patrol, my first real-life experience with *esprit de corps:* we were trusted with the lives of other children because we had at some level convinced our elders that we were trustworthy. I still recall the pride, not to mention the shock, that welled up in me in the spring of 1945 when word came from Miss Corry's office that I would follow Cliff and Frank into the ranks of the School Boy Patrol. It was also my first exposure to a puzzling realization: my indifferent academic record did not preclude opportunities to excel in non-academic pursuits. Through all my years in education, I kept being tapped, not only by my peers but by my teachers, to carry responsibilities I would not have thought were open to me. My appointment to the School Boy Patrol was among the most hopeful gifts I received from my North Ward teachers who, though they were ill equipped to help me academically, saw abilities in me that I did not yet see in myself and moved to reinforce them. In time, their confidence in me would translate into confidence in myself, opening doors that the mediocre primary school child never anticipated.

When I entered first grade, the tall eighth-graders who shepherded us across street intersections, resplendent in gleaming white belts with sparkling silver badges pinned on diagonal shoulder straps, seemed as handsome as soldiers and as imposing as police. They were delegated considerable authority; children who lacked older siblings to orient them to this fact (definitely not my problem) quickly discovered that to disobey a patrol boy was an invitation to visit the principal. Given Miss Corry's temperament, the result was more likely terminal embarrassment than severe chastisement. But for most of us, it was motivation enough not to cross a crossing guard.

My first encounter with one launched a seven-year dream of joining the patrol, fretting the while lest I be deemed unworthy when the time came. Only half-a-dozen crossings, all of them within a couple of blocks of school, required covering, with one or two boys assigned to each. So it was a case of many being called but few chosen. At the time, the privileges and obligations seemed considerable. Patrol boys were expected to be at their posts fifteen minutes before the morning and afternoon opening bells. Children who arrived early at a guarded corner knew they were not to cross until a patrol boy arrived. And (this is the part I liked best) patrol boys were dismissed several minutes before the other children, to allow them time to reach their assigned places.

As if the school's authority was not sufficient, a Meadville police officer visited school each fall to frighten the wits out of us in an effort to ensure our cooperation. Addressing the whole school as we sat in cross-legged class clumps filling the gymnasium floor, he'd relate frightful stories about children who, though warned not to, ran into traffic and were killed. Having already tested that approach for myself, I didn't need the police to convince me.

But not everyone got the message. To this day, the mere thought of it knots my gut with the uncomprehending melancholy that overwhelmed me the morning one of my classmates was killed. Three boys had run out into the middle of a circus convoy, trying to grab onto a tailgate and swing aboard for a ride to school. Grasping for a handhold, my classmate lost his grip and fell into the street, where he was crushed under the wheels of the following truck. The police told some bloody tales in their bid to persuade us to respect traffic. I still remember some of them. But their most lurid tales had only a fraction of the persuasive power of that boy's empty desk in the third row of our classroom. The feeling intensified two days later when his desk disappeared, mute testimony to the finality of death.

For primary school children, all this was pretty intense. We yearned for the glory of wearing the white belt and silver badge, but experience taught us that this was not a trivial job. Failing to do it faithfully could result in probation or dismissal—mortifying experiences for a young ego. Worse, my failure could get a child hurt or dead, a burden I wanted desperately not to carry. Whenever I was tempted to get casual about it, the image of my classmate's empty desk emerged from my subconscious brain and snapped me back to attention.

All the preceding annual recitations of the rules, amplified by the dire warnings from those visiting policemen about the price of ignoring them, added ten pounds to the weight of the belt I buckled on the first day of eighth grade. Whatever impetus I had to honor the rules as a child pedestrian trebled under the weight of that symbol. Standing on my assigned curb as canting sunlight broke over the crowns of trees just starting to exchange summer green for the fire of autumn, I looked with dismay at the flow of children who converged at my crossing just as the morning flow of auto traffic peaked. How would I manage to keep them all straight, to get the children past the vehicles without someone getting hurt? What if I made a mistake and signaled "go" when I meant "stop," like Mother did that morning across from Alden Hall? How would I ever live it down? Visions of the *Tribune-Republican's* headline swam in front of my eyes: "School Patrol Boy's Error Sends City Toddler to Hospital; Opening Day Tragedy; Skinner Youth First in Generation to Fail Meadville's Children." Suddenly, I wasn't sure I wanted the job at all.

The anxiety was short-lived. Watching cars and children stop or go at my signal, flowing among and between each other without apparent difficulty, I quickly recovered my confidence and enthusiasm. I began to discern something about American culture that I would not be able to describe precisely for two more decades: that our society works not because our laws possess some inherent power to compel obedience—clearly they don't. It works because the overwhelming majority of us want it to work. If every traffic sign and crossing guard in the county were removed tomorrow, children and traffic would flow just about as smoothly without them as they do with them. Apprehending this fact didn't even require the whole of my first morning on the job. I wasn't really in control of anything; I was just there as a reminder, a signal to drivers and children, just in case they weren't paying all the attention they should to each other.

I doubt I need to explain what a relief that was.

And with that, my peers and I were again freed to be children ourselves. I could not otherwise have endured the intensity of that first morning. Barely five minutes into the assignment, I had broken out in a fevered sweat and shed my windbreaker so the cool September air could penetrate my shirt sleeves. When the last child passed safely across the front of the last menacing chrome grill, and I followed toward school, the air seemed suddenly chilly again and I pulled my jacket back on, covering the patches of moisture that stained my shirt and brought a shiver to my gait. But I had survived my first morning on duty, and it would never be that hard again.

Indeed, I was an old hand ere Friday signaled the arrival of the first welcome weekend, and my fellow patrol boys and I had already begun to invent the diversions by which we would entertain ourselves when traffic, either kid or car, was slow. Mostly it was conversation, the mindless banter by which children fend off boredom and pass the time when not free to go where they would and do what they want. Few of our topics were such as to cinch them in memory. Indeed, I don't recall a single conversation—a clear indication of triviality. One game we made up, however, remains as fresh as on the day we invented it.

It was the 1945-46 school year. World War II, which had seemed interminable for its horrifying events and terrible losses, had ended suddenly that summer, and the country's giddy celebration rapidly gave way to the hard business of converting back to a peacetime economy. When the war started, my friends and I were innocent fourth- graders; when it ended, we were sophisticated eighth-graders, incipient men of the world, the senior members of our school population. And we could not have been more delighted by the speed with which the automobile industry completed the transition from war footing to normalcy.

Families denied the opportunity to purchase a new car for five or six years (a span most Americans found interminable) poured into local dealerships in record numbers to buy up the new models. Larger than vehicles left over from the depression years, those first-generation, post-war cars were harbingers of consumptive excess overtaking a war-weary nation ravenous to spend. And Detroit, having attained the peak efficiency demanded by war production and obsessed with glitz, was eager to satisfy demand. Glittering with chrome, painted in never-before-imagined knock-your-eye-out two-tone color schemes, tires sporting fat white sidewalls as if automobiles wore spats, the new models rolled onto Meadville's streets and alleys and blew away our boredom like maple leaves caught up by an October wind.

For boys standing on Meadville's street corners to prevent unfortunate convergences of children and motorists, it was a dream come true. Teenaged American boys had had this thing about cars since the first horseless buggy flivered down some dirt lane and filled a neighbor's horse with abject panic. If someone had unbolted the tops of our heads and lifted them off, exhaust would have poured out, borne on the revved-up snort of an internal combustion engine. Never dawned the day when our patrol duties were so arduous that we could not carry on a contest— across the street if we were posted on opposite sides—vying to see who could first identify each car that cruised into view. We knew them all from six blocks away. "DeSoto!" one of us would shout, looking north. "Lincoln Zephyr!" the call came back, looking south. By trial and error, we learned the lot: GM's Cadillac, Buick, Oldsmobile, Pontiac and Chevrolet; Chrysler's Chrysler, DeSoto and Plymouth; Ford's Lincoln, Mercury and Ford; the single-model producers' Jeep, Hudson and Studebaker; and the new but short-lived trials: Kaiser, Fraser, and Crosley. If we didn't recognize it, it hadn't been built.

We had no idea, in those heady opening days of peace when America's industrial might, like God, seemed infinite and eternal, how ephemeral our vehicular trivia would prove to be. The age of planned obsolescence was upon us, making change for its own sake a national obsession. Neither could we foresee, nor would we have believed, that our streets and highways would soon be flooded by increasingly popular imports, manufactured in the very nations we had learned to despise as our enemies during the war so recently and dearly won. At the moment, we were on top of our school in a nation that was on top of the world, and our streets were home to new machines the likes of which humanity had never witnessed, behemoths of incomparable power and elegance.

Even as the field of entries changed, my initial inventory survived: to this day, whenever I get within sight of an antique car show, I scan the gleaming grills and sparkling hood ornaments, trace the lines of roof and fender, and hear faint echoes of an eighth-grader's triumphant shout to his friend across the street: "Chevrolet!" "Mercury!"

CHAPTER 25

Dirty Little Secret

We never admitted it to ourselves. In fact, I managed to grow from infancy to young manhood unaware that my Pennsylvania town was every bit as segregated as the steamiest hamlet in Jim Crow Alabama. And ours was not the lesser indignity. To go about our business ignoring a grinding injustice among us was as morally corrupt as acknowledging it openly—even arrogantly—while working to sustain it. Save for the improbability of a black person being lynched, there was little to distinguish the North from the South in mid-twentieth-century America. Southern segregation was enshrined in law and enforced by fear. Northern segregation was embodied in social consensus and enforced by neglect.

At home, at school, at church, we were "officially" raised to harbor no hostility toward people of any race or ethnic group. But secrets have a way of churning beneath the surface, and we inherited plenty of ideas about our own superiority. It wasn't called that. It wasn't called anything; for the most part we talked around it, but the message was still clear: we were blessed by social standing. Fast upon that self-congratulation followed an insidious bit of false logic: if by social standing, then by privilege, and if by privilege, then by entitlement—as in appropriate and deserved. "We" were where we were relative to "them" because it was in the order of things that it should be so. Thus are children conditioned to hew to a public line of tolerance and affirmation while seething internally with unarticulated notions of the subservience of those toward whom they are "tolerant."

———————

Until I entered high school, I don't recall ever having personal contact with an African-American. And when finally I did, I didn't use that term. In polite society, with which we middle-class white Christians sought always to be identified, the label of choice was "colored." The word was surely less vulgar than the obscenity "nigger," but it would be a mistake to assume that it was used out of a larger consideration for those it labeled. More likely it illustrated the subtle ability of tyranny to cloak itself in the pretense of decency.

At least "Nigger" had the virtue of transparency. No one using it was ever accused of hiding behind carefully crafted hypocrisy. The question must be put: was not our use of "colored" simply a more genteel way to deny dignity to a whole race of people? If we were ruthlessly honest, could we who so comfortably employed the word deny that its underlying purpose was to distort who those people were, to insist that they be identified as the negative of us, the "white" people, as if they were our shadow? And was it not our real purpose to strip them of substance, and by doing so to make them invisible?

Later we would have to learn to say "negro" without blushing. The word had the advantage of arising from anthropology, a clinical label for one branch of the human family as distinct from others. Even Frederick Douglass, as eloquent a critic as ever privileged our socio-political dialogue, used it with ease. But we managed to retain the lie even as we changed the label. We spoke of the Negroes and prided ourselves on this latest evidence that we were not racists; yet we never quite managed, save in academic discussion, to call ourselves—even think of ourselves—as "caucasians." We were white, and whiteness remained the reference point of worth. So we subverted negro and absorbed it into the vocabulary of domination.

Then we were hit with "black" and we almost choked on the word. Not because, as coloration, it was the logical opposite of white—and we, after all, were the ones who had insisted both on our whiteness and their oppositeness. The word troubled us because "they" chose it for themselves, and shadow people aren't supposed to have that privilege, much less to exercise it.

Were we better acquainted with history we would not have been taken so by surprise. In the early centuries of this era, Jesus' followers had adopted, and empowered with dignity, a pejorative laid sneeringly on them by people who feared and hated them; now his followers are pleased to call themselves "Christians." Americans of the Revolutionary period gleefully absconded with a sarcastic label conferred on them by British soldiers in a popular tavern song, and still we pride ourselves on being "Yankees."

In like manner, "black" had been around for generations, but had been born of the same dismissive intent as were all the other labels thought up by someone else to label people rooted in the cultures of Africa. Then lo and behold, those labeled again grasped the epithet, turned it about, burnished it up and packed it with pride. But "our kind" was not ready for it, not just because an oppressed people had grasped the initiative, but because the label they redeemed came at us in the same breath as "power," and we reacted with fear. With rich irony, people who had grasped and used power for generations feared and denounced it when it was seized by others. In our hands, power was appropriate; in theirs, it was dangerous.

The issue was finally resolved in a way that seems to make sense to anyone secure enough to think about it without fear, even if not without feeling, and "African-Americans" adopted a name for themselves that genuinely reflected not only pride but heritage. In doing so, they challenged the rest of us to find something more useful to call ourselves than "white"—a vacuous emblem that always was, and remains, devoid of meaning. That we have not yet rid ourselves of it fully is evidence, should we require it, that this nation is still a work in progress.

———

All of this is light years away from the Meadville of my childhood, but it was an essential digression. I have longed to spit out my feelings about my town and race because, coming of age, I discovered that I had grown up in a place where we prided ourselves on the pretense of liberality while carefully masking our real views behind wretched social convention. It was our dirty little secret.

African-Americans, even those born and raised in Meadville, were not welcome there. They could not buy a restaurant meal. If dusk overtook them as travelers on the outskirts of town, they could not register to stay the night in a hotel. African-American men knew they could not enter a "white" barber shop to get a trim, or women a beauty parlor to get their hair done. If they wanted to attend a movie in the Park or Academy Theaters, they were required to sit in the second balcony (I will not resurrect the outrage they endured by recording the name given that part of the theater).

In a word, African-Americans were excluded: from social engagement, from essential services, from all that made the place a town and the town a home, from everything we embraced as a benefit of growing up and living there. And I, I did not know it. Perhaps that was the intent of it all; if it was, it certainly worked. So opaque was the screen erected around these unwelcome squatters in *our* town that they simply vanished from this child's view as though they never existed.

But they were there, and I still remember the consternation and shame I felt the day I first had to confront it. I don't quite know how it came about, but there must have been a reason. Mother never drove anywhere without a reason. After we had been downtown on some errand, she drove down a disgraceful rut of a path I remember as Canal Street. It extended from the lower end of the business district southwest to French Creek.

I had not yet had opportunity to travel in the South, though I had heard allusions to how desperate living conditions there were for poor people in general, and people of color in particular. But when I finally had that opportunity, nothing I saw appalled me more than what I saw that day in my hometown. Dilapidated frame houses that had not seen a paint brush since long before I was born, that time and neglect had corrupted to ramshackle piles of boards; windows with shattered panes or sashes gone altogether, gaping vacantly like dead men's eyes; doors hanging akimbo on a single hinge, utterly useless for holding the weather at bay; porches so rotted that some had simply slumped into heaps, leaving a door four feet off the ground to be negotiated by climbing up and down an old fruit crate. And here and there, faces staring as we passed. They registered no anger at the white folks' car trying to negotiate the pot-holed track that passed for their street, not even a spark of curiosity about the dumb white kid in the passenger seat gawking out his window at their circumstance. They registered nothing at all, human eyes as vacant as the paneless windows of their wretched houses.

It was almost too much to comprehend. The sheltered privilege of our elegantly appointed North Main Street home suddenly screamed at me in accusation: how could I grow up in this town without realizing that these people are here? How could my town, or my country, tolerate human beings being left to live like this? How do they live at all? And if they have to live like this, what does that say about me and mine?

For the first time in my life, I recoiled from the tension of feeling simultaneously accountable and helpless. I did not imagine that their plight was my fault, but I sensed, even then, that if I simply ignored it, I would somehow come to share the blame. Not that I had the foggiest idea what to do. I couldn't think of a thing, and so launched on a lifetime of discomfort at seeing a wrong clearly in need of redress, but having to admit my own bankruptcy. Time and experienced mentors (people who long since had come to grips with what can and cannot be done, and—sadly—more of them in social work than in the church) eventually would help me to acquire some small capital to work with.

But that was in my future. For the time being, I was growing up never having spoken to an African-American beyond a few oblique courtesies, those wanting-in-substance remarks that we employ to avoid each other while performing the charade of meeting. There were children in their families whom I never met because we attended different grade schools, mine no less the product of Meadville's segregated housing profile than theirs. And though we shared the town's single high school, I have only fragmentary memories of them as classmates. Had most of them dropped out by then? How is it possible that, in attending a school that prided itself on athletic competitiveness, I cannot recall a single African-American student out for football or basketball, or on the cross county or track teams? I remember one African-American who sang in the chorus, non-threatening because she was a girl, reassuring because she was alone (the fact that she was there at all speaks volumes about her courage). So I grew up never knowing an African-American as a friend until my freshman year in college, when Allegheny's room assignment process randomly placed us across the hall from each other on the same dormitory floor.

I propose no great moral to this sad history, and certainly no solution. I am not wise enough for that. My life story, unlike that of Mother Theresa, is not such that the very hearing of it strikes like judgment, compelling our attention in spite of ourselves.

Nor is it my intention, in reopening an old wound, to suggest that Meadville was any worse than any other American town. It was not. The point is that it was no better. To suggest that I grew up in the Northeast—bastion of eighteenth century liberalism, birthing ground in the nineteenth of the emancipation movement—and thereby somehow escaped the poison of crabbed racial attitudes would be dishonest. True, I was spared the most virulent form of the disease, but the consequences of having contracted it at all were not nil simply because my case was mild. And while I did not enter adulthood weighted with a huge burden of distrust and suspicion, I arrived poorly equipped to address such of my responsibilities as were freighted with race, leaving me no recourse but to plunge into half a career of on-the-job training.

To put it in a word, I was cheated—not by indoctrination but by emptiness. The conspiracy of silence sustained by the culture of my town left me scrambling to find what I had missed, to fill in blanks that should not have been left void. Both my personal experience and my reading of our national two-mindedness convince me that I was not alone. Entire generations, the children of ten thousand divided and suspicion-filled towns, grew up ill equipped to do any better, and the ultimate victim was, as it always is, our commonweal.

CHAPTER 26

The Bok Tower Painting

W hile I'm at it, I might as well get the other skeleton out of the closet and confess that I was raised (at least the attempt was made to raise me) with an anti-Catholic bias. In time I would learn the distinction between Roman Catholicism as a religious communion and "catholic" in its formal sense of "universal." I would also come to the conviction that all Christians, certainly including Roman Catholics, are part of the one catholic family of Christ. But that's not what I was taught as a child. While I am as troubled by my anti-Catholic indoctrination as I am about the despicable treatment my community accorded African-Americans, at least the religious bias was spiked with humor—and a delicious bit of redeeming irony.

I can't think of a better way to introduce it than by telling a story on my sweet but naïve Grandmother McCafferty, which is not very nice because she's not here to defend herself, but the story reveals much about the America of my youth. In the late

1950s, *Life Magazine* published a series of special issues, each devoted to one of the world's great religions. While on vacation from theological seminary, I traveled to Pittsburgh to visit Grandma. As we drove to the store one day she said, "You should read the latest issue of *Life*, Don. It has a great deal in it about Christianity."

"Actually, Grandma," I replied, "the entire issue is devoted to Christianity."

"Oh no," she countered. "There's a lot in there about Catholics, too."

The naïveté of her remark startled me, but not the direction of her thinking. If the indoctrination I received at home wasn't as far off the wall, neither was it any more complimentary.

If not denigrated, Catholicism was clearly devalued by those charged with my religious training. The simple mention of it sent adult eyeballs rolling toward the ceiling, a gesture that pronounced it hopelessly inadequate and unworthy of discussion. And silence can be a powerful tool in negative indoctrination: when teaching a lie, the less said the better. Silence precludes a lot of "yes... but" questions.

Less often, I overheard uncomplimentary remarks about a priest or bishop, the negative ante tending to increase according to how far up in the church hierarchy the subject had ascended. I suppose I'm wasting words by pointing out that the most egregious slights were reserved for the Pope.

Not that the animosity was one-sided. If Meadville had not yet become an equal-opportunity community on race, it surely had on religion. Subtle insults moved in both directions, leading to one of my saddest memories about my father.

I came home from school one day somewhat agitated: several Roman Catholic classmates had asserted that I would not go

to heaven because I wasn't a Catholic. It wasn't a teasing taunt;
they were at pains to rub it in, and I could not imagine what I had
done to deserve the derision they were dishing out with such
obvious glee. I had no way of knowing, being a kid and all, that I
had done nothing. I was merely a convenient target, a handy
"outie" against whom they could stake their claims as "innies."
Young children, whose self-esteem is still fragile and close to the
surface, are easily pulled into mindless religious loathing. Even
as the incident occurred, Hitler had succeeded in turning it into a
national preoccupation. No one should be surprised that Protes-
tant-badgering was just as common a practice among my Catholic
schoolmates as was the baiting of Roman Catholic children by my
Protestant peers. After all, it dates back to the Protestant Refor-
mation of the Sixteenth Century—always, of course, in the name
of our loving God. And any religious conflict that thrives for four
hundred years is well on its way to achieving immortality.

As usual, Mother was dismissive. They don't know what
they're talking about, she urged. Just ignore them. Had she left it
at that I might not have dropped it, but I would have felt some
vindication. But she didn't stop there. She saddled me with words
that, through all the intervening years, have remained a stinging
memory. Almost as an afterthought, she added, "Your father once
said he could tell Catholics walking down the street by the vacant
look in their eyes." I wonder: had she not been preoccupied getting supper, or worrying about whether we had enough money
to get through next month, or whatever other of the often trivial,
sometimes harsh things that burdened her mind during the years
following Dad's death, would she have expressed the thought
that way? Or if she simply had weighed her words a moment
before speaking, would she have spoken them at all? She well
realized that knowing something to be true is not necessarily

grounds to speak it; just because Dad said those words was not justification to repeat them. But she did, and I wished for years that she had not.

Even at the time, when I wasn't emotionally secure enough to challenge Dad's interpretation of things, nor intellectually equipped to do so, her words made me intensely uncomfortable. For several days I went around school furtively looking into the eyes of classmates I knew to be Roman Catholic, trying to see if I, too, could discern the vacancy (hoping like crazy that they wouldn't notice!).

Maybe Dad was right; if he was, then it would at least not seem so callous to think such a thing. The experiment was a failure. I could see no vacancy—certainly nothing more pronounced than the adolescent void behind my own eyeballs. I rather thought that we shared about the same degree of obliviousness. But that wasn't the worst of it: my failure forced me, for one of the few times in my life, to fault my father's judgment in a fundamental way. And the pain of it was compounded by the fact of his death. Even if I had summoned the courage, I could no longer ask him what he meant; and even if he was disposed to answer, he no longer could. The matter was stalemated, and there was nothing to be done for it.

In due course I would encounter such remarks again, but by then I had acquired enough insight to recognize them for what they are: evidence of the age-old penchant of free-thinking Protestants to assert, all evidence to the contrary notwithstanding, that the result of parochial education is intellectual sloth. At the time, however, it would be weeks before I could look into a Roman Catholic face without worrying that the flush on my own betrayed an embarrassment I didn't want to have to explain.

———·——

But then there was the gift of the Bok Tower painting. If ever an act of generosity knocked the legs out from under religious chauvinism, this was it.

Of Meadville's two hospitals, Spencer was senior. Founded in 1864 by the Sisters of St. Joseph as an "asylum for orphans," its evolution into a hospital resulted from a failure of human technology. The 1869 wreck of a passenger train on the Atlantic and Great Western, later to become part of the Erie Railroad, overwhelmed Meadville with broken and bleeding people and no medical facility to receive them. The railroad surgeon appealed to the Sisters for aid, and the swiftness of their response jolted the townsfolk into recognizing the need for, and the benefit of having, a hospital. Operated as a religious charitable institution, it opened in 1870 as St. Joseph's Hospital under the administration of Mother Agnes Spencer. And from her name, you may surmise the rest of the story.

A decade later, in response to the medical needs of a rapidly growing county, Meadville City Hospital was founded as a public charitable institution, and soon matured into a full service hospital. Dad joined its medical staff in 1931, and his involvement in Spencer soon became inevitable: in 1935, the medical staff of City Hospital dispatched him to the Lahey Clinic in Massachusetts to be trained in the rapidly developing field of anesthesia. The opportunity being too good to pass up, Mother and Dad packed the entire family off to Boston for the summer. We returned that fall with a remarkable collection of New England memories and the only trained anesthetist in Crawford County. Since most of Meadville's physicians practiced in both hospitals, Dad was soon on call at Spencer as well as City.

The arrangement must have strained his rural Methodist preconceptions to the breaking point. Try as he might, he was unable to ignore the growing realization that the devotion of the

Sisters of St. Joseph, an ardor grounded not just in medical professionalism but in their religious vows, made a discernible difference. Before long he confessed that he preferred to hospitalize
his patients at Spencer because they received superior nursing
care—though I don't think he ever said it too loudly around City
Hospital.

And somehow, the bias he reportedly harbored toward Roman Catholicism in general must never have shown in his relationships with the nuns. They idolized him, which is why they
broke with the standing custom of the day by entering a Protestant church building to attend his funeral. It was a gesture as
elegant as an embrace, but no more touching or enduring than
the Bok Tower painting.

I never learned whether the idea originated with the woman
who painted it, or was suggested by others of her order. When
the gift was presented to Dad, it came from them all, a profound

gesture of affection and appreciation
from Roman Catholic nuns whose religion he denigrated but whose devotion he admired second to none. I
don't know that Dad ever visited
Florida's Lake Wales or heard the tumbling enchantment of Bok Tower's
magnificent carillon. Nor have we any
idea why the artist chose that particular scene, although its Gothic architectural style surely appealed to her sense
of tradition. It hardly mattered. The
tower is an inspiring structure, set in
an expansive and exquisite formal garden; and the artist was skilled enough

to capture it in both mood and detail. It is not a great painting, but it is a good and appealing one, in which the stone and gilt-filigreed tower, surrounded by its semi-tropical landscaping, stands sunlit against an aquamarine sky.

The painting obviously touched both Mother and Dad in ways for which they were not entirely prepared, or able to admit. They gave it a prominent place in the living room, proudly sharing its story with their Protestant friends and neighbors who, perhaps, were moved by it in ways that they, too, had not anticipated. I would like to think so. The painting remained there as long as we lived in Meadville, a source of pride and pleasure for our family; and when Mother sold the house and moved to Chautauqua, it was accorded a place of honor in her new living room, where it hung until her death.

We no longer reflect as often as we once did on the odd paradox implied by our ownership of that painting. Time and maturity heal many wounds. But it is clear that the nuns who gave it to Dad handed him something larger and more enduring than any token of appreciation. They offered him reconciliation—the gift that really does keep on giving and the polar opposite of the divisiveness that our community tolerated for far too long. Just as acts of anger echo from one generation to the next, so a spirit of gentleness, turned loose to blow and browse among us, engenders trust among our children's children.

CHAPTER 27

Not Your Usual
Show and Tell

With Mother working in the biology department at Allegheny, it was inevitable that I would make a pest of myself by stopping by on my way up and down North Main Street, not just to see Mother but to get underfoot of Chester Darling. If Mother fretted about my becoming a nuisance, Chester soon put her worries to rest. He was infinitely patient with Clifford Skinner's youngest, and frankly pleased with my interest in wildlife. He seemed never to be too busy to answer my questions, or to teach me about the inmates of the menagerie he kept in his back office, as mixed a bag of critters as you could hope to meet in so modest a zoo. Before long, he recruited me to assist him in their care and feeding—all but the Gila monster, a lizard both nasty and venomous.

So it developed when I was in seventh grade that he trusted me enough to let me borrow one of his animals to take to school.

We didn't have "show and tell" as such; maybe it wasn't invented yet. But we children were allowed to bring something unique to school on occasion to show to the class, and to acquire some degree of status by sharing our knowledge of it. That said, however, no one was fully prepared for the day I strode into school with a three-foot blacksnake curled around my arm, mesmerizing half the class and scaring the other half out of its collective wits.

Chester and I agreed in advance on the terms of the loan. I must first have my teacher's permission (admittedly a sensible provision: Miss Kelsay wasn't surprised by much that her charges did, but this would have been stretching the point). Then there must be a secure place for the snake to stay when I was not using it to terrif... er, educate the class. Finally, since Chester would not be there when I walked back up the hill for lunch, I was to return the snake to its cage and secure the top carefully. Those conditions agreed to, I entered his office early in the morning of the appointed day, reached into the blacksnake's cage, gripped him gently but firmly behind the head, and lifted him out of the cage.

After writhing about a few seconds, the animal simply accepted me as another tree branch to hang on, coiled around my wrist and arm, and clung there passively. That he was accustomed to being handled probably contributed to his acceptance of being dragged so unceremoniously out of his home. I don't pretend that he enjoyed it; it simply had happened often enough to convince him that fighting was a waste of energy, and snakes are nothing if not proficient at conserving energy. Little wonder. When your diet consists of a small mouse once a week, lying still the rest of the time is not just smart, it's imperative.

Whatever else may be said about that visit, it clearly was not your usual show and tell. No sooner had I retrieved the blacksnake from its temporary quarters and carried it to the front of the room than kids began to crane their necks and lean out from their desks. The braver among them even got out of their seats and edged up the aisle. For whatever reason, Miss Kelsay made no move to discourage this breakdown of North Ward discipline; before long, the whole class was knotted together in the front of the room, the more timid children keeping a respectful distance from what they presumed to be the snake's working end.

For the next few minutes, I was the expert. It was a confusing role for me; my emotions vacillated between the dread of making a fool of myself and the exhilaration of realizing that, for one of the few times in my life, I knew more about something than anyone else in the room. Recognizing their conditioned dread of a snake's bite, I pointed out that blacksnakes are not poisonous (sighs of relief), but constrictors who kill by crushing their prey in concentric coils ("Eeewh!"). Grasping the snake by both head and tail, I held it up like a yardstick so they could see its corrugated belly, explaining that a pair of the animal's numerous ribs end just inside each of the overlapping flaps. A few of the braver students reached out to stroke the belly when I then explained that snakes "walk" by progressively moving their ribs, much like the motion of waves in water.

By now I was on a roll, telling them that snakes are not, as often believed, slimy. Their skin is dry and, since they are cold blooded, cool to the touch unless they have been lying in direct sunlight, which they do to raise their body temperature, making themselves more agile. More hands, even a few from the timorous outer circle, reached in to sample the animal's temperature, nodding agreement with their heads while their eyes remained fixed on my hand, to be sure its grip on the snake's head remained firm. I explained that snake skin doesn't grow with the animal, like human skin does, but must periodically be shed: the skin splits at the head, and the snake hooks it onto a stick or rock and climbs out of it, pulling it inside out just as they might turn a mitten inside out by grabbing it at the wrist and peeling it off.

I saved the best for last. Contrary to what you've heard, I told my classmates, snakes aren't dirty. They are exceptionally clean. In fact, snakes won't crawl over some things that chickens will eat. More than one face betrayed a sudden queasiness of stomach; they wouldn't dream of handling a snake, but among them they had eaten a whole lot of chicken, and they were beginning to have second thoughts.

I hadn't learned much of what I said from Chester Darling, actually, but from two books I had read by Raymond Ditmars, curator of the New York Zoological Garden—better known by its popular name, the Bronx Zoo. (Ditmars had kept snakes since he was my age. I thought it a splendid hobby.) But Chester, who devoted his life to teaching people to appreciate the real mysteries of the natural world and dispelling lame misconceptions, would have been proud.

I was immensely satisfied with myself as I walked up North Main hill that noon, bug-eyed children—especially the youngest ones—flowing along behind me like laughing gulls trailing the wake of a Carolina shrimp boat. As I expected, Chester was gone when I pushed through the massive swinging doors into Alden Hall, but his office door was unlocked for me. No one challenged me as I let myself in, gently returned the road- weary snake to his cage, and latched the top. When I put my face to the glass to check on him, he looked at me, flicked his tongue a desultory time or two as if to say, "Enough, already," coiled up in the litter on the cage floor and, after the manner of his kind, froze.

Pulling Chester's door closed again, it didn't really occur to me, though it might have, that I had just gained another increment of trust from a man who had achieved the status of icon with my parents.

CHAPTER 28

High School

The transition from North Ward to Meadville High School was fairly seamless, actually. The subject matter was more substantial, the homework assignments more demanding. Algebra and plain geometry replaced arithmetic, American history supplanted geography, and spelling gave way to Latin. Too, there was the excitement, if anxiety, of being allowed some latitude in picking our own subjects—decisions that hinged on whether we planned to attend college or seek a job after high school. For a Skinner, there was no decision to make: college lay in our futures as surely as high school followed primary. We were on track, and quitting before we earned at least a baccalaureate degree was unthinkable, and that's all there was to it.

I was most impressed by my teachers, though it had little to do with the quality of their teaching. The difference was biological: half of them were men. Through eight years of public education, I had never had a male teacher. Now suddenly I had six. The difference was apparent the minute I met my homeroom teacher, Mr. Lehman. The sense of that first meeting is difficult to describe. It was way more than the usual hello-how-are-you introduction. Something stirred in me that I didn't understand and couldn't describe. But I felt as though it had been there all along, only asleep, and I was waiting for it to wake up. It helped immeasurably that he was, from the first day, kind and encouraging. The general science instructor, he even took me on as a kind of student assistant. Not teaching science, God help us; I was his gofer, getting equipment and supplies out of the large walk-in closet at the front of his classroom, setting things up and putting them away afterward.

I don't think for a minute that he needed my help. I suspect he recognized that letting me think he did would be of value to me. Finally I had an exemplar, someone who was more than a remembered shadow on the ceiling or a one-week idol from church camp, a man I could talk to, hang around, watch in action, and learn from. And the learning I wanted was only partly related to general science, in which I did well, in large part because of my admiration for the man. But that was just the point: I longed to understand what it might mean to be such a man, and for the first time I had someone to imitate.

I never saw Mr. Lehman after I left Meadville to begin my junior year at Mercersburg Academy, still trailing in the wake of my disgustingly smart brothers. Looking back, though, I think he must have known that each semester only diminished the odds that I would ever achieve a decent high school record. A review of my scrapbooked report cards (thanks, Mother, for reminding me!) makes clear that I survived two years of Meadville High School on the likes of drawing, shop, and chorus, where I earned A's and B's (remember, I could draw, and Skinners could build things and sing). But regarding English, civics, Latin and algebra, I invoke my Fifth Amendment right against self-incrimination.

————•+•————

As a pupil at North Ward, I had watched with quiet envy as high schoolers, on their way to and from the dark brick building that covered half a city block at the north end of the Diamond, brushed right past me as if I was invisible. Their easy manner impressed me and made me feel awkward and insecure. Their humor baffled me because I wanted to understand it enough to break out in suggestive guffaws and hearty hoots at the right reference points, but I didn't understand what the reference points were. Their failure to accept my authority when I was on School Boy Patrol duty infuriated me; worse, it made me feel impotent because there was nothing I could do about it. They moved in another orbit, as distant from mine as Jupiter's is from Earth, and I longed to enter their part of the universe. In a word, I was envious, and the cure would come only when I finally left off being a feeble eighth-grader and became a king-of-the-mountain high schooler like them.

I didn't realize, of course, how badly I was fooling myself, because I didn't anticipate that in vacating my position at the pinnacle of primary school I would plummet to the bottom of the social ladder and have to start climbing all over again. And the high schoolers had a really colorful way of demonstrating it. It was the most bizarre moment of my high school career, and occurred three months before I actually started to attend there.

One sunny morning in early June, just before school dismissed for the summer, every eighth-grader in Meadville's public schools was turned loose with the oddest set of instructions we had received in eight years of primary education: "Report to the high school; they'll tell you what to do." Equally remarkably from our point of view, we weren't chaperoned. We weren't even told to stay together. We were simply sent on our way with that single directive.

So off we went, a herd of gangly adolescents on the cusp of a global outbreak of acne, every last one of us cringing with self-consciousness. We were not impressive, hoofing our way toward the Diamond that day. Had the entire lot of us been lined up by height, with the shortest of us on the right, ninety percent of the females would have been on the left, and arguably more mature, end of the line.

If orientation was the goal, it can't have been very successful. We may actually have been told something about the building, the teachers, and the curriculum. I vaguely recall scrambling all over each other in the auditorium looking for enough unoccupied seats so that we could all sit with our own group of friends: for security's sake we didn't want to be separated. When the shuffling and shifting subsided, a few talking heads made noises at us from on stage. Surely Mr. Bender, the highly respected principal, was among them.

But it was so much water off this duck's back, because the real focus that day was not the building's floor plan or the academic program. It was our social standing. My attention was focused on what I knew was coming after the assembly, when my peers and I would be assailed by members of the rising sophomore class. These days it's called "hazing," and is increasingly frowned upon. In 1946 it was called "initiation," and no one bothered to weigh its appropriateness one way or the other. Whatever you call it, it was a mess.

Having already watched three of her children come home from initiation, Mother issued an unheard-of order at bedtime the night before: "Put on old clothes when you get up tomorrow morning. I don't want one of your good shirts ruined." She needn't have bothered. I, too, had watched Ruth Ann, Cliff, and Frank, each in their time, come home from their own introductions to high school looking like they'd stumbled onto the set of a C-grade western movie and been made up to play bit parts as Indians on the warpath. Which was the reason for Mother's directive: lipstick was the initiation cosmetic of choice.

It's impossible to say just how much Meadville's sophomoric assault troops spent on the stuff every June, but the managers of Meadville's 5¢ & 10¢ and drugstores must have been thrilled. Several hundred smirking high schoolers, lusting for revenge for their own humiliation the previous June and buying up fistfuls of fresh lipsticks, had to have a measurable impact on the town's gross domestic product. And the redder the better. Pink or vermilion would not suffice that day. It must be scarlet, the hue of fresh arterial blood, which wasn't hard to find. Shades of lipstick

were not subtle in those days; a woman who didn't look like her face had been gashed when she left home for work or a date might be accused of forgetting her make-up. Thus indelibly equipped, the sophomores were the artists, and we no-count, pathetic, despicable incoming freshmen were the canvas. And did they paint. Not a boy or girl escaped the building without being aggressed upon by an indeterminate number of sophomores, their eyes crazed with power.

I was prepared for the painting, and knew not to try to wipe it off: that generation of lipstick was as durable as axle grease, and casual attempts to get rid of it would simply smear it onto some other part of my anatomy. I walked home—gingerly—where Mother, keeping vigil, had laid out the necessary cosmetic supplies to help me undo the mess, though in the final analysis it would just have to wear off. Every eighth-grader in town finished primary school flush with the afterglow of this initiation, as if we'd stayed out in the sun too long on the first hot day of summer.

What I wasn't prepared for was the smell. No two lipsticks wielded by our tormentors had the same bouquet, and they didn't blend well. It was like mixing rose and lavender and getting skunk cabbage. As I walked up North Main hill that day in company with my equally smeared and aromatic friends, adults chuckled at us or shook their heads and rolled their eyes knowingly as we passed on the street. For my part, I couldn't help thinking that I must smell like a French... well, never mind. While a definitive term, it's not a very dignified one.

Gym, which had been my least favorite activity in grade school, took on a happier tone in high school, largely because there were locker rooms. At North Ward, gym meant going to a cavernous room at the south end of the building in which, I swear, the heat wasn't turned on from one winter to the next, to play some kind of hard-running game in our street clothes. The only thing we changed was our shoes. That varnished floor could never withstand the kind of hard-soled shodding most children wore to school, especially in the winter. (My clodhoppers—ankle-high leather boxes with soles as thick as a tire and comparable tread, but with nail heads poking out of them—would have taken the finish off that floor faster than a commercial sander.) Beyond changing into our canvas tennis shoes, we played in whatever we had worn to school. By the end of the period, I felt like I had gone swimming in my clothes, and the two hours following were an exercise in clamminess and itch. Not to make too much of a point of it, I despised gym even more than spelling class, so you know how bad it was.

I confess that carrying everything I needed for high school gym class to school was a challenge. I didn't own a gym bag, so I rolled everything into my towel, forming a tight bundle that I clamped under my arm. But the thing was the size of a log, and constantly threatened to fall apart and spill its contents on the floor or sidewalk. Which would be more than simply inconvenient; it could be acutely embarrassing, because my first-ever, brand new jockstrap was rolled into the innermost fold of the bundle, and I just knew that if the roll disassembled itself in public, that item would be the first thing to hit the floor and I'd be the brunt of mortifying jokes. I worried in vain; it never happened, demonstrating again how anxiety usually exacts a greater toll than reality.

Reporting to the locker room the day of my first gym class, I changed into my gym clothes—pausing before the mirror to admire the impact of my new jockstrap on my masculinity, which was not noteworthy—then joined the other boys thundering up the stairs like stampeding cattle. I tore into the gym feeling like I'd just been released from jail. And—oh euphoria—we would get to take a shower afterward.

I didn't always care for the activities, actually—especially when the call was wrestling ("All right, boys, pick your partners") and before I could decide who in this crowd I was willing to get that intimate with, some bully whose knuckles dragged on the floor had tagged me and said, "I get you!" There was no way to win. But I developed a perverse determination not to lose, which turned out to be almost as good. I never could claim an actual victory, but moral victory could be had in denying some over-sized gorilla a win at my expense. Under such circumstances, I concluded, a draw was worth the pounding it took to earn it. So I won a lot of moral victories and had the bruises to prove it.

Except for one delicious turnabout that may have surprised me more than anyone. I stifled a groan when Mr. Ditty announced that the activity of the day was instant death basketball. I was not good at basketball; and harboring the frail ego common to my age and station, I hated going out on the floor with guys who never witnessed a blunder they didn't like so long as it was committed by someone else, or let one pass without loud and sarcastic expressions of appreciation. But it was gym class, and there was nothing to do but to get out there and hope I could save myself from embarrassment by handling the ball as little as possible.

Mr. Ditty lined us up in a long row and ordered a count-off by fives. It was a wise move, without which the best players would have chosen each other and the rest of us would have been hamburger. The teams thus selected—as opposed to organized, which is a whole different thing—the first two teams took the floor. Under instant death rules, the first team to get a basket stayed on the floor while the vanquished returned to the bench and another team went out to challenge the winners. Mr. Ditty's count-off system worked: the teams were so well matched that no group managed to stay on the floor for more than a couple of challenges.

So it went, until my team took to the floor the second time (we lost our first foray in about eight seconds). Had our group consisted of good players, my strategy never to handle the ball would have required little effort; no good player would pass it to me anyway. But we were, by the luck of the draw, a mediocre lot, and before I could avert my eyes to prove how truly inattentive I was being, the ball came hurtling at my gut. I had either to catch it, fumble it away and endure the derisive catcalls from the bench, or get the wind knocked out of me. I caught it. Now what? I tried in vain to find someone to pass to, but my no-better-than-me teammates were too well guarded. I was on my own.

By that point in my life I had adopted some of the obnoxious conceit that boys employ when they have grown to think of themselves as failures. It was my shield against the pain of ridicule. It also tempted me to acts of cockiness that felt good at the moment but did nothing for my social standing. Hardly thinking about it, I looked the boy guarding me in the eye, then glanced up at the basket as if I intended to shoot. Having positioned myself as far from the basket as I could without seeming to have left the game entirely (part of my avoid-the-ball ploy), I had no *intention* of shooting. I just wanted to get rid of the ball, if someone would just get in range. Then in a heartbeat everything changed: several members of the other team observed my ruse and yelled derisively, "Let him shoot! Let him shoot!"

I can remember few times when my blood came to a boil that fast. Tension slammed the brakes on time and everything decelerated to slow motion. The kid in front of me dropped his arms and stepped back to give me a clear view to miss. To a boy, his teammates grinned gleefully and dropped their guards while mine froze, mouths agape. There I was, on the verge of making a total fool of myself, but I felt more relaxed than at almost any time in my life. It was as if absolutely nothing mattered. Looking at the basket again, I shifted the ball more comfortably in my hand.

"Why not?" I thought. "We're gonna lose anyway."

Opposition grins widened; despair clouded the faces of my teammates. Bending down until the ball almost touched the floor,

I cocked both arms and let go a high, arching shot with stuff behind it that I didn't even know I had. Through an interminable fragment of time the ball rose, almost striking one of the caged lights suspended from the battleship-gray ceiling trusses, arched over, and plummeted toward the backboard. Through it all, not a breath was taken, not a heart beat, not an eye left the soaring ball.

In the nanosecond before the roar of dismay from the opposition and the cheers of my team, mingled with admiring hoots of approval from the sidelines—most probably cries of disbelief—I heard the enchanted spit of a ball plunging through the net without touching the rim and striking the floor like a gunshot.

It was, in the annals of Meadville High School athletics, a moment of consummate insignificance. But I will savor it to my dying day. When your athletic triumphs are as limited as mine, you take 'em where you can get 'em.

CHAPTER 29

Friday Night

Right off, Meadville High School taught me why Friday night is the best night of the week—a lesson erected on the twin pillars of dancing and football.

Thanks to Mother's usual candor and to the kindness of my gang, I learned a bit about dancing several years before high school. The year most of my gang turned 13, Marion Shryock invited us to her home for a dance party in her family's rec room. I badly wanted to go, but was clueless what to do when I got there.

"How do you learn to dance?" I asked Mother nervously.

"You just get a girl and go out on the floor and do it," she replied.

It didn't seem like very helpful advice at the time, but it worked. Once I screwed up my courage—a far easier thing with a dozen friends than in a public dance hall or the school gym—I quickly discovered how much fun dancing was. My learning curve went flat as quickly as it started to ascend, however; I didn't get another opportunity to dance until I entered high school. And even if I had, there was still the uncertainty factor: I couldn't figure out why any girl would want to do it with *me*. It didn't help that I was younger than every girl in my class except Sue Hawkey—she whose mother shared conversations with mine across the hall of Old Mat. When we were in the second grade, friends teased that Sue was my girlfriend, or that I was her boyfriend, or whatever. But Sue had continued to attend North Ward during my two-year exile to North End School, and by the time I returned, even she seemed "older." How was I to know that girls mature earlier than boys, or that they would stay out there ahead of me somewhere until I was about twenty-five, by which time twenty-six would seem about as far off as next door? But when I was fourteen and mired in the Swamp of Self-Doubt, fifteen was a light year away.

Beside, there was my complexion. In an age when neither the cause nor cure of acne was understood, it was assumed to be the great egalitarian affliction, universal, gender neutral, and unavoidable. Not so. We might all have had to fight, but some of us were sent into battle with inferior armor. The best description I ever heard of my own epidermal eruption came a generation later when one of my stepsons described a peer as looking as if his face had caught fire and someone stamped it out wearing track shoes.

I explain this not because I felt sorry for myself (which I did). I want credit for myself and for every other teenager who, in spite of personal humiliation, had the courage to step onto a high school dance floor—indeed, to simply walk out the door to attend the dance in the first place.

The opportunity to get beyond all that came in the wake of World War II when someone (I never knew who) concluded that Meadville's youth needed some place to hang out on Friday evenings, and word went out that the Armory, on the west side of the Diamond, would be open for dancing. The sole chaperone was Rosie, a motorcycle policeman posted at the door where we paid a weekly admission fee of 10¢. Rosie was a bruiser who had earned the respect of Meadville's youth by being both tough and fair. His mere presence was sufficient to insure that public order would remain undisturbed (which may have been the whole point: it was difficult to avoid the suspicion that the whole enterprise was meant to benefit the town more than its youth). As for maneuvering on the dance floor, we were on our own.

For the first time in my life, I was allowed to take off with my friends after supper and didn't have to be home until 11:00 p.m. How could it possibly get better than that?

Still, the fruits of my new-found liberty were slow to ripen. The first evening was largely spent among male peers who circled the dance floor like a flock of vultures, terrified by the very idea of actually approaching a girl and asking her to dance. And given the social conventions of the day, the male who failed to take the initiative was stuck with the vultures. It was as close to do-or-die as most of us ever would have to endure.

Had my hormone-fevered brain been capable of absorbing it, I might have taken comfort in the realization that whenever I found the courage to ask girls to dance with me, none ever refused. That should have taught me something. I saw more than one boy turned down, his frail ego brought down like one of Pymatuning's mallards in duck season, shot right out of the air and not likely to recover soon. So I can't have been a total pariah.

In the meantime, it may have been a good thing that overcoming gender anxiety was so difficult. I was, after all, treading the edge of perilous ground, where the time it takes to cross from wisdom to foolishness has to be measured with a stopwatch, but the consequences can endure for a lifetime. One ought to be fearful in the presence of transcendent things. For me, shyness was a shield against stupidity, a counterbalance to urges that I was old enough to feel but not yet old enough to use wisely.

But let's be candid about this: when I did work up enough courage to ask a few girls to dance, any dread I had about the future evaporated: my train had left the station and I was on board. What was curious is how it happened: while I was unnerved by the thought of asking girls my own age to dance, I was less apprehensive about approaching older girls whom I knew to be kind, even to an awkward freshman. So there I was, gliding around the dance floor (well, okay, plodding would be a more accurate depiction) with junior and senior girls about whom I could not possibly entertain romantic delusions. I was out there because I longed to acquire some measure of social finesse; they were out there with me because they were sweet girls. And because we understood the ground rules, we were free to enjoy ourselves. I have never forgotten their kindness. Every awkward pimply-faced adolescent male should be so lucky.

————•+•————

At the same time I was gaining dancing credentials, I moved from a grade school with no athletic program to a high school saturated with letter jackets, school spirit, pep rallies, and sports heroes. And by far the most seductive event of all was Friday night football. The season got off the ground the first week of school, and I was there for every game.

Gabbing my way out North Street with my friends, anonymous shadows swerving in and out among the flow of other anonymous shadows, our words were measured by street lamps in tumbling puffs of breath that fluttered in the frosty air and evaporated—a mocking metaphor of the importance of our dialogue. Up ahead, the vapor of other fast-talking folk, blended with the smoke of a thousand cigarettes, was visible from three blocks

away. It swept over the stadium wall, borne aloft on the escaping
wattage of a dozen banks of floodlights that encircled the field.
At two blocks, the voice of the crowd and blare of the band became a steady din, the first punctuated by laughter, the second
by the rhythmic chirr of the snares and boom of the bass. One
block away, we could recognize faces as they moved from the
shadow of the wall and turned into one of the gates as if walking
up a ramp of light. By that time, we couldn't contain ourselves
any longer, and broke into a dead run lest we miss one more
second of the excitement.

Threading our way, we moved awkwardly along the rows,
trampling an indeterminate number of toes, until we found
enough open seats for us to sit together. The filling of a stadium, as even casual observers know, begins at the fifty-yard
line and spreads toward the opposing goal posts. It never was a
question of finding seats, only of how far down the yard markers we would have to go to find them. Not allowed out of our
houses until we had eaten our dinners and helped our mothers
with the cleanup, and having then to walk about as far as anyone in town to get to the stadium, we were usually consigned to
the 20-yard marker. But that was okay, because we weren't really focused on the games anyway.

It's not clear whether the boys on the field, who trained
hard and played harder, ever realized how little attention their
peers in the stands actually paid to their labors. We were too
busy paying attention to each other, preoccupied with the intricate choreography of adolescents jostling for position. The back
and forth surging of the color-clad teams on the field was nothing compared to the relentless turmoil in the stands, which was
overseen by no referees and took no times out.

As to the playing on the field, we took our cues from adults
who, long since having outgrown the need to preen and posture

for their peers, were actually there to see the game. When they groaned in dismay at a fumbled ball or opposition touchdown, we moaned in unison. When they shouted their disapproval of a referee's call, we bellowed our protest. When they rose in a resounding cheer, we jumped to our feet and roared in support. But as to the play in the stands, we took our cues from no one but ourselves and the inner urgings that drove us. We were, at one and the same time, school-spirited and independent, dependable and inattentive. Only teenagers get away with that.

So we greeted the arrival of the Bulldogs on the field—resplendent in red and black, honed for action and spoiling for a brawl—with exuberant abandon. They were our team, the best high school team in the whole country, or at least in the conference. And we knew it. Well, okay, we hoped it. Did it matter? Not really. They were there for us to believe in, and we believed even as we paid little heed. They gave us something to shout about and to be proud of, to make us think, even if only for a couple of hours on a Friday night, that our town and our high school mattered. It never was about football. It was about self-esteem and belonging.

─────·•·─────

Which is why, by the end of that fall of my freshman year, I determined that I would join in. Play football? Are you crazy? Mother never would have permitted it. Perhaps she was influenced by having watched her husband as he worked the sidelines at Allegheny's home games, tending to the injured on both teams: she was sensible to how a single instant on the field could alter a young man's life for the whole of it, and she didn't like the odds. But even if that were not the case, no member of a family possessing our educational goals and my grades was going to be allowed to get sidetracked by the grinding requirements of interscholastic training and play. I would tread the gridiron, but as a member of the band.

Well, after a manner of speaking. Recall that I was the Skinner who never quite mastered a musical instrument. I had, by that time, begun to gain control over the clarinet that Rudy Bosch gave me. But I never got so good that I could play the kind of music the band played while keeping track of its collective feet, turning in the right direction at each blast of the drum major's whistle, and ending up were they were supposed to get. I might have resumed my bass drum studies, figuring that going boom boom wouldn't prevent me from getting to the right place at the right time, but the job was already taken, and the school owned only one bass drum.

Which left the flag.

The fall of my sophomore year, I reported to the field to fill what seemed like a made-to-order niche. I got to be somebody, and to march with the band—clear out in front, in fact, ahead of the high-stepping drum major and the gorgeous drum majorettes who twirled their batons so fast they disappeared and threw them halfway to the floodlights and caught them again, still spinning, without missing a beat. I had to attend practice only when the band moved to the field to drill for each week's halftime show. And I got to wear one of the gawky uniforms with tight black pants with a red stripe down the seams, and a red straightjacket with white piping, and a round black hat so hard it felt like a Shaker cheese box, with a red pompon on top. I somehow imagined I would look terrific. But when I got it home and stood in front of the mirror, I saw a total nincompoop, and wanted to turn in the uniform and resign from the band.

It would not do. I had absorbed the family dictum that a commitment is a commitment and, once made, must be fulfilled except for the most compelling of reasons, and feeling like a simpleton was not compelling enough. I'd soon discover the solution: if in doubt, don't volunteer. Besides, there was still the gratification that came from being out there under the lights, performing before the steaming audience in company with fifty other kids, each of whom looked every bit as much the imbecile as I did. Let's hear it for the comfort that company affords misery.

And then there was the singular moment that made it all worthwhile. Every game began with the same well-rehearsed ritual that was repeated on who knows how many thousands of Friday night high school football fields. It began in Atlantic coast communities and was passed across time zones, like a baton between runners, to the Midwest and then the mountain states and finally to the Pacific, as hometown crowds, even the adolescents among them, stopped babbling and milling about, stood at rapt attention, faced the flag with hats and hands over their hearts, and sang their national anthem. And I was holding the flag. Proud and erect as a young tree planted where my feet met the ground, mindful for one moment of a larger importance that was undiminished by my stupid uniform and my fragile masculinity, I got to hold high the single banner that was permitted to remain aloft during that dedicatory moment, while all lesser colors were lowered in respect. I had been pledging allegiance to the flag of the United States of America and to the republic for which it stands all my life, but it was when I picked it up and carried it before the people of my hometown that its meaning really began to sink into my skull, and the importance of my birth and citizenship came home to me.

I only carried the flag for one year. By the next football season I had left Meadville to attend Mercersburg Academy, where I was delighted to find the bass drum position open for the asking.

But one year was enough. Besides, some other young person needed to have the opportunity, as I had, to find out just how thrilling it is to carry the quintessential symbol of our citizenship in front of the hometown crowd. I guarantee that whoever took the job the next year, and the next and the next, was never the same afterward.

PART VI

War

CHAPTER 30

A Long and Dreadful Effort

Figuring out what it might mean that the world was at war came slowly to my three-year-old mind; but like a saltwater tide, it came inexorably. Cliff and Lowell Thomas delivered my first lesson. It was 1935 and, per tradition, we had driven to Pittsburgh to spend Christmas at the home of our grandparents McCafferty, where "Lowell Thomas and the News" followed dinner as dependably as light dessert and dilute coffee. The previous October, in one of the most cowardly acts in a decade of villainy, Italy had invaded Ethiopia. Italy was armed with the weapons of twentieth-century warfare. Ethiopia was armed suitably for the twelfth century. Tanks and bombers make short work of horsemen.

On the evening of my tutorial, Thomas was reporting on the progress of Italy's machine guns in the face of determined resistance by naked men armed with spears and grass shields. Three-year-olds poorly understand these confrontations to begin with, least of all their huge injustice. But I had heard of Italy before, never Ethiopia; and wanting to seem involved, I cheered at the report.

For starters, it was an egregious breach of protocol. When Ernest McCafferty sat in his mohair chair, bald head canted toward the tinny speaker that pinched Thomas' sonorous tones as thin as baling wire, peeping children risked a severe reprimand per peep. Granddaddy's reprimanding powers were not to be taken lightly; that he used them sparingly only added to the punch when he did. My ill-advised hooray hadn't even cleared my lips before I knew I was embarrassing myself. But it wasn't Granddaddy who chastised me. He seemed hardly to notice. It was Cliff who, in a whisper that felt like a smack up alongside the head, let me know that I was cheering for the wrong side. I didn't know what I was talking about, he hissed, and needed to shut up. It was a painful first lesson in enemy identification. I soon enough learned who our allies were and who our enemies; but I also learned that I'd better ask before shooting off my mouth.

The growing awareness that followed on that rude beginning expanded with frightful speed as it became clear that the world had fallen over a precipice. Listening to the news was not as customary at home as it was at the McCaffertys'. Mother didn't want supper disturbed, and if her children were to hear reports of violence, she wanted the opportunity to temper them with a hopeful interpretation. It was indicative of the growing seriousness of things that we began more often to listen to the radio during dinner, to learn of the day's developments that, during the early months of the war, seemed unswervingly negative. Hitler's Germany was making one nation after another its victim *du jour* while Japan, already years into the rape of China, was exploding across Southeast Asia and the Pacific, and there seemed no way to stop either one.

The full force of it did not strike many Americans until Germany's invasion of Poland in September 1939, after which Hitler turned back to hammer Western Europe. With the fall of France and the Netherlands, and the frightfully narrow escape of British forces during the evacuation from Dunkirk, all that stood between us and chaos was tiny Britain. It finally dawned on us that diplomacy had failed because the Axis powers intended that it should, and we faced a long and dreadful effort.

What was left of America's internal debate about "getting involved in another European war" was blown to oblivion by Japanese bombs and torpedoes at Pearl Harbor. President Roosevelt's enraged description of December 7, 1941 as a day that will live in infamy made sure that it would be the first and most enduring war date seared into my generation's collective memory. Any likelihood that I would forget was erased by a song composed (overnight, it seemed) in the wake of the attack, and taught to America's school children, we North End inmates among them:

> Let's remember Pearl Harbor as we go to meet the foe;
> Let's remember Pearl Harbor as we did the Alamo.

The last vestige of uncertainty flew off on wings of militant song; we were at war and President Roosevelt made it clear that it would take the effort of every American, including America's children, to win.

———————

We were not at war against Germany and Japan. Our enemies were "Nazis" and "Japs"—labels dripping with enough venom to insure our willingness to destroy them and their way of life utterly, lest they destroy us and ours first. The whole affair could not help but confuse. My brief life had been ingrained with notions of decency and caring. Human beings are good at heart, I was taught, worthy of respect. Abuse of others—indeed of any living thing—was unacceptable. Now, suddenly, I was told that whole nations had proven themselves to be vicious and despicable, deserving of annihilation, and it was not simply acceptable to view them in that light, it was essential.

Ironically, the primary aids in teaching us to hate were comic books, which can't have been much to Mother's liking. She considered them trash, not to mention a waste of the money of which there was none to spare. But they certainly spoke directly to my immature mind. Nothing in comic books was ambiguous. Good and evil were portrayed in absolute terms: we were good, they were evil. Our guys, courageous boys nurtured in the spirit of unsupervised sandlot sports, fought fair; their guys cheated. Our boys killed because war forced them to; theirs killed because they loved to. In combat, our men were gritty and determined—they might be fearful, but never cowardly and ever courageous; their men's faces were contorted with malignant rage, bred to loathing of everything decent. When our guys captured theirs, they disarmed and carried them to the hospital if wounded, or confined them to the stockade if not; when their guys captured ours, they tortured them, shot them in the back, and mutilated their bodies. And we bought it all. It was an early and distressing lesson in how swiftly malice corrupts the human heart.

Mother never said so—at least not to us—but she was clearly grateful that her sons were too young for the draft. She could hardly be blamed for that. Not everyone was so fortunate, and apprehension spread over our town like the angel of death over Egypt on the night of Passover, stealing the firstborn of a generation. I recall none of the exuberant parades like those mounted to see the boys off to Europe during World War I. Baptized in the fire of that cataclysm, we were a sadder and wiser nation in 1941. We already knew that war is horrible, and that our losses would be too. Who could cheer for that? So in pairs and small groups, sometimes as brothers taken together, Meadville boys, and later girls, slipped silently away to war. And one by one their departures were announced by the appearance of small service flags with white fields bordered in red, embossed with a blue star for each member of the family in service. One by one they appeared in the windows of doors and front rooms until it seemed like half the homes in town lived on the edge of dread, a troubling reminder that the real cost of the conflict would not be tallied by the number of bombs and tanks manufactured or by shortages of food and fuel, but in the lives of the nation's youth. And later, when a star here or there changed from blue to gold, we knew that some one of our townsfolk would not come home again.

———————

Nowhere was the exodus more evident than from the Allegheny campus, where the concentration of draft-aged men made their departure more baldly obvious than in the community at large. One cluster of Allegheny students made history before the draft even got off the ground: a photograph of half a dozen fraternity brothers clustered about the radio in the Phi Delta Theta house made the cover of *Life* magazine. The caption claimed they were listening to a report of the Pearl Harbor attack, sensing that their college days were about to come to an abrupt halt. It was a subterfuge, actually, posed by a photographer a day after the attack. It didn't matter. The picture's somber tone faithfully recorded the consternation then spreading over college campuses across the nation.

In one of the fastest transitions in history, Allegheny changed from a coeducational school to a women's college in a single semester: virtually the entire male population, including most of the younger male faculty members, vanished by spring.

It didn't stay that way long. Stripped of half its students, the college was in immediate and serious straits. It was no more recovered from the Great Depression than were the families upon whose tuition payments it depended, and faced the prospect of having to close its doors. The trustees took little time accepting a request to house a basic training unit of the U. S. Army Air Corps. Insofar as possible, the college withdrew to the west side of campus, leaving the east side to the Air Corps. Overnight, North Main Street became something of a Mason-Dixon Line. Recognizing both the college's need to satisfy the anxiety of parents about the security of their daughters and the Army's need to maintain military discipline, authorities agreed on a strict separation: soldiers and coeds alike were prohibited from crossing the street to hobnob in the other's camp. Knowing how determined young people can be when inflamed by raging hormones, severe penalties were promised to any offender who violated the rule: military discipline if a soldier, suspension from the college if a student.

Still, both college and Corps were sensitive to the importance of social contact among young people who know they might not live to celebrate their next birthday, and a system of sanctioned opportunity was agreed upon: every few weeks, the dean of women and the commanding Air Corps officer jointly announced a Saturday night dance in the gymnasium. Those were some affairs: spit and polish for the airmen, formal gowns for the women, a live band—and a full cadre of officers and faculty chaperons strategically positioned about the gym and nearby campus.

By such cooperative enterprise, the college served its country and its women students survived the war.

———•·—·———

Allegheny wasn't the only school where things changed rapidly after Pearl Harbor. Before the children of Meadville's schools had any inkling of what war might mean, we got our first lesson in survival. Had not the Pearl Harbor attack occurred just before the start of Christmas vacation, the lesson probably would have come earlier. As it was, we launched right into it when school resumed in January.

Having just spent two weeks happily forgetting the routine, we struggled out of snowsuits and galoshes, shoved them into the overstuffed and aromatic coat closet, and rustled about trying to remember what we were supposed to do. Finally settled into our seats, we waited for Miss Chapman to announce the first lesson. Would it be spelling, arithmetic, geography? (What is the routine, anyway?)

"Today, children, we're going to begin with an air raid drill."

Whatever that was, it didn't sound good. Wasn't the thing that happened at Pearl Harbor an "air raid?" And if it was, why was our school having a drill for one?

An air raid drill, we quickly discerned, differed from a fire drill in one fundamental regard: a fire drill required us to file out of the building as rapidly as possible; during an air raid drill, however, we would stay inside, packed as closely together as possible in the center of the building. As many of us as fit would go to the basement, while the rest sat against the walls in the center of the main corridor, as far from doors and windows as space allowed. I hoped for the hall. I'd been to the basement. It was a murky place, lit by huge naked bulbs the light from which seldom got past the ranks of pipes lining the ceiling, and what did escape the pipes was swallowed by dank concrete walls. I was a child of the out-of-doors, accustomed to playing year-round under the open sky; while I had no particular anxiety about going into that basement when there was reason, the idea of having a bomb land on our building and dying down there like a chipmunk trapped in its hole didn't appeal to me in the slightest. I preferred to take my chances in the hall, where I could at least see daylight seeping in at the ends of the building.

Air raid drills held another anxiety that fire drills lacked. If the school caught fire and we all had to run out of the building, we'd get to enjoy the spectacle of the sparkling red and chrome trucks laboring loudly up North Main Street, sirens shrieking and red lights flashing ecstatically. We never tired of that. And even if the building burned down, we'd all go home after it was over and wait to be told when and where to report for school thereafter. But if there really was an air raid, and even if no bombs hit our school, what would I do if I walked home afterward and home wasn't there, and the stores and banks and factories were blown-out shells and I couldn't find Mother, and I went wandering around in the debris with no one to notice or take care of me? And with thoughts like those, how were we supposed to think about spelling and arithmetic anyway?

It sure was a crummy way to start school.

CHAPTER 31

Victory Garden

W e never had a victory garden, but we may have been the only family in the neighborhood that didn't. It wasn't for lack of patriotism. It was just that Mother's unswerving commitment to take us to Chautauqua every summer made it impractical. The object was for each household, by raising part of its own food, to reduce its demand on the nation's commercial production and free it up for the war effort. Families would plant and tend their *own* vegetables, and whatever was not needed for fresh table use could be preserved for the ensuing winter.

We'd been doing that last part for years, and more consistently than any of our friends that I ever was aware of. It wasn't just for the economic saving, though that surely added to the utility of it, especially after Dad's death. We did it because both Mother and Dad had been raised in families that had canned and preserved their own food for generations, and they saw no reason to discontinue the custom.

Gardening in our neighborhood was a collective enterprise. Much of the block across Hamilton Avenue from our house had not been built on; while part of it was rough and wooded, an acre of ground cornered by Hamilton and Jefferson Streets was open meadow, ideal for such a project. Adding to its appeal, it was an open, sunny spot, while most of the back yards in neighborhoods like ours were shaded by mature trees—a poor environment in which to raise corn and cabbage. The effort got under way in late spring when a farmer appeared with his tractor and began to plow and harrow the meadow. He made quick work if it, too: it took him little more time to prepare the ground than it did to get his motorized beast to our neighborhood in the first place. The newly turned earth was soon marked off into plots of several hundred square feet, and each family wanting to participate staked their claim to one of the plots. From then on, they were on their own to smooth and rake the soil, mark rows, plant seed, and fertilize, weed, and water their gardens.

The land was quick to betray lazy or inexperienced gardeners. Given the location of the garden plots, watering was out of question for most families unless they rounded up about five hundred feet of hose, which none appeared to be interested in doing. A few laboriously carted buckets of water from home to dribble on their seedlings; but after the plants were established, most simply trusted the wind to suck moisture off Ohio's humid plains and blow it over into Crawford County, which in the main proved to be sufficient. Things got off to a strong start as seed sprouted to rows of young green and reached for the sun, driven by genetically inbred determination.

How well each family would succeed in this enterprise, or not, became evident when the first weeds appeared. In some plots, by simply sticking its top out of the soil, a weed imposed its own death sentence; few survived until sundown. More relaxed gardeners hoed their rows often enough to keep the weeds generally, if not entirely, at bay. But a couple of the gardens disappeared beneath a stand of volunteer herbage so dense that, within a few weeks, it was no longer possible to tell where the rows had been. If those gardens produced a single vegetable, no one likely benefited by it; just locating it required more work than it was worth. By the second year of the war, such families had given up. They weren't cut out to be farmers and they knew it. One summer of weeds was enough.

For those who stayed in the neighborhood through the war year summers, tending their victory garden plots, the maturing of their crops was so subtle they hardly noticed. For us who left just as the lots were being seeded and returned about the time most gardeners were harvesting the last of their produce, it was a night-to-day transformation. The first rays of the early June sun splashed across raked-over soil, casting no more shadow than what was contributed by seed packets posted on small sticks at the end of each row. When the resumption of school brought us home from Chautauqua and we looked out across Hamilton Avenue that first evening, the beams of the setting sun were snagged on golden-dry heads of corn and huge clumps of overgrown tomatoes, and

ground mist floated among well-worked rows of beans and me-
andering tendrils of squash. It looked like the land had risen a
foot in elevation for each month we were away; and we knew,
just by looking, whose garden had contributed most to the war
effort. Had he the time and inclination to visit—and I am confident that he had neither—President Roosevelt would have been
gratified with the result of Meadville's labor.

But should anyone wonder whether the children of our
neighborhood abandoned the primal rituals of small-town American life just because a war was on, let it be noted that enough
squishy, rotting tomatoes were still to be found among the abandoned victory gardens in late October to insure that the demons
of Halloween were amply supplied with ammunition for mis-
chief-making.

And that's probably all I should say on that subject.

————•••————

Though we never had a Victory Garden, we children did participate in another assignment designed to benefit the war effort. It was perhaps the oddest assignment we were ever given.
Mother delivered the charge: we were to go out and gather kapok.

"Gather what?" we asked.

"Kapok," she replied. "It comes from milkweed. It's the fluffy
stuff fastened to the seeds that makes them blow around in the
wind."

"Oh, milkweed. Sure. Why do they need it?"

"To make life preservers. Kapok floats, so they use it to make
life preservers so sailors won't drown if their ships are sunk."

"Sure," we said eagerly. "Uh... how do we do it?"

It wasn't really kapok, of course. The real stuff grew on silk
cotton trees in Malaysia. But we knew nothing of that, or that
the supply had been cut off by Japan's occupation of the Malay

Peninsula, or even that in searching for an alternative, some genius had discovered that milkweed produces a workable substi-
tute. Indeed, there was a lot that we didn't know. But it didn't
matter. The nation needed Meadville's milkweed and we were
ready to help deliver it.

Mother was ready too. She never could bring herself to throw
away mesh onion bags after we'd emptied them, sure that they
would be useful sometime, if not this year then next. And see,
she was right! Equipping each of us with a mesh bag, she took us
to a field off Park Avenue Extension half a mile north of home,
introduced us to a milkweed plant, and turned us loose. There
was milkweed all over the place. The trick was to get to it before
the wind did. Once the three-inch seed pods dried and burst open,
expelling their fluff into the air like paratroopers trailing out the
hatch of a plane, recapturing it would be like trying to corral the
wind. But we were in luck: the government's appeal had gone
out just before the pods had fully matured, and few had split
open. Flailing my way through the undergrowth of brush and
weeds, some of it as tall as I was, I moved from plant to plant,
tearing off the pods and stuffing them into my mesh bag. I could
hear my sister and brothers thrashing away nearby, even though
I could see them only part of the time in that jungle of overgrown
meadow. It didn't take long. Within half an hour we were on our
way home with bags crammed.

The experience confirmed an observation that I'd heard
somewhere—that a weed is simply a plant for which human beings haven't yet found a use. If that is so, then the hunt-and-
gather operation conducted by America's children all over the
Northeast that fall constituted the stamp of approval that transformed the humble milkweed from noxious invader into productive crop. That wasn't something we were privileged to do just
any day.

How many sailors' lives were saved, I wonder, because no one had yet discovered the method by which to eradicate milkweed from our meadows and pastures? And if someone had, what would we have done then?

On the other hand, the thought that we'd done a real service that day was blown away faster than milkweed seed on the squalls of November when we were told that our four bags of milkweed would yield about enough fake kapok to make one half of a life preserver—for a small sailor. I was left hoping that a whole lot of other children were out roaming around in other fields, stuffing milkweed pods into their mothers' empty onion bags.

I needn't have worried. They were out in droves, of which Cliff was our resident participant. As soon as he was old enough, Cliff joined Troop 6, Boy Scouts of America, which held its meetings, at what seemed an elevation of about a thousand feet, in the attic of Stone Methodist Church down on the Diamond. Frank and I would join later, when we came of age; but at the kapok moment, Cliff was our Boy Scout. So he answered the call when the scoutmaster, a gentle chemistry professor from Allegheny named Harold State, issued the call. The next Saturday morning, the entire troop piled into cars and drove several miles out North Main Street to Woodcock Township, where they collected enough ripe and explosive milkweed pods to fill several car trunks.

Meadville's children took an awful lot of milkweed seed off the land that year; and since milkweed is an annual—depending on this year's seed to germinate and grow the next generation—one might wonder whether the following year's crop wasn't severely diminished. Not noticeably, as any Pennsylvanian who knew milkweed from Monday could have assured you. If every child in the state had gone out that fall and gathered every milkweed pod they could lay hands on, it would have made little difference. It is not without purpose that Nature is profligate in these things.

CHAPTER 32

President Roosevelt
Recruited Me

I t wasn't long before President Roosevelt recruited me. I
don't understand how he managed it. I am reasonably sure
that, lounging around the Oval Office, his aristocratic cigarette holder clenched in his teeth, he never turned to Harry
Hopkins to say, "We need to get wahd to Donnie Skinnuh up in
Pennsylvania about his paht in the wah effaht." Nor is it likely
that he would have called on me even if he knew me; to the best
of my knowledge and belief, every adult on both sides of my family voted for his opponent in four consecutive presidential elec-
tions. Yet somehow, through the network of departments and
agencies and boards that are the working sinews of the body politic, the message reached me: the president needed my help to
win this war. It was the advent of my appreciation of the presi-
dency as the symbolic heart of our nation.

My assignments, I learned, were three: to be a selective consumer—or better, a non-consumer; to help fund the war effort;
and to collect junk.

There were other duties, of course, like keeping my mouth
shut about when ships would sail for the European or Pacific theaters loaded with troops or supplies. But that required no effort
on my part. I had no inkling what ships were leaving for anywhere; nor did I ever observe someone lurking about school during recess who just might be a Nazi spy hoping to overhear some
loose remark from me. No matter. The very thought of that mer-
chant mariner pointing accusingly from the war poster as both
he and his torpedoed vessel slipped beneath frigid North Atlantic waves—"Because **You** Talked"—was enough to keep me quiet.
I was grateful that such knowledge was beyond my ken, giving
me no secrets to betray.

The other duties the president assigned me, I would faithfully execute.

Millions of American housewives signed the Consumer's
Victory Pledge: "As a consumer, in the total defense of democracy, I will... buy carefully. I will take good care of the things I
have. I will waste nothing." I don't know whether Mother ever
signed it, but it was hardly necessary; in her case the pledge was
redundant. Among McCaffertys and Skinners, the compulsion to
conserve was congenital.

The most powerful inducement to conserve was the lack of
supply, though even that had its curious side. We were, for example, limited to about half a pound of sugar per person per
week. I couldn't even imagine consuming that much, except
maybe during fall canning season when a cup of sugar routinely

accompanied the fruit into every quart canning jar and another was stirred into each cup of fruit to make preserves. Nor did the absence of whiskey or cigarettes, as distilleries converted to producing industrial alcohol and Lucky Strike Green went to War, have any impact in our abstemious household. I suppose we might have eaten too much meat, but meat was scarce on the best of days, and when it was available, Mother could seldom afford much at the inflated cost that even the Price Stabilization Board could not entirely suppress. And even having the money was of no help if, when some nice pork chops or a beef roast were found, we had used up our allotment of ration stamps—enough for about a pound and a half of meat per person per week—issued by one of the innumerable alphabet-soup bureaucracies set up by the government to regulate consumer behavior.

But like I said, keeping our consumption down required no change of behavior. Mother hadn't wasted enough food in her entire life to sustain a squirrel for a week, I'll admit we missed the butter. But for the sake of the war effort, we made do with the fantastical invention that American agricultural ingenuity had provided to see the nation through: oleomargarine. Okay, so the industry was in its infancy and the stuff was white and looked like a pound of lard in a cellophane bag. We children were not discouraged. Help was on the way. In response to a public outcry for something that at least *looked* like butter, a small capsule of yellow dye was soon packaged inside each bag, giving us something new and novel to fight over: "I get to squeeze it!"

"No you don't. I got it first!"

"MUH-ther, you said I could do it this time!"

How I loved it when I was the chosen one. Gripping the bag, I poked my thumb into the dye capsule until it burst open. It fascinated me because the concentrated dye was red, and who ever heard of red butter? But as the squeeze and knead of my small hands warmed the bag, softening the fatty contents, it squished back and forth more easily, spreading and absorbing the streaks and swirls of dye until at last the whole goopy mess took on the uniform yellow of butter. And when it was thoroughly mixed, Mother let me take scissors, cut the end of the bag open and squeeze the contents into a bowl as if emptying an entire giant-family-economy-size tube of toothpaste in a single squish. (That required supervision: Mother had scant tolerance for oleo-margarine squirted across her kitchen counter and up the wall.) As a final step, the bowl was put in the icebox until the stuff cooled and hardened. When at last it assumed the consistency of fresh chilled butter, the bowl was put on the dinner table and we dug our knives into it and let a glob melt on a hot roll or a pile of mashed potatoes and popped it into our eager mouths, and it tasted almost exactly like... lard.

But we had the satisfaction of knowing that all the delicious butter we *weren't* eating was going overseas to feed our boys in the service. I never could figure out how that worked. The trip from dairy to front line had to take weeks. How could butter go through all that and not end up tasting almost exactly like... oleo-margarine?

Conserving gasoline wasn't hard for me either. I had no way to burn it except maybe by pouring some into an old tuna can and throwing a lit match at it—a practice that Mother discouraged. Our lawn mower required neither gas nor oil to operate, only boy power. We didn't own a second car, and the one we owned had been conserving fuel forever because of Mother's steadfast refusal to drive anywhere that she personally had no desire to go. To top it all off, the classification system the government devised to ration gasoline consumption on the home front restricted families like ours to three gallons a week, which would propel our Chevy sedan about fifty miles. Even in Meadville, where nothing was very far out of our way, it didn't take many trips around town before the car was running on fumes. Clinching the matter, the strictly enforced national "victory speed limit" of 35mph, announced early and maintained for the duration of the war, insured that most of the civilian population would drive not only seldom but slow.

And because of it all, the nation was guaranteed a plentiful supply of food to feed our troops and fuel to feed our tanks and airplanes; and we'd use them to hammer the Axis powers into submission and make them regret that they ever started the war.

———·—·———

It was fortunate for the nation that financing the war did not depend on my allowance, or even those of my sister and brothers combined. Still, my young mind began to wrap itself around the realization of what a truly national effort can achieve. Each week on the appointed day, I carried to school whatever money I had saved and stood in line to buy a few War Savings Stamps. Uniformly drab in color and design and printed on paper so thin we could see through it, the stamps nonetheless equaled in face value whatever cash I laid on the table. Tucking the stamps into my breast pocket (hoping they wouldn't get damp and glue themselves to my shirt en route), I carried them home to paste into my War Savings Stamp booklet—another task for which I showed only marginal facility. Getting the tiny stamps straight on the page ranked right up there with coloring inside the lines.

Each page, properly filled, was worth a dollar. A hundred 1¢ stamps filled a page, but ten 10¢ stamps accomplished the same goal. And a single $1.00 stamp, pasted in splendid isolation in the center of the page, was best of all. Except that I never had a dollar because my whole week's allowance was fifty cents. Just looking at a book revealed which denomination of stamps made up the bulk of its value. Completed books holding $1.00 stamps were thin, their pages as soft and pliable as fresh newsprint. The lesser the value of the stamps, the fatter and stiffer the books became. My books, their pages layered with 1¢ stamps, looked like dime novels that had been dropped into the bath water and dried on the radiator.

But that did nothing to diminish my pride when, a book completed, I walked with Mother into the First National Bank and stood with barely contained excitement as the clerk checked each rigid and water-stained page to insure that it held the required value. Finally satisfied, he handed me a crisp, new United States Series E War Savings Bond. It cost $17.50, but in only seven and a half years its value would swell to $25.00—an entire year's allowance in one piece of paper. I couldn't know that by the time the bonds matured I'd be twice as old and the money would be worth half as much. That was still saving power, and the fact that I accomplished it by giving President Roosevelt part of my allowance to help fight the war only recharged my patriotic fervor.

I wonder if anyone truly knows how much wealth came into the federal war chest as pennies and dimes carried to school by America's children. Or what ever became of all those petrified stamp books.

———————

Then there was junk. Of all the things World War II demanded of the American people, this required the greatest change of behavior. Even Mother had to reconsider her philosophy about waste—one that not only possessed her but that she bred into her children: if some article might again prove useful, even if only remotely, it was saved; but when no use for it could be imagined, nothing delighted her more than getting rid of it. The incinerator, the trash man, and the Salvation Army ranked among her cherished institutions. And if all else failed, there was always the ravine at the bottom of Ben Avon Street, three blocks from home.

Everything you can imagine—and some that you'd rather not—had been thrown down the bank of that ravine in the years since Meadville's northern-most hill was settled. We called it "the dump," a notion left over from the time when America's families were mostly poor and agrarian and everything was used and re-used until it disintegrated, and when no more use could be gotten out of it, it went into some ravine or the outhouse pit. (Few Americans realize that abandoned outhouses are often rich archeological quarries—or care to.) Such thrift regained popularity during the Depression years. Still, America was well on its way to becoming a society that cherished excess and thrived on waste. By the time World War II broke upon us, Ben Avon's ravine was littered with two decades of debris that earlier generations of Americans never even owned, much less discarded.

Overnight, the war changed all that. Such stuff was no longer trash; it was raw material for the war effort. Newspapers weren't to be thrown out or burned, but piled into bundles, tied with twine, and set aside for collection along with flattened boxes and worn out clothing, curtains, sheets, and bedspreads. I was stunned to learn that my tattered pajamas could be used in the manufacture of artillery shells (now *there's* a potent image for a young boy's imagination!). Glass jars and tin cans weren't thrown in the trash where their residue acquired an awesome stench; they were washed and saved, their ends cut out and put inside before mashing the things flat—a made-to-order assignment for small feet gleeful at the opportunity legitimately to stomp loudly on just about anything. (Could Hitler or Tojo have anticipated that the feet of American children would prove so frightful an enemy?) Men changing the oil in their cars no longer poured it down the garage drain or onto a vacant lot, but turned it in to be re-refined. Worn-out tires were hauled out from behind garages (where they mostly served as mosquito maternity wards) to be donated for their reusable rubber. And every scrap of iron, steel and aluminum suddenly acquired value.

In such a climate, it soon dawned on my friends and me that all that debris festooning the ravine was a gold mine begging for exploitation. So one Saturday, equipped with crates and trash cans and a creaky wheel barrow, we descended into the abyss and spent a morning discovering how rapidly trees and weeds grow up through rusty bedsprings or bent bicycle frames, and how hard it is to extricate them thereafter. Nor had we anticipated how quickly things fall apart when given back to nature. Still, we clawed

through enough detritus to emerge with half a dozen containers of cans and bottles and sufficient iron to fill a small truck.

Over the weeks we waited impatiently for the announcement: Scrap Drive next Tuesday! Could anything delight the hearts of children more than knowing that classes would be delayed just so we could display patriotic zeal by dragging carloads of junk to *school*? We came eagerly, bearing boxes of cans and bottles, bundles of newspapers, old radiators, dead tires, sash weights, broken hoes and shovels and rusty car wheels. It was better than a circus parade because it was uniquely our own creation—a procession the likes of which none of us ever imagined or would likely see again. In a single morning, the children of North Ward hauled more than a ton of raw material from home to school and donated it to Uncle Sam with cheers and laughter. Against the overwhelming demands of the war, it didn't seem like much, but our teachers reminded us that we weren't the only ones doing it. In Meadville alone, the children of five other schools were filling their schoolyards with junk, too. And all across Pennsylvania and the rest of the nation, from Maine to California, tens of thousands of other schoolyards were receiving the castoffs of everyday life, soon to be forged by America's industrial genius into tools of war with which to defeat the enemy. As I dumped my box-load onto the growing pile and stood aside to watch as my contribution was buried by others, grinning and cheering with my school mates at the novelty of it all, I began to sense that we were not just a school that day, or a town or even a state. We were a country united in our cause, willing to sacrifice for what we believed in, determined to prevail. Any lingering doubts about our own safety, or our ultimate victory, got thrown onto the scrap pile that day with the rest of the junk. We were going to be okay, and that's all that mattered.

Of all the changes the war visited on Meadville, two infect my childhood memory as the most strange: construction of the Keystone Ordnance Works and blackouts.

South of Meadville, atop a broad plateau west of French Creek (another of Mrs. Dunham's surrounding hills), an industrial plant appeared out of nowhere and began to produce high explosives. To most Meadville folk, the presence of the plant itself made little difference. We knew it was there, but that was about all. Its impact on the town's population, however, was something else: almost overnight our numbers swelled from fourteen to eighteen thousand. That sounds modest enough to someone accustomed to life in an urban center, but it forced the town to absorb a thirty-percent population increase in a matter of months. The housing impact alone was enormous, and pressure on every other community service—schools, hospitals, police and fire departments—inevitably followed.

It never occurred to me as a child that the plant might make my town a target. After the war, when passions had cooled and the uncertainties were subjected to hindsight, we would realize that the body of the country never was in great danger. The oceans that divided us geographically from our principal enemies were formidable barriers. No aircraft of the time was capable of flying such distances, and our enemies lacked the naval capacity to get within striking range sufficient to do any real damage.

German U-Boats did sink cargo ships within sight of the east coast, and the Japanese mounted a harebrained scheme to suspend bombs under balloons and release them from submarines off the west coast. Borne over land by prevailing winds, they were supposed to fall to the ground where they would ignite forest fires and otherwise terrorize the populace. Most of them dropped into the Pacific, and four members of an Oregon family, killed when they found one of the contraptions lying beside a coastal trail and it exploded, were the sole casualties of the whole inept venture. Without dismissing the tragic nature of these episodes, it still must be said that, measured against the scope of global struggle, they were trivial distractions that had no impact on the

final outcome. But we didn't know any of that in the early months
of the war, when the nation's security wasn't a sure thing and
preparations had to be made for what seemed like real enough
threats.

Without ever using that sort of language, Mother went out
of her way to reassure us that the enemy could not reach us and
we were in no danger. Evidence of loss that greeted us at every
turn—gold stars on service flags, accounts published in the *Tri-
bune- Republican* or broadcast from the breakfast nook radio, and
dramatic news reels shown in every movie theater—never translated into anxiety about our personal safety. Nor were my friends
any more alarmed than I was. If the parents of Meadville could
not protect their older sons and daughters from the outrages of
war, they succeeded in reassuring their younger children that our
homes were secure.

Because my young mind absorbed that view of things to the
point of conviction, I viewed air raid drills as slightly ridiculous,
even as Civil Defense officials were taking them seriously. When,
some evening after darkness filled the valley, the siren atop the
central fire station raised its mournful voice in a sustained wail,
our town vanished. Street lamps and traffic lights went off, cars
pulled over to the curb and extinguished their headlights, stores
and gas stations and industrial plants on twenty-four-hour shift
went dark. In our homes, we were given the choice of turning
off the lights or equipping our windows with blackout curtains—
ugly black things that prevented even a shard of light from escaping to inform enemy aircraft of our presence. Unable to afford the curtains, Mother decreed that we would sit in darkness.

Air raid wardens—neighborhood volunteers crowned with
leftover World War I dishpan helmets painted white—shadowed

their way along murky streets to enforce the blackout. One way or another, the gloom must be total. Only when Meadville's Civil Defense team was satisfied did the siren signal all clear, and the valley's sparkle reignited as quickly as it had been extinguished.

I suppose it was a useful exercise, just in case an enemy bomber somehow managed to defy the laws of physics to fly halfway around the world but couldn't identify a more appealing objective, like Pittsburgh's steel mills or Akron's tire plants. And even if our ordnance plant was targeted, it wasn't a sure thing that it would take the hit, that some errant enemy aviator wouldn't obliterate the Market House or the Mercer Street Bridge instead. And then what would we do?

But we cooperated for a less tangible, more compelling reason, one that most adults must have understood and even we kids began to fathom, if imperfectly: that global war is an all-consuming enterprise. We were learning that our country's psychological response was as vital as the munitions we produced, because each sustained the other. If we went half-heartedly about the whole sorry business, there was a real chance that we'd lose, and we had no intention of losing. Our effort must be unequivocal and unwavering. Every one of us had a part to play, even if it was no more than closing the blackout curtains or sitting in the dark for a few minutes, knowing perfectly well that we were in no real danger. Because a lot of Americans were, and while our commitment was about hard work and doing without and the disruption of routine, theirs was being played out in a life and death struggle that could, at any instant, demand their supreme sacrifice. It was the least we owed each other; but it was absolutely the least we owed them.

The best day of all, the day on which we could begin to put it all behind us, came in 1945 when word burst from radios and sent people hurtling into the streets, rushing from house to house shouting the thank-God news that the war was over.

It is perhaps a measure of the nation's unwavering focus that we still, today, hear people say that World War II lasted five years. In fact, measured from Japan's attack on Pearl Harbor in December 1941 to its surrender in August 1945, America's combat role lasted three years and nine months. We can be forgiven for the exaggeration. When our young people are dying and national life centers on the single-minded, grit-toothed task of losing as few of them as humanly possible, forty-five months is forever.

The very best thing we could say about the war—maybe the only truly good thing we *could* say about it—was that it ended.

PART VII

A Year of Seasons

CHAPTER 33

Playhouse

Among Dad's carpentry projects, none engaged his skill more, or made such a hit with us kids, as the playhouse he built for us in the back yard. Built near the top of a fan-shaped concrete ramp that led from the driveway into the garage where my P-51 crashed into the water softener, the playhouse hugged the back property line. A one-room frame structure, it was a perfect replica of a New England colonial cottage: centered, Z-frame plank door flanked by matching windows; a single window on each end and one in the back; white clapboard siding and a cedar shake roof. The windows worked, but Dad imposed no other detail that would throttle a child's fancy. That was the beauty of it: by the simple press of imagination it became settler's cabin, fort, home or hospital. We had only to agree among ourselves what we wanted it to be on a given day to accomplish the transformation.

Ruth Ann thought the playhouse was her personal possession. We boys never fully conceded her title to the place, but her superior size forced us to cooperate, at least until the onset of adolescence shifted her interests elsewhere. Being youngest, Frank and I were at first assigned the responsibility to do whatever we were told, which was all right at the time. In my three-year-old view of things, Ruth Ann at eight and Cliff at six were "big" people; not as big as Mother and Dad or my Sunday School teacher or the baby sitter (authority figures all), but big enough, in the absence of adults, to issue orders about how things should be done, and therefore to be trusted. I supposed she knew about things. I was only a learner. But what I learned wasn't always what I wanted to know.

The most vivid illustration occurred the summer that Dad took the family to Boston to study anesthesia at the Lahey Clinic. Sent outside with customary instructions about putting our imaginations to work so Mother could tidy up our rental home, we took Ruth Ann's lead and began to play house. As usual, she was the mother. However, Cliff was not in this case the father; in a rare instance of type-casting, he played his everyday role as oldest brother, while Frank and I remained stuck in our accustomed parts as subjects of motherly management. And the motherly concern at the moment was that our faces were dirty. This would never do. Even at that tender age, we had been indoctrinated (one wants to say inoculated) with the adage about cleanliness being next to godliness. The phrase never appears in scripture, but it had acquired the status of gospel among Protestants, for whom soap and water were nearly as sacramental as bread and wi... um, sorry about that, bread and grape juice. The reasoning was, "Well, even if scripture didn't say it, it should have!" What the maxim clearly didn't provide, however, was how-to guidance for an eight-year-old mother.

Ruth Ann wasn't wanting in motivation or technique, but in her knowledge of botany. She had not inherited our parents' love

of the biological sciences, in consequence of which her male siblings—as ignorant as she—were sitting ducks. Searching about
among the underbrush for something suitable with which to wash
our faces, Ruth Ann chanced upon some small plants close to the
ground, amply supplied with compound leaves with finely toothed
edges and a slightly glossy surface. Grabbing a fistful, she me-
thodically and meticulously washed our faces with poison ivy.

Next morning, Mother awoke to discover her sons
transmogrified into a pack of newborn rats—pink, puffy and eye-
less. She quickly recognized the tell-tale rash that streaked our
faces, and could trace Ruth Ann's well-meaning scrub marks as
clearly as if she had used paint. Oh, we were a sight to behold,
and a splendid object lesson on the wages of ignorance. The
scratching and whining that went on for the next week must
surely have caused Mother to wonder whether she should have
remained a teacher after all.

———

Fortunately, our playhouse ventures did not generally end
up so badly. Activities were largely gender-oriented. If the girls
got there first, domestic economics were the order of the day,
and brooms, bandages, and teapots were much in evidence. We
boys, on the other hand, leaned toward violence. The world was,
after all, at war during much of my childhood; there were battles
to be fought, victories to be won, enemies to be vanquished. And
even when we couldn't find volunteers to play Germans or Japanese, there were sheriffs' posses to organize and bad guys to run
down and bring to justice.

I always knew how to dress the part, though some substitutions were necessary. Blue jeans, for example, were not on
Mother's list of essential clothing for her children (nor had they
yet acquired the status of a national icon), but a pair of worn

corduroys served nicely—the ones with frayed cuffs and a hole
in the right knee. A plaid flannel shirt was always suitable, over
which I pulled one of Dad's discarded vests, making me one of
history's few cowboys to wear pinstripe. A red bandanna tied
about my neck and turned backward covered my face to ward off
trail dust or, if iniquity was afoot, shield my identity. An old straw
garden hat, its side brims curled up, perched on my head. Finally,
I coiled a length of Mother's clothesline into my belt and strapped
on my handy six-shooter.

Every boy in the neighborhood had a six-shooter, though
they were not uniformly engi-
neered. Only the lucky among us
had "automatics" that advanced the
brick-red roll of explosive paper caps
each time the trigger was pulled, and
as fast as it could be pulled. No gunfighter who ever rode trail between
Abilene and Albuquerque commanded that kind of firepower. At
each squeeze, the gun popped like a
small firecracker and burped a puff
of blue-gray smoke. And it could go

on for fifty pops at a time without even having to be reloaded,
filling the air with the bewitching reek of the 4th of July.

My pistol was not one of them. Mother did not like guns,
rapid-fire or otherwise, and wasn't about to spend more than
absolutely necessary to acquire toy ones for her sons; so the dinky
facsimile, strapped to my hip in its pressed-paper holster that
practically melted every time it rained, put me at a serious disadvantage. I had to tear my rolls of caps into individual squares and
load them one at a time, being careful to ensure that the tiny

black spot of gunpowder was precisely centered, or I'd pay for my carelessness come time to slap leather. No frustration beset this cowboy like pulling the trigger of my single shot Red Ryder pistol only to hear the hammer clack metallically, and impotently, against the chamber. Before I could re-cock the weapon and stuff a fresh cap into the slot, Ronnie Wolff, whose dad owned a hardware store so he always had the best, would round the corner with his automatic and put me in boot hill.

This was not a good thing, because I didn't have boots. I had tennis shoes, with white rubber soles and canvas uppers and red rubber circles glued on the sides over my ankle bones. They looked about as much like cowboy boots as our Chevy sedan looked like C.G. Mercatoris' Lincoln Continental. Things got even more ridiculous when we played during cold weather and I had to wear my clodhoppers, which resembled pointy-toed cowboy boots less than they did Monongahela River coal barges. And the older I got, the bigger they got. Someone once observed that if we Skinner boys didn't have so much turned under for feet, we'd all be seven feet tall. Imagine being a single mother to three teenaged boys who wore size twelve to thirteen shoes. Just keeping us shod took a dreadful toll on the family budget. Long before I was old enough to lose interest in playing cowboy, I looked like Gene Autry in combat boots.

Being reliant upon inferior equipment had its beneficial consequence, however: I learned that smarts go a long way toward neutralizing superior firepower, and I became a very wary cowboy. When on the defensive, I learned to use such protection as the playhouse offered by skittering about the floor like a crab, keeping my head below the window sills and denying my attackers a target. And when we switched sides and I joined the sheriff's posse, deputized to sneak up on the outlaws holed up in their

Connecticut colonial hideaway, I learned to ghost my way along the edge of the ravine, circle the century-old white oak at the corner of the driveway ramp, and snake through the shrubs with such stealth that my single-shot six-shooter was through the window before the miscreants even knew I was in the territory.

It's not that I had a passion to become a great gunfighter; I just detested the thought of being buried in Clodhopper Hill.

----·--

The play house fell into disuse as we grew older and were drawn toward more mature pursuits. The paint on the windows blanched from forest green to faded peel, and the white clapboarding weathered to a murky gray. I'm not sure what long-term plan Dad had in mind when he built it, but the more we outgrew our childish innocence, the more the playhouse became a garden shed. The old rusted wheelbarrow took up residence in one corner, and the floorboards in another were branded with concentric rings left by the old push mower's companion oil can. A growing array of hand tools, lacquered with a patina of grass and leaves and dirt, hung askew from nails driven into the faces of the exposed studs. One item at a time, other things joined the mix, adding to the clutter in the playhouse while relieving pressure on the garage.

It was functionality tinged with sadness. There was no way to arrest the fading of childish chatter and laughter that had bounced off the tympanic walls of the small building, until one day I took off my cowboy costume and hung my holster up for the last time, sensing neither the finality of what I was doing nor the significance of the silence that descended over the back yard. But I was hardly alone: all around the neighborhood, a generation of children who shared common interests to an uncommon degree were laying aside the toys of childhood and picking up, if tentatively, the duties of young adulthood. Some, like Ruth Ann, had already left home, and others would soon follow. We were privileged for a time to share our place of play with them, but that time had expired, and the play had ended, and we were fortunate enough not to realize it.

What stirs me now is not the creative ways we used that colonial box during our earliest years, but how swiftly its season passed. I cannot ignore the reality that the interlude between the day Dad nailed down the last shake and that on which his youngest son turned his back on playhouse make-believe was barely a decade. The words of Thomas Wolfe's poem "You Can't Go home Again" (1940), imprint themselves in my gut:

> You can't go back home to your family—
> to the young man's dream of fame and glory
> to the country cottage away from strife and conflict
> to the father you have lost
> to the old forms and systems of things which seemed
> everlasting but are changing all the time.

The reality, of course, is that while the structure stood for years after the last of my family left Meadville, the playhouse of my childhood—ringing with the rush and laughter of children at play—exists only in time. And I don't know how to travel there. It stands now only on the landscape of my memory, inviting me into a Peter Pan world of inventiveness unleashed, while my more objective, surely less inventive adult mind informs me that I can no longer play there, could never have stayed there anyway.

But I can carry away, and continue to embrace, the lessons I learned there: that it is as rewarding to play hard as to work hard;

that being "boss" is only fractionally as rewarding as being cooperative; that a group's imagination feeds and stimulates the creativity of its individual members while they, in turn, enlarge the imagination of the group, until the whole truly is greater than the sum of its parts.

Oh... and never to wash my face with poison ivy.

CHAPTER 34

Fall of a Sudden

I t was clear, stepping out the door one morning in September, that something had changed—some subtle shift in the run of things that wore no badge of easy identification but said "no longer" to summer. The warmth that had ridden the air since May was gone. From June through August, even on such cool days as nature afforded, the breeze bore a backlog of heat, gift of the ascended sun that at mid-June's apogee rose and set on the northern edges of town, crossing high overhead at midday and baking the valley. And though its arc tilted more to the south each day of the waning summer, at the cusp of September it still shed enough heat to replenish what the night had stolen. Now, suddenly, the balance had tipped. A single night lost more than the previous day had gained, or would again until next year.

I never knew, growing up, the exhilarating sting of desert heat that pricks the skin and wrings the flesh out clear to the bone, piercing stiffened joints and making them supple again. I never knew because I grew up in Meadville, where damp is a way of life.

The "mold capital of the world," a pediatric allergist called it. Periodic notations in Mother's little diaries reduced it to three letters—same letter, three meanings: "HHH" denoted a day that was "hot, hazy and humid." It is an apt sketch of many summer days across northwestern Pennsylvania (recall our sticky departure for Oregon); for explanation, one need look no further than Ohio.

I mean no offense to neighbors in the Buckeye state, but a lot of Ohio is a vast agricultural flatland the three primary crops of which are corn, beans, and humid air. Browsing through an old discarded hymnal one day (clergy are known periodically to engage in such odd behavior), I came across the phrase "When on the steaming glebe I faint...." Having no idea what a glebe might be, I went to the dictionary and learned that the word, English in origin, denotes a plowed field. "Ohio!" I thought. Sautéed in early summer sun, the plowed fields of Ohio let go their burden of moisture to ride the prevailing wind east, supplying my part of Pennsylvania with glorious thunder storms—and endlessly humid air. If it's not "HHH" it's not likely summer, or this is not likely Meadville.

So my flesh told me right off that it was fall of a sudden that September morning when I paused on the sandstone step where our sidewalk entered the driveway. The air felt dry for the first time in weeks, as exhilarating as a shot of energizing elixir. I felt as if I could run and play for hours without having to shove against the swelter that sucks the energy out of a summer afternoon and leaves people panting and fanning and sipping iced tea on front porch swings. It was the time of lung-searing games of football and hikes in color-radiant woods—and burning leaves. Wahoo!

———————

Leaf burning in Meadville was a community art form, akin to a Memorial Day parade or 4th of July picnic. It's what we did in

October. All those trees that painted summer verdant had begun to yawn and stretch, trying to get comfortable for the long sleep of winter. And in settling down, they let go their leaves. They fell by ones and twos at first, a red-gold maple leaf in the yard, a yellow-ochre elm leaf plunging past my nose on the way to school. The pace picked up in mid-October when, color deepening, the leaves teamed up like gangs of kids turned loose on the town. On calm days, when the air regained a touch of summer warmth, they just let go, dropping onto the air like Olympian divers tipping off the high platform, flipping and twisting in a choreographic plunge before drifting noiselessly onto the grass. Soon enough, the air filled with leaves in grand climax, a glittering riffle of stored sunlight kicked loose by every passing gust, and I stood in the middle of the front yard and took a shower in cascading color. Finally, there always seemed to come one cold and rain-soaked gale of a night that stripped the trees of whatever leaves were left, piling them in soggy drifts against stone walls or curling them in windrows around the lees of houses.

At the last, all but the white oaks stood stark and naked against the graying sky. Oak trees have a reputation for toughness to uphold, and were not about to forfeit summer just to please the wind. They stood there, stolidly hanging on to leather brown leaves that rattled through winter storms until time to put on new growth the following spring. Only then did they let go, depositing a late burden of unwanted debris to be raked up and disposed of, and that carefully. Burning winter-sodden oak leaves was like trying to fire a swamp; nor did they compost readily, like maple and ash leaves. They just lay there, steeped in their own tannic acid, defying the ages. I have dug into a compost pile and found perfectly preserved oak leaves that had lain in there for two years. But withal, Meadville's forest was in naked readiness, indifferent to the impending onset of winter.

For those of us living at ground level, the work had just begun. There were a whole lot of trees in Meadville, and each tree grew a whole lot of leaves. When they all came down at once, they made an impressive heap. Leaving them to lie where they fell was a surefire way to kill large sections of lawn. And it was well not to wait too long to get started reducing them to smoke or compost: dry leaves could be swept along by the bushel, even by a child's rake; but one night of drenching rain compacted them to a sodden mass and glued them to the earth. Then they could be peeled up and carried away only by force of back-breaking labor.

Mother knew that well enough. When the accumulating drift of color started to raise the surface of the yard, she was quick with the after-school or Saturday morning command: go rake the lawn. As long as the leaves were dry it was one assignment I relished. There was something deeply satisfying about marching an army of leaves in rank order across the lawn, each sweep of the rake clearing a new swatch of grass. It was, at any rate, a job that required minimal brain power; the mind was free to browse where it would while the leaves processed uncomplaining to the street.

Our leaves couldn't be raked south. Well, they could, but not to good effect; they just ended up in the shrubs along the south property line, and if pushed beyond that, they ended up in the Leberman's yard, which the Lebermans would not appreciate. There was one exception: backyard leaves could be raked down into the ravine and into the compost pile at the southeast corner of the property. But that wasn't entirely satisfactory. Dad and Mother had planted a ring of upright arborvitae to fence the compost pile; and with all that nutrition flooding their roots, the shrubs grew twenty feet tall before I made it to five, and their cumulative girth consumed half the space originally intended for the pile. Twenty bushels of leaves put the top of the pile out of reach. And that comprised, at most, ten percent of the leaves we had to dispose of. Besides, in those days before I apprehended the magic that is compost, I thought it a waste to pile up leaves in a ravine to rot when they cried to be burned.

So the solution of choice remained: push them into the street and go for the matches; and that made the north wind our enemy—the one uncontrollable factor we had to deal with. Its breath unfurled the banners of resistance. By individuals and bunches, the leaves became reluctant, as if they knew that our design was their immolation and they would prefer, all things considered, to lie about and rot rather than to vanish in smoky orange flame. And when the wind came booming, they grew downright insubordinate, and the whole effort was a waste of time. Raking dry leaves into the face of a determined wind was like corralling a French Creek flood with a bucket brigade. It wasn't going to happen. Then there was nothing to do but wait for a calmer day. It was an informative exercise in acquiring patience. As Mother observed—from some body of folk wisdom or other—"Nature never hurries, but she's never late."

———·—·———

If raking leaves was satisfying labor, burning them was pure delight. Has there ever breathed the child who didn't love to play with fire, with or without permission? But to be called upon to do so purposefully—not just with parental permission but insistence—was to live in the best of fall possible worlds.

I learned early that there was a right way and a wrong way to start a fire. In a strange reversal, my tutors were not my elders but a clutch of small children engaged less in fall cleanup than your basic pyromania. They raked together a pile of leaves at the edge of a dry meadow across North Main Street and set fire to it, furnishing the neighborhood's youth an opportunity for heroism and my mind with a memory so vivid that my brain smells smoke at the thought of it. Faster than it takes to tell it, the blaze got away from them. Fanned by a fresh breeze and fueled by a year's worth of dried grass and weeds, the fire took off across the meadow, a consuming sheet of flame that headed straight for the Hornsteins' home and garage, and not an adult was to be found anywhere. A dozen of us, gathered to see what the smoke was about, were dumbstruck at the speed with which mischief breeds disaster, until it dawned on us that we'd really better do something.

With trepidation, I ran to the alarm box bolted to the power pole at my corner of North Main and Hamilton. It had been there my whole life, its red jacket embossed with white letters: "In Case of Fire, Pull Lever." Equally explicit, but freighted with anxiety even while not printed on the box, were counter-instructions from our elders: "Pull that thing when there isn't a fire and you'll go to jail."

We must have believed them. I know I did. That was the only time in my life that I recall the alarm being used, and I was the one whose neck was out. Was I sure I wanted to be the first? One look back at the acrid smoke rolling over the meadow and enveloping the Hornsteins' house settled my mind wonderfully. I opened the small door and tugged on the lever. Hearing no sound, nothing that said "We got your message," I wasn't sure at first that the thing had worked; so it was reassuring, seconds later, to hear the tower bell clang to life atop the fire station in the valley, followed by the wail of a siren signaling the departure of a pumper truck, lights flashing and engine snorting, as it turned out the station door to start its mile-long climb to our rescue.

It was an odd time for it, but I couldn't help reflecting—if a bit hyperbolically—that a single tug of my finger had put the whole town on notice that a crisis was brewing.

Meantime, across the street, my playmates had formed a fire line. No one's garden hose was close enough to reach the meadow. But as it did more often than not, Providence came to our rescue in the unlikely form of a pile of burlap bags lying in a neighbor's driveway. Flailing with all their might, several kids began to beat down the ends of the fire, squeezing it toward the center. Another trio found a shovel and a couple of rakes, and began to rake down the flame from behind and throw dirt on it. I'm not sure we ever consciously weighed what we were doing, which was probably a good thing; in an emergency, instinct is often superior to reflection. So we were startled, if plainly relieved, to find it working. By the time the truck stopped at the curb and four craggy-handsome firemen strode into the field, their high boots swinging with the easy stride of veterans, we were beating the last of the fire into submission a bare three feet from the wall of the Hornsteins' garage and thirty-five yards from the telltale point of its genesis.

We were, by then, from the biggest to the smallest of us, soaked with perspiration, smudged with soot and feeling suddenly sheepish. These firemen were the same hardened professionals who visited our school from time to time to scare the pants off us lecturing about the hazards of fire, but we'd never been this close to them in their working uniforms, where we could actually count the multiple layers of chipped paint on their battered helmets and smell the bouquet of a dozen fires that clung to their rubber coats and canvas coveralls. Had we done the right thing? How many times had a fireman (maybe one of these very men) told us to leave fire fighting to professionals? Doubts about the wisdom of our labor were quickly allayed by the firemen, who couldn't seem to praise us enough as they criss-crossed the meadow, dragging a hose bigger and longer than any I had ever seen and maybe than the sum total of all the hoses I had seen in my whole life, soaking down the smoldering embers while the pumper truck rumbled in support.

Every day for weeks thereafter, until winter's first snowfall dressed the fire's wounds in bandages of white, I glanced proudly at that blackened meadow. Curious how much stroking an ego can glean from a blanket of ashes.

—————

But blackened meadows were rare and, fortunately, blackened houses rarer still. If some home was set afire by a pile of burning leaves I never heard of it. Every fall for generations, Meadville's families raked leaves into piles and set them ablaze, yet rarely created even a minor emergency.

Hamilton Avenue was our burning pit: its paving bricks and curbstones were impervious to flame. Besides, Hamilton was the road less traveled. A bare tenth of a mile long, its sole achievement was to join North Main and Jefferson Streets, and it wasn't even the preferred route for those wanting to make the connection. There were no houses on the north side of the street, where the victory gardens had flourished, and the only cars that routinely traveled it belonged to the three families whose driveways turned in along its south side. So there was little competition from traffic, which was a good thing. Nothing churned a burning leaf pile like a car speeding past about six inches from the flames. In the ensuing swirl, the very air exploded in flame, threatening to take off hair and eyebrows.

Too, the side of our property commanded enough curb to burn half the leaves in Meadville. Piling them a foot or two deep and wide, we strung the leaves out along the curb as far as the supply would reach, which on a good day might total seventy to a hundred feet. With everything in readiness, we'd go for the matches—not the wimpy paper book kind that had to be struck on the packet and either went out or burned our fingers before we succeeded in setting the leaves afire. Leaf burning required the manly, wooden, strike-'em-on-the-pavement kind that movie cowboys used to light a hand-rolled cigarette by swiping it right on the seat of their pants. (I'd tried that too, but it seldom worked. The one time it did, I set off another half dozen matches I'd put in my hip pocket. I never was very good a jitter-bugging, but I cut a pretty good rug that day. That was another wound that went untended, not because Mother would have thought it unworthy of medical intervention, but because I couldn't bring myself to tell her I'd been that stupid. I sat on my unblistered left haunch for a week.)

Spreading out along the row, we touched the pile off at multiple points, each child privileged to satisfy the urge, ingrained in the human psyche a thousand generations ago, to burn something. Once the conflagration was under way, a few swipes with a rake served to keep things going smartly, stirring unburned leaves to the surface and plunging hot embers into the heart of the pile. By so attentive an approach we could burn a hundred bushels of leaves in ten minutes. The ash that was left was as fragile as dew, quickly dispersed by the next good wind or flushed away by the next rain.

Leaf burning was one of Meadville's unifying rites of passage. The entire town knew just when conditions were best, and turned out, all at the same time, to move leaves off yards and into streets and alleys, chatting the while with neighbors and passersby and comparing notes on how splendid the color had been that fall, or not. As the day advanced, the town assumed the visage of a great temple supported on pillars of smoke, but the illusion lasted only until the columns reached the first stratum of moving air and drifted off in one direction or another, according to the dictates of the breeze.

If the day brought an inversion, the effect was even more theatrical, as columns of smoke organized themselves into aromatic, low-hanging clouds and spread out over the valley, separated at first, but enlarging until their edges merged to form a ceiling that stretched from hill to hill, burying the entire town under a fog of its own creation. It was a delicious time of year— too delicious to last. Soon enough, the harbingers of winter came huffing, driving some folks indoors where they wouldn't likely see a neighbor for weeks at a time, until the ascending sun again stirred the soil and set the creeks to shouting with melt-water. And when that time came, we'd hail spring and admire the tender new leaves popping out all over Meadville's forest without once reflecting that, in a mere six months, we'd be plotting their cremation, and the circle would close and the process would begin all over again.

———

An olfactory notation on burning leaves: standing in the dense, almost substantial cloud rolling off a burning leaf pile, I breathed the fragrance of evaporating summer, an intoxicating recipe concocted from earth-rooted nutrients fused with the gasses of a hundred stirring breezes and baked to a turn in the oven of the sun. It was seasonal transition as gourmet feast. Later, when the fire died, and only a black smear of weightless ash remained to remind us, like the chalk outline at a murder scene, where the leaf pile had lain on the street, and I went inside and stripped off my clothes, I just plain stank of smoke. Now that's Decay, in record time and with a capital D!

CHAPTER 35

Softball,
Mudball and Snowball

T he season didn't matter: a game of some sort was going on in our side yard all the time, and weather made a difference only in the choice of the game. This was as Mother and Dad wanted it. Their dream house, while large, did not require a double lot. They bought the second lot because they had three children and a fourth pending, and intended for their children to have a safe place to play, preferably at home. And if the other children in the neighborhood came along in the bargain, that was okay too. So the house was erected on the southern half of the property, and the northern half was graded to form a broad, level swath of grass meant to serve as our playground.

Our parents' wish in this regard was augmented by the fact that many of our friends' yards were under some restriction. There were a few patches behind one house or another, but they were either small or sloped or both, precluding the wide-ranging running games we most enjoyed. And their front yards? In your dreams. Front yards existed to impress the motoring public and to reassure neighbors that their property values were secure, not for children to play on. And that's all there was to that.

Our lawn, by contrast, was a testimony to the power of some strains of grass to survive in the face of brutal neglect. If it originally had been seeded with the customary blend of fine grasses, they were soon beaten into extinction. What was left was akin to pasture grass, robust and resilient, and it needed to be. It endured more pounding than Meadville High School's football field, but for twelve months a year and without so much as a thought of tending. Fertilizer was as alien as truffles and watering was confined to whatever nature deigned to send. "Lawn care" was defined as periodic mowing and raking the fall leaves. Beyond these sensible measures, the stuff was on its own.

Hardly a week passed without some activity. In spring and summer, softball was the contest of choice; in the fall, football. And any time of year was okay for running games like hide-and-go-seek or its first cousin, kick-the-can, which we were known to play through the descending dusk of a warm spring evening until forced to quit because someone sent the can flying into the shrubbery with a particularly vigorous kick just as darkness settled, and none of us could find it.

———•———

Softball, the warm-weather game of choice, required the most cooperation. It's hard to mount a convincing effort with three or four people on a side, and late spring Saturdays required a recruiting campaign. On a good day we'd gather eighteen or twenty kids of both genders for a game. Then came the obligatory choosing of sides, a process governed by immutable rules that came

from I have no idea where but which endured because they worked
and we saw no reason to change them. It began with the election
of captains, which required little effort and never a contest—we
all knew that our chance for a good game was best served by
strong team captains. Then, after the ancient hand-over-hand
ritual, using the bat to determine who got to choose first, the
division of players got under way in earnest. The captains already
knew, just by looking around, who among the available talent
they'd choose first, and the initial bidding was fast and furious.
It slowed when players of intermediate ability were chosen, and
each choice took deliberation, sometimes necessitating whispered
debate among those already chosen for that team; and the while,
the un-chosen stood like biblical goats on the left hand, wondering what was to become of them, then beaming in relief when
named to join the ranks of the elect. The pace picked up again
when the weakest players, generally the youngest, were divided
up. They weren't expected to make much difference, so it mattered little on which side they played.

Early on, I wasn't crazy about the system. I began my career
small and unskilled, so I was usually among the last chosen. Over
the long run, I suppose, this built character, but at the time it was
mortifying. How was I supposed to feel good standing there watching people divide off until I was the only one left, and then who'd
want me anyway? I mean, it's wasn't like I was chosen; I was just
the leftover, consigned to whichever team had to take the last
body whether they wanted it or not.

Still, the system instilled motivation. The desire to improve,
to earn the respect of older kids and move up in the ranks, was
strong. And there were built-in opportunities for advancement:
as age and skill advanced, and older children left the games, I
found myself being chosen earlier, eventually to be among the

first chosen, and finally to be elected captain. Whatever wounds my self-esteem had endured were long forgotten that amazing afternoon when, for the first time, I traded hand-grips on the bat with the other captain. But the downside advanced with me: I discovered that disappointing others was a necessary task of leadership. Bruising the egos of the littler kids was not appreciably more fun than when I was the one upset.

But I came to appreciate the system's practical advantages. In so cohesive a group of friends, everyone knew the rankings: who was good and who was merely okay and who (don't say it aloud) was a liability. That being so, choosing up sides insured the relative equality of teams. In rampant self-interest, each side grabbed the best players it could, but all of us benefited. By the time the choosing was done and someone shouted "Play ball!" the chances for a balanced game were good. The proof of the pudding was the score, which was often heart-stoppingly close, and both winners and losers went home knowing they had played a credible game.

The controlling features of our ball field were accidents of landscape architecture. A low but steep embankment defined the eastern property line. On the west, four giant trees—a pair of white oaks and another of black gums—stood a safe distance in from North Main Street. The Hamilton Avenue curb on the north and our driveway on the south completed the boundaries.

The field thus delineated, we were left with a single uncompromising feature: a cherry tree standing fifteen feet from the Hamilton Avenue curb and midway down the infield. Being somewhat vertical and very hard and all, it made a poor home plate, so it was elected first base. It was quite accommodating, actually. Already mature when our home was built, it unaccountably listed 40 degrees to the north, affording the first base player, or runners stuck there during a lull, the opportunity to recline against the trunk while waiting for some excitement to develop.

Second and third bases were, by contrast, less precisely located, and variable in fabrication. We took little time measuring baselines, and didn't own anything remotely resembling bases to put there anyway. A couple of sticks might have to do. But as often as not, someone volunteered a shirt or jacket—which entailed some risk. The purpose of a base, after all, is to have a place to put feet. It wasn't the wear and tear that concerned us; it was the likely need to explain to one of our mothers.

"How on earth did you get this shirt so filthy?"

"Um... we were, um, playing pretty hard."

"Well, for goodness sake, what were you doing, rolling in the dirt?"

Still, someone always made the sacrifice, else what are friends for?

To claim to remember games in any detail would be a stretch. They all blend together into a single, well-stirred memory rather like a bowl of Mother's corn meal mush: the exciting ones and the not so; some when we barely managed to field enough players to cover the essentials; a few with so many players that we had to create unorthodox positions like inner-outfielder and short-stop back-up. One game, however, is cemented in memory. That would be the day I learned that being pitcher can be dangerous.

We always had a pitcher. In a nation obsessed with baseball, tossing the ball into the air and smacking it on the way down seemed a sacrilege, except when two or three of us got together to shag fly balls. But since home plate was just a scrap of oak board out of Dad's shop, and not a large one at that, one of the older kids—someone with enough skill to put the ball over the plate more often than not—was chosen to pitch for each team.

It was early in my pitching career that the incident occurred, and it left me skittish on the mound for years thereafter. The batter was Sally Dean, and she lived with her grandmother a couple of doors up Hamilton Avenue. According to protocol, I pitched right to her. (Our group disliked standing idly about while some smart-alecky pitcher showed how terrific he was by flailing the ball past a line-up of little kids barely able to swing a bat. It seemed both thoughtless and a waste of good playing time. We thought it more fun to give everyone a chance to get a hit so all of us could play ball. We didn't cut each other any slack running bases or taking advantage of errors, but getting hits was essential to having a game at all.)

In that spirit, I eased forward as Sally stepped up to the plate, so I could pitch the ball a bit slowly and still get it inside her admittedly modest strike zone. I should have kept my distance— or paid closer attention. Whether she was feeling especially determined, or simply had eaten her Wheaties-the-Breakfast-of-Champions that day, I never learned. Nor do I recall what it was that distracted me—some insignificant incident off toward the cherry tree that I would have been better off to ignore. In any event, I pitched a slow and arching ball that went right over the plate and belly high. Sally couldn't have been more ready. She whaled that ball like she meant to send it to the moon. Hearing the unmistakable crack of the bat, but having looked away at whatever, I jerked back toward home plate to see the ball five inches from my nose and approaching at just under the speed of sound. I didn't even have time to blink, much less get a glove up to deflect it. It caught me right on the bridge of my nose. Boy, did that smart!

The result was comparable to what happens when a child reaches up over the edge of a hot stove and grabs hold of a scalding pot: the learning curve ascends at an awesome clip, and the mistake is unlikely ever to be repeated. It wasn't significant, or particularly embarrassing, that little Sally Dean was on the working end of the bat. For the next five years, I couldn't pitch a ball without ducking psychologically, even as I managed to stay physically erect. And I can promise you this: ever thereafter, had someone yelled "Truck!" just as I let go a pitch, I would have stayed glued to home plate until the issue was decided, then thought about jumping out of the way.

When fall turned the mornings cool and the deep green of summer's leaves began to ease toward the rainbow, the urge to play football became irresistible. And we took the game seriously: we played tackle. "Never play tackle football without protective equipment," our parents admonished; "it's too dangerous. Play touch."

Baloney, we said (if only to ourselves). Touch football just wasn't the same. If we couldn't knock each other down and roll around in the dirt, why bother? We believed that the real danger was playing with someone who had part of the equipment, like a helmet or set of shoulder pads, that was more bruising to the opponent than protective of the wearer. If we were going to ignore the advice of our elders and put flesh and bone out there to be pummeled, then everyone would suffer on equal terms. So, for two months every fall, we ran and blocked and tackled as if some conference title depended on it, and never broke a leg or fractured a skull. We hardly even sustained minor injuries, and certainly none serious enough to prompt us to report them to our parents. Don't ask how we escaped. I haven't a clue. But Mother's remark about children growing up by the grace of God comes to mind.

Unlike softball, the rules of engagement in football allowed more play with fewer people. I couldn't begin to count the number of games that seesawed across that yard with six kids on the field—three to a side—although that did seem to mark the low end of the numerical requirement. Two to a side didn't allow a lot of options for plays. Nothing could match a full-blown hard-running hell-bent-for-leather contest with eight or ten kids on each side, with fakes and multiple receivers and flying wedges and "THROW IT TO ME I'M IN THE CLEAR!"

There was one other difference between softball and football: I don't remember ever playing softball in the rain, or calling a football game because of it. Maybe it had to do with the seasons. We played softball mostly in the spring, when rain in Meadville tended to fall in impressive quantities and to be accompanied by a lot of very large lightning bolts. Creatures designed to stand erect—like lightning rods—are stupid to hang around in open fields during thunder storms. Besides, after a squall sopped the grass and liquefied the dust, chasing grounders lost a lot of appeal. But with football, nothing short of a blizzard was grounds to quit. Sunny days were ideal, but a high wind only increased the challenge, chill air kept down the sweat, and damp ground was softer to fall on than dry.

As with softball, I have distinct memories of few games. But there was that moment of supreme triumph, a moment right up there with my solo basketball win in high school gym class.

It was the day of the mudball game. A group of us had gone out to the north edge of town to a field developed by Allegheny College for intramural games, complete with limed goal lines. We were a curious group—Cliff and I and several of our side-yard teammates had run into some "older" guys (seventeen or eighteen) whom I had never met and never saw again. As usual, we paired off into teams: seven on a side, with all of our guys and a couple of theirs against the rest of them. It was my first and only game against a visiting team, and looms large in memory because I was the smallest "man" on the field—a fact that was turned to our advantage. David was about to confront Goliath and win again.

It was cold, and the field was wet. There was no way we were going home that day without looking like we fell into the creek. If the sun was somewhere up there above the heavy overcast that scudded endlessly by at low altitude, we couldn't pinpoint it. Only hard play kept us from getting chilled to the bone. Or, put another way, had we played less hard we would have had to wear so many clothes that it would not have been possible to play at all. So we went at it fast and furious for an hour and a half, until our cloths were sopped and filthy and our stamina was wearing thin. With only seven on a side, substitutions were not an option. But the score was tied and no one wanted to quit without a clear decision. Our team had possession of the ball, but we were backed up against our own goal. It was also fourth down, and under the rules of the game, yardage didn't count. If we didn't break out in four, we'd have to cede the ball to the opposing team. It didn't look good. Then Cliff had an epiphany. "They'll never be looking for Don," he said (without adding the obvious: in tackle football you don't give the ball to the littlest kid). Turning to me, he instructed, "You get through their line, hook right, then take off down field. Everyone else stay back and fake a run around the left. When we've drawn them off, I'll pass to Don."

Man, the thrill of it. My own big brother trusted me enough to throw me the ball on what would surely be our last chance to win the game. I was so giddy I could hardly think. I trotted up to the line knowing that somehow I must not let my team down, but wanting most ardently not to disappoint my big brother. My composure wavered for a second when I found myself across from some guy twice my size, but Cliff's words echoed in my brain: "They'll never be looking for Don." He was so right.

  Stepping up behind center, Cliff called out the signals. The ball was snapped and the whole team fell back and faded left, drawing the opposition with them in a move so elegantly coordinated it would bring tears to the eyes of a professional coach. The leviathan across from me didn't even bother to shove me as he tore by, intent on tearing up our backfield. There I was, in splendid isolation. I exploded off the line, cut right a few yards and headed downfield as fast as my worn legs would still carry me. When I looked over my shoulder, both teams were still battering their way toward the sideline and there wasn't a soul within twenty yards of me. And right then, Cliff threw the ball. No pass ever spiraled more perfectly or arched more precisely. I didn't

even break stride, just gathered it in on the fly like I actually knew what I was doing, grinning at the raucously sweet bellow of dismay from the other team.

  So delighted was I, in fact, that it no longer mattered whether we won the game. That single moment of triumph, built on the trust of my big brother, was all the compensation I needed for the pounding bruises I would take home that afternoon. And bruises were nearly all I did get to take home.

The ball crammed into the hook of my elbow, I ran for the goal line with everything I had left in me (which wasn't much), because I knew those big guys wouldn't just stop and watch me go. Their roar of dismay had not yet faded before they were after me—and they could run a lot faster than I could, even that late in the day. Lungs bursting and eyes blurring from the effort of running the length of the field, I simultaneously caught sight of the faded goal line and heard the thump of some very large feet behind me. I'll never make it, I thought, thighs burning and knees rattling. We're gonna lose after all.

But David was not yet done with Goliath—or vice versa. Goliath caught me, grabbing the back of my jacket and giving me a powerful shove. His large body came down on top of me like a bale of hay falling off a wagon, shoving my face into the grass as he rolled over me. But I didn't even feel it: as I started to go down, I glimpsed the goal line pass beneath us. It wouldn't have mattered if he had driven a truck over me. I was invincible and the day was ours.

I had cause to reassess my invincibility the next morning as I crawled into my church clothes—very carefully—and limped down the attic stairs to breakfast. But I regretted neither the day nor the labor, and never would.

When freezing weather finally brought the football season to an end, we prayed for Meadville's muggy climate to send us the kind of heavy damp snow that was "just right for packing." And when it did, we went to work with a will, pushing and heaving to roll enormous snowballs. At times they grew as tall as we were, their sides cork-screwed like caramel buns for Jack's giant and so heavy that they lifted the snow clear off to the grass, leaving a trail of pallid green. A group effort was required then, two or three of us grunting and heaving in unison to arrange the great globs into rows and sculpt them into a snow fort. An old broom handle stuck into the wall near the door, with a rag flag tied to its top, signaled its completion.

Then, as we stood back to admire our handiwork, aggression overwhelmed harmony, and we spontaneously divided into opposing camps. Shouting vacuous threats and scrambling to accumulate an arsenal of snowballs before the enemy could gather theirs—which never worked because they were always as fast as we, or we as they—we pummeled each other until our cheeks were the hue of mottled apples. Sooner or later, someone yielded to the irresistible urge to employ heavy artillery, grabbed a snow shovel, and dumped a load of snow on some hapless antagonist's head. The response was escalation, not capitulation. As soon as the opposition could locate a snow shovel of its own, the offender could count on being buried in revenge. The combat was unrelenting until body heat melted the snow caught in our collars and sent trickles of frigid water down our shirts and over bare skin, soaking our clothes, and we could stand it no longer. Or maybe we simply wore out from the effort. Either way, we called a truce, dropped our missiles where we stood, and went indoors to make hot cocoa.

Chances were that those snowballs would still be there a week later; and the bulk of a good snow fort, like the wreckage of battle, might survive halfway through spring thaw. There it stood, more dirt than snow, a dingy memorial slumped pathetically in the middle of our barren yard to remind us of some gone and combative day. And when finally even the echo of the fort was gone, the first warm days of spring, drying the lawn, signaled us that it was time to get out the oaken home plate and start all over again.

CHAPTER 36

Sonja Henies We Weren't

T he year I turned six, ice skates for all of us appeared under the Christmas tree. Gender expectations were immediately evident: Cliff, Frank and I got hockey skates—squatty, plumb-strait blades mounted on posts strong enough to hold up the family car, riveted to homely black leather boots so heavy they felt like part of the cow might still be attached to the hide. Ruth Ann received graceful figure skates of fine-grained white leather, with wicked little teeth molded into the leading edges of their elegantly curved blades. I thought it a good division. In my six-year-old opinion, hockey skates were manly and athletic; figure skates were for girls and sissies. I didn't yet know about speed skates, nor would I ever try them. Two minutes after I laced my stiff new hockey skates to my feet and tried to move—in any direction at all—it was clear that the extra steel would have done me no good whatever. But sitting there Christmas morning, secure in p.j.'s and bathrobe, I didn't yet know how little I knew. I just knew that skating would be fun and easy.

Then I set skate on rink for the first time and discovered what happens when a six-year-old, accustomed to walking flat-footed on *terra firma*, steps onto a sheet of ice perched atop twin strips of steel an eighth of an inch thick. It was akin to a baby robin falling out of its nest. Legs shooting off toward opposite poles of the compass and arms flailing in a frantic but futile effort to stay upright, I traveled three feet before sitting down so hard that my brain bounced on the bottom of my skull. Not that my siblings did much better. We gave it our best effort, but Sonja Henies we weren't.

There followed the arduous task of learning to move—not in a fluid manner that could be called "skating" as such, more like squirming along in an effort to get from this point to that without falling down or permanently deforming my ankles. The latter was the hardest part. It didn't take long to adapt to a new set of rules about keeping vertical, but keeping my skate blades vertical was another matter. The entire first month, my weight was evenly divided between my blades and the inner edge of each sole; and since tipping their blades causes skates to veer in the direction of the tilt, both feet sought independently to go toward the middle. I didn't skate in a straight line to anywhere. I got there by zigzagging, as if I were a sailboat on a windward tack.

———•·———

The place was called Shadybrook Park, and it lay at the east end of North Street on the Mill Run flood plain, just beyond the high school football field. It was, at the time, less a park than an idea. A decade of discussion among the city fathers was undone by the fiscal constraints of World War II, leaving the town without the resources to make much more of it than the flat meadow that Mill Run already had spent centuries creating.

Mill Run could have been really helpful by flooding in January or February—not a rip-snorter, just enough to overflow its banks and cover the plain. But it was in the habit of flooding in March and April, so we couldn't count on it for help when we needed it. We depended on the fire department, which was certainly up to the job. One frigid January morning, the pumper truck grumbled out North Street, its crew unusually merry at the prospect of an hour's fun playing around with the hoses instead of fighting a fire. Their orders: drive out to Shadybrook and flood a patch of meadow. Those guys didn't fool around, either. They made us a skating rink as large as a supermarket parking lot.

The result was not sophisticated, you understand. No ground barrier was put down, and no effort was wasted spraying on thin sheets of water, one after another, building to a final surface as smooth as a window pane. These were firemen, and accustomed to dealing in volume. They unrolled their huge canvas hose, clapped it onto the nearest hydrant, and let 'er rip. It required several visits. Half the first flooding sank into the porous soil without even slowing down. But that served to seal the ground deep, laying a base that would, with luck and frigid nights, last into spring.

The stopper thus plugged into the tub, subsequent flooding rapidly increased the depth of the ice until four or five inches lay across the meadow, more than sufficient to withstand the grinding it would have to endure. Not all flooding days were created equal, however. Air temperature determined how smooth the ice, and therefore the skating, would be. If the temperature was brushing the bottom side of zero—as it often was—the water turned to iron before it got halfway across the underlying layers, resulting in a tiered surface with inch-and-a-half joints between layers. This posed a real problem for the unwary like me. Cruising across the broad expanse of ice looking just about everywhere except three or four feet ahead of my toes, I'd trip up over a raised edge and do a belly flopper, or drop off one with a bone-jarring jolt that landed me on the opposite side of my anatomy. Either way, the maneuver was calculated to earn insult atop injury, as every "friend" on the ice applauded as loudly as mittened hands allowed, the quicker-witted among them offering mocking assessments of my skating proficiency.

Once in a while, though, if luck placed the temperature around 20 degrees as the firemen ran their hoses, the water spread smoothly from rim to rim before setting up; and if the winter night came on clear and star-spangled and the bottom dropped out of the thermometer, we woke to an expanse of rigid silk, and half the town turned out to sport over it as if we'd invented the family reunion.

That was all there was to it. No warm-up shack fitted with a glowing iron stove; no pot of steaming cocoa hung over an open fire between the ice and the parked cars; no refreshments of any kind except what skaters brought from home in pockets or thermos jugs. And unless some socially motivated thief lifted a couple of park benches off the Diamond, or someone hauled an old wooden bench down from their back porch, there wasn't even a

place to sit down to lace up our skates. If the winter was generous, the windrow of snow at the edge of the rink, piled there by
crews of volunteers clearing the ice, quickly got packed and
sculpted by warm butts to form a long bench. Lacking any of these,
there was always the running board of the family car. It was definitely a low-budget enterprise, and we loved it.

———·——

The hordes that moved onto the ice on a bright and brittle
Saturday quickly assumed a concentric configuration, and it was
important that novices discern it quickly or risk being run over. At
the center of the ice, those with some skill at cutting figures moved
in constrained patterns, pausing now and then to spin in place
before sailing off backward on an expanding curve like a moon
suddenly freed from planetary gravity. That really impressed me;
every time *I* tried it, I lost out to gravity and landed with a thud.

Around the perimeter, a handful of speed skaters skimmed
the outer limits of the ice, blades as long as my arm flashing in
the deliberate, slow-motion gait of their sport that disguised their
acceleration until they merged into a convoy of blurs.

In between, the remaining forty-nine out of every fifty skaters present—too inexperienced to engage in graceful gyrations in
the inner circle or to achieve the blinding speed required at the
outer, or too clumsy to survive in either—milled about. We Skinners quickly found our place, and settled in among the millers.

It was a powerful inducement to humility. I wouldn't become a proficient skater until 1958, when I acquired a pair of
sissified figure skates and a girlfriend possessed of enough expertise to teach me, and started all over again.

CHAPTER 37

About as much
Thrill as I Could Stand

G iven my proficiency as a skater, it seems entirely obvious why I retained a preference for sledding. For kids, as opposed to motorists, the advantage of winters in a valley surrounded by hills was the hills; we were never at a loss for places to go sledding. North Main Street hill was off-limits, and it wasn't even necessary for Mother to tell us why. Even the dullest among us recognized that the thrill didn't justify the risk.

But there was Sunset Drive, a dead-end street on the city line at the top of our neighborhood with half a dozen houses and not enough traffic to bother counting. Too, while the city plowed the streets, it spread cinders (gritty ash from the town's coal-fired boilers that was collected year-round for just that purpose) only on main routes. Sunset definitely wasn't a main route. Even after the plow completed its run up to the dead end where the city water tower loomed above the naked trees like Gulliver among

the Lilliputians, there was more than enough snow on the bricks
to insure great sledding. And it only got better as gangs of booted
children sledded down and tramped back up, knit caps tugged so
far down that we had to tilt our heads back either to see or to be
identified, while ice crystals accumulated in nuggets on woolen
mittens and leggings until, by day's end, we all looked beaded.
An afternoon of that kind of activity packed Sunset's two blocks
of snow to a consistency one degree short of ice, and insured
whiz-bang, take-your-breath-away sledding.

Some days, there were so many of us it was a miracle that
some child didn't get chopped off at the ankles. Chattering kids
laboring up from the bottom, their words hung out in vapor to
dry on the frost-bitten air, were sent scampering over curb-top
snow banks by some down-bound sledder's "GET-OUTTA-MY-
WAY!" No one minded, really, because the roles were soon reversed. Reaching the top, each wave of sledders turned, ran downhill a few yards, belly flopped onto their Flexible Flyers, and
shouted their own way downhill, transforming their tormenters
into scurriers.

Then there was the remarkable winter when, for reasons
never revealed, the city closed off part of Highland Avenue for a
sled run. It was a winter boy's dream come true.

Whereas North Main Street descended into the valley on a
steady grade, Highland Avenue, only a block east and running a
parallel track, bounded down the hillside in leaps. That topography apparently suited someone just fine, and whoever it was
possessed civil authority. Every afternoon for several weeks, as
school dismissed for the day, a traffic barrier was swung across
the street by the reservoir at the top of Highland's first drop-off.
A quarter of a mile below, a second barrier was posted at the

bottom of a sustained but gentler slope, just before the street tilted over for its final plunge.

Now there was a sledding run worthy of the name. Getting started was no problem; the challenge was to stop. Even though the bottom of the run was less steeply inclined than the top, it was still sloped, and a sled arriving there had already traversed a sharp drop of two city blocks over just the kind of terrain that accelerates a sled to orbital velocity. No one wanted to overshoot and take that final plunge. Out on some country hillside, it might not matter, but the bottom of Highland dead-ended into Randolph Street and cross traffic. Any sledder lucky enough to make it across—never a sure thing—would jump the curb and immediately encounter several houses. And while that terminus was barely half a block from City Hospital, none of us was confident we'd live long enough to benefit from the medical care it afforded.

Fortunately, the city took this into account and spread cinders across the last twenty yards of the run. They made for a grating stop, especially after the snow wore off the underlying brick. On the other hand, they eliminated the need to clean rust off sled runners; any corrosion that hindered a first descent wouldn't be around to impede the second.

My most memorable experience of the braking power of ashes and brick came during the first of two bobsled rides. Mother resoundingly disapproved of bobsleds—she'd heard too many stories of people who'd been maimed or killed on the things. But she wasn't there, and the bobsled was. It showed up in the company of three young men who arrived atop the hill one day just as the premature winter dusk was settling. They may have been in high school, and were certainly no older than college-age. And they were more than happy to invite us younger kids on board, because they had extra room: it was a ten-man bobsled.

I'd never seen anything like it. Standing among the crowd gathered in the puddle of light from a street lamp, I considered the makeup of the thing: a single board seat, one foot wide and twelve long; foot rests, equally long and four inches wide, slung on steel brackets on either side; twin pairs of steel-edged oak runners peeking ominously from beneath as if impatient to get moving. The fore pair was mounted on a swivel post, centered well forward, so the runners stuck out ahead. With some skepticism, I studied the loop of half-inch manila rope by which (I was confidently told) the lead man steered the thing. The rear runners were bolted in place and accompanied by a long brake handle, its lower end tipped with steel teeth that looked as if they could tear the hide off a grizzly bear. In between stretched ten feet of unsupported board looking for all the world like a plank waiting to be walked. That's all there was to the contraption; and though my eye assured me that it was standing stock still, it looked like it was already traveling sixty miles per hour.

Scrutinizing it in the gathering darkness loaded my rib cage with adrenalin, rather like standing atop a barn with homemade wings strapped to my arms, knowing that stepping off would effect either a fantastic thrill or total disaster. The decision was visceral, not mental. I sure didn't want to be on the thing if it piled up. If I was and survived it, Mother would kill me anyway. But I ached for the thrill, and could have it only by risking the mishap. And, as the saying goes, it's easier to obtain forgiveness than permission. I climbed aboard—and that's no mere pun!

At first, with eight of us spread along it, the sled sat there as if was bolted to the pavement. "Everyone push!" the pilot called over his shoulder. We dropped our feet and paddled like a sixteen-legged duck in a fruitless effort to get the thing to move, but it wouldn't. Then several volunteers grabbed the rear end and heaved. Groaning ponderously, the runners ground out a few inches, caught and stuck, broke free and edged forward once more. Just when I was beginning to wonder where the thrill was in all this, I found out. Like a beast roused from a nap and not happy about it, the sled lurched and shot forward as if it was inspired, its runners rumbling so forcefully down the snow-packed street that the entire assembly quivered as if stricken with a bad chill.

It was the same sensation that I had experienced easing over the top on my first, fearful plunge on a roller-coaster. We accelerated until I was having about as much thrill as I could stand. I suppose we weren't going all that fast, maybe forty-five miles per hour; but perched there, gripping the narrow board for all I was worth and fighting to keep my feet on the rails, forty-five felt a whole bunch faster than it ever did in a car. Houses flew by in a blur, the light from their windows seeming to stretch as if it had suddenly grown elastic and gotten caught up in our wake, while the sled shuddered from the stress on its runners. Oddly, the rumble of the sled's shuddering was the only noise: we intrepid travelers, strung out on the seat, made not a sound, as if holding our collective breath in the fervent hope of making it to the bottom without being individually thrown off or corporately bludgeoned in a colossal pile-up. At few moments in my life has my brain been that focused—or that useless. Thundering along in the hands of God and the young man up front, I could only pray that the former was very much in command of the latter. Me, I was in control of absolutely nothing.

Peering ahead through eyes brimming with wind-summoned tears, I became aware that we had reached the stretch where the slope moderated, but we continued to surge forward with no appreciable loss of momentum. Up ahead, the downhill barrier came into view out of the darkness, spot-lit by an overhead streetlamp and approaching so fast that its size appeared to double with each elapsed second. And though I'd not yet heard the phrase,

I intuitively grasped the import of "Once you've got hold of a tiger's tail, how do you let go?" For a fleeting instant, I envisioned plunging right on through the barrier, the first two or three riders getting knocked senseless, and going airborne over the lip of the lower hill. But before I could consider how to excuse myself—like diving headlong onto brick-solid snow doing forty-five while wishing to God I still fit into my wool snowsuit—the sled's runners ran onto the cinders.

I am reluctant even to attempt a description of the racket that shattered the evening's tranquility. It would require ten adjectives strung together in outrageous syntax, destroying what reputation I may have acquired as a writer. Let it be noted that no train suddenly and unexpectedly flagged down by a lantern-bearing yardman because "THE BRIDGE IS OUT!" ever made a more abrasive din than those steel-edged runners grating across the cinders, or spit out a more impressive stream of sparks. The young man in the stern seat never even had a chance to use the brake lever, or needed to. The shattering noise was still bouncing off the houses and fading among the barren, night-blackened trees when the air exploded with hoots and shouts as we piled off the sled, everyone jabbering at once about what a ride that was and did you see when and could you believe that and.... Still, concluding that one such ride was enough, lest I experience both thrill and disaster in the same evening, I declined the invitation to go again. Staggering up the hill on rubber legs, I retrieved my Flexible Flyer—which seemed suddenly to have become very modest—and towed it home to supper. It was a long time before I told Mother about that ride.

———·———

Then there was the ride I never told her about at all because I never even had the courage to tell her about this bobsled, a gleaming blue and yellow three-seater with real hand grips and stirrups and a wind cowling sheltering its steering wheel. I thought it was just about the most beautiful machine I had ever seen. It belonged to a boy who lived a neighborhood over, more acquaintance than friend, who had tired of it and wanted to sell it. What's more, he'd sell it for $20—a price that even I could afford—so I bought it. The thought did occur to me that I had no way to store the thing—not for lack of space but nerve: how would I explain such a purchase to Mother, for whom twenty dollars was still the price of a week's groceries? As it turned out, I was relieved of the dilemma on my first and only ride.

Behind Reis Library, on the Allegheny campus, lay a short but steep slope of lawn, a favorite sledding spot for kids growing up on Meadville's north hill. I had sledded there so often that I knew every lump and hollow, and it seemed the perfect spot to test my new bobsled. Arriving on campus with two friends recruited for my maiden voyage, I discovered that bobsleds have real limitations. Even snow packed down by other sleds and riders offered insufficient support for the bobsled's heavy runners. They simply cut through, dug into the grass, and clung there.

Then I had an epiphany. An inclined sidewalk at the top of the rise curved past the library and crossed Brooks Drive, the main avenue into campus. It seemed a natural: hard surface, modest slope, comfortably negotiable. Hauling the bobsled up to the top, I climbed behind the wheel and my friends packed in behind me. That took a moment; we had first to figure out how to interlock arms and legs so that everything fit. And there we sat. How to get the thing going? Being both new and nervous at the sport, we were reluctant to try the kind of running start that we'd seen in newsreels of the winter Olympics. We had enough trouble folding ourselves aboard when it was standing still; how would we manage it scrambling after a moving sled?

So we employed the time-honored rocking method, heaving to and fro with all our unison might. To our delight, it worked. Easing forward, the sled accelerated to a comfortable speed and glided down the curving walk, its runners whispering seductively on the packed snow. Guiding the sled with the steering wheel was as much fun as I had imagined, and far more precise than hauling this way and that on the wooden bar of my Flexible Flyer. I cut as clean a line down the middle of that walk as ever a pro did coursing a bobsled chute. It was just *so* wonderful while it lasted.

All too soon we reached the bottom of the walk, where innovation lost out to bad planning. In far less time than it takes to describe it, the bobsled dropped off the curb into Brooks Drive with a jarring thump and crossed to the opposite side, where the front runners cut cleanly through the loose snow, slammed into the curb, and sheered right off their post. Forward motion didn't abate for four more feet, however, when the back runners caught up with the front and the whole assembly jerked to a stop that piled my two friends into my backside and my chest into the steering wheel. My breastbone hurt for a week, my friends were unscathed, and the bobsled was terminal. I had no way to repair it myself, and didn't know where to get the parts anyway. One of my friends thought he'd like to try, so I just gave it to him. I was too embarrassed to do anything else.

He never did manage it; it sat rusting behind his garage until his dad, weary of fighting the weeds that grew up around it, dragged it out to the curb for the trash man to cart away. It was a short season for the bobsled, but not as short as mine; I never got on one of the things again.

———————

There was, however, that glorious sled ride to school. I never told Mother about that one either (curious, how much obfuscation there was about my sledding life). It was a glorious January morning during my seventh grade year. A fresh deposit of fluff, six inches of it, blanketed the valley and sparked like freshly sprinkled sugar under a rare and brilliant winter sun. It was Temptation with a capital T, and there would be no resisting it.

With clandestine care, Bill Yengst, Ronnie Wolff, and I had crafted our plan. It was to be an exercise in stealth. We would sneak away with our sleds, meet at the corner of North Main and Byllesby safely out of sight of our homes, and ride down the North Main Street sidewalk all the way to school. Once there, we would secrete our sleds in the narrow corridor behind the building, where snow-burdened branches from neighbor's shrubs, stretching almost to the back wall of the school, provided perfect concealment.

Kissing Mother with a casual "See ya at noon," I left at the usual time by the usual side door route. Once outside, and assured that she was occupied, I crept around to the back of the house, jumped down over the stone wall into the driveway ramp and retrieved my sled, which I had stashed there the previous evening. Continuing on into the Leberman's yard, I crept along the row of lilacs and forsythia that divided our yards and dropped down over the front wall onto the sidewalk.

Hearing no dreaded recall from the front door, I knew I had escaped undetected, and coasted on down to Byllesby with a light heart and a guilty conscience. That's the problem with Presbyterian scruples; they don't wait to spoil your memory of fun after you've had it; they get right out in front to spoil your enjoyment before you even begin. Hearing steps puffing up behind me, I turned to see Ronnie trotting to catch up, and Bill was waiting as we approached the corner.

"Okay," we agreed, "we stick together. If one of us gets hung up or has an accident, the others will stay with him."

We lined up, Bill in the van, Ronnie second, and me at caboose, squinting ahead down the brilliant mile of powder that fell away before us. The coast was clear. One by one we trotted a few steps, bent over to position our sleds in line with the walk, and flopped onto them with a breath-knocking thump. Dry powder swirled away as our runners sliced through to find the packed residue of earlier snowfalls. Bill had the clearest view, Ronnie got dusted, and I was half-blinded in a roiling cloud of fluff. What a ride it was. Even the curbs of the seven side streets that lay along our course gave us no trouble—unlike on my ill-fated bobsled ride. By that late in the winter, curb gutters were packed with snow rolled up by the city's plows and trampled to ice ramps by the daily crush of school-bound feet. Our sleds shot off each uphill curb, hung in the air one microsecond, plunged across the street and rode up the downhill ramp as if they'd been designed for it. We even managed to thread our way through the campus without knocking any students off their feet.

The only danger was the threat of cross traffic. Several side streets emerged around embankments or from behind shrubs that blinded us to what might be coming. As our prone forms were well under two feet high, we knew that the odds of a driver seeing us were lousy to nonexistent, and we had no desire to become even flatter. So we dragged our galoshes at each approach until Bill called the way clear. Luck and gasoline rationing were with us: seven times at seven corners the call rang back, "All clear!" and we plunged ahead, quickly regaining the momentum we sacrificed to preclude getting our names in the *Tribune-Republican*.

The only disappointment was that the ride was over almost before it started. Arriving at school looking like the Abominable Snowman, I couldn't believe the speed with which our sleds had consumed the downhill mile. Walking down and back up that hill twice each school day made us fast walkers, and we customarily made the trip—either way—in fifteen minutes flat. (It was that or be late for school or, worse, miss lunch.) Our sleds covered the distance in less than three minutes, even accounting for cross-street caution. That's probably the main reason we never did it again.

There was, of course, the fact that we could never depend on the snow being just right on a day all three of us managed to sneak our sleds away from home; or depend on deluding all three mothers the next time conditions were that perfect. But it was the mile-long haul back uphill at noon, and having to sneak our sleds back into our respective garages without our mothers noticing, that convinced us that the joy of the trip wasn't worth the effort.

If only we could have convinced one of our parents to drive to school at noon to bring us and our sleds back up the hill, it would have been perfect. I won't even give odds on the chance of that ever happening.

CHAPTER 38

Iron Underwear

Mother must have done our laundry in warm weather. I'm almost certain of it, because I don't recall that we ever ran out of clean clothes. In any event, unfaltering dependability was chief among the ways she demonstrated her love for us. It's just that somehow, when I recall doing laundry, it's always wintertime. Chalk it up to experiential learning of the most rigid kind.

Mother's laundry room was in the basement, sandwiched between the furnace room and the garage in a central hallway. It was, at its west end, a dark hole of a space. The stairs from the breakfast nook ran down the side of a massive chimney foundation into the basement. Across from the bottom step, filling the west wall, were floor-to-ceiling cabinets where Mother's home-canned goods were stored. To the right of the cabinets, its dungeon-like gloom penetrated by the light of one tiny window high up on an exterior wall, was a small pantry that provided supplementary storage. It was a root cellar when the house was erected, a throwback to an earlier era, before refrigeration, complete with dirt floor in which to bury root vegetables for winter storage. That idea didn't last long. The ready availability of potatoes, carrots, beets, and turnips at May's Red & White grocery store, or at the Market House downtown, made burying them in the basement floor a quaint anachronism. Keeping an old tradition alive was not worth that much labor; the dirt floor was soon covered by gravel and ultimately by concrete.

By contrast, the wall at the east end of the hall faced the back yard. Since the land sloped away at the back of the house, that wall was above-grade, allowing for a large window that flooded the back end of the hall with daylight. That's where Mother's laundry was set up—a large, double-basin tub fabricated from half a ton of slate next to which stood the workhorse of the enterprise: a round, galvanized metal washing machine with a ringer hanging menacingly off its side, its twin rollers just waiting to trap an unwary child's fingers and squash them flat as a pancake.

The washing machine's metal lid was a superb shield for a boy-warrior engaged with friends in wooden swordplay—when I managed to get out the garage door with it before Mother saw me and hailed me back into the castle for a disarmament conference. But that didn't last long. Dad's penchant for innovation invaded the laundry, and the old washing machine vanished one Christmas, replaced by a gleaming white, front-loading, Bendix automatic rotary-drum clothes washer with a round glass door. Mother's gain as a laundress was my loss as a knight. Glass doors make lousy shields, especially when bolted to the machinery.

But Mother sure liked the way that machine washed clothes. The very idea of being able to load soiled sheets and towels into it, add detergent, set the dial and walk away while the machine filled and drained itself, washed and rinsed the clothes, spun the excess water out of them, and shut off—all while the mistress of the house was profitably occupied elsewhere, even gone shopping—well, that was almost more progress than a modest woman could handle, but she managed. By that single acquisition, the weekly laundry was transformed from an all-day chore demanding constant attention to a morning's diversion. Or so it seemed when weighed against the hours of heavy lifting and endless wrestling with masses of sopping clothes that she had been accustomed to her whole life.

Drying the clothes, however, remained a challenge. It was the one step in doing the laundry that the new Bendix was not equipped to handle. The clothes dryer had not yet been invented or, if it had, Dad hadn't yet heard of it, otherwise, one surely would have appeared in the basement next to the Bendix. So wet clothing still had to be hung up to dry, one piece at a time.

Weather remained the critical factor. If it was raining, the clothes were strung up on half a dozen strands of clothesline suspended just below the open ceiling joists and running the length of the basement hall, from laundry to canning cupboards. This was, of all options, the least desirable. Not only did it take a day and a half for the mostly dead air down there to dry anything at all; the clothes came back smelling like basement and so set with wrinkles that everything we owned looked like seersucker. Then Mother was obliged to try to iron it all smooth again, a dubious undertaking. Even Grandma McCafferty's electric mangle would have been hard put to press out some of those wrinkles. Besides, once I grew tall enough that it was no longer possible to scoot beneath the lines of laundry, every rainy-day trip through the basement was a passage through the haunted forest during monsoon.

That was the exception. Mother not only preferred to hang her clothes outdoors whenever possible, she insisted on it; and on days blessed with sun and breeze, she adored it. The woman could expound more eloquently on the wonders of hanging her laundry outdoors than most poets could manage describing a sunset. The clothes "dried in no time," she was fond of saying; the wind whipped out the wrinkles, blowing most of the work out of ironing; and everything came back smelling like it had absorbed a week's worth of fresh air in an hour.

But—and this is the salient point—even when there was only marginal sun and breeze, or none at all, the clothes went outside anyway. Precipitation actively falling at the moment the laundry came out of the Bendix might provide sufficient reason to admit defeat and resort to the basement ceiling, but if the sky was merely threatening, or conditions made it likely that the clothes would get re-soaked before they got half-dried, they went out on the line anyway. Then Mother would go cheerfully about her day's business, her weather eye cocked outdoors, ready to sound the alarm if rain actually started to fall. That was our call to battle stations, and all hands turned out to grab the stuff off the line before it got wet again—or any wetter than it still was. By the time I was ten years old, we had it down to such a routine that we could empty the line in one minute flat.

Dad had hung what seemed like an awful lot of clothesline, a hundred feet of it, but it was easily filled by a week's laundry for a family of six. The configuration was three-pointed or, if you like, two-sided. The line started at the wall of the house, where it was hooked into the garage door frame, and followed the edge of the fan-shaped driveway ramp to the centenary sugar maple that stood at the edge of the back yard ravine—a distance of fifty feet. From there it hooked ninety degrees to the north and ran another fifty, across the front of the play house to a post sunk in the yard. Those were long spans for anything as wimpy as clothesline, and a single bed sheet or three bath towels fresh from the

Bendix were sufficient to stretch the line enough to start things dragging on the ground. So Dad made four clothesline poles and stored them, ready at hand, in the corner of the garage next to the door—odd scraps of lumber six feet tall with a notch cut into their tops into which the clothesline could be hooked. They were just tall enough to keep most of the laundry airborne.

The significant point here is that Mother's all-weather temperament, and her obsession about drying her laundry outdoors, insured that we were still hanging our clothes out long after our neighbors abandoned the practice in the fall, and equally long before they resumed in the spring—if indeed we ever quit. I can remember winters when we didn't. And that's how we came to the season of iron underwear.

There we'd be, on some brilliant but determinedly sub-zero February morning, struggling to straighten out articles of wet clothing or linen and get them first over, then secured to, the clotheslines before they and our fingers froze solid. No matter how swiftly I worked, I was never fully successful at getting a warm and wet item out of the steaming basket and over the line before it assumed the consistency of oak. The task was especially difficult with bedding, which had so much surface exposure that it turned to sheet metal faster than I could spread it along the line and pin it down. For the rest of the morning, sheets and pillow cases, towels and shirts and underwear swung from the line as if they had been bronzed. Pivoting back and forth on clothespin hinges, they rose and fell according to the bidding of the breeze, without a hint of flap or curl. It was not a day for small children to run about under the clothesline, tossing things this way and that as they zig-zagged among drying laundry. Plowing into one of those sheets on such a morning was like running into a piece of plywood. The stuff could give a child a black eye.

Finally, around noon, the fabric began to relax and show a bit of curl. Ice—as I learned at Mother's clothesline years before anyone brought it up in a high school science class—evaporates. It is simply water that has gotten stiff, to borrow the apt adjective from Thumper, the opinionated rabbit in Walt Disney's version of *Bambi*. And stiff water is bound by the same laws that govern limp water; the process just takes longer. By mid-afternoon, when the low-slung winter sun dropped behind the bulk of the house, shadowing the laundry in premature dusk, everything was as dry as if it had been hung out on a July morning. A whole lot colder, to be sure, but dry. Sheets bunched up just as easily, towels folded and stacked as neatly as ever. Even underwear could be worn without injuring oneself.

And best of all, everything really did smell like it had absorbed a week's worth of fresh air in an hour.

CHAPTER 39

A Splendid Jumble
of Woods and Quarries

T wo years after entering Allegheny, Ruth Ann transferred to Flora Stone Mather in Cleveland, where she could major in vocal music. On arriving, she met a girl from west central Ohio who was away from home for the first time in her life. As anyone who has visited western Ohio knows, much of it resembles your dining room table. Pull off most roads and climb up on your car's bumper and you'll have an unrestricted view of cultivated land stretching from here to Sunday. Having spent her life seeing nothing else, the girl was startled at how "mountainous" it was around Cleveland. Ruth Ann, not wanting to be rude, but fresh from western Pennsylvania's restless and forested foothills, had to stifle a laugh. Neither had traveled more than a hundred miles to get to Cleveland. And both were right: home is the rule by which all else is measured.

I grieve for children who grow up knowing only the press of concrete underfoot, blistering in summer and frigid in winter, their acquaintance with grassland no wider than a ball field, their knowledge of trees no richer than fragments of city park. These places compare to meadow and forest like paint-by-numbers compares to Monet and Michelangelo. Part of my world was paved with concrete and brick, but not a great deal of it. I think myself privileged that my first and enduring sense of the world was mediated by a splendid jumble of woods and quarries that spoke to all my senses because they were redolent with life. My first exposure was practically in our back yard.

Eleven homes ringed our pentagonal block. The lots were deep, one hundred fifty feet or so. We knew every family, and their children comprised our network of playmates. What made our block unusual was the wooded half-acre at the center of it. We never knew who owned it. I suppose it's possible that it belonged to no one, the result of a surveyor's oversight, though that's hard to imagine in a society as obsessed with private property as ours. To us children, it was a stroke of serendipity: as it seemed to be no man's land, we were free to treat it as all kids' land, venue for serial episodes of hide-and-go-seek or capture the flag, or a place to go and talk of forbidden things, knowing that none of us had ever seen our parents wander beyond the mowed edge or fence that marked the boundary of their own back yard. They would stand in a back door and call, sing-song like, "HOW-ard, DO-ris, SUP-per." For a parent actually to come to a back fence was fair warning that patience was wearing thin: "Bar-BRA, you'd better be in here by the time I count to ten, or else!" It mattered little that "else" didn't mean the same thing in the lexicon of our several families; all "elses" spoke of trouble.

Mother detested shouting, so Skinner children were called only if visible. From somewhere, perhaps acquired as a bank promotion or purchased at Murphy's 5¢ & 10¢, she brought home several flat metal whistles, the size of a stick of chewing gum and two-tone. That's a double entendre: the whistles were painted a different color on each side; and when blown, they sounded two pitches, the first and fourth notes of the major scale (think the first two notes of the trumpet call "Reveille" or the Christmas carol "O Tannenbaum"). Mother being Mother and the consummate mistress of musical expression, these twin notes floating flute-like across the neighborhood conveyed all the subtleties of other parents' voices. It's not easy to make a small whistle snarl, but she knew how.

———•———

There were other woods as well. Our hilltop was covered with them, each an interpreter of times and seasons. In fall, their freshly stripped frames arrayed against a north wind, they swayed and hissed their unison complaint at the prospect of winter, and for ample reason. More than one winter night that started serenely enough was jarred by the gunshot crack of a limb split by its own frozen blood. The grip of woodland creatures on life was most tenuous then; small beasts ventured out less often and returned sooner to grass-lined nests and burrows, or simply slept it off in the grip of evolution's ancient ritual of hibernation. I sensed early on that I, progeny of the naked ape, was far more vulnerable than they. It was a wonderful time to be abroad in the woods, especially on mornings gifted by a breathless fall of wet snow that clung to every branch and twig and filled the forest with silence so palpable that it seemed I must lean forward and push to get through it. But not many birthdays came and went before I sensed the limits of the forest's indulgence: that unless I was exceptionally well-clothed, I had best not overstay the light.

(There was of course the June day when I was about eighteen months old and somehow escaped to run out the door stark naked. My exploration of the natural world in my natural state ended abruptly when Frank ran to Mother yelling, "Don ran outside with his stomach on!" But I don't think even then that I would have been tempted to try it in January.)

Our hardwood forests became transparent in winter, exposing more of the land: horizons and vistas that seemed not to exist in summer became obvious; and the shape of hills was defined less by timber than by geology, making the world a harder place. Sunrise and sunset moved closer to the ground, too. Their crimson and gold rays found their way between tree trunks at the root, reaching beyond to strike the eye without having to leap over leaf crowns to get there, and casting shadows so long that I thought I should carry lunch if I hiked out to find their ends.

———————

Spring was muck time in Pennsylvania's woodlands, the bane of every mother who understood that eternal vigilance was the price of a clean floor. Even a dry spring was muddy. The accumulated moisture of winter, whether from ground frost or snowmelt, conspired with spring rains to fill every wooded hollow with frigid water and frog's eggs. The soprano chirp of peepers filled the night even before the ice had fully melted from around the feet of last season's wind-dried cattails, their tops frazzled as if winter had begun to chew on them but found them unpalatable.

Giggling with birdsong as it came, the greening forest reached northward to screen the hills for a new summer, lifting the horizon and making the world a taller place. Skunk cabbage and trillium punched through ooze and loam to claim their fifteen minutes of fame before the ascending sun burst the overhead buds of maple and ash and beech trees that, impatient for spring, had been swelling since January. After that, the woodland floor would have to wait for fall fully to feel the sun again.

Spring is the season for explorers. Those who would discover new worlds must be on their way with the first greening of the land, lest they run out of time. The mystery of life surrounded me at every season, but never more than in spring, when a cubic yard of muck and marsh held more to discover than a square mile of winter, and a single afternoon yielded more that I did not understand than all the heedless weeks of summer—when I cared less anyway. I suppose it was Mother's love of biology that let her accept, if grudgingly, my spring resemblance of the creature from Dismal Swamp. I still wasn't allowed in the house after one of my forays into spring slop, but she was more than usually tolerant of my coming home more than usually dirty. This was a good thing, because I could be depended upon to get filthy. If ever her Bendix clothes washer earned its keep, it was in springtime.

Coming across a melt pond was a curious experience. I knew the woods around home well enough to know where water was likely to be found, standing or flowing. But spring ponds appeared where no pool existed the rest of the year. As deep-wood snow receded (and it was several weeks later melting than snow that fell on yards and driveways), small ponds emerged as if they had been hiding under there all winter waiting to be discovered. They came in all sizes and configurations: some small as a bucket, others too wide to jump across; some round as a pie plate, others like a length of hose; some barely more than wet spots, so shallow that dead leaves broke their surface without even having to float, others too deep to wade across (at least wearing *my* galoshes) and steeped in liquid mystery.

Those were the ones I looked for: they were frog maternity wards wherein gelatinous clumps varying in size from oranges to kumquats clung, where deposited, to twigs blown down a year or two before and now so waterlogged that they stuck to the pond bottom, a secure hook for some fecund lady frog to hang her eggs upon. Reaching into the 32.1° water, my hand scarlet from having already dredged around in other wet spots that still harbored ice crystals, I cupped a glob in my palm and raised it to the light for an obstetrical exam. Tiny, evenly-spaced crescents of embryonic life appeared in the clouded mass, like shadows in the fog, each with a pin-prick eyeball that looked back, unseeing, from within the fragile and frigid womb of frogdom, and I wondered how any baby could possibly begin life that way and survive.

Wandering that way again a week or two later, I stopped for another look. The pond was shallower now. Spring ponds are ephemeral at best, and this one was already shrinking. The cause, I would someday learn, was not evaporation—not in those moist and deeply wooded hideaways. Pennsylvania's woodland pools died by percolation, their water seeping into the earth to reemerge in another place at another time. The stick, barren now of fast-hatching frog's eggs, still lay in the muck to which I had returned it after my earlier survey of its thousand-twin burden. But the dark water teemed with polliwogs that flitted about in what pond was left, scurrying for cover as my bulk overshadowed its surface, propelled by nothing but a spindly spine of tail. If I hadn't known better, I might have imagined the little critters had figured out how to spin their tails like propellers.

Reaching quickly into the still-frigid water, I scooped one out for a pediatric exam. Bulbous body like a glob of crab-apple jelly with skin on it; enormous eyes bulging from its round end (calling it a "head" seemed a bit of a stretch); pouty mouth sucking at the terrifying thinness of air; tail flailing energetically if uselessly at nothing; and on its bottom side the tiny belly buds that would grow into powerful legs. Yep, it was healthy all right. Ugly as sin, but healthy. Reaching into the water one last time, I opened my hand and watched it wriggle off and swim for cover. I always returned polliwogs to the pond after the very first time that I kept some in the mistaken belief that it would be fun to take them home in a can. It was an early and convincing chapter in nature lore titled "On Leaving Well Enough Alone." Polliwogs die quickly when taken from the nourishing soup of their pond, and exact revenge with equal alacrity. Mother let me learn that lesson right off, knowing it would never have to be repeated. Just to press the point, she made me dispose of the corpses, fetid water and stinking can—but not on our property.

A third visit usually failed to locate any pond at all. Only a hollow of congealing muck remained, with green shoots poking through to reach for the rapidly diminishing light soon to be blocked by that expanding leafy overstory. Not a polliwog was in sight anywhere. Nor, for that matter, was there any evidence of the frogs into which some few of them must have matured. Later days assured me they had, as the sun-drenched heat of still afternoons or the humid warmth of summer evenings brimmed with the tenor arias of leopard frogs and contrabassoon harrumphs of bullfrogs. Then I knew there would be polliwogs the following spring, and hoped there always would be.

It was a mystery to contemplate how frogs—who never struck me as among nature's more intellectually astute inventions—knew which pond would last long enough to insure their offspring sufficient time to grow to froghood. I don't ever recall finding polliwogs flopping about on the floor of a pond that vanished before they escaped infancy. For that matter, I never saw a frog around any of those ponds, early or late. I might have accused them of being bad parents but for the fact that their absence seemed not to concern the polliwogs, which became frogs without the slightest help from the adults of their species. Clearly Mother Nature was more interested in results than in anthropocentric definitions of parenthood. And frog parenting got results.

Still, watching their annual struggle from egg to polliwog to adult, I was grateful not to have been born a frog. It wasn't just having to grow up in a pool of frigid muck. It was having to do it without parents—even my single parent—that I didn't envy.

———•———

Speaking of my single parent, wandering into the woods was among Mother's favorite recreational pastimes, and one of the few that she clearly enjoyed doing with us. Mother derived most of her leisure enjoyment from specialized pursuits like music, or activities that demanded individual focus, like the china painting she took up late in life. But she loved few things more than a brisk hike. Even when she was in her mid-eighties, many a younger person who joined her in anticipation of a leisurely stroll on the beach (or a boring one, as they held back so the biddy hen could keep up) found themselves scrambling as her wiry little legs set a pace that scorched their lungs.

Among the closest spots where legs could be stretched and the town left behind, even though its edge was never more than a few hundred yards away, was the stone quarry atop our hill. And among my most vivid memories of it is the day, soon after the end of the war, that she, Frank, and I took a hike in the woods. It was one of those incomparable fall days when Pennsylvania is at its best. A warm breeze made jackets superfluous, and they were soon tied around our waists by the sleeves. A cloudless sky gave free rein to the sun, which shone through the red and gold leaves of October until the air itself seemed to be aflame.

Starting up Hamilton Avenue, we turned north on Jefferson Street and walked until the pavement ended. It was only two blocks, but as far as the town was concerned it might as well have been two miles. The street just quit, as if the bricklayers had run out of pavers, and narrowed to a dirt lane hardly wide enough to accommodate a car. A dozen strides in, the path curved east and ascended a shallow rise into the trees; and that fast the town was left behind. Another fifty strides brought us to a fan-shaped opening where the woods had been shoved back, and the dirt lane gave way to a field of sand and shattered stone. Here and there, a few shrubs and clumps of wildflowers had begun a recolonization effort, their scrubby condition evidence of considerable, if not particularly recent, human disturbance. Confirmation confronted us in the form of a rusty conveyor belt that sat forlornly off to one side, metal wheels sunk a quarter of their diameter into the sand and weeds choking its moving parts. Clearly, the old contraption had not seen service for several years. A few yards on loomed the reason for the disturbance: a 150-foot-long stratum of pure sandstone canted out of the land from the north and sloped gently upward, perhaps thirty feet, before disappearing under the woods that rode over it from the south. Its face was broken—one wants to say chewed—into a rough-hewn cliff by area workmen who had left fractured pieces scattered about its base as they cut and chiseled curbstones and foundation blocks for Meadville's homes, including ours.

Clambering onto the low end of the wall, we threaded our way up its lip and struck off into the woods, following a sometime trail that angled southeast. It was a lovely little lane, closely shouldered by young maple and ash trees whose uniform size and cramped stance told us that the area had been logged over several decades earlier and abandoned to regenerate on its own. Undulating as it went, the path dipped into depressions that might well have birthed frogs the previous spring but were now buried so deep in fallen leaves that we couldn't see our ankles for ten strides at a time.

Suddenly, the trail ended as abruptly as it had started. I don't mean that it petered out. I mean that it marched right up to the edge of another rock face and quit. Had we been less attentive, we might have gone right over the lip in serial order like lemmings off on one of their disastrous migrations.

It's not clear to me how many Meadville folk, beyond those who had worked it and those of us who lived atop the hill, even knew about the quarry where we had started; but even fewer must have known about the wall on which we now teetered. It was the old stone quarry, Mother explained, the one used and abandoned before stone was cut from the wall we had climbed moments before. If you had dropped me at the edge of England's Salisbury Plain and aimed me at Stonehenge, I could not have been more entranced. Frank and I were down the wall and into the middle of it before the initial shock of reaching its abrupt drop-off had time to wear off.

The old quarry was not as dramatic as the new, less cliff than shallow amphitheater.

The walls, few more than ten feet high, were darkened with age and had acquired a patchwork of lichens and moss. The whole had been undisturbed for a long enough time that trees, rooted in the fractured floor and nurtured by generations of layered leaves, were approaching maturity. A few saplings had even found footholds in cracks in the wall, from which unlikely base they turned to hug the quarry face, ever obedient to the genetic programming that compels a tree, no matter where fastened, to reach for the sky.

Gazing at the scene with an expression bordering on reverence, Mother mused quietly, "How nature reclaims its own." I don't know whether she was quoting some sage or the expression took shape in her own mind, but it certainly was apt.

My fancy was most taken by a vertical channel in the face of the rock. Open at the base like a fireplace hearth, a lip of sandstone folded across it several feet above the quarry floor and continued mostly to cover it to the top of the wall. The whole formed a narrow conduit, as natural a fireplace and flue as ever I could imagine, and far more graceful. Long-cold and rain-hardened ashes at the base gave evidence that I wasn't the first to imagine using it that way. More than one fire had licked at that rock channel, its smoke staining the walls and emerging from the brim of the quarry as if from the rock itself. For a moment, my imagination played with the thought that Native Americans had sat about it roasting corn and nuts over the coals, or cooking small game on skewers of ash wood and smoking ceremonial pipes, long before Europeans wandered into the valley below. But the thought wouldn't hold. I knew who had shattered the vein of rock that once filled the hollow of that amphitheater, carting the pieces downhill into the growing town; and I could guess which of my peers might have come here, out of the sight of parents, to build a fire and play at camping and perhaps roast wieners and marshmallows. It wasn't Native Americans.

But it was a delicious fantasy while it lasted.

CHAPTER 40

No Haircuts that Week

W hen Mrs. Dunham pounded that datum into us about Meadville being in a valley surrounded by hills, she never mentioned ravines or talked about rampaging water. We kids discovered those things for ourselves.

Meadville's ravines tended toward deep and sheer. Gullies fifty feet deep were common. Equally important, a ravine might be no wider from one lip to the other than it was deep; and at a few points, some appeared to be deeper than they were wide!

Meadville was carved out of the primeval northern hardwood forest that stretched in unrelieved splendor from the Atlantic Ocean to the Ohio prairie. Only a remnant survived into my childhood years, but Meadville still prided itself on its magnificent trees. Some then standing sprang from winged maple seeds or acorns that found their way to a patch of fertile earth about the time, in 1815, that Timothy Alden met with a clutch of prominent Meadville citizens to discuss the founding of a college west of the Allegheny Mountains. With plenty of trees to choose from, Meadville's settlers had little need to strip the sheer walls of its ancient ravines, and a lot of erosion-inhibiting reasons not to. So most retained their hardwood cover—and remained largely invisible. Indeed, it was possible for someone unfamiliar with the terrain to step right to the brink of some of them without realizing where they were. In consequence, even among long-time citizens, the ravines did not loom large in Meadville's mental landscape.

But their influence was never far off.

—————•———

As a child, I was drawn to those ravines like a pirate to gold. Like the woods behind our house, the ravines showed no evidence of ownership, and none was posted against trespass. And because they were hidden, they offered boys a haven to do the kind of things that no one but boys wanted very much to do anyway, like root beneath sodden rocks in search of red-speckled salamanders, or paw around in streams like raccoons whose probing fingers see more than their lousy eyes, searching for crawfish and snatching one off the stream bottom before a pulse of its powerful tail propelled it backward under a ledge and out of reach.

Or we just wanted to talk about boy things, the kind of stuff we imagined would cause girls' ears to shrivel and fall off, and to say them without anyone hearing. We were fooling ourselves. Walking past years later, when professional responsibilities at the college precluded my mucking about in the ravines at any time of year, I'd smile at overhearing boys jabbering away, perhaps believing that no one could hear them, either. It wasn't that no one could hear, it's that no one cared, which was just as good.

Here and there among the trees, an erratic sequence of short boards nailed up the side of a massive trunk betrayed the presence of a tree house in the branches above, its altitude and elegance dictated by the bravura of its builders—or lack of it. Some had never progressed beyond the early stages of an idea. Others, finished but long abandoned, were in an advanced state of decay, built by children who'd likely become parents themselves by the time my friends and I craned our necks trying to assess their handiwork.

Climbing such a ladder was always a gamble, the odds of a successful ascent depending on the skill of its makers and how many seasons nature had labored on its decay. More than one exploratory climb ended abruptly when a rotted rung gave way, threatening to return this explorer to the ground in a fraction of the time it took him to ascend. It was common wisdom that if we wanted a tree house, we'd better build it ourselves. But our efforts were generally short-lived, never more than a season. In the very time it took to erect a tree house, its rapidly maturing architects grew older or just lost interest, which accounts for all the abandoned tree houses in those ravines. Boys grew up and went away and the objects of their labor, stilled by inactivity and abandonment, hunkered down like Puff the Magic Dragon and waited for nature to take its course.

Without realizing it, we were engaged in forest preservation. Years after I built my last tree house, I stood beneath an enormous beech at the rim of the gully where my friends and I most often played, talking with a colleague who actually did hold title to part of it. I was explaining the finer points of tree house construction when he cut me off with a laugh. "You may have saved this tree," he exclaimed, pointing to the massive trunk. "I tried to have it cut down, but the loggers refused. So many nails are embedded in these trees, they're afraid of wrecking their chain saws!" Amazing, I thought: all those nails we hammered into these poor defenseless trees inoculated them against chain saw disease.

The real attraction of a ravine was its brook, and all of Meadville's ravines had one. Indeed, brooks were the reason the ravines were there. What I really longed for was spring runoff, when my friends and I descended into our favorite gully two blocks from home. It was as secret as they come, its rim screened by mature trees and edged by undergrowth so dense that passing through it required care, lest the next step prove to be three feet lower in altitude than the last. We descended into it like orangutans, swinging from one sapling to the next while our feet punched into the soft loam. By the time we got to the bottom our boots had accumulated enough soil to double in size, and we could barely walk until we sat down on a fallen tree trunk to scrape them off.

Here the water was worthy of our ambition. For hours of a sloppy Saturday morning, we'd labor with rocks and fallen tree limbs and clods of earth and boards pulled down from some tree house of an earlier generation. Anything movable was hauled into place as we struggled to master the torrent. Our goal was always the same: to create as large a pool as the floor of the ravine would hold before the force of the water was too great for the integrity of our engineering. Sometimes we succeeded, sometimes not. Even when we succeeded, it was never for long. Water is determined stuff, and doesn't require sleep like boys do. While we were home in bed, the stream worked tirelessly to undo our labor, and did. By Sunday afternoon, when we might or might not return to gauge the success of our effort, boards and branches and rocks lay strewn downstream and the brook, burbling its victory song, pronounced itself the master.

This was no big deal when it was boys and a debris dam in a ravine. Elsewhere, raging water had to taken more seriously.

———————

The impact of high water had an intimacy about it. The whole town might be inconvenienced, in an abstract sort of way, by the cumulative effect of its renegade streams; but the actual wetting was isolated and personal, in a home swamped, a business shut down, or a life endangered. For me, rising water meant shaggy hair.

Floods visited Meadville during the springs of my childhood as dependably as skeins of migrating geese autographed the northward sky. Such inundations were born of two accidents of nature, the first meteorological, the second topographical.

Northwestern Pennsylvania was blessed with an abundance of water in all its known states—rain, snow, hail, ice, melt water, streams, ponds, rivers, lakes, puddles and swamps. For the most part this was just fine. It was the primary reason western Pennsylvania was so verdant that, were it less beautiful, it would have been boring. Rural wells seldom ran dry, water rationing ranged from rare to nonexistent, and most years the summer watering of lawns was as necessary as carting coal to Pittsburgh. The stuff was just there, in such profusion that the land sometimes couldn't absorb it all.

Which introduced the second factor: all that water needed somewhere to go. Over eons of time, Crawford County was sliced, sub-divided, and reconstructed by water seeking a way out. The county's main artery was French Creek, named by George Washington in 1753 when, as a twenty-one-year-old lieutenant of colonial militia, he was dispatched by Virginia's Governor Dinwiddie to protest French incursion into territory claimed by Great Britain. On his way to Fort LeBoef, near the stream's headwaters south of Lake Erie, Washington camped at the junction of French and Cussewago Creeks where Meadville would one day stand, the farmer in him taking note of the fertility of the flood plain then used by Seneca Indians to plant corn. French Creek also bore David Mead and several companions to the site where, in 1778, they built a blockhouse to defend against Indian attack and founded Mead's Settlement.

But I digress. Reaching French Creek was the main hydrologic problem; to solve it, the water carved the intricate network of ravines into which my friends and I periodically descended in search of the secrets of the known universe. Twenty-seven of them cut right through the fabric of Meadville. Equally important, several tributaries other than Cussewago Creek—most notably Woodcock—drained into French Creek just above Meadville. So every spring, especially when early rain piled on top of melting snow, the whole network churned with water that raged at not finding a simpler way out, reminding us that it was still busy solving the problem. The larger streams could overrun their banks in a matter of hours, spreading out to reaffirm their ownership of the flood plains they had created. Squatters who challenged that claim did so at their peril, and Meadville had its quota of peril-seekers.

Mr. Sanderson was not one of them. He was our barber, and owned a modest shop on North Street, half a block east of North Main. Mr. Sanderson was not an arrogant man. A bald man who cuts hair for a living has little ground for false pride. He was a good-natured soul whose store, in the best tradition of America's small-town barbershops, buzzed with humor, neighborly gossip and lively debate. While the men who gathered there were surely aware of the hoary admonition about debating religion and politics, they honored half of it: I never heard religion openly discussed. But no facet of the political economy escaped their editorial wit.

Mr. Sanderson and his single partner, a large and powerful man, were not the kind of avoid confrontation. I once listened with mingled amazement and delight as the partner told several regular customers of a recent visitor to the shop who quibbled and carped through his entire haircut. This wasn't right, that wasn't right, and—several times—it's still too long! Can't you do *anything* right? With rapidly diminishing patience the burly barber struggled to satisfy the man's demanding specifications. Suddenly the customer glanced in the mirror and groused loudly, "Now you've made it too short!" For a barber already on the verge, that was the proverbial straw. Gripping the man's head firmly in one beefy hand, he ran his clippers over its middle, from his eyebrows to the nape of his neck, shaving to the skin. Never breaking stride, he jerked off the barber's cloth, grabbed the man by the collar and the seat of the pants, and sent him flying through the door onto North Street.

These were not violent men. Trimming my hair one day, Mr. Sanderson caught the corner of my ear in the teeth of his hand clipper. It stung for two seconds and oozed a drop or two of blood—a minor mishap. But Mr. Sanderson apologized so profusely that he arguably covered every contingency for life. His action was at once disconcerting and reassuring. To be ten and to receive so heartfelt an apology from a grown man impressed me so indelibly that, becoming a man myself, I could never again treat dismissively a child who had been hurt by something I said or did.

Still, were I ever tempted to bellyache about the haircut I was receiving, I had only to envision that man flying out the door, face scarlet and cranium grooved by a reverse Mohawk, to remind me of the value of common courtesy.

But neither Mr. Sanderson nor his partner was brazen enough to mess with the forces of nature. Their periodic run-in with high water resulted from circumstances beyond their control, and was grounded in a peculiar bit of local history: Sanderson's shop, like many others along that block of North Street, occupied Meadville's version of London Bridge. Finding Mill Run an impediment to progress, nineteenth-century developers channeled much of it between vertical stone walls. Thereafter, builders simply laid beams across the walls, erecting buildings and laying streets across the stream as if it wasn't there. As a result, some of Meadville's most valuable mercantile properties—not to mention its central fire station—had a river running under them. It accounted for the sometime quizzical looks on the faces of visitors to town when they encountered small street-side warning signs announcing the tonnage limit of an upcoming bridge, though there was nothing in sight but a city street with all the accouterments thereunto appertaining, like buildings, parking meters and light poles. They had no way of knowing that they were about to cross the clandestine Mill Run, the tunnel for which, where it crosses under a street, qualified under state law as a bridge, to be marked and maintained as such.

It was an ingenious solution—except when Mill Run heard the call of nature. Sufficient to handle the stream's normal flow, the block-and-beam tunnel was utterly unable to contain it in flood. And if any of North Street's merchants entertained any doubt on that score, Mill Run quickly persuaded them by rising right up through their floorboards. Among those so affected was Mr. Sanderson, whose barber chairs, their hydraulic vitals suspended beneath the floor of his shop, were disabled by the churning water.

Forewarned that Mill Run was on a tear, I knew there would be no haircuts that week. And even if I failed to get the word, I still knew the minute I turned the corner off North Main and looked up a deserted North Street to see Sanderson's electrified barber poll hanging as motionless as a candy cane. I had to wait until the concealed stream subsided to obtain the periodic and

costly (25¢) shearing required to pass Mother's sharp-eyed inspec-
tion. It felt odd, as best, to approach Sanderson's darkened door
and read the hand-scrawled notice taped to the window: "Closed
due to flood."

There I stood, the only person on a bone-dry street that in
all other respects looked as it did every other business day, shiv-
ering ever so slightly at the realization that a water demon raced
beneath the so-normal-seeming line of shops, clawing at the con-
fining block walls mere inches from my toes and licking at the
floorboards of my barbershop. I hoped I might hear, tried to convince myself I could feel, the sonorous reverberations of its passage. But I couldn't. The men who built that stone channel did
their work well.

And to be honest, I relished the delicious tingle of danger at
being that close to the torrent because I knew perfectly well that

the channel did not extend beneath the sidewalk on which I was standing.

———•·•———

Any doubt I might have entertained about the speed with which a river can spill out across its flood plain was dispelled the warm spring evening Frank and I attended a movie at the Park Theater. I don't recall what was showing; in any event, it didn't impress us half as much as what greeted us when we left the theater. The main door, which faced Chestnut Street, was recessed twenty feet into the building atop a ramp that sloped up from the sidewalk. Everything seemed right with the world—or at least with our town—when we strode up the ramp, bought our tickets (twice as costly at 50¢ as a haircut, and less durable), purchased the obligatory box of buttered popcorn, and settled into our seats in the silver and pastel art deco auditorium to await the black-and-white news reel, Technicolor cartoon, and OUR FEATURE PRESENTATION.

Two hours later, when we walked back down the ramp, everything was definitely not right with our town: the sidewalk at the bottom of the ramp was under water. Luckily, wading was not required; the water had not yet crossed the whole width of the ramp, and by turning up Chestnut Street we stepped immediately onto dry ground. But down Chestnut, all the way to the railroad station, there was only the black and riffled face of a flood nervously reflecting the glimmer of street lamps. We couldn't comprehend how it got there so fast. French Creek was almost half a mile away, and no one had said a thing about it not staying there. Yet all of a sudden it was here, licking at theater and shop doors halfway up the main street of town.

There is something dreadful about coming suddenly upon water in the middle of the night where you don't expect it, and dreadful becomes demonic when the water is where it does not belong. So even though I knew I could walk right down to the rail yards, because I knew where all the curbs and cross streets were, and that the familiar paving bricks and concrete sidewalks still lay just a foot or two beneath the greasy-faced flood, I was more than a little unnerved. Whatever advantages we may have enjoyed by living on top of a hill, they seldom seemed more evident than on that night. As Frank and I hiked uptown, rounded the Diamond and started to climb North Main Street hill, I thought of the people in the valley below, the foundations of their homes already standing in the unwelcome stream, and was grateful that we were not among them. Each uphill stride seemed a step toward the place that was, of every other in the world, most secure that waterlogged night.

———

Another year and another flood, however, taught me that even when out of its banks, a stream might be turned to personal advantage. I doubt that our unwitting tutor on that occasion would ever deliberately have invited the river into his yard. But finding opportunity riding the breast of calamity, he was not about to thumb his nose at it.

It was French Creek again, not riding as high as the night it came lapping at the Park Theater ramp, but far enough over the Erie tracks to shut down the railroad. Several of us, always willing witnesses to crisis, walked down to see the high water and found ourselves at a south end rail crossing. To the north, the Erie tracks subdivided over and over, expanding like an iron mat to create the rail yards. But they weren't visible that morning; eighteen inches of muddy French Creek water covered them in its latest bid to reassert its ownership of the flood plain.

Several yards out in knee-deep water, in hip boots so big that a single boot might have sufficed, stood a wisp of African-American manhood. Worn of frame but still wiry in spite of what must have been seventy years of material deprivation, he leaned upstream to keep his footing against the current sucking at his stick-figure legs. And the while, he scooped large lumps of coal out of the water as they floated toward him from a pile fifteen feet upstream, and dropped them into a battered wheelbarrow that was two ripples short of becoming a boat. He eyed us, side-long and circumspect. I doubt that he trusted white people very much—or that life had given him reason to. But seeing that we were taking no exception to his activity, his face softened and broke into a broad smile, revealing a mouth missing so many teeth it resembled a well-punched data card. Even had we intended otherwise, we could not have refused that infectious grin. We beamed back at him.

Lump after lump of coal, pulled loose by the incessant tug-ging of the current, fell away from the pile, plopped gently into the flood and floated right to him as though his patient hand was a magnet attracting lumps of iron, and was added to the growing barrow load. It was a perfect arrangement. Had the whole pile broken loose at once, he would have lost the most of it, even if it didn't first knock him sprawling. As it was, the pile came apart piecemeal and so gently that it seemed possessed by providential restraint.

At first blush, I assumed he was a railroad employee saving coal which, were it sufficiently buoyant, might have floated all the way to Pittsburgh, maybe even to the Gulf of Mexico, though it did occur to me that it was an odd use of a laborer's time; the company would have to be paying him more than the coal was worth. He quickly dispelled that assumption. Apparently deciding we meant him no ill he made full confession of his purpose: "If I take the coal off the pile, see, then I'm stealin'; but once it floats off the pile, I'm just pickin' stuff up out of the river."

Indeed. Thus may necessity serve comfort, and suffering conspire to offer its own restitution. One night that fall, when the aggregate warmth of summer had faded to chill and the promise of winter came astride the northwest wind, I hope one family on Canal Street sat baking its shins before a red-hot grate fired with coal not stolen, but received as a gift of the flood.

CHAPTER 41

Nocturnal Beetles Indeed

For such a particular housekeeper, Mother gave in to some strange impulses. I knew that she had majored in biology in college, but even so it surprised me to see her invite a bunch of bugs into her breakfast nook.

We called them lightning bugs, though many people call them fireflies. Whatever. They were one and all members of the family *Lamphridae*, which my desk dictionary defines as "Any of various nocturnal beetles... producing a light in its abdomen." How crassly clinical. How utterly unromantic. They were sprites of June invoking the advent of summer; light-bearers of spring scattering shards of sun to seduce the meadows into bloom; messengers from heaven bearing stars of hope to a winter-weary world. Nocturnal beetles indeed.

Every June, on some warm evening when ground mist moistened the heads of newly-seeded grasses and young leaves had matured just enough to curtain the darkly secret places of Pennsylvania's woodlands, the show began. As if out of nowhere, tiny bursts of light appeared in the short grass, rose to meadow tops, invaded orchards and skimmed wood margins, until the evening was alive with gently pulsing candles that fired up, traveled a foot or two, disappeared, reappeared a few feet on, and vanished again. To see one was fascinating. To see a thousand was magic.

It did not take long to discover the pattern, that each bug flew pretty much in a straight line, and that by marking the direction of its glow when lighted, I could project its movement through the dark and anticipate where it would appear next. After I had cracked the lightning bug code, able to judge both speed and direction so that I could tell where one of the tiny sprites was, even as it flew incognito, catching them was a piece of cake. And it was even easier to pounce on one when it settled into the lawn to play lighthouse, signaling its presence and availability to potential mates by periodic bursts of patterned light, or mimicking the signal of an unsuspecting cousin of a different firefly genre, inviting it to dinner—with the guest constituting the main course.

One evening, on an impulse, I ran to the basement cupboard, grabbed one of Mother's empty canning jars and rushed outside to harvest a bottle of light. One by one, I snatched the critters off the grass or tagged them on the fly. When several dozen sput-

tered and glowed in the bottle, banging their heads against the glass in uncomprehending futility, I ran inside to show Mother, who was working at the breakfast nook table.

She took the bottle from me, held it up to the light, and examined the tiny prisoners within. "Aren't they wonderful!" she exclaimed. "I loved catching lightning bugs when I was a little girl." Then to my utter amazement she reached over, turned off the light, and lifted the lid off the jar. It was like watching a 4th of July rocket in slow motion. The squiggling, blinking ball of light came apart, expanded out the open mouth of the jar like the genie coming out of the lamp, and spread through the room. Before long the air was alive with sparks, and every corner became home to a minuscule lamp. We stood there for a long time, surrounded by the wonder of entomology gone bonkers and grinning into the dark, until Mother said matter-of-factly, "Well, we can't keep them in here. They need to be outdoors."

Then began the ridiculous work of trying to put the genie back into the bottle—a task everyone knows to be infinitely harder than letting it out. I soon gave up on the jar, grabbing bugs out of the air or trapping them against the wall and running to the window with one in each small fist to fling them back into the night. Predictably, freeing them took twice the time and effort required to capture them in the first place, and I never thought it worth doing again. I suppose it was another step along the road to insight: from desiring to possess something to simply appreciating it—like my pollywogs, but without their revolting perfume. My first impulse was to capture and keep, until I realized how quickly a bottle extinguishes the light and crushes the magic. In later Junes, I still ran around the yard capturing lightning, but only for a moment of admiration, an epigrammatic communion with one tiny expression of life's infinite and exquisite adaptations. Opening my hand slowly, I studied each little bug as it stood on my palm, momentarily motionless as if disoriented by the impact of being snatched unceremoniously out of the air. Then, consumed by the irresistible impulses of life and replication, it spread its wings and returned to the night air, a gently pulsing candle that fired up, traveled a foot or two, disappeared, reappeared a few feet on, and vanished again, in the timeless choreography of its kind.

Among the trees where fireflies lurked was a young tulip poplar, one of the few planted at the time our home was built. It stood behind the house, in a narrow wedge of lawn defined by the driveway as it curled around the house to reach the basement garage. Tulip poplars are to trees as corn is to field crops: they grow so fast you can watch it happen. By the time I was old enough to notice, the thing was twenty-five feet tall, and a bird feeder had been hung from its lowest branch—high enough to be readily visible from the breakfast nook windows, but not so high as to be beyond the reach of a child putting out birdseed.

For a child with my proclivities, this created an ideal opportunity: the breakfast nook became my bird-watching blind. It was one hobby that Mother and I shared, but curiously in reverse order: her interest, at first tentative, grew as she observed my enjoyment of it, and evolved into a passion that she pursued for the rest of her life. By the time she died, her "life list" (as birders call it) had grown to more than five hundred species.

I don't know why it became my particular hobby, or even when. I began to identify birds before I have any memory of doing so. Part of it, surely, was the genetic thing. Taxonomy was coded into the McCafferty/Skinner blueprint so indelibly that, for some of us, it constitutes a personality disorder. We count, identify, and record things not out of any need to know, but because they are there. After Mother died, I faced the challenge of sorting through her papers. Courts and attorneys hold that financial and legal documents are the crucial ones, but that's only because they are held accountable to execute the statutory

provisions of inheritance. Anyone with a heart knows that scrapbooks and pictures are far more important. In a first pass at making an inventory of the things that mattered, I found a once-fine
black leather notebook tucked into the corner of Mother's desk
drawer. The frayed edges of its cover and the darkened, ring-bound
pages within announced right off that it was old, though we'll
never know just how old. It was a systematic record of Mother's
cultural life. She had recorded the name of every book she ever
read, every play she had seen, every concert and opera she had
attended—or just listened to on the radio. Turning its discolored
pages, I thought of the scraps of paper and stub of pencil she kept
on the shelf above her kitchen sink with which to record every
cent of each day's expenditures. At regular intervals, she transferred the figures into a budget ledger that she kept year in and
year out, from Dad's death to her own. Once she had worked her
way through the fiscal crisis caused by his loss, there was no financial reason to go to all that trouble. It was even less necessary
after her parents died and left her an inheritance more than sufficient to insure her comfort. I doubt she ever went back to review either the financial record or the cultural one. I suspect it
was her security: the feeling that by naming and listing and recording, she maintained order in her world and her life. Many
would think it silly; but it worked for her, and was a far gentler
system than some people employ to impose control over life as
they wish to live it.

I have managed to go a good many years now without the
slightest guilt at not having logged how much I spent on a parking meter or a cup of coffee on any given day, but it still is not
possible for me to start up or down a flight of stairs without the
numerical recorder programmed into my brain clicking on to count
steps: "One, two, (why am I *doing* this?) three, four..."

I am reassured that I am not alone in this. My nephew and his wife, far from their California home attending medical school in Philadelphia, came one year to spend Thanksgiving with us. At the time, we lived in one of Crawford County's oldest homes. It was begun in 1813 as a small, native clay brick farmhouse, onto which a large federalist home was grafted in 1837. Having devised a way to restore it, at once retaining its authenticity and enhancing its energy efficiency, I was proudly touting our success by showing Mark and Liz a graph on which I had charted, over several years, our diminishing energy consumption. In a delightfully candid outburst, Mark observed, "Geeze, Uncle Don, just like Dad—every kilowatt since birth!" I knew that Frank had caught this genetic quirk, but had not realized that Cliff was infected too.

In the same way, when birds happen across my path, my mind not only sets about identifying them, it tabulates how many of each species are there. It mystifies Patricia to this day that, bolting along some interstate highway at 75mph, she sees an unintelligible blur cross the windshield while I see a western meadowlark. If this is compulsive behavior, I at least enjoy the advantage of deriving pleasure from it. And it all started in the breakfast nook.

Hardly a day passed when I did not stand in the window for a long moment to see which of my avian friends might be visiting, especially in winter when the dependable food supply at our feeder drew birds in large numbers. I mused in fascination at their variety and differences in their behavior—why some exploded away in panic at the slightest provocation while others sat stuffing their crops with seeds—and pondered how such fragile creatures not only survived but thrived in the Pennsylvania winter. For the rest of my life, I would never be without a bird feeder. I even found a way to clamp some makeshift device or other onto several dormitory windowsills on my way through college and graduate school.

I also learned the hard way not to say too much about it. Few of my peers cared, and among those who cared least were a few who were happy to use it to taunt and ridicule. The lesson came early, the consequence of an assignment given my fourth grade class by our teacher, Marybelle Chapman, one Friday: we were to list the birds we saw over the weekend and report to the class on Monday. Never had there been a more perfect assignment! I ran straight home, grabbed pencil and paper and stationed myself in the breakfast nook window. I repeated the ritual a dozen times on Saturday and Sunday. By Monday morning I was the most prepared child in the entire U.S. of A. public school system! Then I got slapped down.

"Well," Miss Chapman opened cheerfully. "Who would like to tell us how many birds they saw over the weekend?"

An awkward moment later, one child timorously reported having seen three birds. And with that, the conversation died standing bolt upright. For most children in the class, the assignment had clearly been a waste of time.

"Anyone else?" Miss Chapman prompted helpfully.

"I saw a robin," one child muttered.

"And a blue jay," chimed another. The room fell silent again, and I started having second thoughts. I had held back, expecting to have a pretty competitive list. But this was ridiculous. A voice in my head told me to keep my mouth shut, but my track record at heeding cautionary voices, internal or external, was not terrific, and I walked right into it.

"I saw twenty-seven species," I offered gingerly, immediately realizing (too late, as usual) that my reproving inner voice was right again. The class erupted in derisive laughter.

"You did not!" one classmate blurted, trampling the rule about not speaking unless called upon. Snorts and guffaws bounced around the room. But what really hurt was the expression on Miss Chapman's face. Clearly she didn't believe me either.

"Here's my list," I said sheepishly, and a bit angrily, handing her the paper on which I had meticulously recopied the names— English and fox sparrow, cardinal and black-capped chickadee, white-breasted nuthatch and downy woodpecker, hairy woodpecker and yellow-shafted flicker, mourning dove and song sparrow, slate-colored junco and blue jay and tufted titmouse (*that* got a laugh!).

"That's very good, Donnie," Miss Chapman said, without much conviction, handing the list back to me. She was not an unkind person, but I realized that she couldn't judge my claim because she wasn't well versed enough. It was discouraging to share knowledge—especially when opportunities to do so were as limited as mine were during primary school—only to realize that no one cared. I quickly refolded the list and stuffed it into my shirt pocket. When I got home, I went straight to the incinerator and threw it down. It would be a long time before I again spoke of my hobby to anyone except Mother who, with the precious kind of gesture that parents sometimes extend to their children without even realizing it, began to ask me to identify birds for her.

To this day, having had the pleasure of observing hundreds of species of birds in their habitats across the nation, from Lake Superior's Apostle Islands to Aransas National Wildlife Refuge in Texas, from Maine's magmatic coast to 10,947-foot Beartooth Mountain Pass in Wyoming, no venue is so rich or exotic, or so satisfying, that it excels in magic the birds I watched out our breakfast nook window.

PART VIII

Stuff Around Town

CHAPTER 42

Send in the Clowns

C ircus! Every child of us felt a thrill on seeing the densely colored posters bloom all over town like spring crocuses. Subtlety was not their purpose. Even an illiterate tyke like me could interpret the brash composite of clowns cavorting among pachyderms and prancing horses bearing pretty girls, while the caged and top-hatted lion tamer, chair in one hand and whip in the other, faced his snarling charges and, high above, tightrope walkers strutted in midair and trapeze artists brushed the roof of the tent. The scene was never repeated in any circus I actually attended, but the reality was hardly less riveting than the posters.

Question: How does a five-year old wait patiently for the circus to arrive? Answer: Badly. "How long until the circus gets here?" was right up there with "Are we there yet?" Parents must have grown so tired of the question that they wished the show had come and gone already—or wasn't coming at all. The very fact that we couldn't wait but had to was, I suppose, integral to growing up. A child who had learned to wait for the circus could wait for anything. Still, in the final analysis, parental anticipation was scarcely less childlike than our own.

The Circus Ground was a meadow between Terrace Street and French Creek, part of the original flood plain (as was demonstrated nearly every spring of my childhood). We waited as eagerly for its burden of moisture to dissipate as we did for the end of school. Even preschoolers knew that the drying of that field and the arrival of the circus were cosmically linked.

Before mid-century, circuses usually arrived by train and pitched their tents a few dozen yards off the right-of-way, an arrangement that insured a privileged life for those of us who lived along the Erie Railroad. We didn't have to travel to the circus, it came to us. And when promoters announced that the visit would begin with a parade, we knew we lived in the best of all possible worlds. Then our anticipation knew no limit. Trying to get children to bed on Christmas Eve may have generated more parental aggravation (though I wouldn't stake my life on it). But while leaping out of bed at the crack of Christmas dawn satisfied a largely psychological need, it was essential on circus day: the parade waited for no man, woman or child. Those too late to capture a piece of curb—or just a few feet of sidewalk in the second or third row—missed out.

Sometime during the night, the circus train came to rest on the siding by the Circus Ground, barely hissing to a halt before the roustabouts tumbled out of the crew car to begin the amazing work of erecting the huge tents. The elephants were led out of their box cars and trotted briskly to the flat cars where, with the precision of a drill team, poles as big as trees, coils of rope as thick as a man's arm, and a mind boggling array of steel hoops, pulleys, and stakes were spread out on the ground as if being laid on a blueprint.

Men and pachyderms, wholly versed in the task and working in taut-muscled harmony, soon raised the giant framework of poles and arrayed the canvas about them on the ground. Then, ropes rigid with the strain and the giant snatch blocks groaning in dissent, the towering spread of canvas climbed into the sky. Soon the tops were spread over the perimeter polls and secured to stakes mauled into the earth by teams of three or four roustabouts who, swinging in turn, pounded with such synchrony that no man struck more than three or four blows. Inside, meanwhile, bleachers were erected, performance rings lain down, lines strung for the high-altitude performers, and straw and sawdust spread about the floors and pathways to prevent human feet from trampling them into a sea of mud. At the last, the side curtains were raised and secured, completing the shelter into which, at performance time, Meadville's citizens would pour in anticipation. Ere dawn drove the stars from the eastern sky, all was in readiness.

———•———

I was never sure how, on parade days, the whole crew got transported from the Circus Ground to the south end of Water Street where the parade began, but I suspect that the train simply backed down the track to the rail yard south of town. There was ample room there to unload the wagons bearing animals that for practicality, public safety, or both, were excused from walking—gorillas and giraffes, hippos and bears and big cats. Patient elephants nudged the wagons off the flatcars and worried them into position, one by one, while teamsters backed quartets of horses or zebras or duets of mules into place and hitched them to their loads. Weary performers, jaded by the repetition of travel, endless performances, and bad food, stumbled down from passenger cars and listlessly found their places, while members of the band tuned their instruments in utter disagreement about key and melody.

Finally, by habit as much as managerial control, everything fell into place. The drum major, whistle shrilling, lifted his glistening baton, snare drums rolled to the cadence of the bass, musicians lifted their instruments, and the whole entourage—faces suddenly radiant as though this very day was without equal and they would rather be in Meadville than any other place on earth—unsnarled itself and flowed into Water Street as if borne on a river of music.

Then what sensory stimulation enveloped me, teetering at curbside a dozen blocks away. First contact was of necessity auditory: the procession's approach was hidden from this child who, leaning as far out as he dared (or his mother would permit), was yet too small to see a thing. Larger persons, mostly older children, hogged the view. Unseen were the white-clad and blue-piped drum major's splendid strut and the scarlet-jacketed musicians, their white-panted legs swishing left, right, left, right as if vassals to the beat of the drum, sunrise glinting off their polished instruments. But I could *hear* them, and hear too, beyond the music, the din of a circus on the move. Clopping hooves echoed sharply off street-front buildings and steel-tired wagon wheels grated across Water Street's granite-hard paving bricks. The barefoot shuffle of elephant feet mingled with the flabbering lips of sighing horses and the Bronx cheer of discontented camels, punctuated by the adenoidal bleep of a rubber-bladder horn squeezed by an oversized clown riding an undersized bicycle with its real wheel hub mounted five inches off center.

All of this my imagination clothed in visual flesh long before it processed into view and the actuality proved itself more astonishing than my naïve mind had dreamed. What a visual feast!

So much to absorb in so little time! Back and forth, up and down, my small eyes probed every facet of the passing pageant, wanting desperately to record every detail before it flowed out of view beyond the bigger kids on the other side of me and vanished into imagination again.

Still, imagination was not unsupported. The procession left an olfactory wake so complex that my feeble nose could easily have spent an hour unraveling its origins. Wagon wood steeped in the cumulative deposits of the occupants and the glaze of ten-thousand miles of coal smoke; the gymnasium flare of a hundred too-seldom-laundered uniforms scented by sweat and tent canvas; animal manure dropped onto Meadville's streets with the unselfconsciousness of the innocent; the humid chemistry of exhaled breath from a hundred large animals patiently engaged in pressing their burdens forward. Not that I cared to fathom all the details of their origins: an inquisitive child quickly learns that some things are best left unexplored. Still, olfactory memory being as enduring as it is, pictures of such a parade would not recall it to mind half as surely as being able again to nose its exhaust.

The march was not concluded, however. A circus on parade exerts a pull as irresistible as that on Hamlin's children during the Pied Piper's final walk through town. The last wagon barely rumbled past before the crowd surged off the curb and took up the march, calling and chattering and cheering on its way, albeit (mindful of the horses and elephants) careful about where to put down its collective foot. For those who have never shared the road with large animals, the experience gives new meaning to the term "road hazard." There was nothing amusing about stepping into a pile of... well, you catch my drift—unless, of course, you weren't the one who did it. The poor victim was laughed out of the parade with little choice but to go home and change shoes.

No one I knew wanted to sit next to such carelessness under a tent in which rising temperature could be counted upon to magnify its bouquet.

So moved the promenade as it marched giddily up Water Street, bore off onto Terrace Street, and turned down the short slope to the Circus Ground, where it coiled about itself like a snake curling up for a nap and ran out of steam.

———————

Giant conglomerates like Ringling Bros. and Barnum & Bailey didn't waste visits on towns our size. Meadville was played by smaller, three-tent companies. In addition to the big top that housed the main show, there was usually a separate tent where children were allowed to mingle with denizens of forest and jungle—at a discreet distance. Long before they reached my town, half of these misappropriated creatures were already in an advanced stage of what, were it observed in a human being, would be labeled psychotic withdrawal. The dumb numb sadness of their eyes spoke volumes about the trauma of being sentenced to life imprisonment without parole, their only offense being what they were. Big cats and bears, caged in small wagons, planted hind paws steadfastly in the center of the floor while their front ends paced in futile wanderlust. But my mind was too young to parse such things, and I delighted in the safe shiver of being eyeball to eyeball with a gorilla or looking halfway to the stomach of a hippopotamus—sights not indigenous to my part of Pennsylvania.

The elephants were easily my favorites. A phalanx of tuskers is imposing even to an adult. From my altitude, their backs appeared to brush the tent top, and they weren't in cages! Emboldened by assurances from grown-ups that the great beasts were gentle and meant me no harm, I clutched my little paper bag of peanuts (purchased from a well-supplied attendant with ample change in his pocket) and—checking to be sure that each behemoth was secured by an ankle ring—moved gingerly to the point where their fully extended trunks met my fully extended hand, without stretch to spare. And there we communed: me thrilling to the mystical touch of creatures at once awesome and alluring, they absent-mindedly siphoning up peanuts with the efficiency of a vacuum cleaner hose.

I don't know how old I was before it dawned on me that were I empty handed, the beasts would regard me with utter disinterest, which is to say not at all. That realization prompted my first conscious experiment in deductive reasoning. Holding out an empty hand, I quickly deduced the earliest of Skinner's Laws: a circus elephant's attention span ends when my supply of peanuts runs out.

In spite of that, my heart shuddered in delight as snorts of hot and humid breath steamed my extended hand. They were nothing if not focused. Each time I fed peanuts into their bristly snouts, their trunks curled swiftly to their mouths and reached back out to me without discernible pause, nostrils quivering for the scent while the nasal tip deftly probed the folds of my small hand in search of another peanut. Long before *National Geographic* taught me about the phenomenal dexterity of an elephant's proboscis, I learned the lesson for myself with the help of nothing more than a circus and a bag of peanuts.

The second of the three tents was off-limits to Skinner children. It housed the freak show, an assemblage of creatures who in some regard departed from the norm, whether by extra parts, dramatic variation in girth, or a physical anomaly that scratched the itch of those hungering for an up-close look at the grotesque. It was not two-headed snakes or six-legged frogs that put my parents off, however; these they viewed with the dispassionate curiosity of trained biologists. It was the inclusion of human beings

among those labeled "freaks." Perhaps it was our father's oath as
a physician, which commanded that every person be received
with compassion. Or perhaps it was simply a shared lesson of
their upbringing that could neither justify nor tolerate the display of human beings as objects to gawk at. Prevailing social norms
made it well-nigh impossible for such folk to secure gainful employment in the world of "normal" people. Their reduction to
components of a circus sideshow betrayed the seamy underside
of society, a boil on the body politic that no one cared to lance
because we had not yet learned to label it a disgrace or figured
out how to correct it.

But if outrage is foundational to reform, then a refusal to be
comfortable with abuse is its first building block. In any event, it
was clear to me even as a child that no amount of huckstering
and hyperbole by the freak show barker would tempt my parents
through the door of that tent. Their example demonstrated the
validity of the proverbial admonition to train up a child in the
way he should go, and when he is old he will not depart from it.
To this day it would not be possible for me to walk into such a
tent without feeling moral outrage—not just that it was there,
but that I was.

About the time the elephants had siphoned up the last of
our peanuts, Mother and Dad urged us away with word that the
main show was about to begin—a directive that, unlike "get ready
for bed," required no repetition. Wide-eyed with excitement, we
fell into line under the barrage of patter from the barker who
went on effortlessly, and needlessly, about the wonders soon to
occur under the big top. Swept through the broad tent door by
the surging crowd, our eyes darting about scanning the bleachers, each of us tried to persuade the rest of the family that this or

that place offered the best view. "Let's sit here!" "No, let's sit over there!" we bantered. "We'll sit here," a parental voice calmly asserted. And that settled that.

Anticipation running rampant, we squirmed our way into our seats lined up in rows so narrow that we could not help but poke our knees into the backs of people in front of us and endure, in turn, the knees of those behind us. Whatever impatience we felt waiting for the circus to get to town was goaded to astronomical heights by the press and throb of the crowd that, in the great temperature-raising democracy under the big top, began to sweat in unison. Finally, after an eternity of ten minutes or so, the ringmaster stepped into the pool of light at the center of the tent, spoke his sonorous and amplified lines, and we were off.

Every circus started with a Grand Opening. One entire end of the tent lifted like a curtain, unveiling a passageway through which the entire circus company poured in an elaborate cavalcade that divided, like a river junction in reverse, to circle the tent in opposing directions. The whole exercise was meaningless, a major expenditure of energy the sole purpose of which was to mesmerize a gullible audience by its sheer spectacle, as if that morning's entire parade had come into view at the same instant. It worked. I may have been cross-eyed, but I loved it!

No sooner had the company reunited, flowing back into the passageway, than it broke into its component parts, performers returning one act at a time to prove that they really could wow and entertain. Young women and men rode horses around the center ring, individually or in tandem, not just a single animal but two or three running flank to flank, not just bareback but standing up, not just cantering along but executing a series of exchanges, flips, and human pyramids as the horses, superbly trained, ran flawlessly beneath them. Then the elephants trotted out, their trainers putting them through tricks I'm sure no elephant mother ever contemplated for her baby. One balanced atop a large ball; another rolled over and played dead like your dog—only an elephant fills a lot more floor! Then they formed a chain, the lead animal resting its front feet on a platform while a second reared up and planted its forefeet on the lead animal's back, followed by a third and a fourth, until half a dozen of the huge animals seemed to fill the whole tent. Finally, the audience held its collective breath as the trainer lay down and commanded an elephant to kneel and stand on its head, pinning the trainer between its trunk and knees.

Through it all I sat wide-eyed and gape-mouthed, distracted only momentarily by vendors passing through the crowd hawking hot dogs and orange soda, cotton candy and chocolate bars. The temptation was fleeting. Our parents were as immune to such enticements as they were to our whining. Their restraint was pragmatic: neither wanted to miss the show while shepherding a child to the biffy, nor did they care to contemplate the outcome of putting bad food into hyperactive stomachs. The best we ever managed was popcorn.

Never mind: here came the big cats, the only act confined to a large pen. I felt some gratitude on that point. I understood that the lion tamer knew what he was doing or he wouldn't be in there with all those huge teeth. But anxiety told me that if one of those animals ever took it in mind to ignore the trainer, leap the pen and run a taste test on the audience, *I* wouldn't know what to do. And given my size, I seemed to me about right for a lion *hors d'oeuvre*—especially with popcorn butter dripping from my chin. It was a degree of vulnerability that I was not accustomed to, and explained my sigh of relief as the act ended and the cage door clanged shut behind the last animal. In all likelihood, it also explained my frenetic giddiness at the arrival of the clowns.

I wasn't alone in this. The decision to send in the clowns immediately after the trained animal caper was an inspired bit of scheduling. It wasn't simply a matter of being funny, though they certainly were that. The ease with which they moved us to laughter lay in their ability to glaze with humor the things that we both aspire to and dread. It was all of life opened up, regarded and ridiculed, and thereby made more manageable. Their appeal lay in their uncanny aptitude, with nothing more than a gesture or an expression, to reach from the sawdust floor to the tenth row bleacher, tickling both our ribs and our sense of empathy. Hindquarters barely connecting with the edge of my seat, I laughed so hard that my vision clouded with tears and I gasped for breath. Somewhere in the world there may be someone who dislikes circus clowns. If so, we never met.

Of course there was the trio batting each other about in wacky slapstick, and the five-story burning house out the top window of which a giant woman wailed to be saved by a clutch of clumsy firemen who didn't appear to know a ladder hook from a hose bib. (The drama climaxed when the woman plummeted into a net, only to be catapulted into the air half a dozen times before touching ground.) The inept fire crew was followed by the obligatory twenty-clowns-in-a-Ford-coupe act: how all those full-grown guys sardined themselves into a vehicle that small was among America's most closely guarded commercial secrets.

But none of them performed with greater skill than the flap-footed and balloon-panted man who, his tragicomic face grease-painted in a perpetual pity-party, simply walked around a few feet from the front row, pausing here and there to fix a single member of the audience with his unwavering gaze. It was sectional humor by a new definition: a single bleacher convulsed in laughter while everyone else was silent, or was responding to something entirely different. Wading along as if the audience were the sea and hilarity the tide, this master clown moved from section to section, washed in waves of laughter.

The main show culminated in the acts we had to crane our necks to watch because they were performed inches beneath the soaring canvas roof. If the day was bright (and my selective memory illumines every circus day with sunshine), the entire audience was by then so aglow with perspiration as to make spotlights redundant. It was a moment of true community, as performers and audience together sweated out the show's most sensational feats.

By individuals and groups, performers climbed ladders so tall their rails appeared to merge before they reached the top. To my eye, charged with anticipatory dread for the umpteenth time that overcharged day, the climb took longer than the act that followed. One by one, the high wire artists walked or cycled across their single cable, pausing in the middle to bounce up, twist around, and land facing the opposite direction while my agitated stomach mimicked each flip and the hair on the back of my small neck grew as taut as the wire they walked or rode or, God help us, bounced on. The trapeze artists brought no relief. With heart-stopping precision, they choreographed their swinging bars to allow them to release one bar in time to flip over or twist around to catch the other as it swung into their outstretched hands. Then they ratcheted up the tension, repeating the trick in tandem, one artist letting go of a swinging bar just in time to grasp the out-stretched hands of a partner hooked to another by bent knees. Or two swinging performers engaged in a game of aerial catch, using a third as the ball.

The only thing that held them aloft, swimming in canvas-filtered sunlight instead of plunging to their deaths, was that thread of wire or bar. Which was, of course, an essential ingredi-ent of their showmanship. Had they performed two feet off the ground, who would have paid to watch? We'd done that in our own back yard, treading the edge of the abyss on a two-by-four propped up on old orange crates, or spinning in the swing Dad hung in one of the massive white oaks in our side yard. Never mind that we almost never made it the whole way across the board without falling, or staggered away from the swing without feeling like we were going to throw up: where's the courage in a risk taken an orange crate's elevation from the ground? So while my evolving grasp of mortality dreaded the prospect of watching a human being plunge from the glory of the tent top to oblivion on the sawdust floor, I sensed that the absence of a safety net heightened the thrill, and adjusted my appreciation accordingly.

And when two or three or five performers ventured onto that bare wisp of support together, like as not in some pyramidal configuration that strained endurance to the breaking point, the silence was thick enough to slice. Only when the last performer stepped from wire to platform, gripped the steel scaffold with one hand and extended the other in a gesture of triumph, did the tension snap and the tent erupt in a roar of approbation. At that moment we knew that the impossible was attainable, if not by us, by them, and we swelled with vicarious pride in their achievement.

––––––––

What a mood grasped the crowd as we surged out of the tent into the afternoon sunlight, jabbering about this or that facet of the show, describing to each other in minute detail what all of us had already witnessed. I carried away enough memories to last a lifetime. Was it great art? Hardly. Had it any redeeming social significance? Not likely. Were we entertained? Absolutely. If the circuses of my childhood—especially those that operated on a shoestring—abused and exploited their human talent, still more their animals, my innocent mind knew nothing of it. Those realizations would dawn later, when I caught up with reality, or reality caught up with me. For then, it was a good and magic time, when human beings were as uncomplicated as I imagined them to be and life ran in Technicolor.

Climbing into bed that night, I lay on my back and stared at the ceiling, reliving the whole delirious day until exhilaration finally wore me out and I fell asleep to dream that someday, I too might fly or (better still?) make the whole town cry and laugh and dream.

CHAPTER 43

Market House

P ushing open the heavy front door that was more window than frame, we set the spring-mounted bell on top
jangling our entry and heard "Good morning, Mrs. Skinner" twice—Mr. May's voice the original, his clerk's the echo.
They were equally warm and courteous. "What can we help you
with today?" Those people knew how to win customer loyalty.

"Well, I have quite a list today," Mother said, placing on the
counter the notes she'd prepared during her kitchen inventory.

"Um-hmm, um-hmm. I think I have all these things in stock,"
Mr. May responded. Leaving her list in the center of the counter,
he moved briskly about the store retrieving two or three or four
items on each sweep, returned to the counter and checked them
off Mother's list with a stub of pencil.

I loved few things more than going to that grocery store with
Mother. Had someone asked me if we had a "supermarket," I
would automatically have divided the word into its components,
and replied, "Yeah, we've got a super market." It was called May's

Red & White, actually, and we went there not only because it was convenient but because the May family lived just around the corner from us on Ben Avon Street, and enjoyed the trust of the community.

I suppose it was an average neighborhood grocery for the time. It occupied the ground floor of a frame building no larger than most of the adjacent homes, halfway up Park Avenue hill opposite Hulings Hall, the Allegheny women's dormitory. Even though the store filled the entire main floor, it was tiny by modern standards. Sandwiched into the inside corner where Prospect Street intersected Park Avenue at an angle, the building wasn't even square—it was missing a pie-shaped segment from its uphill side. Yet into that cramped space Mr. May and his single clerk managed to squeeze all the basics that neighborhood wives required for day-to-day cooking and home care. How they ever managed it is a mystery, but it probably had something to do with no one assuming that a market had to offer everything that everyone in town thought they might possibly want, in three different brands, colors, and flavors. I never recall Mother grousing about not being able to find something she needed. Then again, maybe she and the other neighborhood women knew that Mr. May couldn't squeeze everything into his compact little store, so they didn't ask.

What he did manage to squeeze in was extraordinary. The place was a jigsaw puzzle assembled with a shoe horn; Mr. May utilized every square inch of space where something could be stood, stacked, shelved, lined up, or hung. Especially useful were the shelves that reached from the floor to the twelve-foot ceiling, none taller than it needed to be to accommodate the line of goods it held. So cereal boxes and baking soda occupied different tiers, as did soup cans and bottles of olive oil. Medium-sized bags of dried goods sat on lower shelves, and large burlap sacks stood on the floor. A long counter, set a few feet out from the back wall, featured drawers for spices and other small goods.

I watched in fascination as Mr. May picked up the long-handled calipers and neatly plucked a box of cereal off the top shelf, depressing the lever on the handle to squeeze the tongs on top, gripping the box as neatly as if he'd reached it with his hand. Watching me watching him, Mr. May held the caliper pole out to me, his handsome, wrinkle-rimmed eyes smiling more than his mouth, and asked, "Want to try it?" I took it, startled by how heavy it was. But then it was twice as tall as I was. Reaching up to a shelf, I tried to lift down a box of cornflakes but succeeded only in knocking it off the shelf. His hand as quick as his laugh, Mr. May snatched the box out of the air, returned it to the shelf, and hung the pole on its wall hook. Reaching across to tousle my hair, he winked and grinned: "Maybe when you're bigger."

"Did you want that beef tied up into an oven roast, Mrs. Skinner?" the clerk asked, stepping around the end of the bulky meat case tucked into the angle where part of the building was missing.

"No, thank you, I'm going to cook pot roast for Sunday." It occurs to me that Mr. May probably knew what half the families on Meadville's northern hill were having for dinner on any given Sunday. Maybe grocers needed to be as discreet as our doctors, lawyers, and clergy.

"Very well." I ran to the meat counter as he wrapped the roast, knowing that the next item on Mother's list was hamburger. Reaching into the case, he lifted out a slab of beef, cut it into cubes and fed the pieces into the funnel atop the gleaming white and chrome meat grinder. Laying a square foot of butcher paper on the tray, he reached for the switch with one hand and the large wooden plunger with the other, pressing the meat into the funnel until it reappeared out the holes of the sizing disk to flow, slow-motion, onto the paper. Pausing, he deftly lifted the paper and its burden of ground meat onto the scale. "That's about a pound and a half, Mrs. Skinner."

"I'll take a little more, if you have it."

"Okay." The rest of the meat coursed through the machine, and the call came again, "Just under two pounds."

"That'll be fine, thank you." Packing the meat into a ball, the clerk wrapped the paper around it, secured it with string, marked the price on the package and brought it to the counter where everything was gathered. Jotting the price of each item in the margin of Mother's list, Mr. May double-checked the list against the items stacked on the counter and started to add up the total.

"That's twenty-four dollars and thirty cents today, Mrs. Skinner," he said, looking up to see bills on the counter and Mother's hand fingering through her coin purse for the change. Mother often finished such tallies up side down faster than most clerks did it right side up. While she seldom drew attention to it, she wasn't shy about challenging a clerk whose addition was wrong, pointing out the error in a gracious but no-bones-about-it tone of voice, and never mind whether the error favored her or the store. It was just one of those things the morality of which was long since settled. What's more, I never knew a clerk to win the argument.

All the years we lived in Meadville, Mother shopped for staples and daily supplies at May's Red & White. Only the Market House came close in competing for her loyalty.

———·—·———

Hunkered in among Meadville's downtown buildings a block north of Chestnut Street, the Market House was one of Meadville's enduring institutions—a combination supermarket, church bazaar, and specialty mall that had provided area farmers an outlet for their produce since 1870. At once distinctive and functional, its primary feature was openness. Indeed, most of the interior consisted of a single room. The second floor and the broad, sloping roof were supported by a post and beam frame that took the weight off the walls, allowing the placement of large windows along the length of the building.

Market House
1870

The exterior design served the building's purpose equally well, allowing the sidewalks to serve as an extension of the interior. The arrangement was made possible by two factors: when erected, the building was allowed to occupy its own diminutive city block, surrounded on all four sides by streets and alleys; and an arcade roof, supported by a line of posts and trusses, encircled the building and spread over the sidewalks like an umbrella, reaching to the curb line. This unique plan allowed farmers to back their horse-drawn wagons, later their trucks and station wagons, clear to the curb, and to set their stands right on the sidewalk. They were generally spare, those counters—a rickety folding table or two, like as not castoffs from a church social hall, although a few planks laid atop wooden crates or sawhorses served just as well. But spread with the produce of an August sunrise, they were a cornucopia of color and variety to suit every taste—tomatoes and beans, corn and cabbage, potatoes and squashes of such variety as mimics the rainbow, grapes, apples, peaches, and pears. If it would grow in Pennsylvania soil, it was there for the asking at the season of its harvest.

In my memory, the place had a touch of Brigadoon. Quiet to the point of stagnation four days a week, it stretched and yawned, opening sleepy eyes about halfway on Tuesday and Thursday mornings; but on Saturday, it exploded. Before the sun rose over A. R. Wolff & Son's hardware store across Market Street to burn away the chill damp of the previous night, the dew-soaked yield of several dozen farm gardens, orchards, and vineyards materialized on the sidewalks amid a clutter of boxes, baskets and boards.

To the people of Meadville, early didn't matter. Well, actually, it *did* matter, a lot. Bred on the adage about birds and worms, they knew for a fact that the earliest shopper got the best produce. So they came, almost before the farmers' tires bumped to a stop at curbside, eager to paw the produce with practiced hand and assess it with particular eye, choosing what most pleased them. Then they moved inside to thread their way through aisles bustling with bodies and lined with the products of human labor.

To find that just-right loaf of bread or coffee ring, or study the meats and poultry in Mr. Baldwin's glass-fronted refrigerator case, brow knit and lips pursed as the report of the scale was weighed against the quoted price, finally nodding in satisfaction and walking away with fresh chops or a fat stewing hen bundled in crackly and ubiquitous brown butcher paper—this was how to spend a Saturday morning.

Still, a visit to the Market House was not just about shopping. Of all the places where Meadville's folk invested themselves in neighbor relations via chance meeting, only church exceeded market. A Saturday trip predictably consumed twice the time actually required to buy anything. Anyone with half an hour's-worth of shopping to do, who called to their family on the way out the door, "I'm going to Market for half an hour," wasn't doing the math. Small clutches of women and men, as often as not with a child or two circling their thigh trying to be patient and only partly succeeding, stood about under the arcade or blocked the interior aisles, eagerly and noisily engaged in the business of each other.

No topic was too weighty, or too trivial, to escape notice: the restraints imposed by gasoline rationing, the children's teeth, a neighbor's accident, the improvement in the economy, the high school football team's upset of arch rival Oil City last night. By the time the last shopper started home, shopping bags reassuringly tugging at each arm with the weight of a couple of good dinners, and the last farm truck rolled away from the curb, empty baskets and crates rattling in back and cigar box cash register jangling on the seat beside the driver, more news had changed hands than the *Tribune-Republican* could publish in a week. By such means did ordinary activity feed both stomachs and relationships, and Meadville's market-goers acquire both the benefits of good nutrition and the linkages that human communities depend upon to lend joy to days of blessing and succor when tragedy strikes.

If the Market House was productive to one degree or another throughout the year, its bounty was most evident from late summer to mid-fall, when gardens planted the previous May and June matured and harvest time came fast upon us. Then the buying included not just items for the coming week's dinner table but the necessities of the coming winter's pantry. It was a rare September Saturday when we did not wake to find Mother already on her way out the door to market. An hour later she'd return with a couple of pecks of beans or peaches, pears or tomatoes, beets or grapes—whatever was then at its prime. We'd rush down to the kitchen, hoping she hadn't overlooked the opportunity, while downtown, to stop at the Little Home Bakery to pick up some pastry, perhaps cookies plastered with gooey chocolate icing, for the children of the house. She often had, not just because she knew we wanted one, but because she did.

On such a morning, we didn't even have to ask about the day's chores: it was canning time.

First thing, Mother dispatched one of us to the basement to retrieve a bushel basketful of glass-domed Ball canning jars, each jar's rubber ring stuffed inside for safekeeping, to be loaded into the dishwasher.

Now there was a first-generation marvel. Built into the kitchen counter next to the sink, our dishwasher consisted of a round tank with a large trap door on top and a cone-shaped bottom, its point occupied by a propeller powered by an electric motor suspended beneath. Dishes were loaded into round racks that hung above the propeller, a cup of Kleeco detergent was poured in, and hot water was added from a hose in the kitchen sink. When all was ready, the lid was closed and the motor switched on, blasting the dishes with a powerful spray. (We learned just how powerful the day someone hit the switch while the lid was open. Half the kitchen had to be mopped up and wiped down.) When the load was washed, the motor was switched off and the water drained out a valve beneath. Then rinse water was hosed in and the cycle repeated.

Washing the jars seemed like a lot of extra work. Every one had been washed and rinsed after being emptied for some evening's dinner last winter. Where the preserving of food was concerned, however, things could never be too clean for Mother.

While the bottles were washing, the great, cast-aluminum pressure cooker, its lid bristling with hand screw clamps and steam gauge and pressure release valve, was set on the tall-legged gas stove and filled with water. It had to be started early. Bringing that volume of water to a boil consumed the first act of the Saturday afternoon Metropolitan Opera broadcast coming from the breakfast nook radio.

Those preparations concluded, several of us were put to work at the sink or breakfast nook table or stove, skinning or chopping or slicing or pitting or blanching whatever Mother had brought home from market. Then there were tomatoes or grapes to be boiled and juiced through the inverted cone colander, and salt and sugar to be measured and added.

When all was in readiness, the freshly sterilized jars steaming atop the counter were filled with the fruit or vegetable *du jour*, salt or sugar added, boiling water poured in almost to their tops, rubber rings stretched on their shoulders, and glass domes fastened into place with the wire bale—but never tightly. The bales must not be snapped shut, Mother admonished every year of our youth (as if we were slow learners), until the scalding jars came out of the cooker, lest a jar get over-pressurized during cooking and explode. Finally, seven to a load, the jars were lowered gingerly into the roiling water, the heavy lid was lifted into place, and the hand screws were tightened, bolting it down. Soon enough, the safety valve spit steam, cueing us to snap it shut. Within seconds, the needle on the pressure gauge quivered and started to move, tracking the rise of the internal temperature to the prescribed 240 degrees. I never could understand how the thing sat there, silent and immobile, while all that churning was going on inside. It would have been reassuring if the thing had jumped around on the stove or something, just to make all that pressure somehow believable.

Pressure canning was a long process. At 240 degrees, we couldn't simply pop the lid off the canner unless we intended to blow a two-foot hole in the kitchen ceiling. In the wrong hands, that cooker was a bomb. It must be allowed to cool down first; and sealed up like that, the cooling took a while. Nor could the safety valve simply be flipped open, venting off the steam. The sudden drop in pressure would cause the jars to blow out their liquid, then suck in canning water. That may not have been un-sanitary (no microbe I ever heard of survived being boiled at 240 degrees), but it wasn't very appetizing.

So we busied ourselves until the pressure dropped enough to allow us safely to loosen the hand screws and lift off the lid. But even that wasn't the end of it, or of the need for caution. The final step was fraught with pain; lifting the scalding jars out of the cooker and transferring them to the counter with hand-held calipers was not a job for the faint-hearted. But dropping a jar was worse, and not simply because of the labor lost. Take my word for it, a shattered jar of peaches drowned in boiling sugar syrup makes a really awful mess on your kitchen floor. Nor was the final step any less painful for small children with tender fingers; someone had to hold each bottle and clamp the wire bale shut, insuring a final seal and preventing air from being sucked into the jar as it cooled. My fingers smart at the mere thought of fighting with those infernal bales. But it beat the alternative; I could easily tell, next time I opened the door to the basement storage closet, if a bottle had not been sealed quickly enough. No biology teacher had to convince me of how many contaminating organisms live in a thimbleful of air. I learned it as a child from Mother's pantry.

Once cooled, the bottles were given a final rinsing to remove any residue blown out during the cooking (reducing both sticky-handedness and vermin appeal), and carried to the basement to be lined up, two deep, on the shelves of Mother's canning cupboard. There they sat, dark and cool through the weeks into winter until, one by one, we carried them back up to the kitchen, rinsed them one more time (!) and broke their seals. Then the kitchen filled with the aroma of some late summer Market House Saturday, reminding us of what our labor was for.

I always thought that Mother's home-canned fruits and vegetables, pickles, jams, and jellies were the best I ever tasted. At least I am certain that if I never taste any better, I won't have missed much.

CHAPTER 44

The Apparition

I 'm with Dylan Thomas. It is common knowledge that the snows of my youth, and those that fell on the villages of my chronological peers, exceed by several degrees of magnitude the modest flurries my grandchildren now dignify by the caption "snowstorm." This conclusion is not drawn from a study of the meteorological record; it goes deeper. It is derived from folk memory, an awareness stored in some indeterminate quarter of the human brain wherein, regardless of chronological age, resides the collective mind and memory of childhood. Just so, the winter days of my infancy were arguably more brittle, not for their commonplace burden of cold, but because *my* childhood Januaries were scoured by frigid blasts rising straightway out of Boreas' arctic storehouses.

But temperature and snow depth are not all that is recorded in my memory. They are accompanied by palpable silence, stillness so pervasive it reached into our bedroom windows some winter dawns to tell us, even before we were fully awake, "It snowed!"

Or if it wasn't the silence, it was the light. What is it about light? Stirring from sleep one morning, I became aware, even before I opened them, of some radiance prying at my eyelids with the intelligence that we had been visited during the night by the gnomes of winter. The sun was not yet up, its full flood still dammed up behind the hilltop to the east. But I knew. Lying there in bed, not yet more awake than asleep, my mind raced across the room to look outside. Without waiting to stretch or yawn, my body leaped out of bed to follow, and sure enough, everything beyond the windowpanes was clothed in splendid white.

Actually, the white stuff wasn't all outdoors, as the sharp tang of snow against the soles of my bare feet quickly told me. As noted earlier, Mother and Dad believed religiously in the benefit of fresh air. Indeed, until her death at 90, Mother engaged annually in a short but consequential migration: as the first hint of spring surrounded her lakefront home at Chautauqua, usually in March, she moved from her bed to a cot on a second floor porch; and she stayed there until, some late October morning, a dusting of snow on her bed covers signaled that it was time to move indoors for the winter. By the time self-consciousness awoke in us children, we were already indoctrinated. Every room in which someone slept must have one or more of its casement windows opened outward into the night, anywhere from one-inch-peek to wide-mouthed-gape, depending on conditions; neither weather nor temperature existed for which "closed" was the appropriate setting. The bedroom windows in that house quickly became veterans of every form of weather known to Pennsylvania, from drought-dry to Noah's flood, across a 125-degree temperature gradient. It was good their frames were metal.

So when winter's blizzards came snorting around the house, snow blew into the room, packed the channels of the metal casement, and scattered across the floor. Many a winter morning required the first one out of bed to run to the window and brush snow out of the frame, bare fingers smarting in complaint, before the window could be fully closed.

Too, given the vacillating quality of winter at that latitude, the problem was not confined to snow. If whatever was falling was tending toward snow but was not yet entirely persuaded by the time it touched down on the window frame, the residual warmth of the house quickly melted it—until about 3:00 a.m., when things chilled down enough to make the case compelling. Then the morning's challenge was not snow but ice: trying to close those windows when their channels were clogged with ice was an exercise in futility. On some mornings, the frigid steel handle could not even be coaxed inside the frame, and in the contest between ice and fingernails, ice usually won. There was nothing to do then but leave the window ajar and wait for the furnace to warm things sufficiently to free the casement. That, in turn, made for a noisy bedtime, as we pounded on the window frame to break it loose from the refrozen melt water that locked it shut as securely as its handle. The effort required unerring aim. Why none of us ever put a fist through a pane is among the unsolved mysteries of my childhood.

The window routine took on a special excitement on such mornings, as the chill air deposited by the night warmed and filled with the bouquet of cooking oatmeal. It was almost tactile, that aroma, as much felt as smelled, announcing that Mother was already at work in the kitchen. Yet on the heaviest of such mornings, and in spite of our best efforts to bump and clatter as children must, the house was unresponsive, as though night had wrapped it about with a giant muffler. The din of our voices, as insistent as on other mornings, yelling where's my other sock and hurry up and get out of the bathroom and I can't find my homework, seemed to have lost its resonance. Like Peter Pan's shadow, our echoes had come unstitched and run away. And when, breakfast swallowed in a gulp of anticipation, I ran to the front hall closet and pulled on my galoshes, cinched my scarf around the neck of my wool mackinaw, crammed head and hands into wool hat and mittens, and erupted out the door into the taut air of a new winter morning, I entered a world of unrepentant stillness. Like the fox squirrels holed up in the old sugar maple that loomed above the back yard ravine, the frigid mantle had driven both Echo and her shadow into hibernation.

———————

The walk down North Main Street hill to school on such a morning was a demonstration of acoustical constraint. Snow as uniform as cotton batting blanketed every roof. If there had been no wind to drive it as it fell, and the falling had been delicate enough, shelves of snow extended a foot beyond the eaves of houses as if the air were material enough to support them; or folded over, cautiously, as if they meant to reach clear to the ground without breaking. And every branch of every elm tree lining Main Street from home to hill-bottom was so enlarged by its sheath of gossamer fluff that I thought they must have trebled in diameter in a single night.

Streets had not yet been plowed, nor walks shoveled, when we started for school, and Ronnie Wolff, Billy Yengst, and I flogged along in snow up to our knees. Trails of close-spaced puncture marks appeared where sidewalks normally lay, left by the high, hushed lifting and plopping down again of small feet snaking this way and that as we navigated in the absence of familiar land-marks. Our steps were exaggerated by an effort to keep snow out of our boots. I could feel the futility of it even as I lumbered along, the snow working its way deeper and deeper into my boots until it reached my feet where it melted into my socks and turned my toes scarlet.

The voices of other groups of children, making their way from other muffled homes through other muted streets, struck our ears as having traveled halfway across town to find us. By the time the sounds reached us, little was left of them beyond the suggestion that they had been there earlier and passed on by. When one of us yelled—which seemed a strangely disruptive act, akin to shouting in the library—the cry was swallowed by the stillness without so much as a secondary vibration. For a nano-second it was here, troubling the air between us. That fast it was gone again, as a flash of light aimed at the midnight sky vanishes into the void of the universe, never to be heard from again.

On some mornings, if the planets were in precise alignment, and our conduct the previous week had been exemplary, and our timing was precisely right, we were cosmically rewarded by a vision of The Apparition. Though we all might be looking for it intently, we could never be sure who would see it first, or if we would see it at all. For among The Apparition's endearing quali-ties was the always mystical manner of its coming. It was not like watching a car or truck laboring up the hill; such mundane ma-chines appeared definitively at the bottom where North Main and Baldwin Streets form a wye. The instant a vehicle veered right and started up North Main Street hill, it was plainly in sight. Not only could we see it coming, we could probably identify its make and model year by the time it was two blocks away.

Not so The Apparition. It seemed rather to materialize out of the snow, as if emerging from the very heart of winter. If you were not looking at the place of its manifestation, you were already too late. Too, like Lewis Carroll's Cheshire cat in *Through the Looking Glass*, it did not materialize all at once, but came to us in sequential fashion, and silent as a ghost. First visible were puffs of vapor, regular, like chugs of smoke belched out the stack of a steam locomotive. On the most muted of mornings, especially if snow was still falling, this might be all we could see for half a block, even as its rhythmic huffing and our arching footsteps closed the distance between us.

At some point, a rounded shape formed behind the steam, as if a giant version of Grandmother McCafferty's antique Chinese terra cotta teapot was floating up the hill a few feet off the ground, boiling as it came. In its own time, the dark shape began to differentiate into two: a larger, rounded one nearer us and a smaller, more angular one behind. By then it also became evident, impressions to the contrary notwithstanding, that the larger

form didn't really exist independent of the laws of gravity; it was only the deep snow that earlier prevented us from seeing that it indeed had legs, and so admitted its attachment to the ground. The smaller shape behind it stood, not unlike a man, but stood so silently, so unmoving, even while being propelled forward through no labor of its own, that I shuddered at the momentary thought that I was seeing the boatman from the River Styx.

The distance closed rapidly then, and we children stepped off of the sidewalk—or off of where we presumed it to be—to make way for the horse and plow sled. Not until we had done so, and the horse plodded across our front, did we hear the leathery creaking of the halter, the hollow munch of the horse's mouth worrying the bit, the snort of its tangible breath as it labored up the steadily ascending slope. Behind, bearing its burden of a dozen large rocks and one average man, came the sled—a large wooden box, really, with a V-shaped prow that parted the snow and furrowed it back off the sidewalk with a steady, barely audible hiss. The weight of its passage was less heard than felt, a sub-acoustic reverberation that spoke to us more through our toes than our ears. Braced within, one foot planted on the floor and the other lifted against a massive stone, the driver was borne silently by, his stolid eyes looking neither right nor left. It seemed we were invisible to him, no more substantial than the snow through which his uncomplaining beast dragged him.

The faint sounds that marked the plow's passing vanished as quickly as they had come, and The Apparition receded uphill and vanished into the winter morning that brought it, leaving only its frozen wake to evidence its passage. We continued to stare after it until it again vanished into the heart of winter; then jumped with the realization that if we didn't get a move on, we'd be late for school. Clambering back over the new pile of tumbled snow bordering the walk, we stomped our feet in the welcome clearing, and hurried on down the hill on the almost visible pavement.

Once in school, we received further confirmation that our prancing had been in vain. Twice the effort required to pull dry boots on in the first place was now needed to get them off wet. And heavy wool socks retained the dampness throughout the morning, drying just in time to pull wet boots on over them again and hike back up the hill for lunch.

By noontime it was never the same. Snow that absorbs mystery when falling does not retain it at all well when left lying about. The brief time required for our socks to dry and our teachers to complete our morning lessons robbed the snow of its muffling magic. The windrows cast up by the plow had already begun to settle, losing loft and degenerating into mere piles; heat escaping through poorly insulated attics had been busy all morning melting snow from the bottom up, sending trickles of drip-water down roof slopes to solidify into brittle icicles that grew by ranks on every overhanging eave and gutter; and the elm trees' gossamer shrouds were breaking up piecemeal and plopping gracelessly to the ground.

So the climb up North Main Street hill was boisterous again, because the mystery that attended our morning passage was gone. Nor would I see The Apparition again, that day or the next, maybe even for weeks—not until we were once more visited by the night-owlish gnomes of winter, and I woke to find that silence had crept across the window jamb.

CHAPTER 45

Railroad Town

L et's be clear about one thing: no one who grew up awed by the majesty of steam is able to emote eloquently about diesel. Having grown up with steam, I get about as excited by an oval-nosed box spewing foul-smelling oil smoke as I do at the sight of an Ohio River towboat after standing on the deck of Old Ironsides in the Boston Navy Yard. Part of the attraction of early industrial technology in general, and the steam locomotive in particular (at least for me), was that so much of how it worked hung right out in plain sight, where the genius of its design and the quality of its machining could be appreciated. And no flat and gritty expanse of sheet metal, unrelieved by anything but a pipe railing and a couple of louvered vents, no matter how cute its color scheme, possessed the mystic allure of a well-oiled steam locomotive.

Such machines were living actors on the stage of life in our valley, even among those of us seldom privileged to climb aboard a passenger car, settle back, and watch a seamless vignette of world glide past just beyond the expanse of a plate glass window. In contrast to the frequently-voiced adage that children should be seen and not heard, steam locomotives were often heard but seldom seen in our valley. Still, those heedful of the rhythm of things could, like Sherlock Holmes, tell you a great deal based on a mere fragment of evidence, and the evidence most often took the form of a whistle.

So insistent were those things that often they were all we heard. The roar of a train was intimidating when rolling by yards from my toes. But when I stood in our front yard, or was awakened by the sound of it invading my bedroom at midnight, the machinery's noisome din seemed to have been stripped away; only the whistle survived. And what a herald it was. The very fact that diesel engines came equipped with horns instead of whistles was clear evidence of their subservient station in the pantheon of the gods of steel. What's the big deal about a horn? Every driver in town owned one, and blew it at any reasonable provocation. Besides, diesel horns sounded like sheep missing their vibrato: they went BAAAAAAAAA BAAAA! without color or variation. But only steam locomotives had whistles, and a steam whistle, its cord in the hand of an experienced engineer, strutted on the edge of speech.

I knew of people who had lived on our hill all their lives who, on the basis of nothing more than a distant whistle, could tell you what crossing a train was approaching and whether it was hauling passengers or freight. If it was a passenger train they could—with a glance at their watches—say whether it was on time and the precise moment it would hiss to a halt at the station at the foot of Chestnut Street. There were even a few true champions of all things steam (often railroad people and therefore better informed than the untutored among us) who might tell you whose hand held the chain, loosing a precise combination of longs and shorts and coaxing a particular ascending or descending pitch from the pipe stand atop the cowling, punctuating his signature with a set of staccato whoops.

It wasn't simply a whistle; it was a concert in steam, in comparison to which the monotonic bawl of a diesel horn was about as mystical as a cow's belch.

———·—·——

Before the explosive transformation of America's highways and airports that came in the wake of World War II, the railroad was the chief means for getting from here to there. Without passenger trains, moving troops from the country's interior to the coasts for deployment to war theaters abroad would have been daunting. Every railroad town in America was visited by a troop train at one time or another: eight or ten passenger cars crammed to the sash tops with young men off to war, bound for places that most Americans had never heard of, or would see advertised on brightly colored posters in travel agency windows. Many of the young travelers would never make the return trip home; they were fated to vanish into the bowels of the sea, or to wait out the pleasure of eternity in the soil of one of those strange-sounding places that demanded their killing labor because that's where the enemy was.

But those years were, thank God, the exception, and no one was happier when the need for troop trains ended than the students of Allegheny College, including many of my friends, who depended on the Erie Railroad to get them to and from school, and crammed its cars at the start or finish of every academic term. It commenced a slow trickle along the east coast, as if towns in Connecticut and New Jersey had sprung leaks. One or two at a time, young men and women converged on New York City to board a train that rolled across the Hudson, angled north through the mounded bulk of the Catskills, and thundered across New York's southern tier. At each stop, a few more 'Gators, here and there a clutch of half a dozen, climbed abroad; and before long the aisles were alive with milling students and lively chatter and obligatory inquiries about what did you do on vacation and did you get your term paper written, until the other passengers were wishing they'd boarded any day but this. By the time the train angled southwest into Pennsylvania, students were riding everywhere except on the roof, and when they all piled out onto the Meadville platform, they overwhelmed it with their bodies and baggage.

Every September and December, and January and June, one generation after another played out the ritual, until the Erie discontinued passenger service and the rhythmic click-clack of rail cars approaching the station was replaced by a clutter of family automobiles that, with seasonal reliability, clogged the streets and byways of town and campus.

———•———

My most memorable railroad experience occurred one cool day in March. I was perhaps in seventh grade—old enough that Mother was no longer concerned about where I was, even though she probably would have been justified to be. I was downtown on no errand in particular, or one so inconsequential that, once concluded, it didn't merit the effort required to remember. So I wandered down to the station and out into the rail yards. I knew I wasn't supposed to be there. Only railroad employees were allowed out in the middle of the yards; even if the Erie hadn't made the point sufficiently clear, Mother had, on more than one occasion. Still, I surely wasn't the first Meadville lad to wander out there, and as surely wouldn't be the last, but I was the only one that day.

It was tricky walking. Railroad tracks always looked a lot bigger when they were right there to be stepped over than they did when I was watching a train rumble through a crossing, or even when standing a few feet off as a locomotive, bell clanging its syncopated rhythm and pistons venting waste steam, heaved through the station and ground to a halt just far enough down line to position the passenger cars directly opposite the station door. Maybe the enormity of a train overpowered them. But they seemed enormous enough by themselves that day, and the jumble of ties and switches and their underlying bed of slag didn't make them less so. I thought of the serial movie I'd been treated to on a friend's birthday outing, in which the heroine, noted for her sweetness but not her smarts, got her foot stuck in the converging tracks of a switch and couldn't get loose, and the 5:40 was coming around the bend and there wouldn't be time to brake the churning locomotive even if the engineer saw her in time, and the hero was a hundred yards off and she was terrified. But since

it was a serial movie it ended right there and I never did learn how it came out because I never in my whole life was allowed to attend the Saturday matinee two weeks in a row.

So I stopped thinking about it and focused again on what drew me out into the yard in the

first place: a locomotive and tender sitting a dozen yards away,
all alone among several acres of track. Wisps of smoke from the
stack and soft puffs of vapor flaring from a valve or loose joint
here or there told me it had steam up, but it was otherwise idle
and appeared to be unattended. I didn't see the fireman until I
came even with the cab and looked up. He was leaning on the
steam arm, waiting for whatever trainmen seem always to be
waiting for. We considered each other for a moment, expression-
less. Maybe he expected me to say something, to explain what I
was doing standing there in the middle of the company's track; I
fully expected a stern reprimand and reminder that I had no business being there at all, and to get my buckets back to the station
where I belonged.

"Wanna come up?" he asked impassively.

"Sure, if it's okay."

"C'mon." His matter-of-factness was reassuring.

If I thought the tracks were big when wandering across them,
that locomotive looked like a house. The ladder bolted to its side
was dead vertical, and by the time I put hand and foot on it and
looked up, it seemed to go forever, like I might be climbing Jacob's
ladder right up to heaven. But six or seven rungs up my head
cleared the floor of the cab, and the fireman was right where I
last saw him, leaning on the steam lever.

The last step was the hardest. Moving from the top rung
into the cab required swinging around the outside of the ladder,
a maneuver made suddenly unnerving when I glanced at the
ground and discovered that it appeared to be a good deal further
down from the cab than the cab had first appeared to be up from
the ground. And while I had been in no danger of falling up, it
was clear that it would be easy to fall down, and then wouldn't
Mother have a field day. It suddenly made sense why people treading high and narrow places are told not to look down. Gingerly,

gripping the ladder as if my life depended on it (which I thought it might), I stretched my left foot around into the cab and twisted myself on board like a liquid pretzel. I think one hand might still have been gripping the ladder when the rest of me was already three feet inside the cab.

If the fireman was studying my movements, his face didn't show it, though I thought his eyes betrayed a smile lurking back in his brain somewhere. But he was too kind to ridicule, and probably remembered his own first climb into a locomotive, before it became second nature and he learned how to swing out into the air in a looping step that landed him comfortably on the platform. Or, in reverse, to swing onto the ladder and climb down, maybe even to step off the moving locomotive without ever breaking stride, like he'd just laid down his evening paper and was stepping from his easy chair to the kitchen table for dinner. How I would have loved to be able to do that.

But steam locomotives were not in my future; even if trains were, by the time I was old enough I would have been stuck in a smelly diesel cab, not this itinerant boiler-plated open-air coaling station that bristled with more valves and levers than I had seen in my whole life—even on the water softener I had clipped with Phil Benjamin's Packard coupe. The fireman leaned there, saying nothing unless I asked, and I was too awed to ask. He didn't interfere or lecture; he just let me wander around and look, even when I reached out to lay my hand on the place where a valve or lever was polished brilliant by daily handling, or fingered the whistle chain longingly, or peeked through the small vent holes into the hell of red-hot anthracite that glowed so intensely in the boiler's belly that I had to squint to look at it. And all the while I had the uncomfortable feeling that I was standing between the shoulder blades of a huge beast of burden lying in wait of its master's next command, but seeming quite capable of commanding itself to do whatever it wanted, and then who could possibly stop it? Locomotives, I realized, were very serious business. The entire machine quivered with power on a scale I had never imagined.

Years later, I inquired of one of our sons, at the time a railroad engineer, what he guessed the monetary value of one of his freight trains might be. "Oh," he replied, "it has to be fifty to a hundred million bucks." Then, offhandedly, "They get real upset if you put one of the things in a ditch." Indeed.

I would have given anything if the fireman had said, "Say, kid, let's take a short ride," his practiced arm shoving the steam lever to release just enough of that latent boiler power into the pistons to start the huge drive wheels clawing at the track. But moving was not in his orders at the moment, and standing still was. So standing still was all I ever got to do.

Acknowledging my thanks with a nod so frugal that I barely saw the brim of his gray-and-white striped engineer's cap tip (although, smoke-stained as it was, it was more like black-and-gray), the fireman again watched impassively as I grappled my way around his ladder and lowered myself to the ground. While my climb down probably wasn't appreciably more poised than my ascent, I felt like it was. I strode over the tracks to the station with a lot more confidence, too. The track seemed somehow smaller, the tie and slag foundation easier to negotiate. After all, I was practically a railroad man. I had been in the cab of a steam locomotive. I didn't know a single one of my friends who could make that claim.

Then steam locomotion went the way of the dinosaurs and I grew up and got a desk job.

CHAPTER 46

Hard Luck Hill

We could hardly believe what we were hearing. It wasn't so much that it seemed impossible; it was just so unlike anything I had ever heard that it was hard to rank it as credible. Obviously there was only one way to find out: go and see. To my surprise, it didn't take long to persuade Mother to climb into the car and drive us there. It's difficult to appear reluctant when what you ache to do is to break into a run; for Mother, in light of the circumstance, it proved impossible. "Oh, all right. I suppose it wouldn't hurt. Just this once," she chattered, all the while grabbing a sweater and her purse from the front hall closet and heading down the basement stairs without breaking stride. If I hadn't broken into a trot myself, I might not have made it into the passenger seat before the car shot backwards out the garage door, scratched gravel up the curved driveway, and accelerated down North Main Street hill a lot faster than I was accustomed to when Mother was at the wheel. Pressed into the seat by the acceleration, I gripped the door handle

and looked at her with new appreciation. This outing was going
to be worth it.

————•————

To be perfectly honest, the above description is not entirely
truthful. But it is based on fact. It is a compilation of two incidents, identical in nature if not consequence, and noteworthy
because of the ease with which I convinced Mother to get the car
out and go in search of excitement. Both events occurred at the
same place, at the naming of which all true natives of Meadville
would grin and guffaw and start right in to tell you *their* favorite
story about it. It was officially designated Hickory Street, but was
better known by its popular name: State Road Hill.

From the northeast, Meadville was approached by Pennsylvania State Route 77, a generic rural highway that knit together a
number of small communities built around farming and manufacture. Southwest from Corry, where the run to Meadville began
in earnest, the road traversed half a dozen broad ridges before
pausing briefly atop a plateau on the slope of which Meadville's
city line was invisibly inscribed. There, without warning, the road
nosed over and plunged down a mile-long hill directly into
Meadville's east-side residential neighborhood. Of the hills Mrs.
Dunham lectured us about, State Road Hill must be included on
the list of those sure to get your attention. It could as aptly have
been named Hard Luck Hill.

The larger topography was consistent, actually; that slope
was no more precipitous than most of the others that lay between Corry and Meadville. They all rose and fell smartly, a vehicular roller coaster that soared over ridges and swooped through
narrow fertile valleys, the epitome of "rolling country." State
Road Hill differed in only one regard, but it was some regard:
near the bottom, but before it ran out of slope, the road teed

into Washington Street. It was a swell surprise. Drivers unfamiliar with the terrain came booming down that hill oblivious to what was coming, only to confront a sign planted at the corner. It said, "STOP." Not everyone made it.

Every American community seems to have at least one segment of road that has consumed more than its share of lives and insurance dollars over the years, but defies correction, the kind of place where tire tracks go flailing off in three or four directions to mark the passage of vehicles whose drivers totally lost control. State Road Hill was such a one. It amounted to open season on unwary drivers, and we all knew it.

There were more than enough incidents to keep life interesting at the bottom of that hill, where heedlessness and failed brakes translated into bizarre events. I personally witnessed the aftermath of two of them. The first entailed motor vehicle handling that can only be called inspired. The second caused property damage that, while frightful, fortunately fell short of causing fatalities.

———·—·———

The most extraordinary passage involved a woman driver. This was significant. Like all children of my generation, I was tutored in the chauvinistic belief that men drive, women are inept. This assertion came mainly from men, most of whom did not themselves know a carburetor from a camshaft. But never mind that: common wisdom assured me that the advent of the automobile had moved technology light years beyond a woman's limited technical aptitude. "Woman driver" was a pejorative applied to any person, regardless of gender, whose handling of a motor vehicle inconvenienced another—especially if the other was a man.

The incident in question may have—surely ought to have—
forced some of my generation to reconsider the verity of that
common wisdom. It stands in memory as some of the most exceptional driving I ever heard of. Call it luck, call it grace; call it
impossible. It sure got my attention.

I never learned whether she was a resident or just a visitor to
Meadville. It may not have mattered. Indeed, familiarity with what
lay ahead might actually have increased the level of terror when,
about halfway down State Road Hill, it dawned on the woman
and her single passenger that her brakes had failed. Automobile
brakes were neither as efficient nor as dependable then as they
have since become, and hers were out to prove it. Pressing on the
brake pedal, she sensed that her car, far from slowing, was picking up speed. With increasing horror she also realized that pressing the pedal harder would accomplish nothing: it was already
against the floorboards. Abject panic, I suspect, would not be too
harsh a phrase to describe her feeling; and yet, with the presence
of mind that sometimes blesses one abruptly straddling the edge
of mortality, she fought for control of both car and emotion.

Jabbing the clutch to the floor, she rammed the car into a
lower gear in an effort to use the engine to slacken the pace. At
best it only stabilized the car's speed; the vehicle was no longer
accelerating, but neither was it losing momentum as it bellowed
down the hill. She could only pray that no cross traffic was at that
instant approaching the Washington Street intersection, else
surely it would become one of those fateful encounters when
human beings with no prior association are instantly and eter-
nally bonded by common tragedy.

Mercifully, the intersection was empty, although she had
scant time to reflect on that bit of good fortune. Secondary disaster, in the form of the cross street's inopportune profile, rushed

to meet her at what must have seemed the speed of light. State Road Hill, you see, entered Washington Street at an angle of about 70 degrees. Across Washington, however, Clark Street—Hickory Street's natural extension—exited the intersection not just at the traditional 90-degree angle but did so several feet further to the west. No motor vehicle ever built, no matter the driver, could enter that intersection at high speed and successfully cross onto Clark Street without completing one of automotive history's most audacious maneuvers.

Some would say the woman's car survived that challenge only with the help of an angelic hand. Others, if skeptical of spiritual claims, were nonetheless struck with awe: in less time than it takes even to imagine it, her car crossed the intersection and, tires screaming in protest as she tugged at the wheel with all the strength she could command, swerved into line with Clark Street.

There was no time to congratulate herself on her good fortune, however. A mere two blocks ahead—far too short a distance for the engine, though finally dragging down the car's momentum, to halt their frightful journey—Clark Street teed into North Street and stopped. As in ended.

It was evident from the lay of things that this was not the intention of those who platted that part of Meadville and laid out its grid of streets. Beyond the North Street curb, signs of preliminary work on Clark Street's right of way were clearly evident on the landscape. A few yards further on, however, work had halted where the right of way fell off the edge of Mill Run ravine. It was, along that stretch, an admirable ditch, sheer-sided and thirty-five feet deep. The street stopped cold on its north side and resumed on the south, but never the twain had met.

This created a real problem for the Meadville School District: East End School perched on the slope above the south lip of the ravine, and school district boundaries long ago mandated that children living north of the ravine would attend East End School to the south of it. The problem was how to get them there. The closest bridge was half a mile downstream, requiring a child living a hundred yards from the school door to walk a mile to get to it. The city's solution was a compromise: enough money was appropriated to erect a foot bridge on the Clark Street right of way, joining the north and south banks of the ravine and offering children a short, cross-gully walk to school.

And now the city's solution confronted our hapless driver: her line of motion took her directly onto that foot bridge. Attempting a right-angle turn onto North Street was out of the question; angels or luck may have gotten her across State Street, but the physics against making a ninety-degree turn were, given the circumstances, self-evident and inexorable. The woman had two choices and no time for reflection: she could cross the bridge, which might or might not be wide enough to accommodate her car and might—God help her—have children on it; or let the car plunge into the ravine, which would surely mean injury, possibly death. Had she time for reflection, she might have been struck by a rich irony: her improbable survival thus far now forced her to choose between killing children and killing her passenger and herself.

But there was no time. The way ahead appeared clear; she chose the bridge.

Clearing the curb with a jolting bang, she threaded her car, barely two inches narrower than the bridge, the full hundred and fifty feet to the other end without scraping either side, thanking God that it was indeed empty of children. As her car reached the other end of the bridge, the engine's resistance finally overcame momentum. The front wheels dropped off the curb into Walnut

Street and the vehicle came to a rest. I never learned how long the two women sat there, or what post-trauma tremors must have shaken the car before they summoned the strength to step out of it. But I suspect that at least one male driver coming around the corner onto Walnut Street, forced to swerve to avoid the front end of her car, snorted, "Woman driver!"

By the time Mother and I got there, the women were no longer around. But the car was, its front end still hanging helplessly off the curb. I stood at its nose with the other gawkers, nostrils curling at the rank stench of the overheated radiator and burnt rubber, and wondered how it was even possible. Standing there didn't put me any closer to an answer. And I knew by looking at Mother that she didn't have one either.

The driver in the other incident, if no less skilled, was surely less fortunate, and the consequences were far more destructive. Oh... and I should point out that he was a man.

A stranger to town, he approached the top of State Road Hill early one morning ignorant both of what lay ahead, and that his truck's brakes were unequal to the task about to be demanded of them. With no more than a cursory downshift, he started down hill and learned both things the hard way. Whether his load was too heavy or the hill too steep, or some combination thereof, he had acquired too much speed before he was again able to downshift. Smoking like fire in wet leaves, his brakes quickly reached the critical point and disintegrated.

As with the startled woman, his luck held to the bottom of the hill, where he careened into an empty intersection. But where she was riding maybe a thousand pounds, he was straddling seven tons. Now, it is generally recognized that Sir Isaac Newton was correct when, in his First Law of Motion, he observed that a moving body will continue in a straight line until diverted from it by some external force, and the greater the weight of the body, the more force it will take to deflect it. It requires no great leap of logic to realize that it'll take a mighty impressive force to persuade seven tons of flying truck to change direction. Unfortunately for the driver, he had no such force at his disposal. Piling through the Washington Street intersection at break-neck speed, and not to be dissuaded from its appointed trajectory, the truck crossed to the opposite curb, leaped it with an explosive thud, and cut a diagonal swath across three consecutive lawns. Thanks to its position closest to Washington Street, the first house escaped injury, though not by much. From there on (to employ an apt metaphor) it was all down hill.

The folks in the second house had been up but a short time and were going about their morning routine, blissfully unaware that a very large object, traveling under the influence of Newton's Law, was about to join them for breakfast. The man of the house, in the act of opening the front door to retrieve the newspaper and a bottle of milk left there shortly before by their dairyman, was stunned to have a large truck bellow past, removing his entire front porch together with the posts supporting the roof. This was no mean feat: the porch was thirty feet long and ten deep, and every board of it was reduced to kindling. Impressive piece of demolition, that.

But it wasn't the end of it. As the man stood in the doorway, surveying in shock what was left of his porch—which wasn't much—and thanking God he hadn't stuck his head out for a better look, his porch roof dropped onto the rubble. Its trailing edge didn't hang onto the upper story of the house, however, causing the roof to hinge down like an inverted lid; it came down flat and so neatly that it seemed hardly to have lost its structural integrity.

Which is more than could be said for the third house. The folks who lived there were still in bed—though not for long. Only partly slowed by its dismemberment of the porch, the truck rolled smack into the corner of their house, instantly revealing that the structure was never secured to its foundation by lag bolts or strapping. Indeed, few Meadville homes were bolted down at the time, the belief being that the weight of a house was sufficient to keep it from going anywhere. It seemed a reasonable assumption, and was verified by experience. In this instance, however, the converse of Newton's Law came into play: a weighty object (house) standing perfectly still and having no plans to go anywhere can, under the impress of a sufficiently large moving force (truck), be started on its way.

House, meet truck. Or, more accurately, truck, meet house. Did it ever. The vehicle slammed into that six-room two-story-with-attic building so hard that it shoved the entire structure four feet off its foundation. In this case the family really was shaken, not only at being wakened by the untoward noise but by being knocked out of bed and onto the floor. Scrambling to their feet and struggling to get their bearings in their freshly canted dwelling, they were relieved to find that no one was injured. Outside, the driver had not made out so well. Miraculously alive, he was not unscathed; though his physical wounds would heal soon enough, it was clear that he would be haunted for a long time by the emotional savaging he endured on his harrowing ride. While in City Hospital he was racked by shuddering and nightmares, and it was several days before the nurses could calm him enough to get him to come out from under the sheets.

While I would not for the world have missed going to see that mangled truck, I left with a deeper appreciation of the fact that the world can, on very short notice—or none whatever—become a very dangerous place. It was not simply the annihilation of the truck that convinced me; it was standing in that family's yard looking down through the gap now opened into their cellar. It was pretty ordinary as cellars go, holding pretty much what most cellars hold. But it was private, and was suddenly ripped open and put on public display without as much as a by-your-leave to the family. And it was clear that it was going to be a hard and expensive job to put it back together, and all because, for a fractured second of time, the normal arrangements of daily life got out of kilter. I imagined what it would be like to have my home shattered like that, and our things—even our cellar things—suddenly laid open for everyone to stare at, and our home, in a fateful instant, made uninhabitable. Where would we go? How would we live? Who would pay to have it all made right? And even if all those questions had answers, would we ever feel secure in the place again?

I turned away sobered, even ashamed, as if I had been caught like a voyeur, peeping into places not intended for my eyes. Home, I realized, is secure only in a relative way, more dependent on the good sense and thoughtfulness of neighbors than on locks and keys.

Newton was right: a set of assumptions moving freely through life will continue in its course until altered by a powerful force—like a runaway truck.

―――・――

The truck episode produced two noteworthy anomalies. When the smoke cleared and the dust settled and the police were able to figure out what each piece of contorted wreckage had been before truck and house tangled, the engine block was found resting on the seat of the cab, scant centimeters to the right of where the driver's legs had been. That man was luckier than he had any reason to expect. And on the porch, leaning at the precise angle of the dislodged dwelling but still upright, its cream risen to the top in keeping with the immutable laws of the dairy, stood a quart of milk right where it had been left by the same dairyman who, moments before, had visited the newly porchless house next door. I wonder if Newton could explain that one.

Oh... and a footnote, in confirmation that the problem of State Road Hill is yet ongoing: a mid-July 2001 issue of the *Meadville Tribune* published a picture, in living color, of a mid-sized dump truck that lost its brakes coming down the hill and came to rest in the middle of the foot bridge. Unlike the woman's car, however, it was too wide to thread its way across and tore twenty yards of the four-foot metal fence railing right off the bridge. Who knows what will try to cross that bridge next?

CHAPTER 47

Paper Route

W hen he was fourteen, Cliff got a paper route. Most of the time, this made little difference to anyone but him; on weekdays, the paper was published in the afternoon. Leaving school at 4:00, he made his way to the Tribune Publishing Co. building in the alley behind the Post Office on Chestnut Street, picked up his papers, and started walking. Barring unforeseen circumstances, he arrived home in time for dinner. The Saturday edition, however, was a morning paper. And that, as they say, is a different color of horse: it required Cliff to be at the Tribune office around 5:30 a.m. Since in this, as in all things, the family car did not engage in the taxi business, he needed to be on his way soon after 5:00. And getting up that early required borrowing Mother's Big Ben.

When we were older and left home one by one to attend school, where we needed a loud noise to hoist us out of bed for breakfast or early morning classes, we acquired clocks of our own—receiving an alarm clock was a rite of passage. Until that time, Mother's Big Ben remained the family's sole wake-up clarion. In the main, as befits the head of the house, the clock stood on her bedside table. Only when one of us had a legitimate reason to rise early could the clock be borrowed, and then only for the night in question.

Manufactured before the notion got abroad that a product should self-destruct after a finite period of time, necessitating the purchase of a replacement, Mother's Big Ben was crafted for the ages. Steel-cased, with a heavy glass crystal and a mainspring powerful enough to move its namesake atop London's Parliament building, Mother's Big Ben tick-tocked faithfully for half a century. It was designed by civilized people: its alarm didn't take off at ramming speed like North Ward's fire alarm. It approached its task with dignified reserve, in stages, as if it, too, was just waking from sleep and needed a few minutes to accomplish it. A single "ding" inaugurated the wake-up sequence, followed after a few seconds of silence by two dings; then (pause) one ding and (pause) two again. That much was generally sufficient to rouse us enough to reach over and shut it off before it went any further. Which was a desirable thing; after going on for a minute that way, the clock paused as if to take a breath before launching into overdrive. And when it did, its bell being as substantial in decibels as the clock was in construction, it didn't matter whose bed it was standing by; the entire house was wide awake.

As long as it didn't go beyond that first ding or two, the rest of us didn't much care what time Cliff got up. We rolled over and were soon back to sleep. Until the day, a midwinter day at that, when he decided to get a *really* early start and set Big Ben for 2:00 a.m. Why he did so remains a mystery to this day. Perhaps it is best just to accept it as confirmation that childhood's most memorable experiences are often short on foresight.

I don't recall at what hour he got to bed—not that it mattered. It became clear around 2:00 a.m. that it had not been early enough. None of us was ready to wake up at that hour, least of all Mother. So she made no move to stir from her warm bed when she heard the first tentative chime from Big Ben. But then she had no inkling that its alarm had been set for two o'clock, either. So her consternation began to rise when the one/two sequence kept going. And going. Realizing that any second now the thing would erupt and wake the whole house, she scrambled out of bed and made her way quickly to the top of the attic stairs, where she nearly imploded: there sat Cliff on the edge of his bed, blowing on that clock as hard as he could puff.

Cliff never could explain what he was dreaming about that caused him to interpret the sound of the alarm that way. But it was ever after remembered as the morning that Cliff tried to blow the alarm out.

Oh, yes: it was also the last time he set it for 2:00 a.m. Had he not figured out the impracticality of doing so, I am confident Mother would have explained it to him.

Frank, too, briefly took up the paperboy business, not for the *Tribune-Republican* but for a distributor that handled out-of-town newspapers, mostly from Erie. Always one to put his own unique stamp on things, Frank turned the job into an experiment in gastronomical peripatetics. First it was raisins, which he munched as he walked his route. Incessantly. Day after day. Boxes of them. The California Raisin Board must have been thrilled to see the northwestern Pennsylvania raisin sales curve rise so sharply—and depressed to see it drop just as suddenly. For as abruptly as he took up raisin chomping, Frank abandoned it in favor of chewing cloves, similarly influencing the East Indies spice trade. There's no explaining that one, unless it was an unconscious effort to correct a nutritional imbalance by employing the pungent sharpness of cloves to purge an overload of raisin sugar. Whatever the reason, the long-term results were contradictory: Frank continued to enjoy raisins his whole life, but he never much cared for cloves again.

More than any of us, Frank confronted every newsboy's nightmare: the subscriber who refused to pay. In keeping with the trusting morality of America's small towns, it was assumed that people would satisfy their obligations in a timely manner, without being pressed. Goods and services were delivered, often at considerable expense to the provider, on the good faith basis that customers would pay on delivery. That trust, coupled with a general disinterest in how youngsters were treated in an era when "children's rights" was still an oxymoron, could result in a no-win situation for a paperboy like Frank. He was not paid for delivering his papers, but for collecting from subscribers. Only after the distributor collected his full share did Frank receive his. Nor was he permitted to press an errant subscriber with the only tool available, by terminating delivery; such an action required the authorization of the circulation clerk, who seemed unwilling to offend subscribers even when they were weeks in arrears—an odd case of feeding the hand that bites you. The distributor was willing to serve customers who did not pay because it was the delivery boy's nose that took the skinning.

In consequence, every paperboy sooner or later found himself subsidizing the newspaper for an unpaid subscription. Given the prevailing wage, it took very few delinquent accounts to reduce a boy's pay to nothing. Why Frank took the hit more than the rest of us is hard to explain, but one is suspicious that folks who rejected the local paper in favor of some out-of-town issue probably weren't very thoughtful citizens to begin with. If that seems a parochial judgment, it was reinforced by how often Frank's delinquent subscribers, when refusing payment, were downright nasty about it. Young boys reared in the belief that all adults must be treated with respect are poorly prepared to cope with an adult who gets vicious when asked to pay a legitimate debt. For the distributor then to deduct the shortage from the boy's pay fostered trust in neither the customer nor the employer. Fortunately, this was rare. Most of the good folk of Meadville not only paid on time, but did so with a smile and a word of encouragement. Some even paid in advance, earning an extra measure of trust not only for them but for humanity in general.

In an older and wiser time I came to conclude that such modest encounters cultivate mature and trustworthy citizens who know, because they have absorbed it from very real experience, the validity of the admonition attributed to Jesus: If you're not faithful with small things, why should anyone trust you at all?

My own experience with a paper route was on borrowed time. I never had a route of my own, but Bill Yengst did, and he lent me his. Bill's grandmother lived in Florida; and grandmothers, as we all knew, required visiting—especially over the Christmas holiday and most especially if they lived in Florida! Bill and his younger brother were on vacation from school, their mother had no obligations outside the home to require her presence, their father's professional position allowed him to take time off at Christmas, and they were financially able to make the trip. Most important of all, Florida was balmy at Christmas time and Pennsylvania wasn't.

I was envious, because we'd never been to Florida. In those years we couldn't afford it; and besides, the only grandparents we could claim south of Meadville lived in Pittsburgh, which just wasn't the same.

Bill's anticipation of those annual treks south was marred by a single complication, though it wasn't the need to find someone to take his paper route; he was more than happy to exchange his bag of papers for palm trees and salty surf, especially at the advent of winter. His problem was that he would not be home at the New Year, the one time when Tribune paper boys were allowed to solicit tips from their subscribers. What we did, actually, was sell calendars for the incoming year. These were not, admittedly, calendars that you would want to hang anywhere except maybe in your garage. But the custom of buying a colorless broadside bannered with the paper's name in a huge, artless font, featuring a bland photograph of someplace most Meadville citizens never heard of and wouldn't care to visit if they had, was a long-established tradition. Everyone in town understood that it was simply a cover to allow customers the chance to reward a faithful paper boy—or to slight an unreliable one.

There was no set price. People paid whatever they felt moved to give. Some could afford little, but would dig around in pocket or purse for fifty or seventy-five cents and drop it into my palm with a smile as sweet as a June sunrise. Most gave a dollar or two, and a few generous ones handed over a five or ten dollar bill—a king's ransom for a lousy calendar they didn't want and probably would never look at. Each year that I covered Bill's route, I took in seventy-five to one-hundred dollars in New Year's tips, on top of the weekly pay for delivering the papers. To an adolescent from a fatherless family on the back side of World War II, that was a hefty piece of cash. I hardly knew what to do with it all.

This was the ground of Bill's discontent. His parents insisted that whoever covered his route during his absence got to keep whatever pay came in during that period, including the proceeds of the annual calendar sale. And when Mr. and Mrs. Yengst insisted, protest was futile. Bill faithfully delivered his papers for forty-nine out of fifty-two weeks, only to have the single windfall of the year come while he was away. To his everlasting credit, he never allowed the arrangement to sour our friendship.

In retrospect, it is plain that the money was secondary compensation. Oh, I confess that I didn't mind having it! But revisiting those December days evokes a clutter of feelings at the edge of the Winter Solstice, not the memory of a trip to the bank. Dusk was already settling as the weekday paper came off the press on those vacation afternoons when twilight seemed to impinge on noon, and the hours from supper to breakfast were unrelieved midnight. By the time I loaded my papers into the worn canvas bag from the side of which "*The Tribune-Republican*" had faded to hazy illegibility, hoisted the frayed strap over my shoulder and, listing perceptibly to starboard, started the half-mile hike to the first house on my route, the sun was already behind the western hills, abdicating its duties to a string of streetlights. In the deepening darkness, the two-mile route excited a kind of urgency: I was engaged in the important business of carrying the news to the eagerly waiting citizens of Meadville. If the dark had its measure of foreboding, or the cold cut through my worn corduroy knickers to numb my thighs, it only made the anticipation of the bright warmth of Mother's kitchen, saturated with the humid fragrance of cooking supper, the more delicious.

Nor did I begrudge the time required. Careening up the street with a bag full of papers, a boy was well occupied by day dreaming and paper-rolling. The former was possible because the job was mindless to begin with; the latter was effortless because of Cliff's brotherly instruction on both the technique and importance of rolling newspapers—a pedagogical achievement that consumed maybe fifteen minutes. A few folds, rolls, insertions, and twists turned a paper into a tight cylinder that could be thrown with accuracy. In the time it took to walk the first half mile, the contents of my bag were transformed from a bland stack of newspapers into a deployment of missiles. With a little practice, I could toss a newspaper thirty-five feet, hit a front door (courteously notifying the occupants that their paper had arrived), and land it on the floor within easy reach of the door, all without having it come unrolled.

But for a few exceptions, this method of delivering newspapers was fool proof. One kind of exception resulted from faulty fabrication. If my folding technique failed somewhere between the sidewalk and the door of the target house, the velocity of the missile decreased in direct proportion to how quickly the newspaper was transformed into a collection of badly-made parachutes. This was an impressive but dispiriting sight. Getting the pages back in order was never easy, doing it when they had gotten soaked was a waste of time, and doing it in the dark was impossible.

The second exception was a function of trajectory. Thrown from the wrong angle, or subjected to a sudden burst of wind, a paper could end up in the shrubbery or, worse, on the porch roof. The first was the more easily corrected, even though crawling about in the bushes in search of an errant paper was hurtful to my self-image, especially if some neighbor happened to be watching out the window. In the second case—unless I had an extra paper in my bag—there was nothing to do for it but ring the doorbell and confess. "Uh... I'm sorry, Mrs. Smith, but... um... your paper landed on the roof," as if the thing had flown up there of its own volition. I quickly learned the value of carrying an extra paper or two, for just such contingencies. Chances were good that Mrs. Smith—or more likely her husband—would have marginal interest in climbing out on the roof at night in the middle of December to retrieve their newspaper. More than one *Tribune-Republican* lay on someone's porch roof, its vital information eroding into the gutter letter by inky letter until spring rains reduced the remainder to unrecognizable pulp.

The third shortcoming involved customer relations. Some people, especially those whose houses had no porch or stoop, insisted that the paper be put inside the storm door, where it would be out of the weather and could be retrieved without having to step outdoors. From the customer's viewpoint that seemed entirely reasonable. But it sure broke the rhythm of my stride when I was intent on completing my darkening rounds.

An editorial conclusion: boys concerned for the success of their New Year's calendar sales took care not to ignore these exigencies of the newspaper delivery business.

Ah, but where people had porches, and my arm was in top form and the paper was not so fat that it defied tight rolling, I could cruise up a street bouncing papers off front doors for a block at a time without ever breaking stride. It was a good time to be alive.

Cliff also gave me a corollary reason to master the skill of rolling newspapers: in a word, dogs. Some dogs ignored me as I stepped right over their prostrate bodies in pursuit of my appointed rounds. I might even pause to exchange an affectionate scratch behind the ears (the dog's ears, that is) for a friendly wag. Those were the good dogs.

Others barked a good bit, but did so mainly to fulfill their dog mandate: it was their sworn duty to make a great deal of noise on every occasion when something was out of the ordinary. Somehow, having the same boy come by at the same time every afternoon and toss a newspaper onto their porch in the same manner seemed never to impress them as ordinary. Their mouths went off as dependably as Mother's Big Ben. Those were the loud dogs.

But there was always the chance of an encounter with an animal willing to press the attack. Those were the bad dogs. Most of them, fortunately, were small obnoxious mutts who thought that everything that moved was their enemy. Owners of large testy dogs usually didn't let them run free, but owners of small testy dogs seemed to believe that their animals were harmless. From a medical point of view, that was probably true. The damage they inflicted was more likely to require Mother's mending skill than the surgeon's. Still, it was disconcerting to be striding up the street trying to hit front doors while a snarling dust mop was intent on making my ankles look as if they'd gone through Mr. May's meat grinder. Lacking in mandibular power, they were nonetheless expert in psychological warfare, causing me to be nervous. And nervousness too often resulted in newspapers under the shrubs or on the roof.

It was for these in particular that Cliff counseled me to roll one paper with special care, and to stow it in the front corner of the bag where it could be drawn with the lightning reflex of Tom Mix confronting a bad cowboy. At its folded end, a tightly coiled newspaper possessed a sharp corner which, smartly applied to the snout of a snappish dog, had an immediate and salutary affect. Cliff contended that it generally took only one well-connected swat to retrain a testy dog. Cliff probably didn't realize it at the time, but his observation anticipated "instant reinforcement," a concept that behavioral psychologists would not describe for several more years. Reduced to its simplest form, it means, "one lesson is enough." It didn't improve a grumpy animal's disposition or make it less yappy, but it usually increased the distance between its teeth and my ankles, which was the real point of the exercise.

Rarely, there were large dogs not likely to be impressed by a rolled-up newspaper. Indeed, to swat such animals with anything less substantial than a brick hod might goad then into treating a boy less as alien than as lunch. These were the "dangerous dogs." I encountered only one during my rounds as a paperboy, but the experience was memorable (see "instant reinforcement" above). It also revealed quite spontaneously the defensive capability of the humble paperboy's bag. The animal in question was an Airedale, not an especially large breed but, to a fourteen-year-old boy, large enough. To make matters worse, his owners permitted him to run loose in spite of the fact that he had bitten two other children in the neighborhood. So I felt a certain anxiety walking past that house.

It lay near the end of my route, only two blocks from home. On the day in question, I was strolling up the middle of the street, as I often did in the absence of traffic, when some ancient instinct at the edge of consciousness yelled for me to turn around and to be quick about it. I spun about to discover the Airedale, ears back and belly brushing the ground, ten feet away and coming straight at me. I had been taught the old adage that barking dogs don't bite; and while not fully convinced of that, I will attest that the obverse—that biting dogs don't bark—seemed entirely plausible: the mute stealth of the creature seemed to me a clear sign of his intent, and it wasn't benevolent. Instinctively, I swung the paper bag around in front of me and bent over. The dog ran into it so hard that, had the label not long since faded to a mere stain, it might have imprinted itself on his teeth. Employing the best training my elders had provided concerning dogs, I moved slowly toward him, speaking firmly and commanding him to go home; and while it was not part of any lesson learned from my elders, it seemed prudent to keep the bag between us! Sidling first right, then left as if seeking an opening around that confounded bag but finding none, he finally gave up and turned for home, barking loudly over his shoulder. Had he been human I would conclude that he was convincing himself that he had indeed triumphed. I indulged his vacuous gloat. I was just glad not to have my legs perforated.

Much as I emulated my big brothers' behavior, I never set Big Ben for 2:00 a.m. Mother would not have tolerated the same mistake twice in one generation. In any event, rousting myself out at 4:45 to deliver the Saturday paper was quite early enough for me, thank you. In ways I could never have articulated at the time, it proved a subtle step into maturity. The first time I had to do it, Mother got up and fixed a light breakfast to start me off into the chill predawn of December. When we spoke of it the following Saturday at bedtime, however, I told her not to bother, I'd see myself off. She did not appear next morning, though I could feel her, her tiny frame snuggled under the bed covers, still being Mother, gauging my progress by the familiar kitchen sounds of bread being turned in the toaster and the scrape of a spoon stirring the pot of cocoa. Pulling on my mackinaw and buckling my galoshes that morning, I stepped out the door into the sable stillness, sensing that by taking responsibility for myself I had released her from the burden. It was a lovely feeling. Though only a modest step toward manhood, it still came wrapped in pride.

My five feet of stature seemed ten that morning as I strode down Main Street among the close-packed houses still dark with sleeping families, my psyche extraordinarily alert to the details of my narrow but newly fulfilling world. The streets were empty. During the mile and a quarter walk to the *Tribune* office, not a car or person moved. The air was black crystal, and the lightfall from each street lamp formed a pool of day through which I stepped as if pacing off the minutes of morning. And the silence. My memory retained only two sounds: the crunching of my own feet pressing into the pavement of snow, and the rhythmic clicking of control boxes as I passed each intersection and heard the changing of traffic lights that, in control of nothing at all, pierced the darkness with the intensity of pure color. It was almost sad to realize how soon they would be engulfed by daylight and recede into the background of town life.

Perhaps it was too intense a moment to endure for long. In any event, the spell was broken the instant I shoved open the door and stepped into the humid and paper-smelly *Tribune* distribution room, and took up with the chatter and rustle of the other boys bagging their papers. I knew few of them, nor they me. We lived in different neighborhoods, had different groups of friends, attended different classes if not different schools, and went to different churches. Besides, in barely more time than it takes to tell it, we were all out the door again, headed off in thirty-five different directions, members of the same distribution team but working our solitary rounds as boys in the newspaper business.

Dawn crept up on me as I walked, its first hint little more than the washing out of the inky intensity of the eastern horizon. Looking away momentarily to be sure that I hit some front door in the imperfect illumination of a distant street lamp, I glanced east again to witness the barest blush of rose tinting the gray. Next time it was a streak of red, then yellow, making visible the first details of morning along the streets of town. Here and there it was possible to trace the movement of just-wakened people through their homes, as light erupted from a succession of windows. That small one would be a bathroom, where steam floating around the tightly drawn shade had frosted the frigid glass. And that would be a kitchen, where colored glassware had been set on the sash to catch the sun and brighten some woman's time and labor. Formal drapes partly drawn betrayed a living room, and a chandelier in the middle of a room probably hung over a dining room table. (Whoops! Watch your aim or you'll land one on the roof!)

Dawn was in full flush by the time I crunched up the flagstone steps to our front walk and rounded the corner of the house to let myself in the side door. Mother was downstairs by then, preparing *real* breakfast. And after getting up several hours early to walk four miles of winter morning, the better part of it lugging that bundle of papers, I was more than happy to let her be Mother again. I'd grow up some more next Saturday morning. In the interim, it was still good to be a kid.

CHAPTER 48

Drugstore

I t was unusually warm for a late May afternoon, enough to
bring to mind Dad's quip about being able to fry an egg on
the sidewalk. It probably wasn't all that hot; but the north-
bound spring, which always seemed to slide effortlessly from the
Florida keys all the way up the Carolina piedmont, lost inertia
getting over the Blue Ridge and stalled somewhere around
Morgantown, as if snagged atop West Virginia's stubby mountains. There it hung like a rubber band hooked on a boy's thumb,
stretched to the breaking point. And when it finally let go, it
snapped all the way to Lake Erie in a day and a half.

The taxpayers' money had clearly been wasted on me all
afternoon. I'm sure we were being taught something of eventual
if not cosmic value; that I heard none of it was not the teachers'
fault. Every window in Meadville High School was open as far as
paint-clogged channels and missing sash-weights would permit,
and the building looked like a six-year-old with a couple of half-
grown adult teeth accompanied by a lot of vacancies. It didn't

help. Dogwood blooming on the Diamond and the library lawn across Main Street was so sun-drenched that the light appeared to come from inside it, and the air invading our classroom was so scented by apple blossoms that I thought I might just be able to swim in it. The fantasy of levitating out of my chair and doing the breaststroke right out the window, while the teacher looked astounded and the class cheered, was visceral enough to seem almost real. Besides, all the breeze in Crawford County wasn't enough to cool that schoolfull of fevered teenagers on such a day. So I reflected on the inhumanity of a system that kept me in class while spring was doing a song and dance on the front lawn, and scowled furtively at the clock. Fortunately, the teacher failed to observe me, else I might have found myself staying after school to enjoy the humorless breeze alone. Then again, perhaps the teacher's averted gaze was deliberate. Any observer knows that when a jail must be guarded, the guard is confined as securely as the inmates. I can't imagine that her hankering to get out of that overripe building was less intense than my own; her desire to escape was my salvation.

The four o'clock bell had the clang of a cell door springing open, and I bolted through it like a condemned man just granted clemency. Safely outside, I located a couple of friends who, skipping the preliminaries, looked at me and I at them, and we all said as one, "Ballinger's!" Working loose from the teenaged herd milling about in front of the high school, we crossed into the shade of the Diamond, ignored the walks in deference to the shortest-distance-between-two-points theorem, and cut a beeline across the grass to the corner of Chestnut Street. Careening right at the corner, we spanned the breadth of the walk with youthful bravado, our gangling boy's gait consuming one concrete slab per stride until we turned in at the door of our favorite drugstore.

It's curious how time amends vocabulary. "Drugstore" has almost disappeared from the language, as if some former resident of town, gone to his reward, has been absent long enough that only the old folks remember his name. But it was, in my growing-up years, a foundation block of community along with the likes of grocery store, clothing store, shoe shop, hardware store, gas station, bakery, and butcher shop. And while drugstores were the "pharmacies" of our town, "drugs" didn't begin to exhaust their offerings. We could, of course, obtain everything desirable for first aid home health care: patent medicines, rolls of gauze bandage and adhesive tape, iodine and Mercurochrome, thermometers and hot water bottles (though I thought that a curious name for a rubber bag). But the close-aisled shelves were stacked with a range of other necessities.

Alarm clocks (which, like Mother's Big Ben, did you any good only if you remembered to wind them), writing paper and fountain pens, bottled ink and mucilage, shaving mugs and soap, shampoos and lotions, razors of both the straight and safety persuasions, combs, brushes and barrettes, pipes and tobacco—all were there for the asking. Magazines were there, too, some long since vanished from newsstands and public consciousness: for the family, *Life* and *Look*; for women, the *Ladies Home Journal*; for the serious reader, *Atlantic* and *Harper's*; for the handyman and dreamer, *Popular Mechanics*; and for everyone, the *Saturday Evening Post* with its eagerly-anticipated covers by Norman Rockwell.

For the kids, there was a rack of the new, must-have comic books: *Archie* and *Andy Panda*, *Wonder Woman* and *Nancy*, and the adventures of *Red Ryder*. We couldn't wait for new editions of *Captain Marvel*, each of us wishing with all our might that our own shout of "SHAZAM" might instantly transform us from pantywaist kid to indestructible agent of justice and nemesis of evil.

Like church and school, drugstores were olfactory settings. Each article that helped make a drugstore unique added a particular fragrance to the bouquet, so that even a child could go blind-folded into any drugstore in the land and know immediately what it was.

Indeed, that is still true. Walking into such an old-fashioned drugstore today, when one can be found, is to experience again how the power of smell recaptures history. Such a place looses a flood of memories that draw me back to childhood and home.

It happened in 1998. Driving west in early September, Patricia and I passed through the small Wisconsin town of Dodgeville—a nineteenth-century gem with a near-perfectly preserved main street. The preservation seemed wholly unselfconscious. No late twentieth-century urban planner or councilman seemed to have concluded that the place would be more charming if its original facade was modernized. More likely the sparkle remains because it never occurred to anyone that it could be improved upon. In the middle of Dodgeville's three or four blocks of downtown was a corner drugstore which, like everything around, appeared much as it must have when it first opened. Walking through its door was like stepping through an olfactory time warp. Were it not for the dress of the staff and patrons, and the topical timeliness of their conversation, we might have thought ourselves pulled back half a century.

———— · ————

While Meadville supported half a dozen drugstores at mid-century, each the favorite of its own clientele, two inhabit my childhood: Ballinger's and Wirt's Cut-Rate. It was at Ballinger's that Cliff, as a young teenager weary of lugging 150 newspapers across town in all kinds of weather and attracted by the idea of a regular salary, got his first job. Any idea that his duties would be stationary was dispelled in a hurry, however. The place was in transition—and moving—from Ballinger & Siggins at the corner of Water Street to the newly organized A. L. Ballinger Company, housed in a sparkling new store further up Chestnut Street across from the Post Office. Cliff's first assignment was to lug boxes of drugstore paraphernalia two and a half blocks from the old store to the new.

The completion of the move didn't end the running, however: the mainstay of his job (which Frank inherited when Cliff went off to Mercersburg) was to deliver prescriptions—on foot. Whether either of them accumulated more miles, and wore off more shoe leather, delivering newspapers or drugstore prescriptions is open to debate. The calls came from all over town, and all over town they were obliged to go in response.

I think it safe to say that Frank won the trophy for the silliest of all possible assignments, maybe for all the delivery boys in the history of Crawford County. A woman who might fairly be labeled eccentric called Ballinger's, not once but periodically, complaining of a headache and requesting two aspirin. Delivered. We never understood why Mr. Ballinger agreed to her requests. Perhaps it was the expansive sense of social responsibility displayed by most Meadville business people. Then again, maybe it was the fear of losing a customer who was more than capable of spreading negative remarks all over town about her "former druggist"— though it wasn't clear that anyone would take her seriously. Nevertheless, Frank was handed the small packet containing two aspirin with instructions to hoof the mile and a half round trip between the store and her home. Even at the modest wages then paid teenagers, it's a safe bet that Frank earned more delivering those pills than Mr. Ballinger did by providing them.

But finally, there was the *real* reason for drugstores, the one
that insured their popularity as after-school teenager hangouts:
the soda fountain. Of the two drugstores we frequented, Ballinger's
was by far the more dignified—too much so to attract large high
school crowds. Or at least Mr. Ballinger was. Even to sit at his soda
bar demanded seemliness on the part of any kid wanting to hang
around long enough to finish his soda. Some adults had to work
to get our attention; not Mr. Ballinger. His gaze, so unrelenting it
would make a great horned owl flinch, was akin to Superman's X-
ray vision, except that where the superhero's glance passed right
on through its object, leaving no trace of its presence, we could
feel Mr. Ballinger's stare poking at our backsides. And while he
might be behind the drug counter at the back of the store, and we
on stools at the soda fountain in the front, the weight of his scru-
tiny did not require so much as a glance in his direction to confirm it, and we modified our behavior accordingly.

That may explain why the high school crowd preferred Wirt's
North Street store. Mr. Wirt was no business dumbbell: the location of his store half a block from the high school made it a natural venue for after-school congregating. But proximity alone did
not explain why teenagers jammed the place every weekday afternoon at one minute past four. Meadville's public library was
directly across the street from the school, and no hordes of kids
crowded in there. They went to Wirt's because, if not welcomed
with open arms, they were tolerated, and for teenagers that was
good enough.

Their behavior was a case-study in the ripple effect of economic activity. The consumption of cokes and hot fudge sundaes
alone was sufficient to keep the entire mid-adolescent population of Meadville well broken out, insuring lively sales of acne
medication. More—or so Mother was convinced—it provided job

security for Meadville's dentists. "You're rotting your teeth out," she groused at Ruth Ann. Unfazed by the adult logic of the case, Ruth Ann and her peers, equally unconvinced by *their* parents' logic, packed into Wirt's booths each weekday afternoon, stuffed nickels into the juke box (the music of which could not possibly be heard over such teenaged tumult), and spooned enamel-eroding fudge sauce into their faces.

Not to mention the dependable profits generated for Meadville's Coca-Cola franchise. While Coke was available in the light-green, ribbed glass bottles then popular for picnics or ball games, the preferred venue for soft drink consumption was a drugstore fountain. Students displaying all the symptoms of advanced dehydration erupted out the school door at something approaching the speed of light, navigated the intersection via just about any route except the designated crosswalks, and lined up three deep at Wirt's counter, digging into pockets or purses for dimes—or begging them off friends in exchange for meaningless verbal IOU's—to order up their favorite flavor.

Like a person possessed, the soda jerk filled their orders with an efficiency that would warm the heart of a motion-study expert: grab the familiar flared glass; punch in a couple of squirts of

Coke syrup from the line of pumps built into the counter and, unless the drink had been ordered "plain," add a squirt of the customer's requested flavor—vanilla or lemon or cherry or chocolate; swing the glass onto the tray beneath the fizz-water spigot and pull the handle with one hand while twirling the long-handled soda spoon with the other; cut the flow one centimeter shy of the rim; slide the bubbling elixir, still swirling, onto the counter and into the customer's hand; retrieve the dime and drop it into the cash register drawer en route to grabbing the next glass. It was done without a nanosecond's hesitation. An experienced jerk so mastered this choreography that the individual steps coalesced into a single, unified motion. Had it possessed greater aesthetic quality, it might have earned the grudging approval of a balletomane.

Then there were kids like me who, never much of a cola fan, still found the produce of the fountain to our liking, no matter whose drug store we happened to be in. Our beverage of choice was a "phosphate"—a drink that combined pure flavor and utter simplicity. My favorite was vanilla, a shot of which was stirred into plain fizz-water. You can't get much simpler than that. However, my adolescent sweet tooth did require special instructions to the soda jerk: pump the flavored syrup into the glass and fill it with fizz-water *without* stirring. Barely breaking the surface of the liquid with my straw, I consumed the drink from the top down, from the dry-tart charged water beginning toward an increasingly sweet and flavorful finish, until the final few slurps delivered nearly undiluted vanilla syrup oozing in sugary sweetness across my tongue. Umm! It just didn't get any better than that.

Sadly, soda fountains were made obsolete by giant super market chains intent on absorbing the lucrative pharmaceutical business, or when drugstores themselves expanded to become hybridized supermarkets, leaving no place for neighbors to share something refreshing while engaged in relaxed conversation. Except in rare cases, mostly in the form of small-town coffee shops, nothing quite like drugstore soda fountains exist any longer; and America, in my judgment, is the poorer for it. How many kids know how to make a fountain coke any more, or can find the equipment even if they do? And I doubt there are a dozen Americans under the age of sixty-five who even know what a phosphate is.

Maybe I've lived too long.

Three More Returns

My second arrival in Meadville followed my 1950 graduation from Mercersburg Academy—though "escape" more accurately summarizes the closing of my high school career. Since Mother sold our house the year before, Meadville was no longer home, but I had been accepted at Allegheny. My admission was almost certainly based on family reputation—a factor that would prove no more valid as a predictor of success in college than it was at any earlier level of my education. I was still dyslexic, and still had not overcome either the condition or the discouragement that was its main spin-off. By the middle of my junior year it was obvious that, absent either a miracle or a transformation, further effort would be a waste of time. No miracles being anywhere in sight, I knew I would have to pursue transformation. I didn't know how; I only knew it would not be at Allegheny.

The college was then on one of the most inhumane academic calendars ever devised: fall semester classes ran from early

September to mid-December, broke for a two-week vacation, then resumed for a week before final exams. I doubt that the human mind is capable of designing a schedule less conducive to enjoyment of a holiday. Long before I left campus that frozen December, I knew that the semester was beyond redemption. Walking out of my last class on my twentieth birthday, I went home to Chautauqua, picked up the phone and called my friends and neighbors at local draft board No. 92 in Fredonia, NY. The Korean War was on, and the woman who answered the phone almost suffered a cardiovascular incident.

"You want to *what*?" she exclaimed.

"I'd like to volunteer for the draft," I repeated.

"W-well," she stammered, "when would you like to go?"

"How soon can you take me?"

"I have a group reporting January 20."

"Where do I report?"

"At the federal building in Fredonia, 8:30 a.m."

"Thank you," I said, "I'll be there," and hung up. I'll bet that conversation dominated *her* lunch hour. I took my last final exam on January 15th and walked away from Allegheny, hoping to return some day but in no condition to even think about what that might mean. A month later, Mother forwarded a letter to me at Camp Gordon, Georgia, where I had been ordered for military police training. The dean of the faculty, who had been my father's colleague and was one of the college's most deeply respected men, was obliged to inform me that the faculty had dismissed me for low scholarship. He must have found a hard sadness in writing that letter. For my part, I read it dispassionately and with a single thought: "What took them so long?"

As it turned out, I stayed in Georgia for two years. The officer in charge of training was a Captain Nelson, a veteran of both World War II and the Korean conflict and reputed to be the most decorated officer in the U.S. Army at that time. I can't vouch for the accuracy of the claim (I never heard him say it of himself; it was said about him by his peers), but there was no room between his shoulder lappet and shirt pocket to fit any more ribbons than those he already wore. Concluding that my artistic skill was of more use to the nation than my ability to direct traffic and patrol off-base bars and brothels, Nelson invited me to stay on at regimental headquarters as a draftsman—to create visual aids to help train future generations of military police. That was a stunner; I was unaccustomed to being asked whether I wanted to do *anything* in the Army. I would figure out later that the man simply understood that people are more dependable if committed to a task by choice, and he was right. He would quickly earn my respect and admiration, and I would work as hard for him as for any one in my life. I can count on the fingers of one hand the people who effectively shaped my ability to serve young people, and Captain Nelson's place on the list is secure.

So I stayed at Camp Gordon, and the anticipation of being shipped to a potential combat zone gave way to the routine and boredom of garrison life, allowing me ample time to consider the future.

Two things, I would conclude, changed mine. In entering the Army, I entered an environment where, for the first time in my life, family history meant nothing. Whatever expectation my officers had of me as a soldier had nothing to do with the respect my family enjoyed in our community, or how well my sister and brothers had done in school. I was on my own and would make it, or not, accordingly. It was arguably the most exhilarating thing that had ever happened to me. I determined to make it, for no reason more profound than that I couldn't imagine doing otherwise. Without yet recognizing it, I adopted an attitude articulated years later by my father-in-law, a high school principal: "Finally, it's not the IQ that counts, it's the 'I will'." It wasn't just that I meant not to fail in the Army; I meant never to fail again for the rest of my life.

However, to give due credit to the way that mundane factors alter life (my wool snowsuit is a case in point), I confess that the second change I underwent was more important than the first: I had two birthdays. I was reminded years later, during graduate school, how significant this was: in the question and answer period following a lecture by a skilled criminologist, someone asked what factor is most likely to transform young men from criminals into productive citizens. He didn't even hesitate. "Their twenty-first birthday," he shot back. Simply put, I was growing up; when I returned to Allegheny two years later, no longer the youngest in my class, I brought a level of experience measurably greater than that of any of my new classmates who entered directly from high school. The faculty approved my readmission for January 1955, and I was discharged from the Army with exactly one week to drive home from Georgia, stash my gear, repack for college, and get myself to Meadville—for the third time.

When I graduated from Allegheny in June 1956 and left for Yale, I had no reason to expect that I would ever return to Meadville a fourth time. For that matter, I really doubted I'd return at all, except maybe for an alumni reunion now and then. Much as I loved Allegheny, I couldn't imagine any circumstance that would take me there more often.

Which just goes to show how little my prognosticating skills had improved. I wasn't destined to return simply to visit; I would spend almost half of my professional career at the college—a development that stunned no one more than me. Leave it to the one member of the family who flunked out of college to devote his life to higher education.

And I can say without fear of contradiction (because few people have the experience to challenge me), that flunking out of college was the single most important credential I brought back with me as dean of students. There is an old adage that you can't con an old con. In the same vein, it's difficult for a stumbling student to pull the wool over the eyes of an old flunk-out. Or for the student's parents to do so, which is equally important. Knowing first hand that failure in college is not conclusive evidence of what a student may eventually achieve, I was uniquely positioned to help students fail productively. More, I was able to persuade parents to resist the temptation to try to protect their children from failure. It can't be done; and freeing a child to accept the consequences of bad choices is among the most useful gifts that parents can give. It's admittedly hard, and never fun, but it can be extraordinarily constructive.

Those who doubt the validity of my claim are welcome to browse through a file I keep, captioned "Good Letters." Among its contents are the most tangible rewards I carried away with me from thirty-five years in higher education: letters from students and parents reminding me of our troubled encounters, and informing me of their proud accomplishments since. One even reached me in Oregon two years after retirement, a button-busting accolade from a father so proud of his daughter he took the trouble to track me down to share it. Rehearsing her rocky start at Allegheny, my pointed intervention, and the hard conversations that he and the girl's mother had with me about her future, he wanted me to know that it had all worked out: she had just received a graduate degree, gotten married, and begun a promising career—all in the same week!

It should be no surprise that the most gratifying encounters were live ones, when some student on whom I had been particularly tough came back to say thank you, often to request a letter of reference. But the best occurred in ways I could not possibly have anticipated.

In 1990, five years after I became chaplain of the college, our friend and Allegheny's choral director, Ward Jamison, invited Patricia and me to accompany the college choirs on a spring concert tour that would take us to Florida and back. At the final stop in North Carolina, while milling about among the mob inhaling the continental breakfast in the hotel lobby, I was approached by a student who reported that a man across the room was saying he was an Allegheny graduate, and I had saved his life. That sounded too good to pass up. We threaded our way through the crowd to where the young man was engaged in lively conversation with half a dozen of the singers. When he told me his name I realized why it had seemed familiar when I saw it on the hotel's marquee the evening before: he was to be married that afternoon, and the sign was to welcome the families of the bride and groom who were guests at the hotel.

I confess that I had no recollection of the story he was telling the students: how he arrived at Allegheny without the slightest notion of what he wanted to do with his life, and started his freshman year partying every other night and skipping classes on the intervening days. By December he had compiled an academic record of unparalleled wretchedness. Then Dean Skinner called him in for a conference. He came expecting to be lectured, chastised and belittled, but instead was invited into a pointed conversation about the real scope of his abilities, why he was failing, what could be done about it, and what resources the college had to help him—but only if he took advantage of them. We could assist, but he'd have to want it. It was up to him.

He wanted it. It was the only conversation we ever had; and ever since, he had convinced himself that I saved him from failure and an expulsion that might have ended his first and best chance at a meaningful career. Now he was a junior executive about to return to his room to dress for his wedding, with a future as bright as any of us is entitled to anticipate.

Don't think for a moment that I didn't enjoy every word of his testimonial, or the obvious reaction of the choir students, who were too young to remember me as the dean. When he finished, however, I disputed his conclusion, pointing out that all I did was touch potentials he had brought to college with him, possessions as substantial as the suitcases and boxes he hauled into the residence hall on matriculation day. He didn't succeed because of me; he succeeded because he determined to struggle with that internal coward that makes up a part of each of our childhoods, the part that tries to convince us that we really aren't worth much and will probably fail so why not start early and avoid the rush.

I didn't remember his case because it was only one of hundreds that my profession required me to deal with during three decades on four campuses; and no matter how hard I tried I never was able to keep them straight. But there was no need for me to, as long as the students did. I had only to refuse to let them con me, so that they would be less likely to con themselves into a life of disappointment.

If I was qualified for the job, it was partly because I spent my early life being tutored for it by all the successes and failures I had been privileged to experience, and all the good and caring people I had been privileged to know, since the day I first opened my eyes and looked uncomprehendingly out the window of the Old Mat at a December morning dawning over my town in a valley surrounded by hills.

Coming Home to Stay

Yet once again: when Patricia and I left our damp-eyed friends and family on the restaurant curb that steamy June day in 1993, we fully intended to reside in Oregon for the rest of our lives. It was to be the fulfillment of her long-standing dream, a dream in the realization of which I was more than happy to share. We had by then visited Oregon five times, and I delighted in its variety, beauty, and culture.

Then came what may be the greatest surprise of all: the decision to make the journey to Meadville a fifth time—and not just to visit. We'd done that half a dozen times since moving to Oregon, foremost because three of our children and their families live east of the Mississippi and our most enduring friendships are there. But the fact is that as the final chapters of this writing were being drafted, our Oregon home was filling up with stacks of boxes, packed with our possessions and taped against the depredations of moving; we were preparing to go back to stay.

The decision was made in a curious way, best revealed in a conversation several months before: sharing our thoughts one day about our life in Pennsylvania and our life in Oregon, and what is most important to us, Patricia fixed me with her guileless gaze and said, "We've lived in Oregon for nine years now. It's time to go home."

Knock me over with a moving van! Fifteen years in Meadville, it appears, had worked a change in my bride that we only recently came to appreciate. All this time we thought she was the dyed-in-the-wool Oregonian (they even have an acronym for it: S.N.O.B., for Society of Native Oregon-Born). There are fewer of them than most people realize, and they are fiercely loyal where their state is concerned, some even proclaiming the parochial conviction that no other place in the entire world is remotely comparable. Indeed, in the view of Pacific Northwest purists, the rest of the nation is not even worth visiting.

Which is why it was doubly surprising that my Oregonian wanted to "go home" to Pennsylvania. Perhaps reading over my shoulder as I worked on this book prompted some initial reconsideration, though we certainly had not approached the project that way. Still, it is no secret that human beings see things most clearly when forced to look at them through the lens of contrasting experience. It appears that we are a case in point: for nine years, and even as we thrilled in being part of it, Oregon provided a place to stand, a point of reference from which to look back on both the years of my youth recounted here and on our fifteen years together in Pennsylvania. And that very reflection let us see, in a way we had not earlier recognized, how deeply Meadville had become Patricia's home, as it had been mine all along, no matter where else I lived.

So I compose this postscript while glancing, from time to time, out the window of my study into a lovely patch of Pennsylvania woods that lies behind our new Meadville home—four blocks east of the North Main Street home where I was raised, a ten-minute walk from the Allegheny campus, and barely a hundred yards from the site of the old stone quarries. My flesh grows clammy as I write, victim of an HHH spring day. A new backyard bird feeder, fabricated from scrap cedar I brought from Oregon, has already attracted thirty-two species of birds (including wild turkey), and our yard regularly hosts chipmunks and red, gray and fox squirrels, with periodic visits by field mice, cotton-tail rabbits, raccoons and woodchucks; but no visitors more beguiling than the herd of whitetail deer that regularly pass through the woods and pause to feed in our yard. We've even been advised to watch for an itinerant black bear or two.

Will we go west again to visit? Absolutely. Three of our children and their families remain in Oregon, from whom separation is every bit as painful as was our leaving their eastern siblings in 1993 (there really are some things in life that we can't do anything about). Besides, we are obdurate travelers, and the American West is country so vast and majestic that it defies description and demands to be visited as often as possible. But even as we human beings travel, we need to know where our roots lie, where our sense of community is most enveloping, where our neighbor relations are most engaging. It is the places we are from, not where we reside, that define us.

What I didn't anticipate the first time I brought Patricia to Meadville was that it would come to be the place that she felt *she* was from. I assumed, as did she, that it would never be anything more than the town of her husband's birth and a temporary stopover on our professional journey. It never occurred to us—indeed it could not possibly have occurred to us at the time—that her sense of connection would become so interwoven in the fabric of my northwest Pennsylvania town. The fact is that the people of both town and college earned her loyalty with the unaffected generosity with which they embraced her when she first arrived, not just as the wife of the new dean, but as ol' "Doc" and Ruth Skinner's daughter-in-law come home to share in the life of their town.

And while my powers of prediction are not notably more astute now than they were in 1948—or 1953 or 1956 or 1993— something tells me that this time we really will stay.

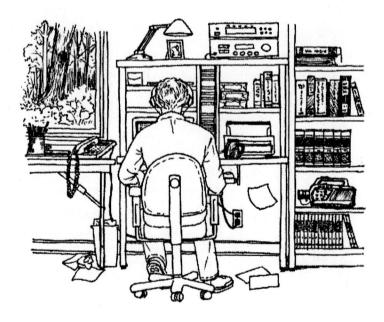

About the Author

Born in Meadville, Pennsylvania in 1932, Don Skinner attended Meadville's public schools through tenth grade and graduated from the Mercersburg Academy, in southern Pennsylvania, in 1950. Returning to Meadville, he enrolled in Allegheny College, dropping out in the middle of his third year to spend two years in the U.S. Army. He graduated from Allegheny in 1956, completed theological studies at Yale University (1959), and earned a doctorate in the social sciences at Syracuse University (1966). The same June, he was ordained in the United Church of Christ. His professional career was divided among three college campuses, culminating at Allegheny as dean of students (1978-85), and chaplain (1985-93). In 1994 he was named *chaplain emeritus* of the college. Retiring to his wife Patricia's home state of Oregon, they spent eleven months building their own home, followed by eleven months recovering from building their own home. In 2002, however, they returned to Meadville where they now make their home. Don and Patricia share five sons, one daughter and thirteen grandchildren. This is Don's third book. Previous titles include *A Passage through Sacred History* and *Prayers for the Gathered Community*.

Printed in the United States
23708LVS00002B/43